THE
SCHOOL LIBRARY
a force for
educational
excellence

THE
SCHOOL LIBRARY
a force for
educational
excellence

BY RUTH ANN DAVIES

R. R. BOWKER COMPANY, NEW YORK & LONDON, 1969

PUBLISHED by R. R. BOWKER COMPANY
(A XEROX COMPANY)
1180 AVENUE OF THE AMERICAS, NEW YORK, N. Y. 10036
COPYRIGHT © 1969 by XEROX CORPORATION
ALL RIGHTS RESERVED.
STANDARD BOOK NUMBER: 8352-0269-0
LIBRARY of CONGRESS CATALOG CARD NUMBER: 70-94511
PRINTED AND BOUND in the UNITED STATES of AMERICA

TO MY MOTHER
FOR HER INDOMITABLE SPIRIT
AND HER LIMITLESS COURAGE
AND
TO MY AUNT JESSIE
FOR HER ABIDING FAITH
AND ENDURING AFFECTION

Contents

ACKNOWLEDGEMENTS   xi
PREFACE   xiii
INTRODUCTION   1
    CHAPTER   1:   The Goal of Education   3
    CHAPTER   2:   The School Library, Force for Actualizing the
                    Educational Goal   17
    CHAPTER   3:   The School Librarian, a Mediating Agent for
                    Educational Excellence   25
    CHAPTER   4:   The Role of the School Librarian as Cur-
                    riculum Consultant   41
    CHAPTER   5:   The Role of the School Librarian as
                    Materials Specialist   59
    CHAPTER   6:   The School Library as an Integral Part of
                    the English Program   97
    CHAPTER   7:   The School Library as an Integral Part of
                    the Social Studies Program   137
    CHAPTER   8:   The School Library as an Integral Part of
                    the Science and Mathematics Programs   159
    CHAPTER   9:   The School Library as an Integral Part of
                    the Guidance Program   187
    CHAPTER 10:   The School Library as an Integral Part of
                    the Study Skills Program   199
    CHAPTER 11:   Evaluating the Effectiveness of the School
                    Library Program   209
    CHAPTER 12:   The School Library Supervisor   227
    CHAPTER 13:   The School Library—A Laboratory
                    for Learning   243

Appendices

APPENDIX A: Basic Background Readings   251
APPENDIX B: Job Description: What School Librarians Do   263
APPENDIX C: Terminology   265
APPENDIX D: Sample Resource Unit: The Civil War and Re-
               construction   273
APPENDIX E: Growth Characteristics of Pupils   288
APPENDIX F: School Libraries as Instructional Materials Centers   294
APPENDIX G: Evaluative Checklist: an Instrument for
               Self-Evaluating an Educational Media Program   298
APPENDIX H: Policies and Procedures for Selection of School
               Library Materials   308
APPENDIX I: Model School Library Philosophy and
               Policy Statement   315
APPENDIX J: Elementary Reading Interest Inventory   320
APPENDIX K: Streamlining for Service   323
APPENDIX L: Social Study Skills: A Guide to Analysis and
               Grade Placement   327
APPENDIX M: Facilities Planning   346
APPENDIX N: Learning to Learn in School Libraries   359
APPENDIX O: Poetry Unit   368

Figures

Figure   I: The Proliferation of Knowledge   8
Figure   II: The Spiral of Education   12
Figure   III: Primarily, The Teacher Must Know   35
Figure   IV: Goals, Content, Method, Media: Vectors Shaping
                 Unit and Course Design   55
Figure   V: Individualizing the Teaching Design   56
Figure   VI: English Materials Laboratory   83
Figure   VII: Social Studies Content Includes Basic Concepts
                 from Many of the Social Sciences   138
Figure   VIII: Forms of Curriculum Organization   147
Figure   IX: Blueprint for Literacy   185
Figure   X: Library Self Evaluation Scale   215
Figure   XI: Find your School Library Service Profile   217
Figure   XII: Find your School Media Center Service Profile   221

Tables

Table   I: Educational Program in Transition   15
Table   II: School Library Program in Transition   23
Table   III: Profile of the Competent, Educationally Effective
               School Librarian   39
Table   IV: Diversification: The Solution to the Problem,
               "How to Individualize Instruction"   57
Table   V: High School Paperback Survey   75
Table   VI: Role of Paperbacks in Schools Today   76
Table   VII: Guides for Selecting Books for Slow Readers   106
Table   VIII: Criteria to be Used in Selecting Books for the
               Adolescent Retarded Reader   107
Table   IX: Library-Based Unit: Biography   112
Table   X: Biographee Profile   116
Table   XI: Classroom Experiences in Listening   124
Table   XII: General Guides to Continuity in Speaking
               Experiences   127
Table   XIII: The Speech Potential of a Ponderable Quote   129
Table   XIV: A Fused Library-Based Unit: Transportation   148
Table   XV: Characteristic Differences in Emphasis Between the
               Subject and Experience Curriculums   157
Table   XVI: Outline of Topics for Library Investigation:
               "Exploring our Universe"   170
Table   XVII: List of Topics for Library Investigation:
               Mathematics   180
Table XVIII: General Principles for Guidance of Children's Think-
               ing   203
Table   XIX: Some Guidelines for Teachers in Developing the
               Skills of Critical Thinking and Problem Solving 204
Table   XX: Patterns of Critical Thinking   205
Table   XXI: Characteristics of an Effective Teacher   224

Checklists

Checklist   I: Book Selection Guide   66
Checklist   II: Textbook Evaluation Form   67
Checklist III: Audiovisual Materials Evaluation Record   69
Checklist   IV: Criteria for Selecting Equipment   70
Checklist   V: Self Evaluation in Media Selection   71
Checklist   VI: Professional Library Resources   80
Checklist VII: Media Programming Components   88
Checklist VIII: Media Evaluation Form for Selecting Resources to
                 Support, Enrich, and to Extend a Reading Unit   105

Checklist   IX: Teacher Evaluation of Individual Student's
                 Listening Skills   125
Checklist   X: Critical Thinking Skills to be Developed Through
                 the Use of Primary Source Materials   146
Checklist   XI: Topic Checklist to Unify and Coordinate Unit
                 Development   151
Checklist XII: Checklist of Problem Solving Practices
                 Recommended for Science Teacher Use   168
Checklist XIII: Determining Feasibility of Assignments   206
Checklist XIV: School Library Checklist   216

Examples

Example   I: Community Resource File   78
Example   II: One Day in an Elementary Instructional Materials
                Center   84
Example   III: The Pittman Learning Guide—History   90
Example   IV: Itemized Media Budget Request   93
Example   V: Biography Reading Summary Report   116
Example   VI: Read for Fun   121
Example   VII: Biography Reading Summary   122
Example VIII: Unit Pretest: The Civil War and Reconstruction   154
Example   IX: The Pittman Learning Guide—Roman Numerals   182

BIBLIOGRAPHY   372
INDEX   379

Acknowledgements

So many have contributed so much to the pages of this book that it is impossible to say with whom "the thought began." I am grateful to each one of the many professional friends who have given so unstintingly of their knowledge, their time, and their energy. The completion of the book is testimony to their generosity.

A special vote of thanks is due to:

My students at the Graduate School of Library and Information Sciences, University of Pittsburgh for serving so willingly as my "reaction agents." In large measure this book is the direct result of their faith and encouragement, for they have been my constant source of courage, challenge, and inspiration; by my students I've been so kindly taught.

Dr. Edward Kruse, Superintendent of the North Hills Schools, and to Mr. Martin Scholl and Dr. Victor Morrone, the Directors of Secondary and Elementary Education, for their willingness to have the North Hills Schools serve as the "proving grounds" for originating and testing many of the concepts, models, techniques, and procedures included in these chapters. The continued backing of the North Hills Schools administrative staff has made it possible to demonstrate in action the truism that a district library program of excellence begins with administrative understanding, commitment, and backing.

The North Hills school librarians for their cooperation and support, their loyalty and patience. Each one has taken an extra share of responsibility to lighten my load; each has contributed directly by designing, structuring, and testing many of the units and models included here. This book is testimony to the value accrued from a school library staff willing to work together as a cooperative team.

John Rowell for his invaluable professional guidance and his willingness to serve as the catalytic agent bringing form and substance to nebulous thought. He indeed has had the power to visualize these thoughts and to actualize these ideas.

Mrs. Elizabeth P. Hoffman for her encouragement and her inspiration as well as for her willingness to field test this book while it was in manuscript form.

Joyce B. Scholl for her rare ability to turn a phrase creatively and, without effort, bring lucidity to these pages. Without her constant collaboration the book could not have been written.

My family—Martha, Mary, Elizabeth, Little Ruth, and Shirley—for their encouragement and willingness to shoulder my responsibilities as well as their own. Their unselfish devotion and unwavering faith have sustained me from the beginning to the end of this entire project.

My teachers—Nita Butler, Ella Martin, and Laberta Dysart—who shared with me their wisdom and their love of learning. Many of the concepts in this book are reflective of their teaching.

Preface

The modern school library or educational media program has long lacked a full-length interpretive portrait. Skillfully executed sketches abound—bits and pieces of the total picture have been painted, but until now, they have not been portrayed in a single panoramic format.

This has been unfortunate for the media practitioner who has attempted to keep on top of a rapidly developing and highly complex profession. It is even more difficult for the student being introduced to and involved in learning the profession.

There are understandable reasons for this unfortunate situation. The proliferation of theories and practices in educational purpose and technique have created new demands on the school library's performance. New educational materials—new in content and format, use and expected result—have required new competencies of the school library's personnel. Even the rapid acceptance of the fact that physical facilities be reshaped, component by component, to emancipate the new functions of educational change have originated new forms of libraries and media systems centers. And all of this newness, this change, these theoretical *and* actual processes created, developed, and directed for the most part by gifted leadership, have been too many, too quick, too incohesive, too independent to have permitted sitting still long enough for that sharply defined portrait. Until now, we have merely had a blurred picture of the school library.

Ruth Ann Davies has come to terms with the problem in this book. Not in over twenty years has school librarianship been as carefully detailed in a book available to everyone who cares. Miss Davies is well-known as a librarian, a scholar, a library administrator, an educator. She is also an artist: a person of enormous creativity who has known the landscapes of the past and onto them paints the pictures of the future. But perhaps more importantly, she recognizes the present and is able to interpret its design, color, proportion, balance.

Her book is at once historical and visionary, theoretical and highly practical, offering a comprehensive picture of school librarianship in the United States as it enters the 1970's. It should be valued for its perceptive archival content. It should be considered as a rational and defensible position paper. It will be increasingly important as the biography of a young and swiftly growing profession. It is a how-to-do-it handbook; it is philosophy in action; it is an inspiration!

Pre-service, in-service school librarians, library educationists, school administrators, classroom teachers and the great variety of education specialists will be able to distinguish the school library as portrayed here. If, as may be claimed by some, it is *not* the whole picture, the counter-claim can be made that it is the sharpest, most complete picture we have extant.

The profession of school librarianship is both vertically and horizontally mobile. It moves. To catch its picture in a book is to freeze it unnaturally at one point in space and time. If all the aspects of this developing institution could be filmed, edited, and viewed simultaneously and continually, perhaps we could keep current. That is impossible, of course, but frequent revision is not. Revision is anticipated and will be welcomed.

In the meantime, the taut canvas upon which changes will be ordered is available here. *The School Library—a Force for Educational Excellence* is an impressive and important addition to our professional gallery.

> John Rowell
> Director, Programs for School Libraries
> Case Western Reserve University, Cleveland, Ohio

Introduction

The purpose of this book is to get the static out of the educational intercom so the message can be heard clearly that today's school library is a force and a source for educational excellence. No longer with impunity can the school library be relegated to the peripheral fringes of educational non-involvement. The direct support of the school library is fundamental to the basic design and optimum implementation of an educational program of excellence. Deny the educational program this integral support and the program is weakened irreparably.

The reader of this book is introduced first to the philosophy, goals and objectives of education itself. These are the imperatives giving direction, purpose, and significance to the school library program. The philosophy, goals, and objectives of the educational program ARE the philosophy, goals, and objectives of the library program. They are one and the same, permanently fused, and therefore inseparable.

In design and content this book reflects the organizational pattern and structure of a course originated by the author at the University of Pittsburgh. "The School Library—Source and Force for Educational Excellence" is an innovative course, for it is offered to students enrolled either in the School of Education or in the School of Library and Information Sciences. This duality of course sponsorship has made it possible for educators to discover the school library's true educational identity and for librarians to gain insight and perspective in viewing the educational enterprise. In this course, school board members, school administrators, guidance counselors, department chairmen, classroom teachers, public and school librarians, and neophyte teachers and librarians meet and learn together and from each other in a climate of mutual concern and respect.

This book has been designed to be highly practical, to extend theory to application. The author has little patience with the intellectual dilettante who delights in theory as an academic exercise. Consciously each learning experience in this book, as in class, has been extended beyond fact to include comprehension, application, analysis, evaluation, and synthesis. The Appendices provide an opportunity for the reader to work with ideas in context and to discover for himself the meaning between, behind, and beyond the words.

Understanding has been extended beyond the cognitive area to include the affective area of learning. The author believes that this area is of grave concern to all who teach, kindergarten through graduate school.

Reading this book should serve as a point of departure along the road to self-directed knowledge building. Each footnote should be an open invitation to further exploration and discovery, a stimulus to self-teaching. Since learning is an "open-ended" process, reading this book must end with a question mark and not a period. It is hoped that the reader will internalize the thoughts presented here, and will determine for himself the validity and the reasonableness of these guiding principles: that a quality, optimum educational program demands the support of a quality, optimum school library program; that an innovative program of educational excellence demands an innovative program of library service commensurate with the support needs of the educational program; that the school library functioning as a multimedia learning laboratory is more productive educationally than a study hall-reference center library; that the school librarian functioning as a teacher is the result of common sense.

No apology is offered for the use of the traditional term school library rather than more contemporary terms such as instructional materials center or media resource center. The choice of the familiar term precludes any reader misunderstanding the specific service to which reference is being made. It is not the terminology which is of educational significance; it is the quality and the extent of the service which give the school library its claim to educational significance. A change of name is not basic to a change in function. It is a change in attitude, a recognition of potential worth, and the redesigning of the existing program to directly reflect the developmental needs of the teaching and the learning program that will vitalize the existing school library. "Services, not words portray the true image of the school library."

The scope of this book is greater than that of a textbook. Deliberately the contents have been widened to include many of the answers essential to on-the-job problem solving. The contents have been structured to anticipate the need for ready, specific guidance on the part of the school librarian, the classroom teacher, and the school administrator as they plan and work together to build a school library program of functional excellence.

The author joins Francis Bacon in admonishing the readers of this book: "Read not to contradict and confute, nor to believe and take for granted, nor to find talk and discourse,—but to weigh and consider."*

* Bacon, Francis. *The Essays of Francis Bacon*. Edited with introduction and notes by Clark Suthorland Northup. Boston, Massachusetts: Houghton, Mifflin, 1936 (Riverside College Classics). pp. 154-155.

1 The Goal of Education

*Civilization, it was once said, is a race between education and catastrophe—and we intend to win that race for education.**

The school library becomes a force for educational excellence when it functions as an integral supporting component of the total educational program. Perspective in viewing the educational significance of the school library begins logically with building an understanding of education itself. For it is the educational pattern, design and structure which gives purpose and direction to the school library program. The library program and the educational program are inter-dependent, one and inseparable. The attempt to develop an adequate understanding of the school library program in isolation from the educational program is comparable to attempting to construct a building without blueprint or specifications. It is the educational program which gives purpose and direction, scope and dimension, form and substance, significance and value to the school library program.

DEMOCRATIC CONCERN FOR EDUCATION

Education is an instrument which our free society has designed and employs to strengthen, to perpetuate, and to safeguard the American way of life. In our democracy direct participation by the citizen in governmental policy-making holds both the promise of freedom and the threat of enslavement. Democratic concern for education is predicated on the assumption that an educated citizenry will be competent to act intelligently and thereby preserve its freedom. Conversely, an uneducated electorate not perceiving dangers inherent in unwise decisions will embrace false doctrines and as a result lose its freedom.

Our founding fathers believed that an enlightened government must have

* *Public Papers of the Presidents of the United States, Containing the Public Messages, Speeches and Statements of the President.* John F. Kennedy, January 1 to November 22, 1963. Washington, D.C.: United States Government Printing Office, 1964. p. 896.

as corollary an enlightened citizenry. Thomas Jefferson considered education to be "the most legitimate engine of government."[1] He warned that "If a nation expects to be ignorant and free . . . it expects what never has and never will be."[2] Likewise James Madison held a deep personal conviction that education was the sure bulwark against self-elected enslavement as a result of ignorance. Madison said, "popular government, without popular information or the means of acquiring it, is but a Prologue to a Farce or Tragedy; or, perhaps, to both."[3] Education was valued by our forefathers as the means of enabling each citizen to secure for himself and his posterity the rights and privileges accrued to him because he was free and because he was an American.

Our society regards education as a means of preparing each generation for productive and effective living. Since society is a living and dynamically changing organism, education of necessity must be capable of changing and growing in order to meet adequately the emerging needs as well as the traditional needs of society. The educational program designed to prepare the past generation for productive living in the horseless carriage age will not suffice in preparing today's youth for space exploration and tomorrow's youth for moon habitation.

GENERAL EDUCATION IN A FREE SOCIETY

Each generation faces the obligation of evaluating critically and realistically America's traditional educational goals and patterns in the light of its own economic, political, social, and cultural needs. Dr. James Conant when president of Harvard University took the responsibility for his generation to re-think critically and reflectively the very purpose and nature of the American educational enterprise. Dr. Conant appointed a Committee on the Objectives of a General Education in a Free Society, commissioning the members of this Committee to "venture into the vast field of American educational experience in quest of a concept of general education that would have validity for the free society we cherish."

The Committee after many months of soul-searching submitted to Dr. Conant a report summarizing its analysis of the American educational scene and endeavor. The Report, *General Education in a Free Society*,[4] is a classic in the field of educational philosophy and should be read and pondered by all who would understand and appreciate the purpose and the promise of the American educational dream (See Appendix A).

The Harvard Report identified for the American citizen the philosophic, the political, the economic, the social, and the cultural vectors giving direction and magnitude, purpose and unity, form and substance to the contemporary educational endeavor. It brought cohesion to our educational efforts by identifying the primary purpose of education: cultivation in the largest possible number of citizens an appreciation of the responsibilities, the privileges, and the benefits which come to them because they are Americans and

---

[1] Jefferson, Thomas. *The Writings of Thomas Jefferson.* Edited by Albert Ellery Bergh. Washington, D.C.: Thomas Jefferson Memorial Association, 1907. vol. 6, p. 392.
[2] *Ibid.*, vol. 14, p. 384.
[3] Madison, James. *The Complete Madison: His Basic Writings.* Edited by Saul K. Podover. New York: Harper, 1953. p. 337.
[4] *General Education in a Free Society: A Report of the Harvard Committee.* Cambridge, Massachusetts: Harvard University Press, 1945.

because they are free. By destroying the concept that equality for all in education would result in "colorless egalitarianism," the report brought a new dimension to the ideal of educational equality. It stated without qualification that a true democracy is obligated to provide an educational program which will serve not only the needs of society but especially the needs and aspirations of each individual in society. The Harvard Report stressed the necessity of a democratic government's providing an educational program where *equality of opportunity* is the rule and not the exception. The report clearly stated that equality in education does not mean an identical education for all. Rather, it means an educational program which recognizes and provides adequately for the vast actual differences among students. Since there is no single form of instruction that can reach all equally, how best to meet the immense range of talent must be solved if we are to avoid denying each citizen his educational birthright—unlimited opportunity to develop to the optimum the promise that is in him as a human being and as a citizen.

Unfortunately America was too engrossed with developing social competence in its schools to follow the advice and act on the recommendations of the Harvard Report. During the late 40's and 50's the extremists in the progressive education movement were still being heard and heeded; this "happiness cult" frowned on intellectualism as a primary goal. Indeed America was not ready to restore seriousness of purpose to general education until Russia launched its first successful Sputnik in 1957. Seeing Russia's scientific superiority in the field of space alarmed and embarrassed the man in the street. He raised the question, "Is America lagging behind Russia in her educational program as well as in her space program?" This question was followed by a second, "Is it not time we evaluate critically what we as a nation are doing educationally?"

The impact of Sputnik shattered America's educational complacency and obliterated America's national indifference to the quality of general education. At last we as a people were dissatisfied with educational drifting and dreaming. Sputnik prepared us to be thoughtfully receptive to the recommendations of the Rockefeller Report, *The Pursuit of Excellence: Education and the Future of America,*[5] published in 1958. Here America found reiterated the basic tenet of the Harvard Report—excellence in all aspects of the educational endeavor is the only goal worthy of our free society. Here was reflected the same concern for equality of opportunity and for optimum achievement evidenced in the Harvard Report. Here was stated the same urgent plea that America realize that excellence cannot be left to chance but must be planned for, worked for, and paid for. Analyzing and evaluating the findings and recommendations of the Rockefeller Report give insight and perspective, for the Report clearly outlines the road to be traveled in carrying American education from traditional mediocrity to innovative excellence (See Appendix A).

The Rockefeller Report stressed that there can be no excellence in our educational endeavor until we rescue the individual from the faceless anonymity of impersonal education. It is the birthright of each American citizen to have his individuality respected. The Report correlated the

[5] *The Pursuit of Excellence: Education and the Future of America.* ("America at Mid-Century Series," Special Studies Project Report V, Rockefeller Brothers Fund.) Garden City, New York: Doubleday, 1958.

optimum development of the individual with the health of society itself, for enabling each citizen to achieve optimum fulfillment is a means of society's re-invigorating itself.

In building insight into the unique characteristics of education in American society, the Harvard and Rockefeller Reports serve as foundation stones. In relating education to the totality of the American enterprise, the Report of the United States Commission on National Goals, *Goals for Americans,* serves as the keystone (See Appendix A). The significance of education in our contemporary society is stressed throughout this report which was specifically designed "to develop a broad outline of coordinated national policies and programs and to set up a series of goals in various areas of national activity."

The Harvard Report, the Rockefeller Report, and the Report of the United States Commission on National Goals[6] bring three dimensional solidity to the American educational ideal. They have defined clearly the educational goal and obligation of our free society—to provide a quality, optimum education for each citizen so that all citizens will be functionally literate. They have focused attention on the need to educate citizens in the art of competent thinking and competent social participation—translating knowledge into a pattern of constructive, reasoned, rational, purposeful, and positive behavior. They have extended the responsibility of education in our free society beyond the preparation of each citizen for intelligent political participation to encompass preparation for purposeful living, for economic effectiveness, for responsible individualism, for successful inter-group relations, for world consciousness, and above all, for self-realization and self-fulfillment.

ATTAINING THE EDUCATIONAL GOAL

Having identified the goal, the next concern is to blueprint the means of attainment. Education to be effective and adequate must be designed and structured scientifically to meet the needs of society and of the individual in that society. An adventure of this magnitude requires a scientific approach in the sense of Warren Weaver's use of this term in *Goals for Americans:*[7]

> ... science is not technology; it is not gadgetry; it is not some mysterious cult; not a great mechanical monster. Science is an adventure of the human spirit. It is an essentially artistic enterprise stimulated largely by curiosity, served largely by disciplined imagination, and based largely on faith in the reasonableness, order, and beauty of the universe of which man is a part.

Designing and structuring an educational program of excellence must bring into play the artistry, the disciplined imagination, the creativeness, the inventiveness as well as the Yankee ingenuity and practicality which have characterized the designing and structuring of American business and technology. The time is at hand; the priority has been assigned; the means must be perfected.

[6] The Report of the President's Commissios on National Goals. *Goals for Americans* © 1960 by the American Assembly, Columbia University, New York. Reprinted by permission of Prentice-Hall, Inc., Englewood Cliffs, N.J.
[7] President's Commission on National Goals. Op. cit., p. 105.

THE SABER-TOOTH CURRICULUM

At the heart of the problem of blueprinting and developing an educational program of excellence is the stark realization of the need for immediate renovation, innovation, and adjustment. Education must be updated to meet the emerging needs of contemporary society. We cannot tolerate the traditional time lag which Harold Benjamin satirizes in *The Saber-Tooth Curriculum*.[8] Benjamin dramatizes the sorry waste of human effort and potential that results when an educational program is chained to the needs of past generations rather than geared to meeting the present needs of contemporary society. He recounts the story of a primitive tribe that organized a school to teach fish-grabbing, horse-clubbing, and saber-tooth-tiger scaring for these were the three skills basic to the survival of the tribe. As generation followed generation a better method of fishing was devised; the horses moved to far away grazing grounds, and the saber-toothed-tiger died off. Yet the three original curricular skills continued to be taught to the young; they were traditional and therefore sacred.

NEED FOR INNOVATION

Authentic concern for educational excellence demands that each educational concept and each educational practice be scrutinized, evaluated, and, if found wanting, discarded. We must be guided by the realization that continuous, judicious reappraisal, and constructive, on-going innovation and renovation are a professional way of life. Education as a concomitant part of society must change as society changes. Traditionally we have been content to treasure the educational status quo with little concern for evaluating what we are doing in the light of the effectiveness or the efficiency of a practice in today's world. In the past there has been widespread reluctance to change.

> Once a "practical invention" (such as the kindergarten) had been devised to meet an underlying need—a process itself occupying fifty years on the average—approximately fifteen years elapsed before 3 per cent of school systems had installed the innovation . . . complete diffusion of successful inventions appeared to take approximately fifty years after the first "authentic introduction."[9]

We cannot afford to chain our youth to an educational program that is fifty years behind the times. Knowledge is proliferating (See Figure I) at such a rate that even a ten-year or a five-year lag is limiting the students to outdated information.

> Never before have the dynamic forces of change spun with such incredible speed. In the nearly 2,000 years since the birth of Christ, there has been first a very slow and then a very rapidly accelerating growth in the accumulation of knowledge. If this accumulation is plotted on a time line, beginning with the birth of Christ, it is esti-

8 Benjamin, Harold. *The Saber-Tooth Curriculum*. New York: McGraw-Hill, 1939.
9 Miles, Matthew B., ed. *Innovation in Education*. New York: Teachers College Press, Columbia University, 1964. p. 5.

mated that the first doubling of knowledge occurred in 1750, the second in 1900, the third in 1950, and the fourth only ten years later, 1960![10]

Today's world is not only highly complex but also highly competitive. The society that refuses to educate its citizens realistically, creatively, and

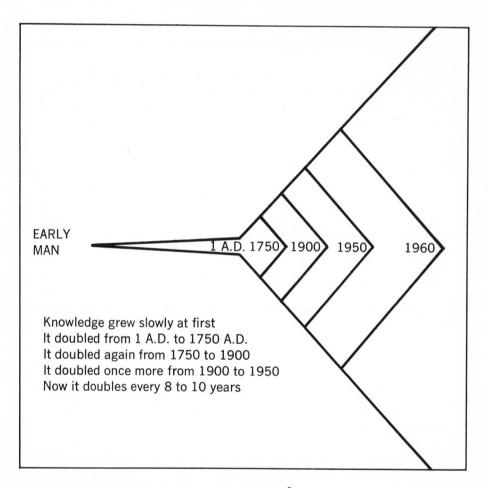

FIGURE I.   THE PROLIFERATION OF KNOWLEDGE*

effectively is doomed. No longer can we dissipate the intellectual potential of our citizens with social, economic, and political impunity. An educational program of excellence designed to develop each citizen for productive,

[10] National Education Association. Project on Instruction. *Schools for the Sixties.* New York: McGraw-Hill, 1963. p. 50.

* *The Encyclopedia: A Resource for Creative Teaching and Independent Learning.* Chicago, Illinois: Field Enterprises, © 1968. p. 6.

creative, purposeful living must be structured to meet the needs of citizens in today's world in preparation for the world of tomorrow. No longer can we afford to chain our students to the educational practices designed for the past and unrelated to the present and the future.

VENERATION OF THE TEXTBOOK

All too often our youth are chained like Prometheus to an archaic educational program. One paleolithic shiboleth condemning today's youth to an inadequate education is the veneration of the textbook. Traditionally the textbook has been regarded as the fountainhead of knowledge, the alpha and the omega of the educational program. And as long as outlining the textbook paragraph by paragraph, and page by page is the accepted method of teaching and verbatim memorization and verbatim feedback the accepted method of learning, the textbook more than suffices. It is only when the goal of education embraces depth and breadth of understanding that the textbook is found wanting.

The reluctance of American educators to change is all too evident when one considers the time lag between recognizing and compensating for the inadequacies of the textbook. As early as 1839, Horace Mann deplored limiting pupils to the information in the text. He warned:

> Pupils, who, in their reading, pass by names, references, allusions, without searching, *at the time,* for the facts they imply, not only forego valuable information, which they may never afterwards acquire, but they contract a habit of being contented with ignorance.[11]

Again in 1915, Henry Johnson, professor of history at Columbia University, pleaded with teachers to lead their children beyond the content of the textbook.

> While the textbook in the United States is the chief instrument of school instruction . . . a conviction has developed, especially during the last twenty years (1895–1915) that the textbook should be supplemented by collateral reading. The need of reference books was strongly emphasized by the Madison Conference (1892) 'Recitation alone' it was declared, 'cannot possibly make up proper teaching. . . . It is absolutely necessary from the earliest to the latest grades, that there should be parallel reading.'[12]

Likewise the Harvard Committee warned that:

> . . . texts often fail. They sum up too soon. It is right to let a student know roughly where he is going, but wrong to save him the journey. Too many courses tell him throughout what he is seeing,

[11] Mann, Horace. *Life and Works of Horace Mann.* 5 vols. Boston, Massachusetts: Lee and Shepard, 1891. vol. 3 "Annual Reports of the Secretary of the Board of Education of Massachusetts, 1839–1844." p. 49.
[12] Johnson, Henry. *Teaching of History in Elementary and Secondary Schools.* New York: Macmillan, 1915. p. 323.

so that he memorizes the account of a trip which he never took. His head was buried in the guidebook.[13]

At last we have come to recognize that the textbook is not the most but the least that can be said on any subject. Today we admit that a quality educational program will employ the textbook only as a point of departure, as an outline indicating topics of major significance worthy of the pupil's further consideration and exploration.

VALUE OF NON-PRINT MEDIA

Just as the textbook is not complete in and of itself, so printed material is no longer the single source of information. A quality educational program provides knowledge-building and knowledge-extending resources without concern for format, container, or wrapper. When hearing is essential to understanding, then a disc or tape recording is provided. When seeing is essential, then a filmstrip, slide, or study print is provided. When seeing and hearing are essential, then a motion picture or a sound filmstrip is provided. Our concern for excellence precludes our limiting knowledge to any one source or kind of information. Our concern is not for the package but for the knowledge-building contents of the package. An educational program of excellence is not restrictive but embraces all types and kinds of resources. Today's student should be as accustomed to using non-print media as he has been to using the textbook in the past.

CLASS APPROACH TO TEACHING

The time hallowed impersonal class approach to teaching is another archaic practice chaining today's children to an educational experience of limited effectiveness. Traditionally all children in a given classroom are taught the same content, in the same way, and at the same rate. All children, regardless of ability and promise, study the same textbook, complete the same assignments, take the same tests. All experience a program designed to fit no one in particular. The class approach to teaching—that lock-step, never look to the right nor to the left, keep eyes glued to the textbook, hurry to complete the text before the end of the semester approach—has been designed to move the bright, the average, and the slow through the textbook at the same rate. And if the teacher can gauge the rate just right, the average can walk through the text, the slow can stumble through, and the bright, who could have run through so easily, can just stand around and wait.

The class approach has been defended in the past as a means of perpetuating the oneness of society—one way for all. This philosophy implies that democracy is obligated to provide for "colorless egalitarianism" in its schools. This practice is contrary to the very promise of democracy that each citizen will have as his birthright respect and concern for his individuality. Each student when guaranteed an optimum education is being guaranteed the right to be taught as an individual, the right to learn in his own special way, the right to achieve self-realization and self-fulfillment. The class-

13 *General Education in a Free Society: A Report of the Harvard Committee.* Op. cit., p. 109.

oriented program is not democratic, for it denies the rights of the individual student, limiting "the development of individual excellence in exchange for a uniformity of external treatment."[14] The promise of an optimum education demands that teaching and learning be individualized, that each student receive an education commensurate with his special needs, his interests, his goals, his abilities, and his concerns.

A STRUCTURED EDUCATIONAL PROGRAM

The lack of an over-all directional plan for the sequential development of a fundamental body of knowledge, grade by grade, and subject by subject, is yet another hereditary educational deficiency. Traditionally, from the days of the one room school, teachers have been considered "kings" in their own classrooms and have been vested with the divine right of determining the totality of the educational program in their kingdoms. In large measure what the student has been taught has been determined by each teacher and, all too often, has reflected teacher-interest and teacher-disinterest rather than the developmental needs of the student as he experiences a continuous, on-going educational program. There has been little continuity experienced by the learner as he moves from room to room and from grade to grade. The lack of continuity and articulation in the educational program has condemned the learner in the past to a fragmented education of bits and pieces, a collection of disjointed, skeletal facts lacking interconnectedness, cohesiveness, form, and substance.

BLUEPRINT FOR EXCELLENCE

A quality, educational program cannot be left to whim or chance. Quality must be both planned and worked for. A quality program begins with a quality blueprint which identifies the scope and dimension of the total program, kindergarten through grade twelve. A blueprint for excellence clearly identifies all elements basic to the program, and having identified the elements, orders them into patterns of logical, progressive sequence. An educational program of excellence is strongly structured to guard against any inadequacies occurring in the plan. How can understanding be complete if basic structure be misplaced or missing?

Jerome Bruner, Harvard professor of educational psychology, in his book, *The Process of Education*,[15] pleads for scientific planning of the educational program. He advocates that the scientific design and structure of the educational program provide "continuity, unity, balance and harmony" in the total educational experience. He recommends that the teaching and learning processes continually broaden and deepen knowledge in terms of basic and general ideas. This would require that courses of study for each discipline be "re-written and teaching materials revamped so that the pervading and powerful ideas and attitudes relating to them are given a central role."[16] The educational program, he states, must be designed to introduce and reintroduce at each grade level the appropriate fundamentals. And the entire

14 *The Pursuit of Excellence: Education and the Future of America.* Op. cit., p. 22.
15 Bruner, Jerome S. *The Process of Education.* Cambridge, Massachusetts: Harvard University Press, 1960.
16 Ibid., p. 18.

program must be organized so as to relate the parts to the whole for "unless detail is placed into a structural pattern (of interrelatedness) it is rapidly forgotten."[17] The key to retrieval is organization. An educational program of excellence is designed and structured ever to broaden, ever to widen, ever to relate, and ever to extend understanding through a logical progression of inter-locking, cohesive and mutually supportive experiences (See Figure II).

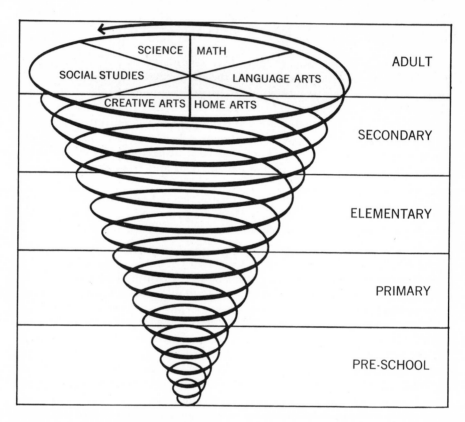

FIGURE II.   THE SPIRAL OF EDUCATION:
AN INTEGRATED, ON-GOING, SEQUENTIAL,
INTER-RELATED, OPEN-ENDED, CONTINUOUS PATTERN*

THE DISCOVERY METHOD

Dr. Bruner includes in his program design not only the teaching and learning of fundamentals, but he includes "the development of an attitude toward learning and inquiry, toward guessing and hunches, toward the possibility of solving problems on one's own."[18] The program he envisions would

17 Ibid., p. 24.

* *The Encyclopedia: A Resource for Creative Teaching and Independent Learning.* Chicago, Illinois: Field Enterprises, 1968. p. 7.
18 Ibid., p. 20.

encourage students to discover understanding and to find satisfaction in and through self-directed knowledge-building. Discovery, he says, adds *zest* to learning. "There should be a sense of excitement about discovery—discovery of regularities of previously unrecognized relations and similarities between ideas, with a resulting sense of self-confidence in one's abilities."[19]

The discovery method of learning is a sharp departure from the traditional practice of memorization of facts. In the past, facts have been not only the means to understanding but the end of understanding. But memorizing is not understanding; it is only rote recall and is as educationally significant as the meaningless talking of a parrot trained to call back memorized words and phrases. If our goal of training each citizen for functional literacy is to be reached, we can no longer tolerate nor can we condone the educational malpractice of senseless or meaningless memorization. We must build into our program ample opportunity for each student to learn to think effectively, critically, reflectively, and creatively. Our responsibility extends beyond presenting facts to providing the opportunity for the learner to work with ideas, experiment with ideas, apply ideas, analyze ideas, synthesize ideas, evaluate ideas,[20] and above all, to have the student derive personal satisfaction, pleasure, and challenge from working with ideas. Effective learning results in effective thinking. An educational program of excellence is designed and structured to promote, foster, and encourage each student to think effectively with competence and satisfaction.

QUALITY TEACHER

An educational program of excellence can well begin with a quality blueprint, but in actuality the promise of excellence inherent in the plan depends largely on the quality of the teacher. The teacher, "the instrument for educational excellence," is responsible for translating the educational design into actuality. He it is who enables the child to build his "house of intellect" commensurate with the promise that is in him. The problem of meeting individual differences, needs, abilities, and interests is not only one of courses but also one of method. The course of study is, of necessity, impersonal and has significance for the individual learner only if the teacher personalizes the teaching plan by customizing experiences to meet the needs, the interests, the goals, the abilities and the special concerns of the individual student. "The traditional democratic invitation to each individual to achieve the best that is in him requires that we provide each youngster with the particular kind of education which will benefit him. That is the only sense in which equality of opportunity can mean anything."[21] The good teacher, respecting and valuing the individuality of each student, will encourage each student in a class to travel in his own way toward the common goal of understanding. A quality educational program requires a creative teacher concerned for the personal well-being and the intellectual development of the student. Just as effective learning results in effective thinking, so creative teaching results in creative learning.

[19] Ibid., p. 20.
[20] Bloom, Benjamin S., ed. *Taxonomy of Educational Objectives: The Classification of Educational Goals. Handbook I, Cognitive Domain.* New York: David McKay, 1956. p. 18.
[21] Gardner, John W. *Excellence: Can We Be Equal and Excellent Too?* New York: Harper, 1961. p. 75.

"Love of learning, curiosity, self-discipline, intellectual honesty, the capacity to think clearly—these and all other consequences of a good education—cannot be insured by skillful administrative devices. The quality of the teacher is the key to good education."[22]

The teacher of excellence holds authentic concern for the optimum development of the learner as a human being. In humanizing his teaching, the teacher provides ample opportunity for each student to build a positive attitude toward self and toward society. He encourages the student to look at himself in a mirror and to measure his self-image against the hallmarks of decency, integrity, and honesty. Personal concern for the moral and spiritual well-being of the student is basic in our democracy for we are committed to preserving the dignity of man. Impersonal teaching reduces the learner to the level of a machine—a computer receiving information to be stored away in brain cells and held ready for retrieval or recall. The quality teacher translates the democratic respect for the dignity of man into his teaching program. He respects and values the learner as a living, thinking, dreaming human being capable of self-respect, self-realization and self-fulfillment. It is both the responsibility and the privilege of the teacher in a democracy to encourage each student to build a positive attitude toward himself as a person and as a citizen of his nation and of his world. "Know thyself" is the constant which keeps the teaching program in sharp focus as teachers help, direct, inspire, and challenge each learner to recognize and achieve the promise that is in him.

Traditionally teaching has been a one-man show with the teacher playing the part of playwright, producer, scene shifter, and star. Many students have suffered as a captive audience watching a less than gifted teacher acting a too demanding role. An educational program of excellence precludes amateur theatricals. The drama of teaching and learning should transcend the talents, artistry, imagination, and creativity of any one teacher. A drama of heroic proportion requires many actors. From writing the scenario through the complete production the educational drama must be the shared responsibility of a teaching team—each member of the team filling the role for which he is best suited.

INDIVIDUAL EXCELLENCE

The goal of providing a quality, optimum education for each citizen must be realized if we are to educate our citizens for competent participation in today's world. John W. Gardner in his book, *Excellence: Can We Be Equal and Excellent Too?* pleads that competence be assigned a high priority rating for:[23]

> Keeping a free society free—and vital and strong—is no job for the half-educated and the slovenly. Free men must be competent men. In a society of free men, competence is an elementary duty. . . . But excellence implies more than competence. It implies a striving for the highest standards in every phase of life. We need

[22] President's Commiission on National Goals. Op. cit., p. 82.
[23] Gardner, John W. Op. cit., pp. 159-160.

individual excellence in all its forms—in every creative endeavor, in political life, in education, in industry—in short, universally.

The quality of the citizen as a person must be of prime concern to educators in a free society. Decency, integrity, and dedication to the ideal cannot be legislated. The fate of democracy rests not on the documents written to direct the function of the government but rests on the thoughts and actions of each citizen. Each generation holds the fate and the future of the American way of life. "Every incompetent citizen is a menace to the freedom of all."[24] Education is the hope held by our free society that the fate and the future are secure and that the ideal will be strengthened and perpetuated.

An educational program capable of meeting the needs of contemporary society and capable of developing the potentialities of individuals for creative, productive living cannot be limited to the content, philosophy, materials, and methods appropriate for past generations. An educational program of excellence is more than a retread on the traditional framework of outmoded educational practices and thought. A program of excellence is designed and structured scientifically to integrate that which is educationally sound and valuable from the past with that which is educationally promising in the present. We are living in the midst of an educational reformation where the climate is right for educational innovation, where traditional educational ineffectiveness is being supplanted by innovative excellence (See Table I).

TABLE 1

EDUCATIONAL PROGRAM IN TRANSITION

FROM TRADITIONAL PRACTICES	TO INNOVATIVE PRACTICES
From the textbook as the totality of knowledge	To the textbook as a point of departure
From teaching restricted to the printed word	To teaching employing the multi-media approach
From class oriented teaching	To individualized instruction
From subject development unrelated grade to grade	To curricular programs structured for continuity and interrelatedness
From overemphasis on facts	To emphasis on comprehension
From emphasis on memorization	To emphasis on learning to learn
From learning limited to the skill and cognitive areas	To learning emphasizing the affective as well as the skill and cognitive areas
From restrictive conformity in teaching and learning	To creative inventiveness in teaching and learning
From classroom teacher working alone	To cooperative team planning and team teaching
*From librarian working as a paraprofessional	To librarian working as a planning and contributing member of the teaching team

* See TABLE II: School Library Program in Transition
24 United States Commission on National Goals. Op. cit., p. 120.

2 The School Library, Force for Actualizing the Educational Goal

*As a library program becomes more meaningful, it is more closely identified with the total instructional program, so that its ultimate success is really to put itself, as a separate program, out of business.**

A quality school library program is an instrument for educational excellence. The "educational program is strengthened in direct proportion to the quality of the school's library service" for the school library is the "keystone of a quality educational program."[25] Since the school library is an integral component of the educational program, the educational goals, objectives, and aims are also the school library goals, objectives, and aims—they are identical, one and inseparable. Because the primary goal of general education in our free society is to educate citizens for functional literacy, the primary goal of school library service is to facilitate the attainment of this goal. The operational objectives of the school library program are to enrich, to support, to vitalize, and to implement the educational program as it strives to meet the needs of each student. The constant aim of today's school library is to encourage and to enable each student to achieve the optimum of his potential as a learner, as a citizen, and as a human being.

SCHOOL LIBRARY OBJECTIVES

The American Association of School Librarians recommended in the 1960 *Standards for School Library Programs*[26] that the school library program

* Murray, Marguerite. "Knapp Project Evaluated." *Library Journal,* September 15, 1967. p. 3127.
25 Pennsylvania Governor's Committee on Education, 1960, Task Force on Curriculum. "The School Library—Keystone of Quality Education." *A Guide for School Librarians.* Harrisburg, Pa.: Department of Public Instruction, Division of School Libraries, 1969. pp. 1-2.
26 American Association of School Librarians. *Standards for School Library Programs.* Chicago, Illinois: American Library Association, 1960.

be developed to complement and reflect the developmental needs of the educational program. These objectives are constants and will not be outdated or superceded though the quantitative standards will be changed.

> Every school library has the primary objective of contributing to the achievement of the objectives formulated by the school, of which it is an integral part.
>
> The general objectives of dynamic school library service are common to all schools. They apply to elementary and secondary schools alike, to independent and parochial schools, to rural schools and to urban. They are in harmony with the overall objectives of education which they serve.

The purposes of the school library are to

1. Participate effectively in the school program as it strives to meet the needs of pupils, teachers, parents, and other community members.
2. Provide boys and girls with the library materials and services most appropriate and most meaningful in their growth and development as individuals.
3. Stimulate and guide pupils in all phases of their reading so that they may find increasing enjoyment and satisfaction and may grow in critical judgment and appreciation.
4. Provide an opportunity through library experience for boys and girls to develop helpful interests, to make satisfactory personal adjustments, and to acquire desirable social attitudes.
5. Help children and young people to become skillful and discriminating users of libraries and of printed and audio-visual materials.
6. Introduce pupils to community libraries as early as possible and co-operate with those libraries in their efforts to encourage continuing education and cultural growth.
7. Work with teachers in the selection and use of all types of library materials which contribute to the teaching program.
8. Participate with teachers and administrators in programs for continuing professional and cultural growth of the school staff.
9. Co-operate with other librarians and community leaders in planning and developing an over-all library program for the community or area.[27]

The attainment of these objectives requires a library program designed to permeate the totality of the educational program. An educational responsibility of this magnitude precludes the traditional "catch as catch can" functioning of the school library.

A STRUCTURED LIBRARY PROGRAM

If the school library is to become educationally effective and significant, its program must be planned and developed as an integral component of the

[27] Ibid., pp. 8-9.

overall educational design. The same high degree of artistry, disciplined imagination, creativeness, inventiveness, and ingenuity required for shaping an academic program of excellence must be employed when designing and structuring the school library program. Things equal to the same thing are equal to each other; a library program must equal in all aspects—scope, dimension, and proportion—the implementation needs of the total educational program.

An educationally effective library program requires an operational blueprint which relates library services, facilities, and resources to the overall educational program and to each of its component parts. The educationally effective and efficient library program is designed and structured to synchronize library service with the developmental needs of the educational program and the personal needs of the students.

DIRECT INVOLVEMENT OF THE LIBRARY

In the past the school library has not been in the "mainstream" of the educational endeavor. Traditionally the school library has been relegated to the role of study hall or reference center, serving solely as a place to house students and books. Involvement of the library in the teaching and learning enterprise in the past has been the exception, not the rule. So long as the educational program concentrated on textbook memorization, the library was not required to function in any other manner. But as the educational program evolves from traditional mediocrity to innovative excellence, the concept of the school library has to change from study hall, reference center to learning laboratory, from peripheral non-involvement to direct participation in all aspects of the educational program. Direct involvement of the library in the teaching and learning program has necessitated its functioning as a learning laboratory where the use of resources, facilities, and services is no longer sporadic, unplanned, and incidental but where the use of those resources, facilities, and services is purposeful, planned, and directly related and interrelated to a viable teaching and learning program.

LIBRARIAN AS ACTIVE TEACHER

Direct involvement of the school library in the teaching and learning program has changed the status of the school librarian from passive spectator to active participant in the educational endeavor. As study hall monitor and book curator the school librarian of the saber-tooth curriculum days had little responsibility of an educational nature. Today's school librarian is a teacher, a teacher in training, certification, service, and attitude. Today's school librarian serves in the triple capacity of team teacher, media programming engineer, and curriculum energizer. The school librarian's responsibility extends beyond organizing and maintaining a materials collection. His responsibility includes planning cooperatively with fellow teachers and working directly with students as teachers, librarians, and students work toward the common goal of educational excellence. No longer can the school librarian be relegated to the status of "hat-check boy in the halls of culture," for he no longer is an educational convenience. Today's school librarian is an educational instrument employed in vitalizing, energizing, and powering the educational program (See Appendix B).

LIBRARIAN AS A COOPERATING TEACHER

When the school librarian becomes directly involved in the teaching program the services, facilities, and resources of the library are integrated and coordinated with classroom teaching and learning. The classroom teacher and the librarian functioning as a team share the responsibility for designing and implementing a program to achieve the following educational objectives which despite their age have never been superseded as educational basics:

> The development of effective thinking;
> The cultivation of useful work habits and study skills;
> The inculcation of positive social attitudes;
> The acquisition of a wide range of significant interests;
> The development of social sensitivity;
> The development of increased appreciation of music, art, literature, and aesthetic experiences;
> The development of better personal-social adjustment;
> The acquisition of important information;
> The development of physical and mental health;
> The development of a consistent, positive philosophy of life.[28]

Together the teacher and the librarian design a media usage pattern to realize these objectives.

ADEQUACY OF LIBRARY RESOURCES

The promise of providing a quality, optimum education for each citizen cannot be realized if students are to continue to be restricted to what William Chase of the United States Office of Education has characterized as the traditional "2 x 4 education—between the two covers of the textbook and the four walls of the classroom."[29] A quality educational program provides far greater depth and breadth of understanding than the contents of any textbook. Likewise an optimum educational program requires resources beyond the textbook, for the textbook can generalize but cannot individualize teaching or learning. The school library must compensate for inherent textbook and classroom inadequacies. Effective teaching and effective learning require the resources, facilities, and services of a school library. How can the promise of an optimum education be met if students be limited to textbook content and classroom resources? A teaching and learning program of excellence leads out of the classroom and into the library where library resources and services can individualize, personalize, and humanize the educational endeavor. In the words of the 1960 *Standards for School Library Programs*:[30]

> Whatever form the soul-searching regarding the education of youth may take, sooner or later it has to reckon with the ade-

[28] Smith, Eugene R. et al. *Appraising and Recording Student Progress.* New York: Harper, 1942. p. 18.
[29] Editors of *Education U.S.A. The Shape of Education for 1964: A Handbook on Current Educational Affairs.* Washington, D.C.: National School Public Relations Association, National Education Association, 1964. p. 47.
[30] American Association of School Librarians. Op. cit., pp. 3-4.

quacy of the library resources in the schools. Any of the recommendations for the improvement of schools, currently receiving so much stress and attention, can be fully achieved only when the school has the full complement of library resources, personnel, and services. This fact holds true for the multitrack curriculum, ability groupings in subject areas, the expanded and intensified science program, the toughening of the intellectual content in all courses, advanced placement and accelerated programs, the development of the disciplines of critical thinking, the teaching of reading, the provision of a challenging education for superior students, the meeting of needs of all students no matter what their abilities may be, ungraded elementary school classes, and similar practices and proposals.

In the education of all youth, from the slowest learner in kindergarten to the most intelligent senior in high school, an abundance of printed and audio-visual materials is essential. These resources are the basic tools needed for the purposes of effective teaching and learning. That the achievement of the objectives of a good school program requires the resources and services of a school library has been recognized and demonstrated for many years by school board members, administrators, teachers, parents, and other people in communities having such schools. These individuals, too, have long realized that the school library program contributes something more to the over-all education of youth than materials and services geared to curricular needs. The scope of knowledge has become too vast to be covered extensively within the boundaries of classroom instruction, superior though that instruction may be. Through the school library, these boundaries can be extended immeasurably in all areas of knowledge and in all forms of creative expression, and the means provided to meet and to stimulate the many interests, appreciations, and curiosities of youth.

MULTI-MEDIA APPROACH TO TEACHING

There should be no sight and sound barriers in today's school library, for an educational program of excellence demands the multi-media approach to teaching and learning. Library resources can no longer be limited to printed materials; a school library program designed to implement a quality educational program must provide all types and kinds of instructional resources regardless of media format. The library equipped to meet the developmental needs of the educational program and the personal needs of the students must provide all manner and kind of media essential both to developing the curricular design and to meeting the needs, interests, goals, abilities, progress rate, and concerns of the students.

"SCHOOL LIBRARY BILL OF RIGHTS"

The American Association of School Librarians has stated in the "School Library Bill of Rights" that in selecting media the responsibility of the school library is:[31]

31 Ibid., p. 75.

To provide materials that will enrich and support the curriculum, taking into consideration the varied interests, abilities, and maturity levels of the pupils served;

To provide materials that will stimulate growth in factual knowledge, literary appreciation, aesthetic values, and ethical standards;

To provide a background of information which will enable students to make intelligent judgments in their daily lives;

To provide materials on opposing sides of controversial issues so that young citizens may develop under guidance the practice of critical reading and thinking;

To provide materials representative of many religions, ethnic, and cultural groups and their contributions to our American heritage;

To place principle above personal opinion and reason above prejudice in the selection of materials of the highest quality in order to assume a comprehensive collection appropriate for the users of the library.

THE LIBRARY AS LEARNING LABORATORY

The school librarian brings to the teaching plan the promise of realizing the teaching goals while meeting individual student needs. The goal of encouraging and enabling each student to think critically, reflectively, analytically, and creatively requires that each student receive individual guidance and practice in each of these areas of thinking. The goal also requires that substance for thinking be provided. You do not learn to think in a vacuum; you do not learn to think creatively without having at hand the raw material from which to fashion and shape thought. The school library is not a storehouse of ready-made thoughts nor is it a depository of ready-made solutions to problems. The school library is a learning laboratory where the resources for thinking and the techniques of thinking are joined into a pattern of purposeful, intelligent, profitable media usage.

The school library functioning as a learning laboratory provides active guidance to the student in his search for understanding. This guidance extends not only to student search for and choice of materials but includes the profitable use of those materials. Encouraging and enabling each student "to learn to learn" in the library, giving him guided practice in comprehending, analyzing, synthesizing, and evaluating ideas are constant concerns of an educationally effective librarian (See Appendix N). Since the goal of the educational program is to train students for effective thinking, the responsibility of the library must extend beyond organization and distribution of materials to encompass the most effective and efficient use of materials.

In the library functioning as a learning laboratory the student receives competent, informed guidance in how to read, how to listen, and how to view with purpose, profit, and satisfaction. He is also taught how to question, how to validate, how to select, how to relate, how to associate, how to integrate, and how to communicate ideas. Beginning in the elementary school library, the student is taught how to think and how to organize and express thought. Taking pencil in hand when opening a book and copying word for word, a practice all too common in school libraries in the past, should not be condoned in a learning laboratory library. Verbatim copying is not only intellectually dishonest on the part of the student but is professionally dishonest when ignored by teacher and by librarian. Copying requires no conscious thought process: the student is no more involved with the transfer from word to thought-image than the photocopy machine is organically changed when it mechanically transfers print from master to reproduction sheet. When the student is permitted to accept and perpetrate copying as learning, both teachers and librarians have failed to fulfill their proper function as educators. A student does not know innately how to unlock ideas hidden away "between, among, and behind the words." He must be taught how to learn. It takes special training and accumulated experience to learn how to run the thought maize with positive direction, absolute efficiency, and total effectiveness. The librarian as a teacher has professional responsibility not only to provide knowledge building resources but especially to provide competent guidance in the most profitable, effective, and efficient use of those resources.

SCHOOL LIBRARIAN AS THOUGHT ENERGIZER

The school librarian has been assigned the responsibility in today's school of encouraging and enabling each student "to learn to learn" (See Appendix N). The librarian is no longer chained to the charging desk; he no longer is concerned primarily with the circulation of materials but with the circulation of ideas, with encouraging the transfer of thought from written or spoken word into the student's own thought pattern, into the student's own stream of consciousness. *Today's school librarian is not a purveyor of things but is an energizer of thought.* Professionally he is committed to make learning more personally satisfying, more permanently meaningful, more lastingly significant (See Table II).

TABLE II

SCHOOL LIBRARY PROGRAM IN TRANSITION

FROM TRADITIONAL PRACTICES	TO INNOVATIVE PRACTICES
From the library as an auxiliary service	To the library as an integral component of the total educational program
From the library as a study hall	To the library as an educational force
From the library as a materials distribution center	To the library as a learning laboratory
From the library limited to a printed collection	To a library providing all kinds of instructional media
From the incidental use of library facilities, staff, and collection	To the planned, purposeful and educationally-significant use of library facilities, staff, and collection
From the librarian serving as study hall monitor	To the librarian serving as an educator
From the librarian as a curator of books	To the librarian programming for the most effective and educationally rewarding use of all types and kinds of instructional media.
From the librarian as an impersonal dispenser of material	To the librarian as a learning expediter personalizing the services of the library
From the librarian working in isolation	To the librarian serving as a cooperating and/or team teacher

From the librarian working incommu-   To the librarian directly involved in
nicado   curriculum planning, revision, and de-
                                        velopment

The school library has been assigned a leadership role in translating the democratic ideal of a quality, optimum education for each citizen from promise to actuality. Actualizing the promise has necessitated a library reformation of the scope and dimension commensurate with the needs created by the contemporary educational renaissance. As the educational program evolves from traditional mediocrity to innovative excellence, the function of the school library changes from study hall-book distribution center to learning laboratory, from peripheral non-involvement to direct participation in all aspects of the educational program. The status of the librarian has changed from studyhall monitor and book curator to team teacher, learning expediter, and media programming engineer. Today's school librarian extends the library's resources beyond traditional printed materials to all sorts and kinds of media essential to the developmental needs of the curriculum and to the personal needs of the students. The major function of today's school librarian is to join the resources for thinking and the techniques of thinking into a pattern of purposeful, intelligent, and profitable usage. Today's school librarian must view his contribution to actualizing the educational promise as a sacred trust for "the extent to which many children and young people of today will be creative, informed, knowledgeable, and within their own years, wise, will be shaped by the boundaries of the content of the library resources within their schools."[32]

[32] Ibid., p. 4.

3 The School Librarian, a Mediating Agent for Educational Excellence

The tasks I have suggested for the librarian require a person with high-level professional training. They make the library an educational environment for maximal learning. They require a librarian who understands the broader range of materials of instruction now available and who is sensitive to the total curriculum of the school. They make the librarian a co-worker in an enriched program of education. They build the idea and the ideal of an educative environment.*

The school librarian exerts an influence not only on the quality of the library program but also on the quality of the educational program. Since the service of the library permeates the totality of the teaching and learning program, the quality of leadership, guidance, and service provided by the school librarian influences and affects directly the quality of both the teaching and the learning program. The school librarian is a teacher in service and significance. Since "no educational program can be better than its teachers"[33] and since "one of the key factors in achieving our (national) goals (is) the quality of teaching,"[34] the quality of the school librarian becomes a key factor in implementing an educational program of the high degree of excellence required to meet our contemporary societal goals.

A QUALITY LIBRARIAN

What is a quality school librarian? First and foremost, a quality librarian is a competent and effective teacher—a teacher in training, certification, service, commitment, and attitude. He brings to his position training in teaching techniques and methods, an understanding of how learning takes place, and knowledge of subject content and curricular design. Second, a quality librarian is an instructional media specialist bringing to his position extensive knowledge of types, kinds, and content of instructional media, specialized training in how to organize and administer a media collection, in how to build self-knowledge of media and curriculum content, in how to

---

* Dale, Edgar. "Educating for Flexibility." *ALA Bulletin*, February, 1963. vol. 57, no. 2, p. 134.
33 *The Pursuit of Excellence: Education and the Future of America.* Op. cit., p. 23.
34 Hanna, Paul R., ed. *Education: An Instrument of National Goals.* New York: McGraw-Hill, 1962. p. 22.

relate and match media to teaching goals and learning needs, in how to program for the most effective and most efficient use of media (See Chapter 5).
The school librarian holds membership in both the teaching and the library
professions. He is an educational generalist and a media programming
specialist. The quality school librarian seeing and respecting the duality
of his professional service, places equal significance on each role, realizing
that, like the two sides of a coin, neither role is valid without the other.

JUDGING PROFESSIONALISM

The professional qualifications of the school librarian can well be judged
by measuring his training, service, commitment and attitude against the
hallmarks established for judging professionalism. The following definition
found in *Webster's Third International Dictionary* provides these hallmarks:

profession: A calling requiring specialized knowledge and often long
and intensive preparation including instruction in skills
and methods as well as in the scientific, historical, or
scholarly principles underlying such skills and methods,
maintaining by force of organization or concerted opinion
high standards of achievement and conduct, and committing its members to continued study and a kind of
work which holds for its prime purpose, the rendering of
a public service.

The school librarian must meet the above requirements if his service is to
be of true professional stature.

PROFESSIONAL PREPARATION OF LIBRARIAN

The American Association of School Librarians has clearly defined for its
membership the necessity of the school librarian's preparation to serve both
as a teacher and as a media specialist. In the *1960 Standards,* the American
Association of School Librarians endorsed the following major and basic
principles: which have been re-grouped here for ease of reference.[35]

> A broad, general education is essential for the school librarian.
> This basic background is first started in college and continues
> throughout the lifetime of the school librarian.

> The type of professional preparation best suited for the school li-
> brarian is that described in the official statement prepared by the
> Joint American Association of School Librarians, the Association of
> College and Research Librarians, and the Department of Audio-
> Visual Instruction of the NEA, in 1958. . . . The knowledge and
> basic skills required for instructional materials specialists to do
> professional work in education, and the most likely sources of ob-
> taining basic competencies, are as follows:
> 1. SUCCESSFUL TEACHING EXPERIENCE. Instructional materials spe-
>   cialists should first of all be experienced teachers. This experi-
>   ence may be acquired by years of classroom teaching, or, in

[35] American Association of School Librarians. Op. cit., pp. 59-62.

the case of those who enter the profession without experience, through an organized internship program following the completion of their course work. It is essential that instructional materials specialists secure experience on curriculum committees and that they gain experience in guidance and supervision.

2. FOUNDATION AREAS. Instructional materials specialists should have course work in:
   (a) educational administration and supervision;
   (b) principles of learning;
   (c) curriculum development;
   (d) guidance and counseling; and
   (e) mass communications.
   Furthermore they should demonstrate a working knowledge of research methods as applied to instructional materials.

3. SPECIALIZED AREAS. Instructional materials specialists should have course work and in-service experience in the following areas relating directly to the nature and effective use of materials:
   (a) analysis of instructional materials, their nature and content;
   (b) methods of selecting and evaluating materials, through study of individual media as well as through cross-media study by curriculum unit or grade level;
   (c) utilization of materials;
   (d) production of appropriate instructional materials, including laboratory work with specific media; and
   (e) processes for the organization and maintenance of materials and equipment.

The professional preparation of the school librarian meets the certification requirements of his state, of the regional accrediting agency of his state, and of the school system in which he is working.

The basic program of general and professional education recommended for the school librarian is a five-year program. The fifth year may be based on an undergraduate minor in school librarianship in a college or university with an approved program of this type.

REQUISITES OF TEACHING

As a teacher, the school librarian must bring to his position an understanding of the professional nature and challenge of teaching. He must appreciate the necessity of the teacher being original, inventive, and creative, not merely informed. William H. Burton in *The Guidance of Learning Activities*, clearly defines the requisites of teaching.[36]

36 Burton, William H. *The Guidance of Learning Activities: A Summary of the Principles of Teaching Based on the Growth of the Learner.* 3rd ed. New York: Appleton-Century-Crofts, Educational Division, Meredith Corp. 1962. pp. 267-268.

Teaching is not a routine or rule-of-thumb process; it is a genuine intellectual adventure. The mechanical use of formulas and devices, slavish dependence upon methods and techniques recommended by training institutions or by fellow teachers will not beget learning. Teaching demands instead the ability to adapt boldly, to invent, to create procedures to meet the ever changing demands of a given learning situation. Teaching demands continuous, imaginative anticipation of the mental processes of others, the ability to think quickly, to phrase questions and answers so as to stimulate thinking, the ability to keep intricate and subtle learning activities organized and moving toward a desirable outcome without at the same time dominating or coercing. Teaching necessitates a broad background of technological information.

Teaching cannot possibly be done on the basis of common sense or experience alone. A surgeon could not possibly learn how to operate for appendicitis on the basis of common sense and raw experience. Engineers do not build tunnels from two sides of a mountain to meet squarely in the middle on the basis of common sense or raw trial and error. To do either of these things on the basis of common sense or experience alone would result in many deaths and in huge waste of money. These things are done successfully on the basis of lengthy, difficult professional training which includes a period of experience under guidance. Naturally, later experience and critical analysis of that experience play a large part in improving skill, but this experience and analysis are enlightened by the preparatory training in basic technology. Furthermore, there is demanded in addition the ability to make courageous adaptations of known procedures to unexpected conditions and unusual variations, and the ability to invent new procedures. So it is with teaching. A teacher can no more teach little children to read on the basis of her common sense or uncritical experience than can the surgeon operate or the engineer carry out projects. An even closer parallel can be drawn between the diagnosis of illness by the physician and the diagnosis of learning difficulty by the teacher.

How then will the actual necessary skills be developed? Largely through the resolute critical analysis of one's own experience. This analysis is possible only with teachers who see clearly that teaching is in fact dynamic instead of static, an exciting intellectual enterprise, and whose self-analysis is illuminated by adequate general and technological background. Teaching, more than most human activities, demands the use of judgment, imagination, initiative, and enthusiasm. Particularly does it demand the use of freely working, creative imagination.

The librarian who would serve as a teacher must respect and value teaching as an adventure of the spirit as well as an adventure of the mind.

CHARACTERISTICS OF A MASTER TEACHER

The quality school librarian must have the characteristics attributed to the "master" teacher. The following characteristics are listed in the *Educator's*

Encyclopedia as being those expected of the master teacher.[37] The word "librarian" has been added in parenthesis to show that the teacher and librarian must share these characteristics in each case.

The master teacher would be expected to perform his responsibilities outstandingly in all aspects including those that follow:

ESTABLISHMENT OF OBJECTIVES. The establishment of teaching objectives should consider the whole child, his needs, his readiness, his interests, his abilities. The outstanding teacher (and librarian) formulates and selects the objectives of his own program with full realization of these pupil considerations and with full cognizance of the objectives of the educational program of the school district.

GUIDANCE OF PUPILS. Once the objectives have been determined, the outstanding teacher (and librarian) will guide his pupils in defining their own objectives, help them to realize them, and seek to aid them in working independently toward their established goals, insuring that they are working to the fullest of their capacity.

SYSTEMATIC PLANNING. The master teacher (and librarian) will seek to plan systematically, so that appropriate learning experiences are provided to lead toward the objectives of the district, of his own classes, and of his own pupils.

ORGANIZATION OF SUBJECT MATTER. The teacher (and librarian) will systematically plan and organize subject matter in sequential, continuous, and developmental order. In this planning, the master teacher (and librarian) will consider patterns of child growth and development as well as academic needs for the future of the pupil.

SELECTION OF MATERIALS. In order to successfully provide important learning experience, the master teacher (and librarian) will be fully aware of all materials that are at his disposal to further the educational program. He will determine the most appropriate materials for the learning experience he wishes to provide and select them for use in his instructional program. . . .

USE OF A VARIETY OF TEACHING AIDS. Just as he selects the most appropriate materials, the outstanding teacher (and librarian) also takes advantage of a variety of teaching and learning aids. These undoubtedly include community resources, magazines, newspapers, demonstrations, models, specimens, exhibits, and the like. . . .

USE OF A VARIETY OF TECHNIQUES. The outstanding teacher (and librarian) knows that various techniques must be used in teaching. He will use many of these when they are appropriate to the lesson at hand. . . . In fact, the outstanding teacher (and librarian) uses every device or technique he knows about, but he uses them at various times and for specific purposes.

MAINTENANCE OF CLASSROOM CLIMATE. The master teacher (and librarian) realizes that the classroom (and library) climate can be one of the most valuable assets to the teacher-learning situation. He

37 Smith, Edward W., et al. *The Educator's Encyclopedia*. Englewood Cliffs, New Jersey: Prentice-Hall, 1963. pp. 209-210.

strives to maintain a healthy climate, free from tensions and yet with a maximum amount of pupil self-control.

EVALUATION OF PUPILS. A continuous plan for evaluation of pupils is provided by the superior teacher (and librarian). This plan includes the use of a variety of instruments for purposes of testing and appraisal. (The librarian has the obligation to encourage student self-evaluation and self-appraisal.)

COUNSELING OF PUPILS AND PARENTS. Realizing the need for full cooperation between the home and school, the outstanding teacher (and librarian) will continuously counsel parents and pupils about the individual's educational progress.

WORKING WITH STAFF. The teacher (and librarian) works harmoniously with fellow staff members, not only in his own school but throughout the district when the occasion demands it. He is loyal to his colleagues, to the school, and to the pupils in the school.

EXPLAINING TO PUPILS. Explanations and instructions offered to pupils are presented in clear and understandable ways by the outstanding teacher (and librarian). Pupils seldom need further explanation, but they feel free to seek individual assistance when they do.

PRESENTATION OF PROBLEMS. Problems are represented in the classroom (and in the library) in an interesting and stimulating manner. These problems are offered with a full realization of individual differences, so the various rates of learning are provided for: The slower child is offered suitable problems, and the faster-learning child is fully challenged in solving problems within his ability range.

MOTIVATION OF PUPILS. Pupils are thoroughly motivated by the master teacher (and librarian) to take action to achieve the goals that they themselves have established under his guidance.

DEMONSTRATION OF ENTHUSIASM. The outstanding teacher (and librarian) is enthusiastic about his responsibilities and his teaching assignments. He takes full part in all the activities that are part of his duties, and he is quick to sense the need for cooperation and assistance in activities that do not fall within his areas of responsibility.

MAINTENANCE OF APPROPRIATE APPEARANCE. The superior teacher (and librarian) gives attention to his own appearance. . . . he is careful in his dress to provide an example of neatness and cleanliness to his pupils and his co-workers. His voice is pleasant and his manner is conducive to good learning situations and human relations.

SETTING OF STANDARDS. The master teacher (and librarian) sets standards for individual and group work in his classroom (or library). These standards are realistic and determined as the result of his knowledge of the pupils for whom he is responsible.

PROMOTION OF MORALE. Throughout the school day and beyond it, as he partakes of his share of responsibility for activities, the master teacher (and librarian) seeks to promote high morale in students and co-workers alike. He establishes rapport with both groups so he can be effective in guiding their enthusiasm along proper channels.

USES OF DEMOCRATIC CONCEPTS. The classroom (or library) for which the teacher (librarian) is responsible is ordinarily exemplified by full realization of democratic concepts of discipline and behavior of pupils. Pupils have understanding of the need for self-control; the teacher has established a democratic atmosphere that is not permissive, but is representative of pupil–teacher planning.

PROVISIONS FOR INSTRUCTIONAL IMPROVEMENT. Fully aware that he has much to learn about the teaching-learning process the master teacher (and librarian) is usually one of the first to participate in professional efforts of the staff to improve the instruction of the educational program of the school. In addition, the master teacher (and librarian) is willing to share his own successes and failures with his co-workers, as an aid to him and to them.

PROVISIONS FOR REMEDIAL INSTRUCTION. Pupils who need help are provided with remedial instruction by the outstanding teacher (and librarian). This help is given during regular class time whenever possible; when time does not permit it, the master teacher (and librarian) stands willing to offer his help outside of regular class hours even at the sacrifice of his own time.

POSSESSION OF A SENSE OF HUMOR. A sense of humor applied at appropriate times is usually one of the assets of an outstanding teacher (and librarian). The sense of humor is not only at home in the classroom (and library), but also when associating with fellow workers.

KNOWLEDGE OF PUPILS. The master teacher (and librarian) knows the pupils in his classes as individuals. He knows their interests, needs, and abilities, because he has used school records, interviews with parents, conversations with other teachers, and many other sources to gain this knowledge.

INTERPRETATION OF THE SCHOOL. Knowledge and accuracy are used by the outstanding teacher (and librarian) in order to interpret the school and the community at all possible opportunities.

KNOWLEDGE OF THE SCHOOL AND THE COMMUNITY. The master teacher (and librarian) knows the school and the community, and he can answer questions about either. He uses his knowledge as an aid to his understanding of each and his ability to use the resources of each in the teaching-learning situation.

PARTICIPATION IN PROFESSIONAL ORGANIZATIONS. The master teacher (and librarian) is usually active in local, state, and national professional organizations. This activity may be limited to membership, but he takes advantage of all opportunities to attend conferences and meetings for his own information and for the professional growth of himself and his co-workers.

PROMOTION OF PROFESSIONAL ETHICS. Professional ethics are not only understood, but also practiced by the outstanding teacher (and librarian) in his behavior and relations with pupils, parents, and the staff.

ATTITUDE OF LIBRARIAN

The librarian by attitude sets the tone for the library itself. Today's school librarian should be the antithesis of the stereotype study hall librarian. The traditional morgue-like atmosphere which permeated the school library in the past has nothing in common with a library program designed to create, sustain, and reward interest in learning. The library functioning as a learning laboratory should be a happy, bright, inviting place, no matter how old the building, or how small or vast the space, for the factor determining the library climate is not the physical features but the attitude of the librarian himself. The atmosphere of the library reflects as a mirror the self-image of the librarian. If the librarian is happy in his work, he welcomes the opportunity to work with teachers and students; the library atmosphere will be reflective of his attitude. Students and teachers cherish the librarian who gives cheerfully and willingly of his time, his energy, his competence, and his concern—they will beat a path to the library door and count themselves blessed to be there.

LIBRARIAN AS A TEAM TEACHER

No longer can the librarian anticipate serving in cloistered isolation from the drama and the business of teaching. The magnitude of today's educational enterprise requires the shared competencies of faculty teams rather than the single competence of even the most gifted and most talented teacher. The school librarian must bring to his position an awareness of his role and his function as a planning, working, and cooperating member of the educational task force.

The school librarian as a contributing member of a teaching team will share the responsibility for designing, structuring, implementing, evaluating, and re-designing teaching units; i.e., stating unit goals and objectives, determining topic scope and sequence, specifying basic concepts, skills, understandings, appreciations to be developed; designing basic teaching and learning strategies, and selecting media to support the implementation of the unit plan.

The school librarian must be conversant with the unit method of teaching—the method which organizes "subject-matter content and outcomes and thought processes into learning experiences suited to the maturity and needs (personal and social) of the learners, all combined into a whole with internal integrity determined by immediate and ultimate goals"[38] (See Chapter 4). The librarian serves as a media specialist when he relates library resources to teaching and learning support needs. The librarian's modus operandi is developing library-mediating plans to facilitate and expedite the implementation of the teacher's plan. The librarian in scheduled consultation with a single classroom teacher:

> Determines the contribution the library is to make to the overall teaching plan (See Appendix I);
> Determines specific teaching objectives to be accomplished through the use of library resources and guidance (See Chapter 4);

[38] Burton, William H. Op. cit., p. 329.

Identifies basic concepts and skills to be introduced, reinforced, or extended (See Chapter 4);

Structures learning guides; reading, viewing, listening checklists; summary forms; reaction charts; critical evaluation scorecards; etc.;

Determines appropriateness of assignments and the availability of suitable materials (See Chapter 5);

Sets target dates for each phase of the library support program;

Designs specific teaching strategies requiring library support (See Chapters 4 and 5);

Designs specific learning experiences and activities requiring library resources (See Chapters 4 and 5);

Designs specific unit and support activities (See Chapter 4);

Designs strategies for meeting student needs, interests, goals, abilities, progress rate, concerns, and potential (See Chapter 4);

Identifies specific media uniquely appropriate for each of the teaching and learning designs (See Chapter 5);

Programs for the most logical use of media in progressive, sequential order (See Chapters 4 and 5);

Designs appropriate culminating teaching and learning activities (See Chapter 4);

Designs appropriate evaluating activities to determine the effectiveness of the library support program (See Chapter 4).

The librarian planning with a faculty team suggests specific resources which will meet specific team teaching procedures and goals:

This motion picture or sound filmstrip could be used as a class introduction to the unit;

This series of study prints might be of value in developing basic terminology for the below average reader;

This series of overhead transparencies might have value in introducing these basic concepts;

This reading guide might prove useful in orienting the students to techniques of summarization;

This reference tool might be introduced effectively at this time;

This resource kit might prove of value for the teacher when teaching this unit.

The librarian planning with a teaching team relates the service of the library to the overall teaching plan by suggesting possible library usage patterns both for topic development and for class, group, or individual knowledge-building. When developing the basic unit design the team relies upon the librarian to incorporate library resources and support activities essential to the implementation of each phase of the unit. From preliminary planning sessions the librarian and fellow team teachers gain a clear understanding of the total teaching plan, of the interrelation of each part to the whole, and of the specific contribution library resources, services, and guidance must make to facilitate the development of the total unit plan.

TEACHER-LIBRARIAN COOPERATION

Whether the school program be organized for formal or informal teaming, teacher-librarian cooperation is basic to an educational program of excellence. Direct communication and cooperation are the operational bases for meaningful, effective, and efficient integration of library resources and service with the teaching program. The librarian working in isolation from the planning of program can never provide for teacher, class, or student the degree of effectiveness possible when pre-planning exists. Just as planning is basic to good classroom teaching, so is planning supportive to good teaching in a library functioning as a learning laboratory. In the chart "Primarily, the Teacher Must Know" (See Figure III), Murray and Dorris Lee, experts in curriculum design and implementation, graphically illustrate the mediating power of teaching resources in meeting educational goals and student needs. The promise of a quality, optimum program precludes leaving to chance the availability and use of knowledge-building and knowledge-extending resources. It is only logical that the librarian who is charged with the responsibility for implementing the educational program be informed as to the scope, content, and implementation needs of that program.

LIBRARIAN PERSONALIZES TEACHING

Since the school librarian is a teacher, he must bring to his position both respect and concern for the individuality of the student. He must place a high priority on customizing and personalizing the services of the library. He must provide an environment reflective of the needs of students, establish a climate conducive to maximum learning, and appreciate that for many the library may be the only place where the student may taste success, where his disabilities are not on public display and where he can work at his own speed in his own private way. The librarian who holds authentic respect for the individuality of the student must realize that the library can serve as an avenue of escape from the pressures of mass education. Here the student can choose his own area of specialization, define his own limits, and set his own pace; here he is in competition only with himself; the pressure of group, class, and ability competition is mercifully absent. Here the student can find an outlet for his own interests, inventiveness, and creativity; here he can bring substance to his dreams; here he can find an outlet for his love of poetry, music, drama, art; here he can improvise, experiment, and explore without fear of ridicule by his peers.

The librarian who would personalize his services as a teacher must humanize his approach to teaching. He must hold and demonstrate authentic concern for the intellectual, personal, moral, and spiritual well-being of each student no matter how rich or how poor, how bright or how dull. He must build his knowledge of an individual, not only by observation but from day to day contact, working directly with the student as mentor, counselor, and friend. The librarian who would personalize, customize, and humanize the services of the library must have as his constant goal a sincere desire to make learning in the library a means of each student's achieving self-understanding, self-realization, and self-fulfillment.

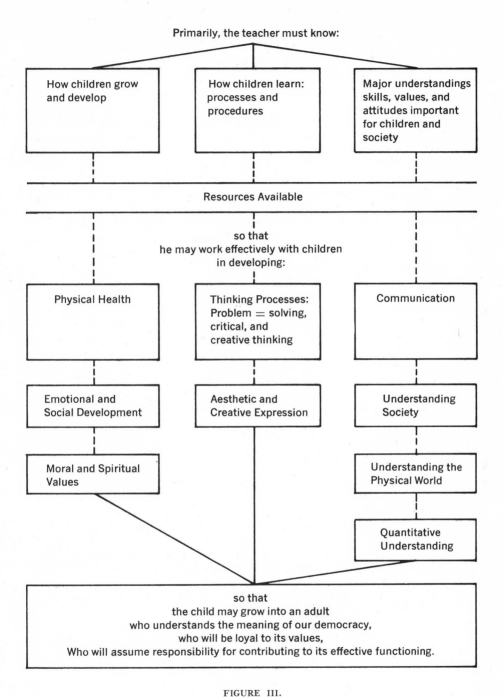

FIGURE III.

PRIMARILY THE TEACHER MUST KNOW:*

* From J. Murray Lee and Dorris M. Lee. *The Child and His Curriculum*. New York: Appleton-Century-Crofts, 1960. p. 12.

INDIVIDUAL STUDENT DIFFERENCES

The school librarian who would become a mediating force—the force for conveying understanding and communicating knowledge—must recognize and respect the individuality of the learner. Effective teaching begins with a recognition of and a respect for the unique complexity of each human being. Each learner is a complex blending of myriad physical, intellectual, emotional, social, cultural, and environmental factors. No matter how homogeneous the community, whether it be slum or affluent suburbia, the school membership is made up of individuals, with:

varying cultural backgrounds;
varying economic backgrounds;
varying social backgrounds;
varying environmental influences;
varying degrees of sensitivity;
varying degrees of incentive;
varying degrees of drive;
varying degrees of awareness;
varying degrees of stability;

varying degrees of receptivity to learning;
varying degrees of creativity;
varying intellectual capacities;
varying cognitive styles;
varying perception patterns;
varying emotional patterns;
varying reaction patterns;
varying interests and
varying goals.

The librarian who holds authentic concern and respect for the individuality of the student will deal realistically but humanely with each student providing learning experiences and/or resources compatible with the student's needs, interests, goals, abilities, concerns, and progress rate (See Appendix J).

PRINCIPLES DIRECTING LEARNING

The school librarian who would expedite learning must have a clear understanding of the principles directing the learning process. Ralph Garry, Professor of Educational Psychology, Boston University, has identified 13 cardinal principles[39] to be followed by teachers as they plan for and guide student learning (See Chapter 10):

ESTABLISH A PREDISPOSITION TO LEARN. If the learner sees purpose in what he is learning and has some knowledge of the value of the task, he will pay attention and learn more. Attitude is a generalized set. Lack of confidence, dislike of school or teacher, and failure to find value in assignments unfavorably affect children's efforts to learn.

(Just as the textbook is not self-motivating and therefore requires the guidance and the inspiration of the teacher so does the card catalog lack the capability of motivating student interest. The librarian is the motivational force which sells the student on the value of using library resources when solving a problem, satisfying his curiosity, or completing an assignment.)

CLARIFY THE TASK; DEFINE THE PROBLEM. The learning situation should be such that unnecessary errors are avoided. Errors which

[39] Garry, Ralph. *The Psychology of Learning*. Washington, D.C.: Center for Applied Research in Education, 1963. pp. 76-77.

contribute to knowledge of results may help, but those which result from confusion only produce more confusion.

(The librarian realizing that each child is a unique learner can appreciate that assignments made to a class frequently are not understood by each individual in the class. In order to minimize student frustration and waste of energy and time the librarian can willingly help the student to clarify the assignment, to determine the dimension of the problem, and to select the most promising method to be employed in solving a problem—See Chapter 10.)

PROVIDE A MODEL, A DEMONSTRATION, VERBAL GUIDANCE, AND CUES. A demonstration of the skill provides a model to be simulated; verbal guidance and cues help the learner direct his efforts by informing him of what to do and how to do it.

(The librarian cooperates with classroom teachers in designing models to be followed by students in organizing, analyzing, evaluating, and communicating ideas. As the student works in the library, the librarian encourages or reminds the student to relate the model to the task at hand—See Table X, Examples IV, V, VI.)

ALLOW ADEQUATE TIME AND DISTRIBUTE PRACTICE. Spaced practice with rest periods facilitates learning. Short initial periods which are generally lengthened as skill develops are desirable. The early phases of practice periods are more effective inasmuch as efficiency decreases as fatigue and boredom increase. Mass practice to attain peak performance.

(The librarian as he introduces or reinforces study skills guards against the tendency to teach too much, too fast.)

PRACTICE THE TASK AS A WHOLE IF IT IS SIMPLE OR SHORT; BREAK COMPLEX TASKS INTO NATURAL COMPONENTS. Children tend to learn better by the part method; adults by the whole method if they have had some experience with it. In the whole method, progress is not readily apparent, a factor which can be discouraging to young children. Complete mastery of each part is not needed before introducing the sequential part.

(The librarian as he guides the student in his search for and use of materials can help him to identify and sequentialize the components of a problem thereby encouraging him to see and to anticipate the logical course of topic development.)

INSURE ACCURATE OR CORRECT INITIAL RESPONSES. Avoid errors as far as possible and check them on their first appearance, unless to do so inhibits the motivation or effort of the learner.

(The librarian in orienting the student to a knowledge-building activity can alert him to certain pitfalls to avoid and can encourage him to check back when unsure of procedure.)

ENCOURAGE MEANINGFUL ASSOCIATIONS. Associations within the material encourage the development of an internal organization. Learning is facilitated by a contextual organization. Transfer of training from previous experiences is desirable.

(The librarian can facilitate student perception and awareness by encouraging the student to associate and relate new understanding with appropriate past learning experiences and then to synthesize past and present learnings into a coherent pattern of interrelatedness.)

PROVIDE FOR RECALL AND RECITATION. Meaningful recall in any degree is conducive to favorable attitudes, contributes to meaningful learning, and allows for more effective distribution of practice. Too-early recall however leads to guessing and retards learning. (The librarian can facilitate learning by prompting student recall of previous use of tools, skills, or similar patterns of learning.)

PROVIDE IMMEDIATE KNOWLEDGE OF RESULTS. Accurate information as to progress is as valuable as reward in promoting learning. Delayed knowledge of results . . . is not as helpful.
(The librarian can encourage the student to evaluate his own work by helping him measure it against appropriate criteria.)

OVERLEARN ONCE MASTERY IS ATTAINED. Retention is increased, positive transfer of training promoted, and interference with other learning reduced by any degree of overlearning. Drill should be meaningful, be similar to the situation in which the skill is to be used, and should command the attention of the student.
(The librarian can assure retention of study skills by seeing that the skills are integrated with the teaching and learning program and are introduced, reintroduced, and practiced in meaningful context.)

REWARD LIBERALLY AND EARLY. Rewards reinforce behavior. They are best when they are an intrinsic part of the activity. Artificial incentives are useful in maintaining effort until some sense of achievement and mastery evolves.
(The librarian can reward the student by following through after the student has completed his work in the library to discover how a report, a debate, a demonstration has gone; by commending the student for a job well done.)

APPLY THE SKILL OR LEARNING. Have children make use of what they learn in order to foster retention and produce transfer of training.
(The librarian when planning with teachers can design learning activities which will reinforce and extend previous learning thereby demonstrating the utility and continuity of knowledge.)

HELP THE LEARNER TO ANALYZE HIS PERFORMANCE. Realistic appraisal and critical analysis are importantly related outcomes of learning.
(The librarian can encourage the student to evaluate critically and objectively the adequacy of his achievements and understanding and then to plan for systematic strengthening of noted weaknesses.)

LIBRARIAN AS EXPEDITER OF LEARNING

The school librarian applies his knowledge of how learning takes place as he works with curriculum committees developing teaching and learning experiences, as he plans with fellow teachers for the integration of library resources and services with their teaching plans, and as he directs and guides classes, groups, and individual students in use of library resources. The contemporary emphasis on independent study neither excludes nor excuses the librarian from working with the student (See Appendix N). Just as the textbook requires the inspired and informed guidance of the classroom teacher so a library resource frequently requires the specialized competency and guidance of the librarian (See Table III). Paraphrasing John Dewey, there is no sense in having an experienced mature adult

TABLE III.

PROFILE OF THE COMPETENT, EDUCATIONALLY
EFFECTIVE SCHOOL LIBRARIAN

A school librarian to serve competently and effectively must

Be a teacher in preparation, certification, service, and attitude

Bring to his position a broad, academic background

Have specialized training in the psychology of teaching and the psychology of learning

Have specialized training in curriculum study and design

Have specialized training in organizing and administering a media collection

Be willing to build knowledge in depth of the school's instructional program

Value the opportunity to participate actively in all phases of the teaching and learning program

See the reasonableness, the value, and the necessity of integrating the library program with the educational program

Hold genuine respect and authentic concern for the personal and educational welfare of each student

Be conversant with curricular content and design

Be capable of translating curricular needs into commensurate patterns of media usage and library service

Be capable and willing to customize, personalize, and humanize the services of the library

Be capable of working cooperatively with fellow teachers to integrate library resources, services, and guidance with the classroom teaching and learning program

Be alert to educational changes and willing to tailor library services to meet those changes

Be capable of growing and changing in a positive, realistic, creative, disciplined way

Be willing to renovate as well as innovate

Find satisfaction, stimulation, and challenge from participating in the teaching and learning enterprise

around if he is not to aid the less experienced immature learner to progress.[40] The librarian teaches the student how to use knowledge-building and knowledge-extending resources with profit, challenge, and satisfaction. The availability of resources does not make the library educationally significant; it is in the effective and efficient use of the resources that the library

[40] Dewey, John. *Experience and Education*. New York: Macmillan, 1938. pp. 31-32.

becomes an educational agent. The librarian designs and develops the library program to make teaching more dynamically effective, to make learning more permanently meaningful, more lastingly significant, and more personally satisfying. Direct involvement in the teaching and learning program has changed the function of the library from a materials storehouse to a learning laboratory and has changed the role of the librarian from curator of things to expediter of learning.

LIBRARIAN'S SELF-IMAGE

The librarian who would serve effectively as a teacher must be self-motivated by a continuous compelling zest for learning. He must regard his service as a creative challenge—a never-ending quest for added understanding and deepened insight. He must possess an infectious enthusiasm for learning which permeates his work with teachers and students. He must derive satisfaction from exploring the new, the untried, the unfamiliar as well as from uncovering in the familiar something new, significant, and unsuspected. He must possess an insatiable curiosity about the hidden value and potential utility of every library resource. He must value media not as things but as ideas, delighting in searching for, identifying, analyzing, grouping, and organizing ideas into patterns of logical, cohesive interrelatedness. He must derive stimulation and satisfaction from the realization that his work is never done: new materials must be searched for and evaluated; old materials must be re-evaluated in the light of current needs; new curricular trends, content, and methods must be studied and reflected in the library program; new faculty and students must be welcomed and their interests and concerns discovered and translated into commensurate patterns of library support service. The librarian who elects to serve in an educational environment should be capable of finding challenge and satisfaction in learning and in helping others to learn. He must view his service as an adventure of the mind and of the spirit, a demanding but rewarding adventure in creative self-realization, self-expression, and professional self-fulfillment.

4 The Role of The School Librarian As Curriculum Consultant

The curriculum worker . . . has one basic responsibility—fashioning learning opportunities. *Details of his contribution will differ, depending upon his nearness to the classroom; but, no matter what his status, the curriculum worker finds himself taking part in ordering and reordering four basic elements out of which a learning program is created. These elements are time, space, material resources, and human resources.*

The tempo of *educational change* must increase in direct proportion to the speed of man's proliferation of knowledge. There is too much that needs to be taught and too much that must be learned to permit the worshipful continuance of the educational status quo. The one constant in contemporary education is change—change that is necessitated by man's explosion of knowledge barriers (See Figure I). Heeding the warning of the historian Toynbee, that "the nemesis of creativity is the idolization of an ephemeral technique,"[41] the thoughtful educator discards the outmoded when he has discovered better ways to meet the needs of society and the future needs of the citizens of that society. Planning for meaningful change is a professional way of life, for "competency in teaching is not possible at all without an ardent desire to grow and to improve both personally and in professional knowledge and skill; willingness to give up easy, well known routines; willingness to study the new and go through the arduous and difficult process of learning new ways."[42]

LIBRARIAN AS AGENT FOR CURRICULAR CHANGE

The administrator who values the library as an integral part of the educational program will expect the librarian to be an agent for change and to take an active part in all phases of curriculum study and revision. The fol-

* Miel, Alice. "Learning More About Learning: A Key to Curriculum Improvement." *Learning More About Learning.* Edited by Alexander Frazier. Washington, D.C.: Association for Supervision and Curriculum Development, 1959. p. 1.
41 Toynbee, Arnold J. *A Study of History.* Abridged by D. C. Somervell. New York: Oxford University Press, 1946. vol. I, p. 326.
42 Burton, William H. Op. cit., p. 249.

lowing educational growth activities commonly expected of teachers will likewise be expected of the librarian:[43]

> SERVING ON CURRICULUM COMMITTEES for such purposes as to select textbooks, to recommend the purchase of audio-visual aids or other instructional resources, to develop teaching guides, to prepare resource units, to determine specific goals for each grade, or to study ways to improve some aspects of the . . . curriculum.
>
> PARTICIPATING IN WORKSHOPS to develop new materials, to learn how to use a new curriculum guide, to become acquainted with new instructional resources, to plan ways of improving instruction, to learn how to deal with special problems of gifted or slow learning children, and others.
>
> (PARTICIPATING IN) GRADE LEVEL MEETINGS to make recommendations for the purchase of materials, to suggest goals to be achieved, to study suitability of textbooks or other instructional resources, to study ways of utilizing community resources, and others.
>
> (PARTICIPATING IN) PROFESSIONAL GROWTH CONFERENCES, INSTITUTES, AND MEETINGS to become familiar with latest trends, practices, or procedures in teaching . . .
>
> (PARTICIPATING IN) RESEARCH ACTIVITIES to try out tentatively prepared guides or instructional material, to experiment with new units, to evaluate books or instructional resources.

Traditionally planning the education program has been the responsibility of the local school district. Some states recommend or mandate general course requirements but delegate to local school districts the responsibility for determining course organization and content. All too frequently in the past the local district relied on the textbook as the course of study letting the contents of the textbook determine what was to be taught in any subject at any grade level. Contemporary concern for excellence requires that the educational program be planned and structured to provide unity, continuity, balance and harmony in the total program, kindergarten through grade 12. It is increasingly common for local school districts to develop their own comprehensive curriculum guides and to involve their teachers and librarians in each phase of curricular study and design.

Today curriculum change is regarded as a long-range, continuous, organized, and on-going activity involving

> "a systematic method of study, evaluation, and communication. To reach some end or objective, a series of tasks must be accomplished in some prescribed order. Such tasks, or stages of development in curriculum change, are—
>
> IDENTIFICATION OF A PARTICULAR NEED TO CHANGE
> (Original idea or initiative may come from anybody)
> Evaluation of existing program
> Criticism of status quo

[43] Jarolimek, John. *Social Studies in Elementary Education*. 2nd ed. New York: Macmillan, 1963. p. 29.

STUDY OF ALTERNATIVE PROPOSALS FOR CHANGE

SELECTION OF PROPOSED CHANGE

(May be for one subject, one procedure, and only one school, rather than the total system)

PILOT STUDY DESIGNED

Trial of proposed change

Equipment and instructional materials proposed

High involvement of total staff

APPRAISAL OF DATA COLLECTED FROM PILOT STUDY

Further tryouts, modification of proposal

CONTINUOUS STUDY BY ALL STAFF INVOLVED

Adequate inservice activities, time, and consultant help

COMPREHENSIVE EVALUATION

TO DETERMINE NEED FOR THE PROPOSAL

Decision to adopt, adapt, or reject

IMPLEMENTING ACTION

Integration into the school system (For one or more buildings tentatively before integration into total system)

There is a steady progression *from* the time of identification of a particular need to change . . . *to* partial integration of the change into the curriculum of a school system. At any given time most of the staff of a system should be expected to be involved in one or more of the stages in some study. Studies should proceed on a jagged front; not all staff and not all schools will be involved in the same activities or the same study."[44]

Direct involvement of the librarian in each phase of the above outlined program is to be expected by the administrator and welcomed by the librarian. Since the school library is in the "mainstream" of the educational endeavor, it is imperative that the school librarian not be by-passed, and that he assume a strong leadership role when the educational program is being re-designed.

In order to serve competently as an effective educational agent for curricular change the librarian must bring to his position a functional knowledge of the ingredients of the instructional program: philosophy, goals, objectives, content, methods, resources, evaluation, and implementation (See Appendix C: Terminology). He must be competent to relate his knowledge of curriculum to his specialized knowledge of resources as he shares with fellow teachers the responsibility for designing and structuring teaching and learning experiences. He must be mindful of each aspect of the total inservice program, building into the school's professional library collection those resources which will support both formal and informal faculty on-the-job curricular studies and professional growth activities.

The contemporary definition of the term *curriculum* clearly requires the involvement of the librarian as a contributing member of every curriculum study or development group.

[44] Conner, Forrest E. and William J. Ellena. *Curriculum Handbook for School Administrators.* Washington, D.C.: American Association of School Administrators, 1967. pp. 315-316.

. . . the *curriculum* is considered to encompass the instructional
activities planned and provided for pupils by the school or school
system. The curriculum, therefore, is the planned interaction of
pupils with instructional *content,* instructional *resources,* and instructional *processes* for the attainment of predetermined educational objectives.[45]

Resources are the librarian's stock-in-trade; designing and implementing
instructional *processes* are two of his specialized competencies; therefore,
the librarian becomes a key figure and has a major responsibility in curriculum development.

RESOURCES AND TEACHING UNITS

The librarian as curriculum consultant is not only called upon to provide
in-service study groups with criteria, checklists, models, etc., but also to
take a leadership role in applying these as the study group evaluates or
structures instructional programs. It is important that the librarian have a
clear understanding of the distinctive difference between a *resource unit*
and a *teaching unit.*

Resource units may properly be thought of as collections of suggested teaching materials and activities organized around large
topics such as "Health," "Recreation," "Transportation," and
"Conservation." They are frequently prepared by committees of
teachers, curriculum workers, state department of education, graduate classes, workshops, institutes, or commercial agencies. Resource
units are not developed with any particular group of children in
mind; in fact, the materials may be used in several grades. They
cover broad areas of content and always contain more information
and suggestions than could be used with any one class. Since they
represent general rather than specific procedures, they suggest a
variety of ways of achieving the same goal. In a very real sense, resource units should serve as a source of material and suggestions for
the teacher when he is planning his teaching unit. The teacher may
draw from the resource unit what is appropriate in terms of a specific situation and a particular group of children[46] (See Appendix D).

Teaching units differ from resource units in several respects.
Ordinarily, the teacher preparing the unit has a specific group of
children in mind and has at his disposal a wealth of information
about their abilities, interests, levels of reading, special weaknesses,
and strengths. The teaching unit is planned in terms of those
known characteristics of the particular class which will be involved
in the unit. The topic under study in teaching units is not as
broad as it is in resource units. While resource units are general in
nature, teaching units are specific[47] (See Tables IX, XIII, XIV,

[45] Putnam, John F. and W. Dale Chismore, eds. *Standard Terminology for Instruction in
State and Local School Systems: An Analysis of Instructional Content, Resources, and
Processes.* State Educational Records and Reports Series: Handbook VI. Third draft.
Washington, D.C.: U.S. Department of Health, Education, and Welfare, 1967. p. 3.
[46] Jarolimek, John. Op. cit., p. 61.
[47] Ibid., p. 65.

XVI, Checklist XI). The librarian will be expected to provide in a professional library a file of resource and teaching units for the study and consideration of the faculty.

BASIC CURRICULUM GUIDES

The following are basic guides* which the librarian may be expected to provide as models for curriculum study groups:

SAMPLE I:

CHARACTERISTICS OF AN EFFECTIVE PROGRAM[48]

PURPOSES

Purposes considered most essential in our times are clearly defined with specific attention to the following and their interrelationships:

Information, concepts, and generalizations from the social sciences

Skills and abilities essential to the study of human relationships and to the meeting of civic responsibilities

Attitudes, appreciations, and behavior patterns of greatest importance in a democratic society

FOUNDATIONS

The social sciences are viewed as the primary foundation of the social studies and as basic sources of information regarding societal changes and child development and learning.

The program is based on studies of the needs, beliefs, and changing conditions of society.

The program is planned and developed in accord with the best available knowledge of the learning process and child development.

CONTENT

Criteria are used to select up-to-date content from the social sciences, related disciplines, and current affairs in relation to the purposes and major areas of study included in the program.

Specific facts and information are organized in relation to basic concepts and generalizations to be developed in units of instruction.

ORGANIZATION

Continuity of learning is maintained from level to level through an organized program of instruction beginning in the kindergarten and extending through the school system.

Depth and breadth of learning are assured and needless repetition is avoided through the assigning of specific areas of emphasis to each grade.

Flexibility and adaptability are maintained within the framework of the over-all program in order to challenge each child's

---

* Note: While several of these guides pertain to social studies each can be adapted readily to other subject areas.

48 Michaelis, John U. *Social Studies for Children in a Democracy: Recent Trends and Developments*. 3rd ed. Englewood Cliffs, New Jersey: Prentice-Hall, Inc., 1963. pp. 30-31.

capabilities and to meet needs and conditions in the community. Instruction in the social studies is related to other areas of the curriculum in ways that contribute to the achievement of definite goals.

A curriculum guide and units of instruction which provide guidelines for developing the instructional program are available to teachers, and are designed to stimulate creative approaches to teaching.

INSTRUCTIONAL RESOURCES, METHODS, AND ACTIVITIES

Criteria are used to make a discriminating selection of resources, methods, and activities that may be used to:

    Achieve basic objectives of the program

    Meet individual differences of learners and local needs and conditions

    Challenge the capabilities of each child and stimulate creative teaching

EVALUATION, REVISION, INTERPRETATION

Provision is made for the use of a variety of procedures in evaluating children's achievement in terms of basic objectives.

Continuing appraisal is made of the effectiveness of the program of instruction.

The program is revised in the light of evaluation, new knowledge from the social sciences, changing societal conditions, and new knowledge from studies of child development and learning.

Parents and other laymen are kept informed as to the nature of the program, its strengths and weaknesses, and changes that are made to improve it.

INSTRUCTIONAL PERSONNEL

Teachers have the depth and breadth of preparation that enable them to provide instruction in the areas of study included in the program.

Supervisory assistance is provided to help teachers meet instructional problems.

In-service education is provided to improve instruction in the social studies.

SAMPLE II:

PLANNED INSTRUCTIONAL OUTCOMES FOR PUPILS[49]

Items of information under this heading may be used to identify general instructional outcomes for pupils for which provision is made in the instructional program, e.g., knowledge and understanding, appreciations and attitudes, skills, appropriately developed readiness, occupational competence, and improved physical fitness. These planned outcomes—reflecting anticipated growth or change in physical, intellectual, emotional, and social behavior or performance—frequently are referred to as "objectives."

ACCULTURATION. Greater capability for pupils of a minority group

49 Putnam, John F. and W. Dale Chismore, eds. Op. cit., pp. 176-179.

to assimilate and to adapt to the general cultural patterns of the community.

APPRECIATIONS AND ATTITUDES. A greater awareness of the value and significance of aspects of the subject-matter area (including aesthetic appreciations), and a greater readiness to respond in a mature manner to phenomenons related to the area.

APPROPRIATE BEHAVIOR. Patterns of acting, thinking, and feeling which are more consistent with those of selected cultural groups to which the pupils belong, consistent especially with the norms and standards set to govern pupil behavior within the school.

CAREER GUIDANCE. Greater understanding of one's educational and career opportunities, which leads to the formulation of realistic goals.

COGNITIVE THINKING. Greater skill in organizing and utilizing one's intellectual resources for arriving at the most appropriate solutions to problems.

CREATIVITY. Enhanced performance in original and self-expressive activities, including greater facility with inventive thinking that explores original and/or alternative solutions to problems.

CRITICAL JUDGMENT. Greater ability to evaluate an idea, situation, or body of information in terms of meaningful (germane) objective and subjective criteria.

EDUCATION FOR LEISURE. Interests and skills appropriate for pupils' leisure-time activities at the present time and in the future.

EXPERIENCE IN SERVICE TO OTHERS. Greater familiarity with the satisfactions, rewards, and problems of providing service to others.

GENERAL DEVELOPMENT IN AREA. General growth and development in the knowledge, understandings, appreciations, attitudes, and skills related to the subject-matter area.

HISTORICAL AWARENESS AND/OR BACKGROUND. Greater awareness of the nature, importance, and relationships of significant historical events affecting the subject-matter area.

KNOWLEDGE AND UNDERSTANDING IN AREA. Greater knowledge of the significant facts, and increased comprehension of the basic ideas associated with the subject-matter area.

KNOWLEDGE AND UNDERSTANDING OF CITIZENSHIP. Increased knowledge and appreciation of one's rights and responsibilities as a member of his school, community, state, and nation.

LEADERSHIP ABILITY. Greater ability to serve effectively in leadership capacities in group activities.

LITERACY. The ability to read, write, and compute at the level of performance expected of an "average" sixth grade pupil in order to become better able to meet adult responsibilities.

MENTAL HEALTH. Improved soundness of mental health and overall personality development.

MORAL AND ETHICAL VALUES. Greater adherence to the principles of morality and the ethics implicit in the highest ideals of American democracy.

OCCUPATIONAL COMPETENCE, INITIAL. The skills, understandings, and appreciations needed for successful initial entry into a specific occupation or cluster of closely related occupations.

OCCUPATIONAL COMPETENCE, UPGRADED OR UPDATED. The skills, understandings, and appreciations needed by workers already in an occupation to upgrade or update their occupational competence.

PERSONAL SATISFACTION. A sense of reward and pleasure resulting from involvement in an activity and/or from enjoyment of the product or results of the activity.

PHYSICAL FITNESS AND HEALTH. Improved soundness of physical health, muscular strength, physical endurance, kinesthetic skills, and resistance to disease.

READINESS. A willingness, desire, and ability to participate in activities related to the subject matter area, depending upon the necessary level of pupils' physical, mental, and emotional maturation.

REHABILITATION. Restoration to a previously attained state of physical, mental, social, or emotional well-being.

REMEDIATION. Improvement or overcoming of any particular marked deficiency not due to inferior general ability, including a deficiency in content previously taught but not learned. When referring to the teaching of skills or other aspects of content for the first time, this may be referred to as habilitation. In occupational programs this includes instruction intended to correct educational deficiencies or handicaps which might prevent pupils from benefiting from their occupational instruction.

SELF-UNDERSTANDING. Greater understanding of one's abilities, interests, environmental factors, and educational needs.

SKILLS ASSOCIATED WITH AREA. Greater ease and precision of physical and/or mental performance in activities related to the subject-matter area.

SKILLS OF INQUIRY. Greater ease and precision in the use of an appropriate systematic approach for seeking information related to the subject-matter area, including the use of observation, experimentation, and questioning.

SOCIAL ADEPTNESS. Greater ease and skill in interpersonal relationships.

SOCIALIZATION. Increased understanding and acceptance of the customs, standards, traditions, and culture of the cultural groups of which pupils are members—including groups comprised of the family, school, community, and the nation as a whole—and active cooperation with these groups as appropriate.

UNDERSTANDING OF BASIC PRINCIPLES. An understanding of the basic principles underlying the subject-matter area.

WORKABLE SELF CONCEPT. A more realistic self-image, incorporating aspects of personal development.

DESIGNING COURSES OF STUDY[50]

The course of study for the local school system should go beyond the state framework to include detailed suggestions for the teachers to use in planning, guiding, and evaluating . . . instruction. Among the topics commonly included in courses of study are the following:

1. Point of view or basic beliefs underlying the program
2. The local setting and adaptations to community needs and conditions
3. Objectives of the . . . program
   a. Major concepts and generalizations
   b. Basic skills
   c. Attitudes and appreciations
4. Organization of the instructional program
   a. Principles of organization
   b. Definition of scope to show strands running through the program
   c. Sequence of themes and units of instruction for each level
   d. Recurring topics
5. Basic principles and procedures of instruction
   a. Planning and developing units of instruction
   b. Specific techniques for developing generalizations, skills, attitudes, (and appreciations)
   c. Procedures for meeting individual differences
   d. Techniques for utilizing instructional materials
6. Essential instructional materials and their place in the program
   a. Textbooks and other reading materials
   b. Maps, globes, films, and other audio-visual materials
   c. Community resources
7. Evaluation of outcomes of instruction
   a. Guiding principles for use at all levels
   b. Techniques for use at different levels

SAMPLE IV:

OUTLINE OF A RESOURCE UNIT[51]
(SEE APPENDIX D)

I. SIGNIFICANCE OF THE TOPIC.

This is a short statement explaining why the particular topic is of importance in the education of pupils. Aspects of the topic to be emphasized and highlighted are noted.

II. BRIEF OUTLINE OF THE TOPIC.

Indicates the subject-matter scope of the unit. This may be a conventional outline, a list of questions and problems, or an outline in terms of major and related understandings to be developed.

[50] Michaelis, John U. Op. cit., pp. 172-173.
[51] Jarolimek, John. Op. cit., pp. 62-63.

III. POSSIBLE OUTCOMES.

These should be stated in terms of the understandings, attitudes, and skills *which would be possible* to achieve in the unit. The list will be long; teachers will choose only a few from this list for use in preparing a teaching unit.

IV. INVENTORY OF POSSIBLE ACTIVITIES.

This section is the main body of a resource unit and is often the most helpful to the teacher for use in planning a teaching unit.

A. Suggested Introductory Activities. These are included to help the teacher initiate the unit in a way that will be meaningful and purposeful, allow for exploration of pupil interest, and to facilitate teacher-guided pupil planning. For example, the resource unit might suggest the use of:

1) An arranged room environment, bulletin board, display table, real objects, books.

2) Films, filmstrips, or other visual aids.

3) A field trip or a resource person.

4) Exploratory reading.

5) Exploratory dramatic representation.

6) Pre-test to discover backgrounds (See Example VII).

B. Suggested Developmental Activities. These are designed to help the teacher guide the work after the children get started. They include such types as the following:

1) RESEARCH-TYPE ACTIVITIES. (Reading, interviewing, listening to the radio, seeing motion pictures, and other visual aids.)

2) PRESENTATION-TYPE ACTIVITIES. (Reports, panel and round table discussions, showing of visual aids, making graphs and charts.

3) CREATIVE EXPRESSION ACTIVITIES. (Handwork, drawing pictures, writing stories, plays, and poems, singing and playing music.)

4) DRILL ACTIVITIES. (Used when students in the group encounter obstacles to further progress. For example, a class might need special work on use of references, map-reading, or other skills.)

5) APPRECIATION ACTIVITIES. (Listening to music, reading for fun, looking at pictures.)

6) OBSERVATION AND LISTENING ACTIVITIES. (Sharpening the senses of the pupils as an aid to learning.)

7) GROUP COOPERATION ACTIVITIES. (Training in democratic group procedures, division of labor among groups leading to cooperation in carrying out plans.)

8) EXPERIMENTATION. (Learning to try out new ways of doing things, laboratory work, with emphasis on equipment the pupils can make as well as on more elaborate types of equipment.)

9) ORGANIZING AND EVALUATING ACTIVITIES. (Discriminating

among and selecting, ordering, and appraising the work done by themselves.)

C. Culminating or Continuing Activities. This section should offer suggestions to the teacher as to how the unit should be brought to a successful conclusion. This would include summary, review, transfer of learnings, sharing with others, and suggestions for continuing study. Several suggestions should be presented in order that the teacher have a wide choice of appropriate culminating activities.

V. EVALUATION SUGGESTIONS.

These include sample tests, pupil self-analysis inventories, rating scales, observation techniques to be used *throughout* a unit of work. Stress should be placed on trying to find evaluation techniques which bring out not only what the students *learn* about a topic but what they *do* about it.

VI. LISTING OF MATERIALS FOR REFERENCE PURPOSES.

This part of the resource unit should include lists of readings (books, magazines, newspapers, etc.) audio-visual aids, community resources, art and music materials, and the like, whenever they are appropriate to the topic under consideration in the resource unit.

SAMPLE V:

OUTLINE FOR UNITS OF INSTRUCTION[52]

TITLE:
___Descriptive of a major area of study.
___Focused on a topic, problem, or theme.

BACKGROUND INFORMATION:
___Indicative of content to be emphasized.
___Related to main ideas, problems, or questions.
___Accurate and up to date.

OBJECTIVES:
___Related to purposes of the subject.
___Directly related to the unit topic.
___Terms, concepts, generalizations.
___Basic skills.
___Attitudes and appreciations.

INITIATION:
___Focused on main idea or problem to be studied first.
___Outgrowth of the preceding unit.
___An arranged environment.
___Teacher suggestion.
___Current happening.
___Community or audio-visual resources.
___Other.

MAIN IDEAS, PROBLEMS, OR QUESTIONS:
___Main ideas identified as organizing centers for content and learning experiences.
___Or, problems identified.

52 Michaelis, John U. Op. cit., pp. 252-253.

__Or, questions identified.
__Arranged in a sequence.

LEARNING EXPERIENCES:
__Critically selected.
__Related to main ideas, problems, or questions.
__Related instructional materials noted.
__Arranged in a sequence as follows:

OPENERS:
__To introduce each main idea, problem, or question.
__Different types suggested such as
__Recalling related earlier experiences.
__Examining and discussing related pictures and objects.
__Others.

DEVELOPMENTAL ACTIVITIES:
__Related to each main idea, problem, or question.
__Grow out of opening activities.
__Arranged in a problem-solving sequence.
__Varied activities suggested such as
__Reading.
__Independent study.
__Group work.
__Creative.
__Writing.
__Reporting.
__Dramatization.
__Rhythmic expression.
__Art.
__Music.
__Construction.
__Other.

CONCLUDING ACTIVITIES:
__Related to each main idea, problem, or question.
__Designed to lead to the development of generalizations.
__Different types suggested such as
__Completing charts.
__Sharing reports.
__Dramatization.
__Quiz program.
__Class newspaper.
__Completing notebooks.
__Other.

CULMINATION:
__Needed to round out and summarize key learnings stressed throughout the entire unit.
__Provision for participation of each child.
__Contributory to evaluation of objectives set for the unit.
__Different possibilities suggested such as
__Leads to the next unit.
__Program.
__Pageant.

__Other.

INSTRUCTIONAL MATERIALS:

__Critically selected.

__Related to each main idea, problem, or question.

__Different types suggested such as

    __Books.

    __Periodicals.

    __Maps and globes.

    __Community resources.

    __Audio-visual materials.

    __Art.

    __Music.

    __Construction.

    __Demonstration.

    __Other.

EVALUATION:

__Related to objectives.

__Made a part of experiences related to each main idea, problem, or question.

__Different techniques suggested such as

    __Tests.

    __Charts.

    __Checklists.

    __Discussion.

    __Observation.

    __Other.

BIBLIOGRAPHY:

__Materials for children listed.

__Background materials for teachers listed.

__Complete information given.

SAMPLE VI:

CRITERIA FOR EVALUATING UNITS[53]

Cite evidence that the unit:

1. Is closely related to the typical interests and needs likely to be found in the on-going life of the learners.
2. Will bring learners into contact with aspects of life which are of both immediate and continuing social significance.
3. Is appropriate to the maturity levels within the group; is challenging without being too difficult; will be revealing to pupils of their own unique capacities and limitations.
4. Is possible within the available resources of the school, the immediate community, and the accessible environment (direct experience).
5. Will provide naturally for use of materials dealing with other places, other peoples, other times (vicarious experience).
6. Will provide naturally for a great variety of individual and

[53] Burton, William H. Op. cit., p. 375.

cooperative group activities—physical, mental, emotional, and social; thinking-feeling-doing.

7. Will lead (as far as can ever be foretold) to socially desirable learning outcomes; understandings and insights, attitudes, appreciations, and values, skills, and behavior patterns which will very likely be used by citizens generally.

8. Will stimulate (as far as can ever be foretold) critical thinking and evaluation of the learner's own procedure in selecting purposes, in planning means of achieving them, in selecting materials and processes, in accepting outcomes.

9. Will lead to other desirable learning experiences.

10. Is of such length as to be comprehensible as a unit by the level of maturity involved; that is, is of such length that the pupil can have insight into it.

11. Is related to the general course of study goals and framework.

SAMPLE VII:

CRITERIA FOR LEARNING ACTIVITIES AND EXPERIENCES[54]

Each proposed activitiy should be scrutinized to see if it is:

1. Recognized by children as usable in achieving their purposes.

2. Recognized by the teacher as leading to socially desirable ends.

3. Appropriate to the maturity of the group; challenging, achievable, leading to new learnings, providing for application of old learnings.

4. Varied enough to provide for balanced development of the learner; many types of individual and group activity.

5. Possible within the resources of school and community.

6. Varied enough to provide for individual differences within the group.

Instructional resources are incorporated into the structural design in each of the examples cited above: program, course of study, resource or teaching unit. In designing any instructional plan, media as well as goals, content and method must be specified; these are the vectors which give direction and scope to the basic structural design (See Figure IV). Goals determine both purpose and direction of unit and course; content determines the fundamentals, skills, values, and attitudes to be taught and to be learned; method determines techniques and procedures to be employed to facilitate content teaching and learning. Media are the substances, the sources, the raw materials to be used in teaching the content and in reaching the goals. Omit resources from the basic design and you will have crippled the plan to the point of ineffectiveness.

Direct participation by the librarian in curriculum study, design, and revision is necessitated by the vast complexity of the task. In *The Process of Education,* Jerome Bruner warns that even after course content has been rewritten so that the prevading and powerful ideas and attitudes are given

[54] Ibid., pp. 364-365.

a central role, two basic problems still remain: how to match "materials to the capacities of students of different abilities"[55] and how to "tailor funda-

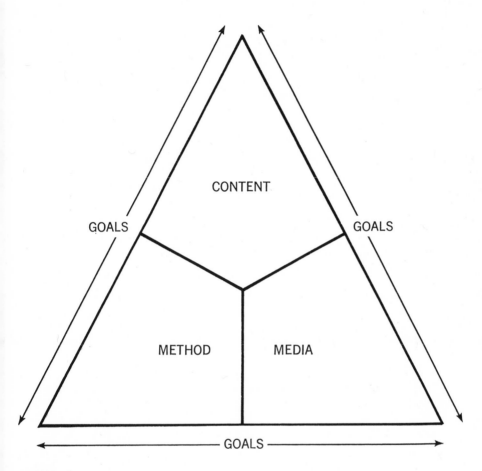

FIGURE IV

GOALS, CONTENT, METHOD, MEDIA:

VECTORS SHAPING UNIT AND COURSE DESIGN

mental knowledge to the interests and capacities of the children?"[56] (See Appendix E). The specialized competency of the librarian is essential to solving both of these basic problems. It is the librarian's special province not only to search out and identify resources to develop understanding of a fundamental, but also to search out and identify those resources uniquely suited to the interests and capacities of the individual learner (See Appendix N). Tailoring fundamental knowledge to the needs, interests, goals, abilities, concerns, and progress rate of the student is of vital concern to the

55 Bruner, Jerome S. Op. cit., p. 18.
56 Ibid., p. 22.

librarian. It is both the librarian's responsibility and privilege to provide resources which will personalize and humanize the teaching plan (See Figure V).

When planning course content it is imperative that a great diversity of ways for the student to succeed be structured directly into the basic design (See Table IV).

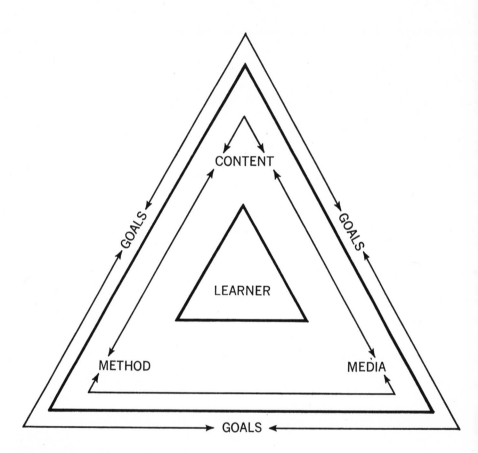

FIGURE V

INDIVIDUALIZING THE TEACHING DESIGN

> When the curriculum is being planned, each unit of work should be tested to see how many roads to success are built into it—how many ways for individuals to contribute diversely to the common whole. . . . The test, then is: Does the youngster go home from school most days, with the feeling of at least some little success lingering in his memory?[57]

[57] National Education Association. The Joint Project on the Individual and the School. *A Climate for Individuality.* Washington, D.C.: National Education Association, 1965. p. 36.

TABLE IV.

DIVERSIFICATION: THE SOLUTION TO THE PROBLEM,
"HOW TO INDIVIDUALIZE INSTRUCTION"

THE PROBLEM:	SOLUTION:
Same goal for all, yet each student is a unique learner	Individualize the teaching-learning program to enable each learner to reach a common goal in his own unique way
SUB-PROBLEMS:	**SOLUTIONS:**
Each student in any given class differs in abilities from every other class member	Devise a variety of appropriate, significant, challenging experiences commensurate with class ability range; wide enough in latitude to challenge and satisfy both the slowest and the quickest learner
Each student in any given class differs in environmental and cultural backgrounds from every other class member	Provide learning experiences, activities, guidance and resources which will compensate for any learner's environmental or cultural disabilities
Each student in any given class differs in progress rate from every other class member	Provide appropriate experiences, activities, guidance, and resources, so that each learner can begin on his own maturity level to learn at his own comprehension rate
Each student in any given class differs in drive from every other class member	Provide appropriate experiences, activities, guidance, and supporting resources, which will create, motivate, and sustain interest in "perceiving, behaving, becoming"
Each student in any given class differs in creativity from every other class member	Provide appropriate experiences, activities, and resources which will encourage the expression and development of each learner's creative potential
Each student in any given class differs in personal goals from every other class member	Provide appropriate experiences, activities, guidance, and resources which will encourage each learner to strive for self-realization, self-fulfillment, and self-understanding
Each student in any given class differs in needs from every other class member	Provide ample opportunity for each learner to find within each school experience assurance of authentic concern for his developmental needs as a student, as a future citizen, and as a human being

. . . it is hard for anyone to grow to full stature until he can come into full and free communication with the people and the world about him, until he can invest his full energy in something outside himself, taking all the risks of rebuff and failure.

Schools can help enormously. A deft teacher can encourage individuals and groups toward idealistic ventures that have a high chance of success, sympathetically cushioning the occasional fall and putting it into perspective. There is some power in a boy or girl that can be realized and appreciated only by spending it. Some individuals need a great deal of social contact; some find their unique destiny in creative expression, in philosophy, or in scientific research; some at quite an early age do not need love or companionship so much as the pursuit of an intellectual and creative goal. All these individuals the school program and the school staff must identify and aid.

Once more, the test. In his years of schooling how much is each youngster helped to reach out beyond himself, to perceive some ideal, and throw himself into working for it?[58]

Authentic concern for excellence demands that educators "develop a philosophy and a technique of continuous reappraisal and innovation."[59] Striving for an ever better educational program is the unifying and motivational force which prompts and directs curriculum study and development. Excellence is possible only if adequately planned for and consistently worked for. An educational program of excellence requires the direct involvement of the librarian in all stages of the teaching and learning program. Without the supporting services of the librarian and the resources of the library, no educational plan can be actualized fully.

To strengthen the teaching and learning program, Lloyd Trump recommends that librarians should be "thrust deeper into the teaching and learning process . . . (should) play key roles in helping teachers decide how, when, and where to use books along with a variety of technological devices . . . (should) be part time members of teaching teams so that their services can be more closely interrelated with the teaching process."[60] Mr. Trump envisions tomorrow's library out of the backwater and into the mainstream of education where the school library's identity in the conventional narrow sense will be lost for "its service will permeate the totality of education."[61]

58 Ibid., p. 37.
59 President's Commission on National Goals. Op. cit., p. 85.
60 Trump, J. Lloyd. "Changing Concepts of Instruction and the School Library as a Materials Center." *The School Library as a Materials Center: Educational Needs of Librarians and Teachers in Its Administration and Use.* Edited by Mary Helen Mahar, Washington, D.C.: U.S. Department of Health, Education, and Welfare, 1963. p. 5.
61 Ibid., p. 6.

5 The Role
Of the School Librarian
As Materials Specialist

In helping our students learn enough to make the critical decisions which lie ahead, we will need the full resources of all existing systems of communication as well as a knowledge of their unique strategies.*

The primary purpose of organized education is to teach the student to think and to translate his thinking into a pattern of logical, constructive, purposeful behavior. Thinking does not occur in a vacuum; it requires raw materials from which to fashion thought. Thinking is a dynamically creative process involving the analyzing, sifting, grouping, organizing, and shaping of ideas into patterns of significance. "We know quite well that the various abilities used in critical thinking cannot be developed in isolation but must be developed in conjunction with each other through use of appropriate materials and situations."[62] School library resources are the materials *appropriate* for creative, significant thinking—they are the plastic stuff from which thoughts are shaped and fashioned. The school library functioning as a learning laboratory is the *appropriate* situation for significant thinking; it supplies not only the raw materials but also the tools, the incentive, the guidance, and the climate essential for creative thinking.

HISTORICAL PERSPECTIVE

The educational necessity of employing appropriate materials to extend learning beyond textbook and classroom has long been recognized as essential for effective learning. Horace Mann in 1839 recommended establishing school libraries to compensate for the informational limitations of the text.[63]

---

* Bills, Robert E. "Believing and Behaving: Perception and Learning." *Learning More About Learning*. Op. cit., p. 54.
62 Burton, William H. et al. *Education for Effective Thinking*. New York: Appleton-Century-Crofts, Educational Division, Meredith Corp. 1960. p. vi.
63 Mann, Horace. Op. cit.

The Madison Conference in 1892 wrote in its Report "Recitation alone cannot possibly make up proper teaching. . . . It is absolutely necessary from the earliest to the latest grades, that there should be parallel reading."[64]

The concept of the school library serving as a laboratory for effective learning is likewise not a recent one. In 1913 Lucille Fargo speaking before the National Educational Association presented the concept of the school library functioning as "a laboratory and a workshop, (a means of) putting into the hands of the pupils the necessary tools for further achievement."[65] In 1915 Mary E. Hall writing in the *Library Journal* quoted a Grand Rapids High School principal as saying:

> The school library of the future will be the proof of the extent of the transformation of a high school from the medieval system of the past to the new standards and ideals in high school education of this twentieth century. I believe I am safe in saying that the school library will be the proof of the educational value of the new curriculum. When our schools have outgrown their cloister days and are aiming to prepare our boys and girls for the life they must live in a work-a-day world the library will be the open door to the opportunity of the present.[66]

Miss Hall then explained how the "new" library differed from the "old" in supporting the curriculum:

> The old high school library was static. The new is dynamic. The old was largely for reference and required reading in history and English; the new is all things to all departments, if in any way it may serve the school. It is not only a reference library, but a *training school* in the best methods of using library aids in looking up a topic. . . . The new library is dynamic, because it is not content with storing, and organizing and recording the loan of books and other material, but because it uses every method known to the best college and public libraries for encouraging their use, *stimulating interest in good reading, arousing intellectual curiosity,* and *broadening the horizon of the students.*[67]

The necessity of the "new" library providing both print and non-print materials was also specified by Miss Hall:

> In the new high school library many of our schools have found it well worth-while to bring together all lantern slides, pictures, victrola records and post cards, and to organize them according to modern methods of classification and cataloging so that they may

[64] Committee of Ten. Op. cit., p. 323.
[65] Fargo, Lucille F. "Training High School Students in the Use of the Library." *Addresses and Proceedings, 1913.* Washington, D.C.: The Association, 1913. p. 760.
[66] Hall, Mary E. "The Development of the Modern School Library." *Library Journal.* September 1915. p. 672. As quoted in: *Selected Articles on School Library Experience* by Mary Wilson. New York: H. W. Wilson, 1925. p. 70.
[67] Ibid., p. 72.

be available for all departments and at all times as they are not available when kept in departmental collections.[68]

Many educators advocated the multi-media approach to teaching at the turn of the century. Henry Johnson, Columbia University professor of history, wrote in 1915 that casts, models, pictures, maps, charts and diagrams as well as printed materials were essential to teaching history effectively. He deplored the reluctance of American administrators to provide an organized school program for instructional media acquisitions and use:

> The need of such aids was clearly set forth as long ago as the eighteenth century, and has been almost continuously emphasized ever since. In Europe the response has been so generous that there is now scarcely any known phase of past civilization which is not represented. In the United States, until recently, the chief reliance has been on maps and pictures, but other aids are now coming into use. The American Historical Association led the way with an exhibit in New York in 1909. The *History Teacher's Magazine* for February, 1910, carried an account of this exhibit to teachers in every section of the country and thus spread information which up to that time has been mainly confined to observers of history teaching in Europe. . . . Two important pieces of work remain to be done. The first is to prepare a really exhaustive guide to aids especially adapted to American schools. The second is to provide a series of illustrated exercises showing definitely when and how the aids ought to be used. As matters now stand at present many schools seem to be wasting their substance in the acquisition of unsuitable material and wasting their time in unsuitable use even of suitable material.[69]

Professor Johnson's observation in 1915 that schools were wasting "their substance in the acquisition of unsuitable materials and wasting their time in the use even of suitable material" foretold the need to organize a functional multi-media library program. Unfortunately the typical fifty-year lag between recognizing an educational need and adequately meeting that need has been all too apparent in the history of the conversion of the school library from a printed storage center to a multi-media learning laboratory.

EVOLVEMENT OF THE INSTRUCTIONAL MATERIALS CENTER CONCEPT

In recounting the evolvement of the school library as a multi-media learning laboratory or instructional materials center the following are significant milestones:

1937   Newark Public Schools (Newark, New Jersey) established a Department of Libraries, Visual Aids, and Radio to provide a unified print and non-print media service in each of its school libraries.

1939   The Joint Committee of the American Library Association

---

68 Ibid., p. 75.
69 Johnson, Henry. Op. cit.

and the National Education Association defined standards
for school library service which advocated "a well balanced
collection of books, pamphlets and audio-visual aids appropriate to the objectives and needs of the school."

1945   The American Library Association's Committee on Post-
War Planning stated in its publication, *School Libraries for
Today and Tomorrow,* that one purpose of the school library was to "help children and young people to become
skillful and discriminating users of libraries and of printed
and audio-visual materials."[70]

1947   The Library Institute conducted by the University of Chicago in developing the theme, "Youth, Communication, and
Libraries" stressed the necessity for libraries to provide all
"ideas" no matter in what form or in what format they
were contained.[71]

1949   The American Library Association published *Audio-Visual
School Library Service* by Margaret I. Rufsvold which emphasized that audio-visual as well as printed resources were
essential to an educationally functional school library program.[72]

1956   The American Association of School Librarians endorsed
by unanimous vote during the ALA conference at Miami
Beach the statement that the school library should serve the
school as a center for instructional materials (See Appendix
F).

1958   The Joint American Association of School Librarians—Association of College and Research Libraries—Department of
Audio-Visual Instruction of the N.E.A. Committee defined
the prerequisites for the attainment of professional status by
instructional materials specialists (See Chapter 3).

1958   The National Defense Education Act provided funds to purchase instructional media to support the teaching of mathematics, science, and foreign languages, and funds to train
teachers and librarians in the use of instructional media.

1960   The American Association of School Librarians defined in
Standards for School Library Programs the quantitative and
qualitative standards for school libraries serving as multi-
media learning laboratories.[73]

1961   The Council on Library Resources provided a $100,000
grant to fund the School Library Development Project designed to provide leadership and guidance to the fifty states
in their implementation of the *Standards.*

1962   The Knapp Foundation, Inc. awarded a $1,130,000 grant
for a five-year project to demonstrate the value of a full

[70] American Library Association, Committee on Post-War Planning. *School Libraries for
Today and Tomorrow.* Chicago, Illinois: American Library Association, 1945. p. 10.
[71] Chicago University. Graduate Library School. *Youth, Communication and Libraries:
Papers Presented Before the Library Institute at the University of Chicago, August 11-16,
1947.* Chicago, Illinois: American Library Association, 1949.
[72] Rufsvold, Margaret I. *Audio-Visual School Library Service: A Handbook for Librarians.*
Chicago, Illinois: American Library Association, 1949.
[73] American Association of School Librarians. Op. cit., p. 7.

program of school library services employing multi-media.

1963   The National Education Association Project on Instruction recommended in its report, *Schools for the 60's,* that there be one or more well planned instructional materials centers in each school system and in each school building.[74]

1964   The National Defense Education Act was extended to include materials essential for the teaching of social studies, reading, and the language arts.

1965   The Elementary and Secondary Education Act through Title II provided federal funds for the specific purpose of establishing and strengthening school libraries.

1965   *Quantitative Standards for Audiovisual Personnel, Equipment and Materials (In Elementary, Secondary, and Higher Education)* was adopted by The Department of Audiovisual Instruction, NEA.[75]

1969   A joint committee of the American Association of School Librarians (ALA) and the Department of Audiovisual Instruction (NEA) published *Standards for School Media Programs* up-dating 'the quantitative requirements for school media programs (See Figure XII).

"THE MEDIUM IS THE MESSAGE"

A quality library program employs resources not as "things" but as "ideas." The value of each resource lies in its knowledge-building, its knowledge-extending and its knowledge-imploding potential. In coining the phrase "the medium is the message,"[76] Marshall McLuhan dramatized the necessity of looking beyond the wrapper of any piece of material to the ideas latent within the package itself. For it is *not* in stocking books and pamphlets, newspapers and microfilms, filmstrips and motion pictures, disc and tape recordings and all other print and non-print media that the library becomes an agent for educational effectiveness. It is the availability of the appropriate package of knowledge-building and knowledge-imploding ideas when that availability is *timely* and *significant* to the learning task at hand that makes the library a source of educational power.

Since the school library employs resources not as "things" but as "ideas" to debate the necessity of having both print and non-print media available is as inanely archaic as to debate how many angels can dance on the head of a pin! Who would debate the necessity of having sufficient light in classroom or laboratory? Print and non-print media are sources of intellectual light essential to dissipating the darkness of inadequate or incomplete understanding. The student will see "in the glass but darkly" without appropriate media to light his mind's eye.

DISTRICT LIBRARY PROGRAM

Since library resources and services are essential to the health, vitality, and success of the educational program, the planning and development of a

74 National Education Association. Project on Instruction. Op. cit., p. 98.
75 Department of Audiovisual Instruction. *Quantitative Standards for Audiovisual Personnel, Equipment and Materials.* Washington, D.C.: National Education Association, 1966.
76 McLuhan, Marshall. *Understanding Media: The Extensions of Man.* New York: New American Library, 1964. pp. 23-25. Used with permission of McGraw-Hill (original publishers).

district library program cannot be left to chance. To assure a district library program of uniform excellence, it is recommended that each district design and structure a master plan for library development (See Appendix I). This master plan should include: a statement of school library philosophy, goals, objectives; a statement of policy concerning media selection and usage; a statement of routine procedures for handling complaints about library materials. Designing and structuring the district school library master plan should be a cooperative team enterprise involving librarians and representatives of both the administrative and teaching staffs.

The following procedural outline can serve as a guide to those planning, designing, and structuring a district library program:

> A planning-steering committee composed of librarians and representatives from the administrative and teaching staffs is appointed by the chief school administrator.

> The planning-steering committee is vested with the responsibility for developing a district program of library service reflective of the developmental needs of the educational program.

> The planning-steering committee builds its background knowledge of the function, purpose, scope, dimension, and requirements of a quality school library program by studying:
>
> *Evaluating the School Library: Suggestions for Studying the School Library in Action*[77] (See Chapter 11)
>
> *Standards for School Media Programs*[78]
>
> *Criteria Relating to Educational Media Programs in School Systems* (See Appendix G)

> The planning-steering committee consults with the state, the regional, or the county school library supervisor or members of his staff to obtain competent guidance and counsel.

> The planning-steering committee visits other school districts to observe quality programs in action.

> The planning-steering committee prepares for district faculty consideration, modification, and subsequent approval:
>
> A statement of school library philosophy, goals, objectives;
> Media selection policies and procedures;
> A statement of routine procedures for handling complaints about media;
> Criteria checklists for the evaluation of media;
> Recommended procedure to be followed in teacher-librarian planning;
> Recommended procedure for school librarian and classroom teacher to cooperate with the public library;
> Recommended procedure to be followed by classroom teachers when making assignments requiring the support of library media.

[77] New York Library Association, School Libraries Section. *Evaluating the School Library: Suggestions for Studying the School Library in Action.* New York: New York Library Association, 1962.

[78] American Association of School Librarians and the Department of Audiovisual Instruction. *Standards for School Media Programs.* Chicago: American Library Association and Washington, D.C.: National Education Association, latest edition.

The planning-steering committee structures a checklist of qualitative and quantitative criteria to be used in evaluating the adequacy of the district library program.

The district faculty employs the DAVI evaluative checklist to construct a *profile image* of district library service (See Appendix G).

The district faculty studies the *profile image* and makes recommendations for strengthening noted weaknesses.

The planning-steering committee prepares a tentative five year school library development plan and submits the plan to the chief school administrator for administrative staff and board study, modification, and final approval (See Checklist XIV).

The planning-steering committee summarizes in a policy statement its recommendations for district school library development (See Appendix I).

Additional guidance in developing a district policy statement for the selection and use of instructional materials can be gained by studying the monograph, *Instructional Materials: Selection Policies and Procedures* prepared by the California Association of School Librarians.[79]

SELECTING LIBRARY MEDIA

The school librarian can strengthen the teaching and learning program if he will build a media collection commensurate with the needs of the community, the curriculum, the faculty, and the student body. A library collection of educational significance is never the result of chance or accident. The professionally honest librarian knows there is no short cut to building a functional school library collection; there are no "pre-fab" collections that could possibly meet the unique characteristics of any community, any school faculty, any curricular program, or any student body. Just as a course of study must be customized and personalized to meet the class and individual student needs, so must the library collection be customized and personalized to meet the individual school's needs. The professionally adept librarian respects basic lists of recommended media as valuable inventories of standard accouterments, all meeting specifications for excellence, but each needing to be tried on for curricular size and student fit. Materials to be used to support the educational program should be judged objectively, preferably at first hand, with care, discrimination, and discernment.

In order to build a quality, functional collection of instructional media that will be adequately supportive to the teaching program, a wise librarian will involve fellow faculty members in media selection. Direct involvement of teachers in choosing materials serves a double purpose: it enables the librarian to profit from the teachers' specialized knowledge; it also enables teachers to extend their knowledge to encompass new ideas imbedded in new materials. Likewise, in order to select resources reflective of student interests and abilities, the wise librarian will involve students as members of media selection juries. Involvement of students in media selection is of inestimable value both to the librarian and the students; it enables the

79 *Instructional Materials: Selection Policies and Procedures.* Daly City, California: California Association of School Librarians, 1965.

librarian to achieve a high degree of objectivity in selection—to look at materials through the "eyes" of potential users; it is also an educational experience for students, providing them with an opportunity to learn and to practice techniques of critical thinking.

CHECKLISTS PROMOTE UNIFORM OBJECTIVITY

To facilitate uniform objectivity in evaluating instructional resources, it is recommended that each district develop specific criteria with matching checklists to guide district media and equipment selection (See Checklists I, II, III, IV, and V).

CHECKLIST I

NORTH HILLS SCHOOL DISTRICT
PITTSBURGH, PENNSYLVANIA—15229

BOOK SELECTION GUIDE

AUTHOR_____   TITLE_____

Publisher_____   Copyright Date_____Price_____

Fiction_____Non-Fiction_____   Reference_____Grade Level_____

Evaluator_____   Recommendation_____

EVALUATION: E—Excellent G—Good F—Fair P—Poor

PHYSICAL FEATURES	E	G	F	P	COMMENTS
Size: Suitability					
Binding: Quality					
Attractiveness					
Paper: Quality					
Print: Readability					
Margins: Adequate					
Illustrations: Quality					

CONTENT					
Style					
Literary quality					
Organization					
Presentation					
Scope					
Pupil appeal					

SPECIAL FEATURES					
Table of Contents					
Index					
Glossary					
Maps, Diagrams, Charts					

POTENTIAL USE

Specific curriculum tie-in _____

Specific reader interest_____

Unique contribution_____

CHECKLIST II

SUPERINTENDENT OF SCHOOLS, DEPARTMENT OF EDUCATION,
SAN DIEGO COUNTY, CALIFORNIA.*

TEXTBOOK EVALUATION FORM

AUTHOR_____

TITLE_____

SERIES_____

PUBLISHER_____

PUBLICATION DATE: FIRST EDITION_____ PRESENT EDITION_____

PLEASE UNDERLINE PERTINENT ITEMS

SCOPE

    Geography (what areas?)_____

    History (what countries?)_____
    Spelling
    Arithmetic
    Reading (developmental)
            (literary)
    Language
    Science
    Health
    Music
    Other

GRADE LEVEL for which it is intended—K——12.

VOCABULARY CORRELATION—If primary health, science or social studies
                            is vocabulary correlated with basic reader
                            series? Yes_____ No_____
                            If Yes—with which series?_____

CONTENT
    Factual
    Authentic
    Biased (in what way?)_____
    Objective
    Up to date

STYLE
    Literary   Readability—good, fair, poor
    Technical   Clearly expressed

ORGANIZATION
    Chronological   Unit centered
    Topical   With usual chapter headings and
    Problem centered   sections

* Form L-19. Supt. of Schools. 6-59.

TEACHER AIDS

Bibliography   Unusual words marked
Index   Correlated audio-visual material
Glossary   Manual available
Suggestions for activities   Workbooks available

VALUE TO CURRICULUM

Adapted to local instructional needs?

How?_____

Suitable for supplementing basic instructional program? Yes_____ No_____

In what area?_____

At what grade level?_____

Suggestions for use_____

_____

_____

Useful for enrichment or extended reading?   Yes_____ No_____

Special uses_____

_____

ILLUSTRATIONS

Black and white   Suitable to subject matter
Color   Suitable to grade level
Photographs   Actually supplement the text
Diagrams   Well placed
Maps

MECHANICAL

Binding	Printing	Paper
Cloth	Typesize—	Color—
Paper	Satisfactory	White
Other	Too large	Other
Sturdy	Too small	Satisfactory
Stitched	Unusual type	Too thin
	Color	Glossy
	Black	
	Other	

Margins—adequate_____ too narrow_____ general appearance—

attractive_____

uninteresting_____

SUGGESTED USE

Teacher reference_____

1 per classroom   _____

5-10 per classroom _____

15 per classroom   _____

RECOMMENDATIONS

    Recommended—Interest level (grades) _____

                   Reading level (grades) _____

  Not recommended———————————————————————

  Remarks—If not recommended, please explain why:

_____

_____

_____

_____

_____

Date_____Reviewer_____School_____

CHECKLIST III

Purchase Order Card Made_____

Approved List Card Made_____

AUDIOVISUAL MATERIALS EVALUATION RECORD*

TITLE_____Type of Material_____

SERIES_____No. Frames_____

PRODUCER_____Sound Time_____

SOURCE_____Copyright Date_____

PRINT IN: _____Color   PRICE: $_____Individual Item

              _____Black & White $_____Series

This section to be filled in by the sub-committee chairman:

We have previewed this material, and:

1. Quality of material:

    a. Is the content accurate and up-to-date?   Yes_____   No_____

    b. Does the material fit in with the aim and content of

       the curriculum?   Yes_____   No_____

    c. Are the concepts presented suited to the grade level? Yes_____   No_____

    d. Will use of the material arouse and maintain pupil

       interest?   Yes_____   No_____

    e. Will the material stimulate the slow learner yet chal-

       lenge the accelerated pupil?   Yes_____   No_____

    f. Is sound clear and understandable?   Yes_____   No_____

    g. Is physical quality of material: good_____mediocre_____poor_____

2. Number of classrooms in which this material was previewed_____

_____APPROVED FOR INDIVIDUAL SCHOOL LIBRARIES

_____APPROVED FOR PURCHASE FOR AUDIOVISUAL CENTER

       LIBRARY

* Houston Independent School District. Houston, Texas.

_____From current allocation

_____Keep on approved list for consideration at a later date

Print should be: Level of use:

_____Color   _____Primary

_____Black & white   _____Intermediate

                                  _____Junior High

                                    _____Senior High

                                    _____Inservice

_____NOT APPROVED FOR PURCHASE   REASON_____

PLEASE RETURN *THIS* COPY WITH THE
MATERIAL PREVIEWED.

           Sub-committee Chairman   Date

           Committee Chairman   Date

CHECKLIST IV
CRITERIA FOR SELECTING EQUIPMENT*

1. Portability

_____ Is the piece of equipment easy to handle and move around?

_____ Is it reasonably light in weight in comparison with others?

_____ Is it compact?

_____ Are handles placed conveniently for easy carrying and lifting?

2. Ruggedness

_____ Will this piece of equipment give good operating service with a minimum of trouble?

_____ Does it have a sturdy appearance?

_____ Is it free of vibration during operation?

_____ Are the joints, supports, braces, and connections tight and strong?

_____ Is the construction material appropriate and heavy enough?

_____ Are the carrying handles anchored securely?

_____ Are the control mechanisms strong?

3. Cost

_____ In comparison with others, and in terms of other criteria, is the cost reasonable and competitive?

4. Ease of Operation

_____ Can teachers and students operate the equipment effectively?

_____ In general, is operation of the equipment easy to teach?

_____ Are the control mechanisms easy to use?

_____ Are the control mechanisms few in number?

_____ Are the controls accessible, in full view, and plainly marked?

_____ Is the equipment free of operating pecularities such as loose parts that have to be removed and reinserted?

5. Quality of Performance

_____ How well does the equipment meet desirable performance standards?

* Erickson, Carlton W. H. *Administering Audio-Visual Services.* New York: Macmillan, 1959. pp. 166-168.

_____ That is, whatever the equipment is supposed to do, does it do it well?
_____ Can the equipment be depended upon to perform at desirable levels consistently?

6. Effective Design

_____ Is the design attractive?
_____ Is it free of unfinished or rough exterior parts?
_____ Is it free of imperfections and errors in construction?
_____ Is the finish functional and attractive?
_____ Is the finish easily marred?
_____ Was the equipment designed with school use in mind?

7. Ease of Maintenance and Repair

_____ Can the necessary minor adjustments be made easily and quickly?
_____ Are parts that need cleaning frequently conveniently accessible?
_____ Are the parts standard and easily available for purchase?
_____ Is it easy to remove the sections likely to need repair, that is, without complete disassembly?

8. Reputation of Manufacturer

_____ Is production of school equipment a major concern of the company?
_____ Is the research, planning, and development record of the company favorable?
_____ Is it likely that the company will continue in business for the school field?
_____ Are the manufacturer's personnel policies and his relationship with dealers commendable?

9. Available Service

_____ Are repair and emergency service facilities nearby?
_____ Are adequate stocks of spare parts maintained locally?

CHECKLIST V

SELF EVALUATION IN MEDIA SELECTION*

Good school library service is in direct proportion to the quality of the media collection and to the competence and dedication of the librarian. A quality media collection meets adequately both the developmental needs of the curriculum and the needs, interests, goals, and abilities of the students.

A competent school librarian exchanges the library budget for the best resources available. The following provocative questions are reproduced here to provide guidance in analyzing media selection practices:

	YES	NO
1. Could you defend each purchase on the bases of need, suitability, and/or intrinsic worth?	_____	_____
2. Do you make an effort to keep your personal enthusiams and prejudices from influencing unduly your choice of media?	_____	_____
3. Do you maintain a list of curricular topics lacking adequate coverage so that you are reminded to search for materials to meet these topic development needs?	_____	_____
4. Do you maintain a consideration file to which you add suggestions for purchase as you review books, preview non-print media, and read reviews?	_____	_____

* Pennsylvania Division of School Libraries. *A Guide for School Librarians*. Harrisburg, Pennsylvania: Department of Public Instruction, 1969. pp. 40-41.

5. Do you seek to maintain balance in your buying so that   _____   _____
over a period of a year all areas of the collection have
been considered for new titles, added copies, weeding,
and replacement?

6. Do you have a realistic picture of the abilities of your   _____   _____
students based on your knowledge of their accumulative
records?

7. Do you know the students as individuals so that you   _____   _____
can search for materials suited uniquely to individual student needs, interests, goals, and abilities?

8. Do you attempt to cover all areas of the curriculum   _____   _____
with materials of different levels of difficulty?

9. Do you duplicate titles judiciously, suiting the number   _____   _____
to a demonstrated demand and choosing only those of
proven worth?

10. Do you avoid selecting the mediocre and the marginal   _____   _____
both in print and non-print media?

11. Do you constantly relate materials under consideration to   _____   _____
materials already in the collection to avoid the purchase
of "just another"?

12. Do you devote some time to re-evaluating materials in   _____   _____
the collection, weeding those no longer of educational
significance and those no longer of student interest?

13. Do you encourage teachers and students to participate   _____   _____
in selecting library materials?

14. Do you visit the state, regional, county and/or local   _____   _____
library to examine print and non-print media before
making your purchase lists?

BUILDING LIBRARIAN'S KNOWLEDGE OF THE EDUCATIONAL PROGRAM

The following guidelines should be employed by a librarian faced with building or reinforcing his knowledge of a school's educational program:

I. Confer with the curriculum director and/or building principal.

Discuss the prevailing educational philosophy, goals, and objectives.

Discuss the organizational pattern of the teaching program.

Discuss possible patterns for integrating library usage with the teaching and learning program.

Request opportunity to schedule visits to classrooms and to participate in class discussions.

Request the opportunity to meet with each teacher in a scheduled planning conference.

Request copies of each course of study for the library curriculum file.

Request for permanent loan copies of the teacher's edition of each textbook currently used.

II. Confer with each teacher in a scheduled exploratory planning conference.

Identify units to be taught throughout the school year.

Explore topic inclusion and areas of emphasis for each unit.

Discover teacher's method of presentation.

Discover textbooks being used for each class.

Discuss possible patterns of library usage by class, by groups, by individuals.

Discuss possible patterns for integrating library media support with the classroom teaching and learning program.

Discuss possible strategies for study skill integration with the classroom teaching and learning program.

Request teacher's cooperation in evaluating, testing, and selecting library media.

Request teacher's suggestions as to specific kinds of material to be included in the library collection.

Request copies of teacher-made guides, outlines, etc.

III. Analyze course content for each subject at each grade level.
Determine for each unit:

Scope and sequence of topic inclusion and development;

Pattern of concept development and linkage;

Specific teaching and learning experiences and activities;

Appropriate patterns for integrating the use of library resources with the teaching and learning program.

IV. Analyze textbook coverage.

Determine scope and sequence of topic coverage in each unit.

Determine adequacy of topic development in each unit.

Identify activities recommended for each unit.

Identify supplementary resources recommended for each unit.

V. Structure a master checklist of topics, strategies, and activities included in each unit plan.

Unify textbook inclusion and teacher suggestions.

Provide for specific skill introduction and reinforcement.

Provide for cross subject integration.

Provide for divergent capabilities of students.

VI. Build knowledge of the students' needs, interests, goals, abilities, concerns, and progress rates.

Confer with students in scheduled classroom visits:
    Identify student hobbies and/or recreational interests;
    Identify student reading interests (See Appendix J);
    Ask for student help in evaluating, testing, and selecting materials.

Confer with reading consultants, guidance counselors, classroom teachers, and/or homeroom teachers:
    Identify individual student I.Q. and achievement scores.

Structure a checklist of student interests and needs:
    Indicate special interests, abilities, disabilities, concerns.

VII. Build knowledge of the cocurricular program.

    Identify types and kinds of student organizations.

    Identify types and kinds of activities.

    Confer with club sponsors and officers.

VIII. Select materials to match.

    Curricular development needs.

    Teacher interest and emphasis needs.

    Student personal and educational needs.

    Cocurricular program implementation needs.

DETERMINING APPROPRIATENESS OF RESOURCES

Teachers and librarians face a professional challenge when selecting resources to support the teaching and learning program. The availability of an ever increasing wealth of media places a stern demand on those who would facilitate learning through the employment of instructional media. It is not in *providing* materials that we meet our educational obligation to the learner; it is in providing the *most appropriate* material when the use of that material is feasible, purposeful, significant, timely.

When determining the appropriateness of supporting media, the following criteria should be applied:

    _____ Is this resource of "real" educational significance and value?

    _____ Is this resource motivational in design and content?

    _____ Is this resource of the highest caliber in format, design, and content?

    _____ Is this resource suitable to the maturity and experience level of this grade?

    _____ Is this resource adequate to challenge the diverse capabilities of the learners?

    _____ Is this resource compatible with student interests, needs, goals, abilities, disabilities, concerns, progress rate, or creative potential?

    _____ Is this resource uniquely adaptable for use by a special class, a special group, or a special student?

    _____ Is the use of this resource supportive to the developmental needs of this unit, concept, or activity?

    _____ Is the "message" of this resource self-evident?

    _____ Is this resource likely to be effective in facilitating and expediting the realization of unit teaching goals?

    _____ Is the use of this resource justifiable in amount of time required in relation to amount of time available?

    _____ Is this resource self-sustaining and complete, or must it be reinforced or used in conjunction with other media?

PAPERBACK BOOKS

The paperback has become a teaching resource of increasing significance and respectability. Today the paperback is judged by teacher and librarian as *appropriate* for student use. The paperback is respected because of its appeal to the reader, its wide availability, its reasonable cost, its flexibility, and its convenience. In 1966 the American Textbook Publishers Institute and the trade journal, *Product Information for Schools (P/I)* conducted a survey on the use of paperbacks in public and Catholic high schools.[80]

TABLE V

HIGH SCHOOL PAPERBACK SURVEY

		Public	Catholic	Total
1. Are paperbacks included on lists of materials approved for purchase?	YES	92.1%	96.4%	93.7%
	NO	7.9%	3.6%	6.3%
2. Do you purchase paperbacks for	TEXTS	46.3%	76.5%	57.7%
	LIBRARY	71.8%	73.5%	72.7%
	SUPPLEMENTARY	93.0%	95.6%	97.0%
3. In which fields do you use paperbacks?	ENGLISH	99.6%	98.5%	99.2%
	SOCIAL STUDIES	81.9%	84.6%	82.9%
	SCIENCE	45.8%	52.9%	48.5%
	FOREIGN LANGUAGES	23.3%	43.3%	30.9%
	MUSIC AND ART	8.4%	20.6%	13.0%
	HEALTH AND PHYSICAL EDUCATION	9.3%	6.4%	8.5%
	MATH	22.9%	38.8%	28.1%
	READING	4.0%	..	2.5%
	RELIGION	..	21.3%	8.0%
	OTHERS	4.0%	4.4%	4.1%
4. Does your school give, loan or ask students to purchase paperbacks used in course study?	GIVE	12.9%	6.8%	10.7%
	LOAN	59.6%	32.3%	50.3%
	PURCHASE	66.2%	91.0%	73.6%
5. Does your school have classroom libraries with paperbacks?	YES	58.9%	51.8%	56.2%
	NO	41.1%	48.2%	43.8%
6. If "Yes" in which classes?	ENGLISH	93.4%	86.3%	90.9%
	SOCIAL STUDIES	63.3%	50.7%	58.9%
	SCIENCE	33.1%	39.7%	30.6%
	FOREIGN LANGUAGES	14.7%	20.6%	16.8%
	MUSIC AND ART	6.6%	8.2%	7.2%
	HEALTH AND PHYSICAL EDUCATION	3.7%	4.1%	3.8%
	MATH	16.7%	19.2%	17.2%
	READING	4.4%	..	2.9%
	RELIGION	..	15.1%	5.3%
	OTHERS	1.5%	..	1.0%
7. Does your library buy paperbacks?	YES	77.2%	75.2%	76.4%
	NO	22.8%	24.8%	23.6%
8. Are paperbacks for your library pre-bound with a reinforced binding?	YES	28.1%	36.6%	31.3%
	SOMETIMES	20.3%	17.9%	19.4%
	NO	51.6%	45.5%	49.3%
9. Can your library buy paperbacks even though they may not be on an approved list?	YES	65.4%	65.2%	65.3%
	NO	34.6%	34.8%	34.7%

[80] *Product Information for Schools.* 2nd quarter 1966. pp. 36-39

10. Does your school have a:				
	BOOKSTORE	45.9%	83.5%	59.6%
	BOOK FAIR	28.9%	31.7%	30.5%
	BOOK CLUB	18.6%	13.0%	16.5%
11. Do you expect to buy paper- backs for any new programs supported by federal funds?	YES	61.4%	52.8%	58.3%
	NO	38.6%	47.2%	41.7%

In 1967 four organizations supported and participated in a survey to determine the educational status of the paperback. The American Association of School Librarians, The American Book Publishers Council, The American Textbook Publishers Institute and *School Management Magazine* survey revealed the following information:[81]

TABLE VI

ROLE OF PAPERBACKS IN SCHOOLS TODAY

Paperbacks are used	Schools With Stores	Schools Without Stores
In elementary curriculum	56%	32%
In secondary curriculum	82%	71%
In elementary library	44%	26%
In secondary library	67%	60%

WHY PAPERBACKS ARE USED IN ELEMENTARY SCHOOLS

If you use paperbacks, check the most important reasons that motivate you to use them.

FOR YOUR LIBRARY

32% Less expensive than hardbound books, so our budget goes farther.

24% Practical for short term use.

29% Students like them.

10% Many paperback titles are not readily available in hardbound.

1% Require less space than hardbound books.

AS TEXTS OR SUPPLEMENTARY TEXTS

21% Less expensive than hardbound books, so our budget goes farther.

12% Students like them.

33% Give teachers more flexibility in dealing with individual differences of students.

18% Give teachers more flexibility in curriculum (can make changes from class-to-class and year-to-year).

31% Provide useful and inexpensive supplements to regular textbooks.

[81] *School Management Magazine,* September 1967. Vol. II, pp. 1-6.

WHY PAPERBACKS ARE USED IN SECONDARY SCHOOLS

FOR YOUR LIBRARY

34% Less expensive than hardbound books, so our budget goes farther.

23% Practical for short term use.

30% Students like them.

26% Many paperback titles are not readily available in hardbound.

4% Require less space than hardbound books.

2% Do not have to be processed and cataloged.

AS TEXTS OR SUPPLEMENTARY TEXTS

21% Less expensive than hardbound books, so our budget goes farther.

14% Students like them.

32% Give teachers more flexibility in dealing with individual differences of students.

38% Give teachers more flexibility in curriculum (can make changes from class-to-class and year-to-year).

33% Provide useful and inexpensive supplements to regular textbooks.

PERIODICAL COLLECTION

A rich resource necessary for the support of the curriculum and for meeting the recreational reading needs of the students is the school library's periodical collection. An invaluable selection tool for the guidance of librarians faced with the need to build a periodical collection is *Periodicals for School Libraries: A Guide to Magazines, Newspapers, and Periodical Indexes*. This comprehensive guide provides purchase information for and detailed content analysis of more than four hundred periodicals worthy of consideration for school purchase.

> Designed to serve the needs of school librarians and teachers, this compilation covers all grade levels, kindergarten through twelfth grade; it comprises a large number of titles to keep pace with the realities of curricular demands and with the recommendations of the *Standards for School Media Programs:* and it includes a number of off-the-beaten-track titles to act as a challenge to the imagination of students and a spur to their intellectual curiosity.[82]

Building a permanent periodical reference collection is mandatory for any high school aspiring to academic excellence. It is now accepted practice that librarians purchase periodicals on microforms rather than continue the traditional practice of binding back issues of periodicals. Since the purchase price of microfilm, microfiche, and microcard is approximately the same as the cost of binding a periodical, and since microforms occupy but from 4% to 6% of the space required by their bulky bound counterparts, it is no longer deemed wise to spend money or to waste shelf space on bound periodicals.

[82] Scott, Marian, ed. *Periodicals for School Libraries: A Guide to Magazines, Newspapers, and Periodical Indexes*. Chicago, Illinois: American Library Association, 1969. p. viii.

Students thoroughly enjoy information retrieval via microfilm, microfiche, or microcard; they find this approach compatible with their space-age reliance on electronic gadgets as a natural part of everyday living. Since students going on to college will undoubtedly find microforms in their college library, the high school has an obligation to prepare its students to use microforms intelligently.

COMMUNITY RESOURCE FILE

In addition to maintaining an index to the library's media collection, the librarian also has the professional responsibility for organizing and maintaining a file of local community resources and contacts of educational significance. Maintaining this community resource file should be a common concern of both teachers and library staff. Each time a field trip or school journey has been made or a speaker from the community has come to the school, the teacher should complete an evaluation sheet indicating the educational value and merit of this experience (See Example I).

PROFESSIONAL LIBRARY

In addition to providing materials to support the education of students, the school library should provide materials to support the continuing professional education of the faculty. A professional library is a necessary investment in quality education, for it is an effective means of encouraging and enabling teachers to grow intellectually on the job.

In the fall of 1964 the American Association of School Librarians and the National Commission on Teacher Education and Professional Standards formed a joint committee "to produce ideas and information of immediate and practical value that would help achieve the objective of making the latest and most relevant books and other materials easily accessible to all teachers."[83] Fullfilling its obligation this joint committee published in 1966, the first edition and in 1968, the second edition of *The Teachers' Library: How to Organize It and What to Include*. This comprehensive handbook provides detailed information on how to get a teachers' library started, how to finance, organize and administer it, as well as how to encourage its use.

EXAMPLE I

COMMUNITY RESOURCE FILE

NAME:	Buhl Planetarium and Institute of Popular Science
LOCATION:	Allegheny Square, Pittsburgh, Pa. 15212
TELEPHONE:	412–321–4300
CONTACT:	Arthur L. Draper, Director
HOURS:	Daily: 2:15 p.m. skyshow
	8:15 p.m. skyshow
FEE:	Group rate: 25 or more students, 30¢ per student
	less than 25 students, 35¢ per student
	teachers admitted free

[83] American Association of School Librarians and The National Commission on Teacher Education and Professional Standards. *The Teachers' Library: How to Organize It and What to Include*. rev. ed. Washington, D.C.: National Education Association, 1968. p. 1.

WHEN TO SCHEDULE:	At least three weeks in advance of anticipated field trip
PUBLIC TRANSPORTATION:	Buses from downtown Pittsburgh: #16-D—Crosstown #16-E—Reedsdale Cost: 30¢ each way
TYPE OF PROGRAM OR LEARNING EXPERIENCE:	Skyshow and lecture Science Fair
GRADE LEVEL SUITABILITY:	7th grade unit: "Man Learns About the Stars" 9th grade unit: "Space Science and Exploration" 7th-12th grade: Science Fair participation
CURRICULUM TIE-IN:	Astronomy, meteorology, space exploration
EVALUATION:	Field trips to the Buhl Planetarium are well worth scheduling; lectures are always informative and enthusiastically received by the students. No two years are alike; a different skyshow is developed for each of the four seasons.

The Teachers' Library provides complete bibliographic information for the selection and purchase of books, pamphlets, periodicals, journals, films, and filmstrips. Curriculum guides and courses of study are not included. Therefore, the librarian charged with the responsibility of maintaining a functional library for the teaching staff should systematically search each issue of *Curriculum Materials.** This comprehensive handbook is compiled each year by the Conference of the Association for Supervision and Curriculum Development as a guide to its annual exhibit of curriculum materials. It contains no less than 1,000 different educational guides including policy and philosophy statements, handbooks, manuals, special reports, resource units, and courses of study. No librarian concerned with providing fellow faculty members with curricular guides can afford not to invest $2.00 a year to purchase this basic index to current curricular publications.

Likewise, the librarian concerned with incorporating in the professional library current research findings should search the publications distributed by the Educational Research Information Center (ERIC). This nationwide network of information centers was established by Congress in 1967 to put results of educational research into the hands of educators at nominal cost and on an up-to-date basis. The ERIC network as of January, 1969, included 19 decentralized clearinghouses, each responsible for a specialized collection.**

A professional library collection should include information pertaining to all facets of the educational program. The following checklist, *Professional Library Resources,* can serve as a means of determining items to be considered for inclusion and as a means of determining the adequacy or inadequacy of present holdings (See Checklist VI).

* *Curriculum Materials.* Washington, D.C.: Association for Supervision and Curriculum Development. National Education Association. Annual.
** For information concerning the location of each ERIC clearinghouse check the latest edition of the *Bowker Annual* published by the R. R. Bowker Co., New York, New York.

CHECKLIST VI

PROFESSIONAL LIBRARY RESOURCES

Information pertaining to:

_____ Administration	_____ Junior colleges
_____ Adult education	_____ Learning processes
_____ Advanced placement programs	_____ Media selection and use
_____ Audio-visual materials and techniques	_____ Mental health
_____ Bibliographies	_____ Merit rating
_____ Book selection	_____ Methodology
_____ Buildings and grounds	_____ Moral and spiritual values
_____ Certification	_____ Philosophy
_____ Classroom organization	_____ Pilot programs
_____ Co-curricular activities	_____ Principles of discipline
_____ College and university programs	_____ Principles of planning
_____ Community resources	_____ Principles of teaching
_____ Compensatory education	_____ Professional ethics
_____ Conference and workshop reports	_____ Professional growth
_____ Courses of study	_____ Professional organizations
_____ Creativity	_____ Professional publications
_____ Curriculum guides	_____ Programmed instruction
_____ Curriculum study and design	_____ Psychology
_____ Disciplines	_____ Public relations
_____ Educational television	_____ Reading
_____ Educational theory	_____ Remediation
_____ Educational trends	_____ Research studies
_____ Elementary education	_____ Resource units
_____ Equipment	_____ Routine and policy manuals
_____ Evaluative criteria	_____ Scheduling
_____ Exceptional children	_____ Scholarships and grants
_____ Federal aids and grants	_____ School law
_____ Finance	_____ School libraries
_____ Free and inexpensive materials	_____ School organization
_____ General education	_____ School publications
_____ Government publications	_____ Secondary education
_____ Guidance and counseling	_____ Special education
_____ Handbooks for parents, teachers, students	_____ Standards
_____ History of education	_____ Student teaching program
_____ Homeroom organization	_____ Study skills
_____ Human development	_____ Supervision
_____ Incentive programs	_____ Teacher education
_____ Individualization	_____ Teacher exchange program
_____ Innovation	_____ Team teaching
_____ Inservice education	_____ Testing
	_____ Textbook selection
	_____ Ungraded schools
	_____ Unit development
	_____ Vocational education

CLASSROOM LIBRARIES

Teachers and students alike require basic tools readily at hand in the classroom as they work together to build understanding. Just as textbooks are accepted as classroom tools basic for learning, so should dictionaries, atlases, almanacs, and encyclopedias be considered basic tools essential for learning how to learn in the classroom. An educational program designed to develop functional literacy requires both the planned and systematic teaching and purposeful application and practice of study skills as an integral part of the on-going classroom teaching and learning enterprise. Today's classroom teacher, if professionally competent and concerned, will carefully and consistently incorporate within his daily lesson plan ample opportunity for students to learn and to practice study skills within a context of timely significance and functional utility (See Chapter 10; Appendix L).

In addition to basic reference tools, each classroom should be equipped with print and non-print media especially supportive to the subjects and grades being taught in that room. For example: a social studies room should be equipped with appropriate maps, charts, globes, gazeteers, handbooks, pamphlets, periodicals, etc. particularly related to the course of study and the needs of the students; a science room should be equipped with microscopic slides, specimens, models, diagrams, charts, books of experiments, dictionaries, and handbooks, required by course content and essential to the learning needs of the students. One rule-of-thumb to guide the decision as to what is appropriate for a classroom library is: place in the classroom those resources used frequently by the teacher throughout the school year to facilitate his teaching and used frequently by the student to expedite his learning. To stock a classroom with basic reference and subject related media is not a needless duplication of material and, therefore, is not a waste of money. Students do not learn to think in a vacuum; they do not learn how to learn unless the tools essential for knowledge building are available for immediate use when and as necessary. When tools are out of sight, they are out of mind. A classroom study skills program is but a nebulous hope unless basic resources are available to bring immediacy of utility to the teaching and learning of the skills themselves.

It is regretable that in our anxiety to initiate school library service we have all too frequently weakened classroom teaching by draining basic tools from the classroom. In addition to a definite budget for the purchase of library resources, a definite budget should be allocated for the purchase of basic classroom print and non-print materials. Whether an index of classroom library holdings is maintained in the library or in the principal's office is not of great import. Frequently the budget for the purchase of classroom resources is spent cooperatively by teacher and principal. Therefore, it does seem logical for the principal to maintain the record of classroom holdings and to supervise the care and maintenance of these materials.

SUBJECT LABORATORIES

J. Lloyd Trump, Associate Secretary, National Association of Secondary School Principals, N.E.A., recommends redistributing the school day to provide the student with greater opportunity for self-directed knowledge building. He suggests the following allocation of time:[84]

40% large group instruction
40% independent study
20% small group instruction.

[84] Trump, J. Lloyd. Op. cit., p. 3.

The student during the time alloted for independent study would be free to go to the library (IMC) or to a special math, English, social studies, science, music, art, etc. laboratory to use resources uniquely appropriate to his quest for understanding in that particular subject area. In addition to resources the student would also have available in the subject laboratory the "supervision of competent adults qualified in the subject matter being studied."[85]

Giving the student the freedom to choose if and where he will study is an encouraging departure from the rigidity of assigned studyhalls. Likewise, having a "social study hall" available where the student may go to relax, play chess, or just socialize is a more realistic approach to meeting the needs of the student than the traditional, antisocial study hall of the past.

Usually the librarian is vested with the responsibility of helping the principal and/or department chairman select the resources to be housed in the subject laboratory (See Figure VI). Processing and indexing the holdings of the subject laboratory likewise are a delegated responsibility of the library staff. In this case, the card catalog in the central library should index the holdings of each subject laboratory, and the cards clearly indicating the location of the material.

STAFF: ONE MAN BAND OR SYMPHONY ORCHESTRA

A library program of educational excellence requires the services of sufficient numbers of librarians, technicians, para-professionals, and clerical assistants to man the program adequately. Traditionally the school library has been the total responsibility of a single librarian, one whose main obligation and sphere of influence was to organize, maintain, and circulate books while supervising a study hall. Today's librarian is a teacher who plans with fellow teachers, instructing groups and classes, and working directly with individual students. The librarian's educational role is too important for him to be assigned clerical tasks. No district can afford to pay professional salary for non-professional service!

A library program designed for optimum service precludes a staff of but one librarian. The library program, if it is to function to capacity, must have the support of sufficient numbers of professional librarians, instructional aides, and clerical assistants. The district has the responsibility to free the librarian from clerical routines by providing centralized processing service to accomplish the non-teaching tasks of ordering, accessioning, and preparing materials for use (See Appendix K). It is a savings in time, money, and effort to centralize the mechanics of media preparation.

A library program of educational excellence requires also the services of librarians with the diverse competencies requisite to supporting the educational program. Lloyd Trump added to his recommendation that librarians move into the mainstream of the educational program, that the library staff be of sufficient number and diversification in training to provide the variety and kinds of services essential to bring adequate support to the educational program. He stated that it is "unnecessarily expensive" to pay a librarian a professional salary and then have him performing non-professional tasks.[86]

When the librarian is directly involved in the teaching-learning program,

85 Ibid. p. 2.
86 Ibid., p. 5.

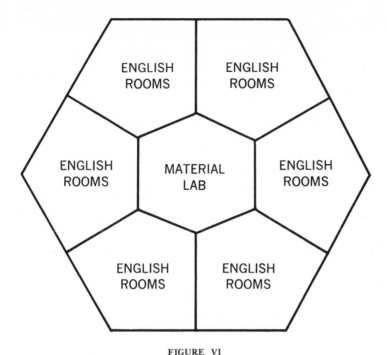

FIGURE VI

ENGLISH MATERIALS LABORATORY*

he should not be expected to work with more students in any given period than the average class load carried by a classroom teacher. He should be freed from all mechanical and sub-professional responsibilities to work as a media specialist personally involved in and professionally contributing to the teaching and learning program.

SCHEDULING

The library schedule should be an "open" one—that is, no time is permanently prescheduled by the principal. The "open" schedule permits the librarian and the teacher to schedule class and group use of the library on the basis of immediacy of need. In the saber-tooth curriculum days, the library served as study hall, scheduling convenience, and disciplinary agency. Those who needed to use the library couldn't get in because the magazine-thumbers, Latin class drop-outs, and physical education dodgers jammed the seats—a costly and abortive misuse of an educational facility.

Since the use of library resources is supportive of teaching and learning plans, it is imperative that all essential materials be available when their use is appropriate, significant, and timely to the developmental task at hand. Since the librarian is a teacher charged with the responsibility of planning cooperatively with fellow teachers for the most effective and efficient use of media, it is imperative that the librarian be available for face-to-face, *scheduled* communication with the teacher. The librarian must be "free" to plan

* Hook, J. N. *The Teaching of High School English.* 3rd ed. New York: Ronald Press, 1965. p. 53.

with teachers without interruption for the teacher's time is too limited to permit any disruption of scheduled conference time.

The librarian is a teacher whose major responsibility is facilitating each student's learning to learn with purpose, profit, challenge, and satisfaction (See Appendix N). This responsibility demands a "free" library schedule so that the library will be available for use and the librarian will be "free" to give the student—class, group, or individual—his undivided attention.

Preplanning and prescheduling for most effective use of the library is advocated not alone by librarians but also by educators recognizing the necessity of library support for a quality educational program. Charlotte Huck and Doris Kuhn in the second edition of *Children's Literature in the Elementary School* specify that the school librarian must be available to work directly with children throughout the school day. In order to clarify and accentuate the concept of the "open" schedule they include a sample schedule of a day in an elementary library or instructional materials center (See Example II).

EXAMPLE II

ONE DAY IN AN ELEMENTARY INSTRUCTIONAL MATERIALS CENTER*

8:00 An intern teacher works with the librarian to select materials appropriate for study of developing nations in Africa. Magazines, pamphlets, and newspapers are used as well as books, films, and tapes. The file of TV tapes in the central school center reveals an interview with a visitor from Nigeria filmed the previous year.

8:15 The library is open so children may come in to return and check out books, to look at displays, to read, to use the carrels. If a pupil missed a television lesson, he may see it by presenting a card from the teacher indicating the number of the lesson he should see. Some children work on reports in study carrels. Those activities continue throughout the day. The library clerk is present to assist.

9:10 Two fifth-graders ask for help in locating information about a boundary dispute with Canada.

9:20 Three fourth-graders want material about Elizabeth Coatsworth, a favorite author. The vertical file contains information, material from the publisher, and a copy of a letter written by the author to another child.

9:25 Ten children go to the listening area for a filmstrip and record presentation of *Blueberries for Sal*. They will compare the Weston Woods presentation with the book.

9:30 The librarian goes to a second-grade classroom for a book sharing period. She listens to a program about bear characters in books. Paddington, Pooh, August, Sal, Goldilocks, the Bears on Hemlock Mountain are some of the "characters" who tell of their adventures, their authors, and illustrators. This was a culminating experience after the librarian had introduced "Bears in Books." In the library six children listen to a tape recording of a folk tale. Three boys study "slide tape" material on astronomy.

* Huck, Charlotte S. and Doris Young Kuhn. *Children's Literature in the Elementary School.* 2nd edition. New York: Holt, Rinehart and Winston, 1968. p. 561.

10:00 A first grade comes for a story hour. The librarian tells a story in the listening area.

10:15 The music consultant checks out recordings for a lesson in appreciation. The librarian has left a new biography of Leonard Bernstein on the table so he may use it or call it to the attention of the children.

10:45 The librarian meets with a third-grade group for a planned lesson on use of the card catalog. The lesson was reinforced with programmed materials.

11:30 The librarian has a luncheon meeting with a parent committee and the public librarian to plan a program on books for children.

1:45 The entire group of ninety children in the intermediate team-teaching unit hears the librarian present a lecture about various editions of Aesop's fables through the centuries. In the library, fifth-graders compare reviews of books in *The Horn Book Magazine* and *Young Readers Review*.

3:00 The librarian meets with the other members of the team-teaching group to evaluate the presentation and to plan further activities.

MEDIA PROGRAMMING

The philosophy of "open-ended" learning is directional to the librarian's function as a media programmer. For in open-ended learning each learning experience is not complete in and of itself but is a single component of a complex, on-going, inter-related quest for further understanding. In "open-ended" learning each learning experience ends not with a period but with a question mark. "Open-ended" learning requires the cross-media approach to teaching for it is through the employment of a combination of appropriate supporting media that meaningful learning experiences accumulate. Depth, breadth, and adequacy of understanding are the directional goals of "open-ended" learning. To reach these goals learning must become a continuous growth process encompassing comprehension, analysis, application, evaluation, and synthesis. Instructional media, the school library's stock in trade, are both the source and the force for regenerative thought carrying understanding beyond inception through incubation to application.

In a program designed to promote "open-ended" learning the librarian's educational responsibility goes far beyond identifying, evaluating, selecting, obtaining, organizing, and dispersing instructional media. These are the mechanical, not the educational aspects of school librarianship, dear though were these routines to the librarian of the saber-tooth tiger days. The prime educational responsibilities of any school librarian are to identify the educationally significant ideas latent in each resource and then to plan for the timely releases of those ideas when that release is appropriate, supportive, and necessary to a specific quest for understanding. The librarian has the professional obligation to translate teaching and learning strategies into supporting patterned programs of media usage. It is the librarian's unique function to group ideas into patterns of logical, significant, cohesive, balanced inter-relatedness. Blueprinting a plan for the sequential use of materials in building adequacy of understanding is called "media programming."

In building a media usage program for the systematic development of ideas, the librarian not only selects appropriate materials but determines what combination of media can best meet a specific developmental need of the instructional plan or meet a special learning need of an individual, a group, or a class. The use of materials that is unplanned, unpatterned or unrelated is a waste of time, aborts energy, and destroys interest. To need specific information and not be able to locate it is not only a waste of time but frustrating to the point of dissipating interest and patience. Freedom to learn does not imply the lack of a structured learning plan for knowledge building (See Appendix N). William Burton warns that "No one ever learned to think under conditions of uncontrolled, uninhibited freedom . . . Freedom, like discipline, can become an end in itself, activity for activity's sake . . . The results of painless freedom are lack of *continuity* and *system,* acceptance of fuzzy, inadequate reasons for one's beliefs, and eventually a demand for continual stimulation by new trivia."[87] Pointless browsing among a wealth of instructional media without plan or purpose is educationally as effective as playing blindman's bluff in the library stumbling in a haphazard, random manner from resource to resource without direction, plan, continuity, or purpose. The sporadic, unplanned use of media is not educationally defensible. Just as planning is basic to developing an effective teaching program, so is planning basic to the effective and efficient use of media by teacher and by student.

The following principles undergird the planned use of instructional media:[88]

> *All instructional aids should be used for specific and defined purposes within an on-going series of activities, whether they be assigned or initiated by the pupils.*
> *A given instructional aid should be chosen to serve a direct need of the learner as that need appears in the series of learning activities.*

> Aids and materials are not used merely because they are "interesting," "real," or "concrete," but because they explain or clarify a needed understanding, contribute to the development of an attitude, explain a motor or machine process. The next principle is equally important.

> *Instructional aids should be chosen in terms of the pupils' maturity and experience, and in accord with individual differences within the group.*

> Is the language used within the reading and speaking vocabularies of the learners?
> Is the material portrayed close enough to pupils' past experience to be readily assimilable?
> Is the manner of presentation understandable to the pupils?
> Is the material sufficiently comprehensive to secure varied responses, thus enabling various types of children to react on their levels and in their own way?

[87] Burton, William H. et al. Op. cit., p. 291.
[88] Burton, William H. Op. cit., pp. 427-428.

Is there possibility of differentiation in the follow-up?
Is there possibility to continue growth along the lines already apparent at the given level of maturity?

Instructional aids should be examined for accuracy and validity as well as for appropriateness to need and maturity.

Is the material accurate and up-to-date?
Is it of desirable quality?
Is it acceptable under aesthetic as well as utilitarian standards?
Is it easily available?

The use of given instructional aids should be carefully planned.

The teacher should preview or otherwise examine the material in order to be sure that it fits the need which has arisen or which he plans to stimulate.
Teacher and pupils together should prepare themselves to use the materials intelligently in the light of the need which it is to serve.
A list of questions may be developed.
An outline of points to observe may be developed.

The use of instructional aids should include a definitely planned follow-up.

This may be through further discussion or analysis in the light of the questions or points to observe or through an evaluation device.

Preference should be given to those supplementary materials which approach most closely the comparable direct experience.
Instructional aids should be chosen within reasonable limits in terms of cost.

The above principles direct the librarian's selection of materials and his designing media usage patterns. Media programming is a new, high level of technological sophistication required of any competent librarian. Today's librarian must know content as well as *when* and *how* best to use that content.

The school librarian employs the science of media programming as he designs a media usage pattern for the systematic solving of an intellectual problem. Before attempting to support the teaching and learning of any phase of the program, the librarian first builds his knowledge of what is to be taught; in what sequence it is to be taught; when, where, to whom, by whom, and how it is to be taught. Having built his background knowledge, the librarian will then be ready to select materials and design a pattern for the purposeful, sequential, inter-related, productive use of the materials by teacher or by student.

The checklist, Media Programming Components, can serve as a guide to the school librarian as he sets about identifying the essential components to be included in a media usage program (See Checklist VII).

CHECKLIST VII

MEDIA PROGRAMMING COMPONENTS

1. WHAT IS TO BE TAUGHT? (Specification of Content)

_____	Appreciations	_____	Processes
_____	Attitudes	_____	Skills
_____	Concepts	_____	Structures
_____	Fundamentals	_____	Terms
_____	Generalizations	_____	Theories
_____	Principles	_____	Understandings
_____	Problems	_____	Values

2. WHEN CAN IT BEST BE TAUGHT? (Timeliness of topic presentation)

_____ In which grade
_____ In what unit
_____ Where within the unit
_____ Introduction
_____ Exploration
_____ Summarization
_____ Culmination

3. TO WHOM CAN IT BEST BE TAUGHT? (Appropriateness to learner maturity)

_____	To above average student	_____	To below average student
_____	To average student		

4. HOW CAN IT BEST BE TAUGHT? (Method of instruction)

_____	By comparative analysis	_____	By listening
_____	By demonstration	_____	By manipulative and tactile activity
_____	By directed observation		
_____	By discussion	_____	By modeling
_____	By dramatization	_____	By practice
_____	By drill	_____	By problem solving
_____	By experimentation	_____	By programmed instruction
_____	By field experience	_____	By project
_____	By a field trip	_____	By reading
_____	By group work	_____	By recitation
_____	By imitation	_____	By seminar
_____	By laboratory experience	_____	By testing
_____	By lecture	_____	By viewing

5. IN WHAT SEQUENCE CAN IT BEST BE TAUGHT? (Sequence of topic presentation)

_____	In logical progression	_____	In branching concept and interest order
_____	In motivational order		
_____	In priority order	_____	In summarizing order
_____	In conceptual interlock order	_____	In reinforcing order
		_____	In synthesizing order
_____	In basic concept development order		

6. WHERE CAN IT BEST BE TAUGHT? (Physical environment conducive to learning)

_____	In the auditorium	_____	In the large group instruction area
_____	In the classroom		
_____	In a community facility	_____	In the library

_____ In the conference room   _____ In the seminar room
_____ In the gymnasium   _____ In the small group
_____ In the laboratory   instruction area

7. BY WHOM CAN IT BEST BE TAUGHT? (Locus of teaching responsibility)

_____ By the classroom teacher   _____ By the head of department
_____ By the community resource   _____ By the librarian
         consultant   _____ By a subject specialist
_____ By the guidance counselor   _____ By a teaching team

8. WITH WHAT RESOURCE OR RESOURCES CAN IT BEST BE TAUGHT?
    (Medium of instruction)

_____ Art print   _____ Microslide
_____ Book   _____ Model
_____ Chart   _____ Motion picture (16 mm,
_____ Community contact   8 mm)
_____ Depth study kit   _____ Pamphlet
_____ Diorama   _____ Periodical
_____ Disc recording   _____ Programmed instruction
_____ Filmstrip   _____ Real object
_____ Flannelgram   _____ Slide
_____ Globe   _____ Study guide
_____ Graph   _____ Study print
_____ Kinescope   _____ Tape recording
_____ Laboratory manual   _____ Televised program
_____ Map   _____ Transparency
_____ Microcard   _____ Videotape
_____ Microfilm

SYSTEMS APPROACH TO MEDIA PROGRAMMING

The systems approach to media programming utilizes instructional media in a logically patterned learning sequence. The preplanned, systematic use of media is based on the premise that:

Learning can be facilitated, expedited, and effectualized by the strategic use of appropriate media if that use is developed in a logical, progressively sequential order of meaningful, balanced inter-relatedness;

Learning can be motivated by having the student see the learning task in its entirety, seeing each part as an integral supporting component of a total learning design;

Learning to learn requires that the student view a learning experience as a challenging, on going, continuous, regenerative process of cohesive inter-relatedness so that he knows where he is going and has a reasonable idea of how he is going to get there;

Learning to learn requires guided practice working with significant ideas; resources contain ideas and, therefore, are a means to an end; the learner must perceive clearly the end to be achieved through the use of each resource before he begins his search for understanding;

Learning resources used indiscriminately without plan or purpose have little or no educational significance or value;

Learning that is purposeful, challenging, and pleasurable is more permanently meaningful, more lastingly significant;

Zest for learning is motivated by success in learning; a learning program should be designed and structured to promote learner success and to minimize learner confusion, frustration, disappointment, and failure;

Learning programs are not impersonal when they build into their design opportunities for student choice of material, student choice of activity, and student reaction.

An innovative learning guide designed by Shirley A. Pittman* employs the systems approach to media usage. Miss Pittman has had marked success using learning guides with elementary and secondary children in the areas of social studies, mathematics, language arts, science, and health. The Pittman Learning Guide is designed for self-paced learning and employs guide questions, references to specific resources, as well as optional and branching activities. Each student receives a learning guide on 8" x 5" cards; the student follows the directions on the cards as he builds his understanding through a series of learning experiences. Examples of these learning guides follow (See Chapter 8 for other examples).

EXAMPLE III

PITTMAN LEARNING GUIDE—HISTORY

Card 1

The History of Our America
Unit: America Moves West
Topic: What was the Pony Express?

Sub-topic 1:   When did the Pony Express begin and what were the qualifications required of the riders?

                SOURCE A—
                Miers, Earl S. *Wild and Woolly West*. Rand McNally. 1964. pp. 143-147.

and/or

                SOURCE B—
                Adams, Samuel. *The Pony Express*. (Landmark Series) Random House. 1950. pp. 3-53.

Sub-topic 2:   What route did the Pony Express follow? How long did it take the mail to go from St. Joseph, Missouri, to San Francisco? How much did it cost to send a letter in 1860 and in 1861?

                SOURCE A—
                Buehr, Walter. *Sending the Word*. Putnam. 1959. pp. 68-72.

AND

                SOURCE B—
                Miers, Earl S. *Wild and Woolly West*. Rand McNally. 1964. Map. pp. 150-151.

* Shirley A. Pittman, Librarian, McIntyre Elementary School, North Hills School District, Pittsburgh, Pennsylvania 15229.

Card 2

Sub-topic 3:   Who were some of the Pony Express riders and what adventures did they have?

SOURCE A—
Collier, Edmund. *The Story of Buffalo Bill*. Grosset & Dunlap. 1952. Chapter 12 "Riding the Pony Express."

and/or

SOURCE B—
Larom, Henry V. *Bronco Charlie, Rider of the Pony Express*. Scholastic Book Services. 1951.

and/or

SOURCE C—
McCall, Edith. *Mail Riders: Paul Revere to Pony Express*. Children's Press. 1961.

(1) Bill Hamilton pp. 85-98.
(2) Billy Campbell pp. 99-109.
(3) Bob Haslam pp. 110-127.

Optional Topic 1:   What kind of horses were used for the Pony Express?

SOURCE —
Mellin, Jeanne. *Horses Across the Ages*. Dutton. 1954. pp. 68-72. (Notice pictures on pp. 69, 71)

Card 3

Optional Topic 2:   Would you like to visit the Pony Express Stables Museum?

SOURCE —
Tour Book: South Central States. American Automobile Association. 1968-1969. p. 73,

Would you enjoy telling about the pony express by:
Preparing a poster advertising for Pony Express riders?

Writing a newspaper account of the opening of the Pony Express service?

Writing a newspaper account of a thrilling event experienced by a Pony Express rider?

Writing a letter describing your job as a Pony Express rider?

Making a map or a transparency showing the route of the Pony Express?

Review what you have learned about the Pony Express by:
Listening to the Enrichment record, *The Pony Express*
Viewing the Enrichment filmstrip, *The Pony Express*

MEDIA BUDGET

Inevitably the cost of instructional materials must be interjected into any discussion of library curriculum support. A quality library program requires the availability of a quality media collection; to build the media collection to functional strength requires an adequate capital investment plus an adequate continuing maintenance budget. Professional qualitative and quantitative standards provide guidance to the school administrator, business manager, and librarian as they set about determining the budget requirements of the school library. The cost of establishing and maintaining an adequate media program escalates as the purchase power of the dollar declines; therefore, standards must be updated to reflect the current cost of maintaining a functional media collection. In 1969 the American Association of School Librarians (ALA) in joint enterprise with the Department of Audiovisual Instruction (NEA) revised the 1960 *Standards for School Library Programs* to reflect more adequately the media needs of the curriculum and the purchase power of the dollar. The qualitative and quantitative standards set forth in the *Standards for School Media Programs* are predicated on the principle that a quality school library program cannot be bought with a substandard budget (See Figure XII).

In the past there have been those who have advocated structuring a school library budget by predetermining a definite percentage allotment for fiction and for each of the ten major divisions of the Dewey decimal system. Such an arbitrary approach cannot reflect the actual growth patterns and needs of the curriculum. The law of media supply and educational demand should be the determining factor in setting up a school library budget. The adequacy of the supply of appropriate print and non-print media in relation to the developmental needs of the educational program (current and anticipated) and the personal needs, interests, goals, and abilities of the student body should be the guide to budget planning.

In setting up a new school library the cost figure for purchase of the initial collection should be determined by totaling the cost of specific print and non-print media essential for teaching each unit in the school's curriculum and for meeting specific needs and interests of the student body and of the community (See Example IV). The cost of materials in relationship to educational value makes good sense to a school administrator; he can see what the money is going to buy; he can equate the educational value with the money invested. An itemized media budget is more effective and convincing than an unspecified "pig in a poke" budget request.

QUARTERS

A quality school library program requires functional library facilities. The library must be adequate to house students, staff, and collection comfortably, to facilitate every investigative and learning activity necessary to curricular support and to student interest satisfaction. To accommodate the many phases of its educational role, the school library plans must be designed specifically to provide the form which will support its educational function. An instrument designed to facilitate and strengthen library planning is offered in Appendix M to provide architects, administrators, and librarians with objective guidance in relating specific functions, procedures, and facilities to space allocation, to traffic and usage patterns, to faculty and learner needs, to general and specific resources, equipment, and furnishings.

EXAMPLE IV

ITEMIZED MEDIA BUDGET REQUEST

TO: _____(chief administrator)_____

FROM: _____

DATE: _____

The following media are essential for adequate support of the teaching of

Grade: _____Eleventh_____

Discipline: _____American History_____

Unit: _____"Interpreting Primary Sources or_____

_____Learning to Think Historically"_____

Print	*Price*
Adler, Mortimer J., ed. *The Annals of America.* Encyclopaedia Brittannica, 1969. 22 volumes.	$149.50
Angle, Paul M., ed. *The American Reader, From Columbus to Today.* Rand, 1958. 703 pp.	$ 7.50
Angle, Paul M., ed. *By These Words: Great Documents of American Liberty Selected and Placed in Their Contemporary Setting.* Rand, 1954. 560 pp.	$ 5.95
Aptheker, Herbert, ed. *A Documentary History of the Negro People in the United States.* Citadel, 1964. Paperback, 2 volumes, $2.25 each.	$ 4.50
Arnof, Dorothy S., ed. *A Sense of the Past: Readings in American History.* Macmillan, 1962. 500 pp. Paperback.	$ 2.32
Bailey, Thomas A. *The American Spirit: United States History As Seen by Contemporaries.* Heath, 1963. 964 pp. Paperback, 2 volumes, $3.75 each.	$ 7.50
Bartel, Roland, ed. *Selected Source Materials for College Research Papers.* Heath. Paperback, $1.75 each.	$ 12.25
Anderson, Sylvia F. and Jacob Korg. *Westward to Oregon.* 1958.	
Bartel, Roland and Edwin R. Bingham. *America Through Foreign Eyes, 1827–1842.* 1956.	
Bingham, Edwin R. *California Gold.* 1959.	
Bingham, Edwin R. *The Fur Trade in the West 1815–1846.* 1960.	
Doubleday, Neal F. *Mark Twain's Picture of His America.* 1960.	
Kogan, Bernard R. *The Chicago Haymarket Riot.* 1959.	
McCormick, Edgar L. and Edward G. McGehee, *Life on a Whaler.* 1960.	
Brown, Ralph A. and Marian R. Brown, eds. *Impressions of America.* Harcourt, 1966. Paperback, 2 volumes, $1.60 each.	$ 3.20
Brown, Richard C., ed. *The Human Side of American History.* Ginn, 1962. 310 pp. Paperback.	$ 2.00
Chute, William J., ed. *The American Scene: 1600–1860. . . .* Bantam, 1964. 462 pp. Paperback.	$ 0.95
Commager, Henry S. and Allan Nevins. *The Heritage of America: Readings in American History.* Revised edition. Heath, 1949. 1227 pp.	$ 9.50
De Huszar, George B. and Henry W. Littlefield, eds. *Basic American Documents.* Littlefield, 1961. 368 pp. Paperback.	$ 1.95

Donald, David, ed. *A Documentary History of American Life.* McGraw, $ 23.60
1966. Paperback, 8 volumes, $2.95 each.

Eliot, Charles W., ed. *American Historical Documents, 1900–1904.* Collier, $ 5.00
1938. 462 pp.

Emery, Edwin, ed. *The Story of America as Reported in Its Newspapers* $ 19.95
from 1690 to 1965. Simon, 1965. 311 pp. Paperback.

Hacker, Louis M. *American Capitalism: Its Promise and Accomplishment.* $ 1.45
Van Nostrand, 1957. Paperback.

Handlin, Oscar, ed. *Immigration as a Factor in American History.* Pren- $ 1.95
tice, 1959. 206 pp. Paperback.

Handlin, Oscar, ed. *Readings in American History.* Knopf, 1957. 715 pp. $ 6.95

Handlin, Oscar, ed. *This Was America. . . .* Harper, 1949. 602 pp. Paper- $ 2.95
back.

Harnsberger, Caroline T., ed. *Treasury of Presidential Quotations.* Follett, $ 6.95
1964. 394 pp.

Hart, Albert B., ed. *American History Told by Contemporaries.* Macmil- $ 45.00
lan, 1929. 5 volumes.

Hofstadter, Richard, ed. *Great Issues in American History.* Vintage, $ 3.30
1958. Paperback, 2 volumes, $1.65 each.

Hollingsworth, J. Rogers and Bell I. Wiley, eds. *American Democracy:* $ 7.50
A Documentary Record. Crowell, 1962. Paperback, 2 volumes, $3.75
each.

Lefler, Hugh T., ed. *A History of the United States: From the Age of* $ 1.85
Exploration to 1865. Meridian, 1960. 410 pp. Paperback.

Levy, Leonard W. and Merrill D. Peterson, eds. *Major Crises in Ameri-* $ 9.00
can History: Documentary Problems. Harcourt, 1962. Paperback, 2
volumes, $4.50 each.

Logan, Rayford W. *The Negro in the United States: A Brief History.* $ 1.45
Van Nostrand, 1957. 192 pp. Paperback.

Macdonald, William. *Documentary Source Book of American History,* $ 7.50
1606–1926. Macmillan, 1926. Third edition. 713 pp.

Meltzer, Milton, ed. *In Their Own Words: A History of the American* $ 9.90
Negro. Crowell, 1965. 2 volumes, $4.95 each.

Meyers, Marvin, et al., eds. *Sources of the American Republic: A Docu-* $ 8.20
mentary History of Politics, Society, and Thought. Scott, 1960. Paperback, 2 volumes, $4.10 each.

Miller, William, ed. *Readings in American Values. . . .* Prentice, 1964. $ 3.75
369 pp. Paperback.

Morris, Richard B. *Basic Documents in American History.* Van Nostrand, $ 1.45
1956. 190 pp. Paperback.

Morris, Richard B., ed. *Great Presidential Decisions: State Papers That* $ 7.50
Changed the Course of History. Revised edition. Lippincott, 1965.
432 pp.

Perry, Richard L., ed. *Sources of Our Liberties: Documentary Origins of* $ 5.00
Individual Liberties in the United States Constitution and Bill of
Rights. American Bar, 1959. 456 pp.

Williams, William A., ed. *The Shaping of American Diplomacy: Read-* $ 8.95
ings and Documents in American Foreign Relations. Rand, 1956.
Paperback, 2 volumes.

Wish, Harvey, ed. *Slavery in the South. . . .* Noonday, 1964. 290 pp. $ 2.45
Paperback.

Total $398.72

Filmstrips	*Price*
Education in America. Museum Extension. 1 filmstrip. Color.	$ 6.00
Folk Songs in American History. WaSp. 6 filmstrips with 6 records, 12", 33⅓ rpm. Color.	$ 52.00
Industry Changes America. Museum Extension. 1 filmstrip. Color.	$ 6.00
Total	$ 64.00

Recordings	*Price*
American History in Sound. 2 records, 12", 33⅓ rpm. Harcourt.	$ 8.00
Great American Speeches. 2 records, 12", 33⅓ rpm. Caedmon.	$ 11.90
The Sounds of History. 12 books each with recording, 12", 33⅓ rpm. Silver Burdett. Each book with recording, $5.95.	$ 71.40
Supreme Court Cases. Educational Audio. 3 albums, each with 2 records, 12", 33⅓ rpm. $11.90 per album.	$ 35.70
Total	$127.00

Total price of print materials	$398.72
Total price of filmstrips	64.00
Total price of recordings	127.00
GRAND TOTAL for primary resources for eleventh grade American History	$589.72

THE LIBRARIAN AS A MEDIA PROGRAMMING ENGINEER

The library program that is educationally effective functions as a multi-media learning laboratory. The librarian charged with the responsibility of administering the multi-media learning laboratory must respect media not as *things* but as *ideas*. Because library resources are ideas the librarian must include in the library collection all types and kinds of authentic carriers of appropriate information regardless of format. The librarian must systematically and scientifically build the library's media collection to match the school's curricular support needs and the students' personal and educational needs. The librarian must plan cooperatively with fellow teachers for the purposeful, timely, significant, and appropriate use of media in support of the teaching-learning endeavor. He is in function a media programming engineer. He couples his knowledge of curriculum and of materials with his knowledge of individual student needs, interests, goals, abilities, and progress rate. Through his specialized professional competence to use learning resources as teaching tools, the librarian must structure a scientific plan for the most effective and efficient of these resources.

Such a library program promoted by such a librarian is not the result of accident or chance; it is an educational necessity forced upon the modern school scene by the demands of modern innovative educational programs designed to carry learning for each student beyond rote memory to functional literacy.

6 The School Library As an Integral Part of the English Program

*We shall have to become acquainted with many new materials of instruction, with newer methods of utilizing them, with better ways to understand our students, and devices for evaluating our instruction. The English teacher, armed with a grammar, a literature anthology, and a piece of chalk, may have been acceptable in my high school days, though he was rarely popular; but in the demanding days ahead, he will be as out of date as the quill pen.**

When man received the gift of speech he was richly blessed, for speech is the means of man's becoming a participant in the drama of human events. Man's voice has made him a social being capable of communicating with his fellow man. Speech is the vehicle of self-expression; for through speech man can express his thoughts, his desires and his love. Without the gift of speech man would be a dumb animal cursed to suffer the travail of inarticulateness, the pain of unshared thoughts, of unsung songs, and unspoken prayers.

When man devised writing, he raised humanity to a level little lower than that of the angels. Through writing man became a participant in the total drama of mankind transcending time, place, space, and memory. Because of the gift of spoken and written communication "no man is an island," for language makes universal man's kinship with his fellow man, a joint inheritor of the wealth of the accumulated history and wisdom of the ages.

COMMUNICATION AS A BASIC SKILL

The school with sincere concern for nurturing the individual promise of its students must assign top priority to building excellence into the total English language arts program. It is largely through experiences provided in formal English teaching that the student will become an effective communicator. If the school fails to enable the student to develop fluency, facility, and integrity both in thinking and in communicating thought, the student will go through life as a functional illiterate, maimed and impoverished. The school must fulfill its obligation to encourage and enable each

* Mersand, Joseph. As quoted in *The Teaching of High School English* by J. N. Hook. Op. cit., p. 461.

student to read, to write, to listen, to speak, and to think with competence.

The librarian shares with the English teacher the responsibility for designing, structuring, and implementing a program for the most efficient and effective teaching of the art and science of communication. To do an effective job, it is imperative that the librarian become thoroughly conversant with all phases and elements of the English program: philosophy, goals, aims, objectives, and guiding principles. Intelligent action on the part of the librarian requires knowledge in depth of the "whys" and the "wherefores" of the English program.

GUIDING PRINCIPLES FOR ENGLISH PROGRAM

These are the guiding principles undergirding the teaching of English in today's schools:[89]

> The English program consists of courses and activities designed to develop the skills of reading, writing, listening, and speaking, which are of value to all students in their personal, social, and occupational life. This program stresses accuracy and comprehension in reading; clarity and fluency in speaking; and correctness, logical arrangement, and effectiveness in writing. Attention is directed to the development of a ready and varied vocabulary and a well-pitched, pleasant speaking voice.
>
> The English courses also emphasize the language processes of democracy, such as group thinking and discussion, critical use of mass modes of communication, and the responsibilities which freedom of speech and the press place upon the speaker, writer, listener, and reader. Every effort is made to relate English to a wide range of experiences, curricular and those out of school.
>
> English is essential in the total program of studies because it is our chief means of communication. It helps enrich the individual's life by developing personal satisfaction in reading, creative expression, dramatization, and enjoying with discrimination the products of the stage, screen, radio, and television. Training in the appreciation of literature develops a student's emotional maturity by aiding the growth of his esthetic senses and by increasing his understanding of the motivations of human behavior. Literature is a particularly apt medium for teaching cultural values and the differences in social class mores and value systems. The experience engendered by a variety of instructional materials and by the mass media of communication stimulates growth in desirable understandings, propaganda analysis, appreciation, and language habits.

GOAL OF THE ENGLISH PROGRAM

The constant goal of the English program is to enable each student to read with competence, write with competence, speak with competence, listen with competence, and think with competence. Reading, writing, speaking, listening, and thinking all require content. The library supplies the con-

[89] National Study of Secondary School Evaluation. *Evaluative Criteria for Junior High Schools.* Washington, D.C.: National Study of Secondary School Evaluation. Distributed by the American Council on Education, 1963. p. 93.

tent to be employed when students are taught how to read, write, listen, speak and think effectively. The librarian shares the English teacher's responsibility for teaching students how to abstract thought from content and then how to communicate that thought competently and effectively with disciplined imagination and integrity.

AIMS OF THE ENGLISH PROGRAM

It has been estimated that no fewer than 2,000 aims have been listed as significant in the teaching of English.[90] William Burton has reduced the possible 2,000 to three all encompassing aims:[91]

1. To improve the pupil's ability to express his ideas, both in speech and writing, with clear, idiomatic, and interesting language.
2. To increase the pupil's ability and desire to understand and appreciate literature.
3. To increase the pupil's ability to read or listen to expository material critically and with comprehension.

BASIC TRENDS

Five basic trends are discernable in today's English language arts program:[92]

The learning of English is now seen largely as a process of inquiry and discovery.

New approaches to learning English concentrate on concepts related to the "Structure of the Subject" and avoid attempting to cover the entire field.

New methods of teaching English require a variety of learning and teaching materials.

The time devoted to English studies varies with individual need.

The interrelated content and skills of English must be taught in a continuous, unified program.

A program designed to encourage inquiry and discovery requires a variety of teaching and learning resources. Likewise a program designed to meet the learning needs of the individual student must have the support of the school library:[93]

Learning today provides seriously for anticipated differences in individuals. . . . and depends upon intelligent use of a great variety of materials. If young people are to read extensively on their own, *strong school libraries are essential.*

READING PROGRAM

The school librarian shares with the English teacher the responsibility of teaching each segment and phase of the English program, but in no other area of the English curriculum is his responsibility greater than in his labors

90 Hook, J. N. Op. cit., p. 5.
91 Burton, William H., et al. Op. cit., p. 348.
92 Conner, Forrest E. and William J. Ellena, eds. Op. cit., pp. 64-67.
93 Ibid., p. 65.

to support the teaching of the reading program. Teachers and librarians face together this greatest responsibility and challenge in facilitating the development of both the formal and informal reading programs for reading is the basic tool for continued self-education. "Some subjects are more important than others. Reading is the most important of all."[94]

BASIC TENETS OF THE READING PROGRAM

A librarian competent to integrate the resources and services of the library with a developmental reading program needs to be conversant with the following basic tenets:[95]

1. Reading is a complex problem involving:
   thinking with the printed word as stimuli;
   reorganizing own experiences;
   reacting to the experiences of the writer;
   using the ideas and thoughts of what is read to develop and modify thought and behavior.
2. A developmental reading program is a sequential program of instruction which:
   reinforces and extends the previously acquired reading skills;
   develops new skills and appreciations needed by pupils if they are to understand and enjoy the complex forms of reading which new programs and new experiences demand;
   seeks to provide opportunities for students to grow in reading ability;
   recognizes many different purposes and needs in reading and tries to plan for meeting of those needs;
   tries to relate reading effectively to other experiences in the individual's program;
   seeks to *extend* students' interests.
3. A reading program of excellence includes these four areas:
   a *basic skills* program which must be planned, teacher-guided, and systematic in development;
   a carefully planned *literature* program;
   a planned program of teaching reading in the *content areas,* with practice and instruction in skills needed;
   a *news-reading* program.

CHARACTERISTICS
OF AN EFFECTIVE READING PROGRAM

Focus on Reading, a joint publication of the New England Reading Association and the New England School Development Council, stresses the significance of the school library and its resources. Among the characteristics of an effective reading program, this publication includes the following which clearly indicate the necessity of active school library support:[96]

1. A suitable, stimulating environment in classroom and school: a "reading atmosphere"; and *good library facilities.*

[94] President's Commission on National Goals. Op. cit., p. 86.
[95] Adapted from Mac Campbell, James C. and Eleanor Peck, eds. *Focus on Reading.* Cambridge, Massachusetts: New England School Development Council, 1964. pp. 28-29.
[96] Ibid., pp. 29-30.

2. Materials that are varied and *multi-level* in *all* grades, with a wider range in the upper grades where ranges in student ability become greater. *Enough materials* should be provided to meet individual needs.
3. Good teaching staff morale and attitudes. (Reading teachers willingly pre-plan with librarian for reading enrichment.) Responsibility for reading must be shared by all.
4. Reading taught in the content areas, as a part of the subjects:
    a. Multi-level and varied materials used.
    b. Unit approach, to permit individual growth and achievement for every child.
5. Systematic and balanced program, with all types of reading and purposes of reading included.
6. Instruction adapted to a wide range of individual differences.
    a. Flexible grouping.
    b. Varied materials.
    c. Individual as well as small group instruction.
7. Systematic evaluation of progress.
    a. A good testing program, including standardized tests, informal inventories, and other evaluative techniques, used chiefly for diagnosis to lead to effective teaching.
    b. Staff concerned with results, and informed as to the meaning of all appraisals of progress. (Librarian receives summaries of test scores.)
8. A good in-service program for teachers should be provided. (This necessitates a professional library collection.)

The librarian directly involved in guiding students in their search for reading materials should take the following suggestions to heart:[97]

1. ... we must not allow a situation to develop in which excessive *pressure* is placed upon either the child or the teacher.
2. There is no *one* method of teaching reading.
3. Content of reading materials should follow as far as possible the *students' interests*. They will not make progress unless they can find meaning and purpose in the materials which they must use.
4. The skill-building program must be well integrated, not isolated.
5. Teachers (and librarians) should understand the significance of "reading levels": basic level, instructional, frustration, and expectancy. Children should *not* have to read at frustration level.
6. The skills program begun in the primary grades should be maintained, and new skills introduced wherever they are needed, in grades 4–12 and beyond. There is no stopping point if children are to meet the demands of today's areas of constantly growing knowledge (See Figure I). The goals of any program should reach far into the future needs of the individual.

ENRICHING THE READING PROGRAM

The ultimate goal of the reading program is to equip pupils for independence in exploring the realm of children's literature for recreation and

[97] Ibid., pp. 30-31.

information. To attain this goal all of the youngsters' reading activities are directly and indirectly pointed toward the acquiring of lifetime interests and habits in personal reading.

The basic reader serves not only to develop reading competence but to create interest in independent reading both for pleasure and information. Each unit in the reader is built around a theme chosen because of its strong pupil appeal. This unit theme is a motivational device which serves as a springboard to independent reading. The classroom teacher who is alert to the motivational power of the reading theme will capitalize on this interest by planning with the librarian for scheduled class or group laboratory sessions in the school library. The librarian welcomes this opportunity to acquaint the children with reading, viewing, and listening experiences appropriate to the further development and exploration of the reading unit theme. Here is a perfect opportunity to acquaint the children with all the wonderful informational and recreational reading resources that might never be discovered if the children were left to search on their own. Self-directed knowledge building does not imply total student competence to work without informed guidance, nor innate student ability to sense quality. In the field of reading the best is not always known to the child and he, through ignorance of possible choices, can well limit himself to less than the best.

GUIDES FOR SELECTING LIBRARY MATERIALS TO ENRICH READING UNITS

Reading an example of literary excellence by the teacher to the class or by the pupils themselves can serve as a springboard to further reading. The purpose of a common reading experience is to stimulate interest in further reading as well as to develop an appreciation of and a taste for quality literature. It is also a means of providing each pupil with a fundamental knowledge of literary style, form, pattern, and merit. Materials beyond the reading text and classroom resources are necessary if the pupils are to have the depth, breadth, and variety of reading experiences essential for fostering a lifelong love of reading. The school library can well serve as a reading laboratory where the pupils under the competent guidance of the school librarian explore the fascinating world of books and discover the joys of reading. The following guides give unity and direction to the librarian searching for material to enrich the reading program:

> Encourage the children to read the entire story, biography, poem, legend, fairy tale, or play if only a selection has been read to or by them in the classroom.

> *Example*

> When they have read in the sixth grade Ginn Basic Reader, *Wings to Adventure,* the excerpts from *The Impractical Chimney Sweep* by Rosemary Anne Sissons, from *Afraid to Ride* by C. W. Anderson, from *Triumph for Flavius* by Caroline Dale Snedeker, from *Stikeen* by John Muir, from *Lion Hound* by Jim Kjelgaard, and from *The Christmas Rocket* by Anne Molloy, children should be encouraged to read the complete book from which the portion in the reader was taken.

Encourage the children to discover why the writer wrote a story, fable, poem, legend, biography, or other literary work.

Example

Before the class reads the brief story of Robin Hood in the fifth grade Ginn Basic Reader, *Trails to Treasure,* the librarian can alert a member of the class to the explanation given by Elizabeth Rider Montgomery in *The Story Behind Great Books,* as to the reason Howard Pyle, an artist, came to write as well as illustrate *The Merry Adventures of Robin Hood.*

Encourage the children to visualize the writer as a personality.

Example

When the children are reading the fairy tale "The Ugly Duckling" in the fourth grade Scott, Foresman Basic Reader, *More Times and Places,* the librarian can suggest that the children read a biography of the author. *Hans Andersen, Son of Denmark* by Opal Wheeler would acquaint the children with this fascinating storyteller as a person.

Encourage the children to gain added understanding of a literary work by viewing, listening, or reading.

Example

When the children have read the five Aesop's fables in the fifth grade Scott, Foresman Basic Reader, *More Days and Deeds,* the librarian can provide a number of additional Aesop's fables in both prose and poetry form, and can encourage the children to view any or all of the nine Curriculum filmstrip series, "Aesop's Fables," and to hear the two Disneyland recordings, "Stories of Aesop" and "Animal Stories of Aesop."

Encourage the children to extend their knowledge by exploring related information in other subject areas.

Example

When the children have read about Heinrich Schliemann's search for the ancient city of Troy in the sixth grade Ginn Basic Reader, *Wings to Adventure,* the librarian can use this reading experience as motivation for reading the history of the Trojan War as well as books about other archaeologists.

Encourage the children to read other writings by the writer whose work has been read in class.

Example

When the children have read the poems "Bird Talk" and "The Rag Bag" by Aileen Fisher in the third grade Ginn Basic Reader, *Friends Far and Near,* the librarian can alert the children to the many beautiful books written by Aileen Fisher such as: *Listen Rabbit, Going Barefoot, Like Nothing at All, Cricket in the Thicket,* and *I Like Winter.*

Encourage the children to read other stories which parallel the theme or plot of the story they had read in class.

Example

When the children have read the story "Benjie and the Pilot" in the fourth grade Ginn Basic Reader, *Roads to Everywhere,* the librarian can suggest other stories such as *Call It Courage* by Armstrong Sperry which also develop the theme of overcoming fear and displaying courage.

Encourage the children to read other works which parallel the setting of the class reading experience.

Example

After the children have read in the fourth grade Ginn Basic Reader, *Roads to Everywhere,* the story about Lapland, "Lars and the Wolves," the librarian can suggest other books about Lapland such as *The Arctic Tundra* by Delia Goetz and *Jon the Unlucky* by Elizabeth Coatsworth.

Encourage the children to read literary forms which parallel and reinforce the common reading experience.

Examples

After the children have read an animal story, the librarian can suggest that they read other animal stories.

After the children have read a myth or legend, the librarian can suggest that they read additional myths or legends.

After the children have read a biography, the librarian can introduce a variety of individual and collective biographies to the children.

After the children have read a lyric or narrative poem, the librarian can stimulate their interest in reading other poems.

SELECTING MEDIA TO ENRICH
THE READING PROGRAM

The reading teacher and the school librarian share jointly the responsibility for selecting media to support the teaching of reading. In evaluating the resources the following criteria serve to relate media evaluation to the needs of the reading program:

   Is this material relevant to the theme of the reading unit?
   Is this material worthy of the pupil's time and attention?
   Is this material appropriate in vocabulary, concept, and format for this age, grade, and maturity level?
   Is this material a means of integrating reading with the other language arts and/or curricular subjects?
   Is this material motivational with strong pupil appeal?

CHECKLIST VIII

MEDIA EVALUATION FORM FOR SELECTING
RESOURCES TO SUPPORT, TO ENRICH, AND TO EXTEND A READING UNIT

DATE_____

READING MEDIA EVALUATION FORM

PREVIEWED BY:_____SCHOOL_____

BASIC READER _____UNIT #_____TITLE_____

TYPE OF MATERIAL   (Indicate by checking):

Art print	_____	Map	_____	Realia	_____
Book	_____	Motion picture	_____	Resource kit	_____
Chart	_____	Phono disc	_____	Study print	_____
Filmstrip	_____	Phono tape	_____	Transparency	_____
Flannel graph	_____	Poster	_____		
Graph	_____	Programmed medium	_____	(Other medium)	

TITLE_____AUTHOR_____COPYRIGHT DATE _____

PUBLISHER/MANUFACTURER_____COST_____

PILOT USE BY   (Indicate by checking):
   Class_____ Group_____ Individual Pupil _____

YOUR EVALUATION:	YES	NO
1. Is this material relevant to the theme of the reading unit?	_____	_____
2. Is this material worthy of the pupil's time and attention?	_____	_____
3. Is this material appropriate for this age and grade level? SPECIFY GRADE _____	_____	_____
4. Is this material appropriate for concept for this age and grade level?	_____	_____
5. Is this material appropriate in format for this age and grade level?	_____	_____
6. Is this material a means of integrating reading with the other language arts?	_____	_____
7. Is this material a means of integrating reading with other curricular areas? SPECIFY_____	_____	_____
8. Is this material motivational with strong pupil appeal?	_____	_____
9. Is this material educationally significant?	_____	_____
10. Is this material worthy of inclusion in the library collection?	_____	_____

Is this material educationally significant?
Is this material currently in print and/or available?
Is this material justifiable in cost?

The effectiveness of these criteria can be enhanced if they are placed in a formal checklist such as the Reading Media Evaluation Form which follows (See Checklist VIII).

MATERIALS FOR THE DISADVANTAGED LEARNER

As the librarian searches for reading materials, he is mindful of the special needs of those who are disadvantaged socially, culturally, emotionally, or intellectually. It is recommended by the United States Office of Education that schools in disadvantaged areas provide the services of a librarian and the facilities and resources of a building library.[98]

> The school organization and administration, teaching staff (librarians), curriculum content and activities, and special services must be focused patiently and effectively on developing the social and intellectual backgrounds and skills which are essential to success in school, and on enabling each student to progress *at his own rate* with dignity and integrity to the end that he will wish to make the most of his educational opportunities.[99]

The complexity of the task facing the teacher and the librarian of the disadvantaged child requires the availability of instructional media uniquely suited to the personal, social, cultural and educational needs of the child. The teacher and the librarian must search for materials that will speak directly to the child at his own perception level. The librarian searches for materials that will enable the reluctant and disadvantaged reader to find satisfaction in and through reading. In large measure the hope of leading a disadvantaged child to overcome his environmental inadequacies lies in the use of instructional materials which will capture, sustain, and reward the child's interest in learning to learn (See Tables VII and VIII).

TABLE VII

GUIDES FOR SELECTING BOOKS FOR SLOW READERS*

CHARACTERISTICS OF BOOKS FOR SLOW READERS

Why does the slow reader need special help in choosing books?
He has to use more physical effort in reading.
He may need to overcome unfavorable emotional associations with reading, reflected in suspicion of books and of the person who suggests them.
His experience and background may be limited. He is often characterized by absence of curiosity and lack of ability to visualize situations and characters.
His interests may be more mature than his reading ability. His reading skills are often woefully inadequate.

* The American Association of School Librarians. Chicago, Illinois: The American Library Association, 1959.
98 Macintosh, Helen K. et al. *Administration of Elementary School Programs for Disadvantaged Children*. Disadvantaged Children Series No. 4. Washington, D.C.: United States Department of Health, Education, and Welfare, 1966. p. 15.
99 Ibid., p. 5.

What should his books be like in *appearance:*
a thin book does not look too "hard" to read;
an attractive cover;
sharp, clear type with generous spaces between the lines to make reading seem easy;
bright pictures which help to tell the story but do not tell it all.
What should his books be like in *style* and *vocabulary:*
easy vocabulary with much repetition (consisting largely of familiar words with a few new ones here and there to be fitted in through context);
simple, direct sentences and short paragraphs;
natural style, simple but not condescending;
fast moving pace which pulls the reader along;
much dialogue (in fiction and biography).
What should his books be like in *content:*
Fiction
real life situations with familiar concepts to give the reader confidence (the unknown, the remote, the fanciful discourage him);
simple plot with few characters, uncomplicated situations;
interesting beginning;
fast moving story, with excitement, action, suspense (to keep the reader wondering what will happen next);
humor (books that make him laugh are most successful in winning over a slow reader);
for boys, subjects such as dogs, horses, other animals, sports, aviation, Indians, cowboys, outdoor life;
for girls, many of the same subjects, plus fairy tales and stories of family and school life.
Nonfiction
easy-to-comprehend presentation of needed facts and information;
profuse, graphic illustrations to help the reader grasp the meaning of the text.
What books, then?
In order to meet the needs of slow and reluctant readers, the school library should apply a wide variety of very easy and very interesting reading materials, including:
Single copies of attractive readers not used as classroom sets.
Titles selected from lists of books with high-interest level and low-reading level. More and more books for slow readers are being published, containing good material consciously adjusted in vocabulary and sentence structure to the needs of learners at various levels but not "written down" to the slow reader.

TABLE VIII

CRITERIA TO BE USED IN SELECTING BOOKS
FOR THE ADOLESCENT RETARDED READER*

Some of the specific interest factors in content are:
1. Stories about teen-agers like themselves with whom they can identify: characters from different socio-economic backgrounds and from other racial and national groups.
2. Realistic experiences related to pupils' own lives.
3. Suspense.

* Strang, Ruth et al. *Gateways to Readable Books: An Annotated Graded List of Books in Many Fields for Adolescents Who Find Reading Difficult.* New York: H. W. Wilson, 1966. p. 17.

4. Action and adventure; exciting episodes of courage and skill.
5. Genuine emotion, giving insight into how people feel when they behave in certain ways and into what motivates them.
6. Humor.
7. Significance—content that helps young people to understand their world and their life today.
8. Information about something they can do or can become.
9. Character and personality building qualities.

Some of the interest factors in style are:
1. A quick, dramatic beginning.
2. Much conversation; few long descriptive passages, but sufficient description to make the scene and characters real.
3. Logical organization, not complex and confusing.
4. Simple, straightforward, clear sentences.
5. Few difficult, unfamiliar words—words often explained by the context.
6. Style natural and somewhat colloquial, not stilted and artificial.
7. Illustrations that clarify the text; pictures, diagrams, maps, and charts inserted close to the text and helping to interpret it.
8. Literary merit—unity, coherence, and emphasis; colorful and vigorous style.

Some of the physical make-up desired involves:
1. Size—adult in appearance, but short enough to prevent pupils' being discouraged by length.
2. Print—deep black, clear letters, easy to read.

READING LITERATURE

Students need not only *"to learn to read* but to learn *to read literature . . .* Reading of literature is one of the special 'disciplines' on which intellectual growth is founded."[100] The library is directly involved in any developmental program for the study and enjoyment of literature, for the library is the "content" of the literature program. Class reading from a literature anthology cannot suffice in teaching students to read, interpret, and enjoy literature no matter how fine the anthology might be. In any serious attempt to introduce the student to his literary heritage the anthology merely serves as an introduction, a point of departure which leads out of the English classroom and into the school and public library.

The following guides will aid the librarian in structuring programs of library enrichment to extend student literary experiences beyond the contents of the anthology:

Provide the opportunity for students to read the entire work if only a selection has been the class common reading experience.

Examples

Having read in ninth grade English the account of the battle of Achilles and Hector as retold by Olivia Coolidge in *The Trojan War,* students should be given opportunity to read a translation of the *Iliad* by Homer.

100 Cook, Luella B. "Criteria for Selecting and Evaluating Reading Materials" in *Materials for Reading: Proceedings of the Annual Conference on Reading.* vol. XIX. Chicago, Illinois: University of Chicago Press, 1957. p. 133.

Having read in tenth grade English the selection, "Gareth and Lynette" from *The Idylls of the King,* students should be given opportunity to read the complete work.

Having read in eleventh grade English the selection, "Stonewall Jackson" from *John Brown's Body* by Stephen Vincent Benet, students should be given the opportunity to read the entire poem.

Having read in eleventh grade English a portion of Emerson's "Self-Reliance" students should be given opportunity to read the entire essay.

Having read in twelfth grade English the "Prologue" to *The Canterbury Tales,* students should be given opportunity to read part or all of Chaucer's collection of tales.

Provide materials which will give insight into the origin of the work.

Examples

Before reading a Paul Bunyan legend in the eighth grade American folklore unit, students should be given opportunity to learn the origin and be oriented to the occupational and geographical significance of the legends through reading the chapter, "As American as Hot Dogs—Paul Bunyan" in Elizabeth Montgomery's book, *The Story Behind Modern Books.*

Before reading short stories in the eighth grade short story unit, students should be given opportunity to discover what prompted the writing of "The Man Without a Country," "The Lady or the Tiger," "The Celebrated Jumping Frog of Calaveras County" in Elizabeth Montgomery's *The Story Behind Great Stories.*

Provide materials which will acquaint students with the writer.

Examples

When Edgar Allan Poe is introduced in the eighth grade short story unit, students should be given opportunity to read a biography like *The Haunted Palace or Life of Edgar Allan Poe* by Frances Winwar or to see a filmstrip like the Eye Gate House presentation "Edgar Allan Poe" and to see a portrait like S. J. Wolfe's charcoal sketch of Poe.

When Elizabeth and Robert Browning are introduced in the twelfth grade, students should be given opportunity to acquire appreciation of these two poets and to contrast and compare characterization as found in biographical sketches such as *Flush* by Virginia Woolf, *How Do I Love Thee?* by Helen Waite, and *Elizabeth* by Frances Winwar, in letters like the Browning correspondence from M. Lincoln Schuster's *A Treasury of the World's Great Letters,* in recordings like "The Barrets of Wimpole Street."

Provide materials which will motivate interest, heighten understanding, encourage visualization and bring added dimension to the common reading experience.

Examples

When reading Robert Louis Stevenson's *Treasure Island* in eighth grade English, students should be given opportunity to recreate the action of the story by seeing the Eye Gate House Filmstrip, *Treasure Island,* or hearing the RCA Victor recording, or seeing Walt Disney's motion picture, *Treasure Island.*

When reading Shakespeare's "Julius Caesar" in twelfth grade English, students should be given opportunity to build knowledge of the hero by reading a biography such as Manuel Komroff's *Julius Caesar,* to reconstruct the action of the play by hearing recordings of *Julius Caesar* like those of the Cambridge University Marlowe Society or Dublin Gate Theater, to visualize the costuming and setting by studying an Edward Wilson painting of a scene from the play, and then to summarize the play itself by seeing the MGM motion picture, *Julius Caesar.*

Provide a variety of editions of the common reading experience.

Examples

When reading *Huckleberry Finn* by Mark Twain in seventh grade English, students should be introduced to the Norman Rockwell illustrated edition.

When reading *Rip Van Winkle* by Washington Irving in eighth grade English, students should be introduced to editions illustrated by Arthur Rackham and by Maud and Miska Petersham.

Provide additional works by the writer of the common reading experience.

Examples

Having read in the eighth grade short story unit, "The Lady or the Tiger" by Frank Stockton, students should be given opportunity to read the sequel, "The Discourager of Hesitancy."

Having read *The Tale of Two Cities* by Charles Dickens in the tenth grade historical novel unit, students should be given opportunity to read, in addition to other fiction by Dickens, his letters and his journals.

Having read poetry by William Wadsworth in twelfth grade English, students should be given opportunity not only to read but to hear other Wadsworth poems like the Caedmon recordings by Sir Cedric Hardwicke.

Provide other works comparable to the common reading experience in theme, plot, setting, characterization, and literary form.

Examples

Having read *Treasure Island* by Robert Louis Stevenson in eighth grade English, students should be given opportunity to read the three sequels: *Back to Treasure Island* by Harold Calahan, *The End of Black Dog* and *The End of Long John Silver* by David Moore and to extend their enjoyment of Stevenson's original plot through books like *Pirate Queen* by S. Meyer and *Blackbeard's Ghost* by B. Stahl.

Having read in eighth grade the Revolutionary War novel of an apprentice, *Johnny Tremain* by Esther Forbes, the students should be given opportunity to read novels of similar theme and circumstance like *The Devil's Tail* by Edith Hurd, *The Wavering Flame* by Erick Berry, or *The Surgeon's Apprentice* by Theodora Koob.

Having read Alfred Tennyson's *Idylls of the King* in tenth grade, students should be given opportunity to read or hear *Camelot,* the Alan Lerner and Frederick Loewe modernization of the Arthurian legend.

Having read *The Canterbury Tales* in twelfth grade English, students should be given opportunity to read Henry Wadsworth Longfellow's *Tales of a Wayside Inn* and to contrast and compare Chaucer's style of presentation with that of Longfellow's.

Having read in twelfth grade Advanced Placement English *John Brown's Body* by Stephen Vincent Benet and class reference having been made to Benet's use of soliloquy, students should be given opportunity to become acquainted with the use of soliloquy by contemporary writers of musicals like Richard Rogers and Oscar Hammerstein in *Carousel* and *The King and I*, Alan Lerner and Frederick Loewe in *My Fair Lady* and *Camelot*, and Lionel Bart in *Oliver*.

Provide materials which will meet individual student needs, interests, and abilities.

Examples

When reading biography in ninth grade English, students should be given the opportunity to discover biographies with special personal appeal such as:

Gene Schoor's biographies of athletes like Babe Ruth, Ted Williams, Red Grange, Casey Stengel, Jim Thorpe, Willy Mays;
Shannon Garst's biographies of western personalities like Wild Bill Hickok, Wyatt Earp, Annie Oakley, Sitting Bull;
David Ewen's biographies of musicians like Irving Berlin, Arturo Toscanini, Leonard Bernstein, Jerome Kern;
Elizabeth Ripley's biographies of artists like da Vinci, Van Gogh, Goya, Picasso;

Marguerite Vance's biographical novels highlighting famous love stories like *The Lees of Arlington, The Jacksons of Tennessee, Patsy Jefferson of Monticello, Martha, Daughter of Virginia.*

Having read in ninth grade English *The Trojan War* by Olivia Coolidge, students should be given opportunity to explore widely in book and nonbook sources uniquely compatible with their personal interest such as:

The Society for Visual Education (SVE) Innovation Records, *Mythology of Greece and Rome,* designed to recreate aurally in four albums of two records each the stirring sagas of ancient gods and heroes;

The Encyclopaedia Britannica Educational Corporation set of ten study prints, *Historical Reconstructions of Ancient Greece,* designed to delight students interested in visualizing this classical civilization.

Provide opportunity for students to acquire beyond the common reading experience understanding of literary form and merit as a basis for critical judgment and evaluation.

Examples

Having read in tenth grade English *The Tale of Two Cities* by Charles Dickens, students should be introduced to elements of criticism of the historical novel like those found in *A Handbook to Literature* by Thrall and Hibbard, revised and enlarged by Holman; in *Literature Study in the High School* by Burton; and in *Cavalcade of the English Novel* by Wagenknecht.

Having read in the eleventh grade English anthology the poetry of Walt Whitman, students should be introduced to a critical evaluation of Whitman's contribution to American poetry like that in *The Winged Horse* by Auslander and Hill; in the Introduction to *Poems of Walt Whitman . . .* by Lawrence Powell; or in the Introduction to *Walt Whitman's Leaves of Grass* by Malcolm Cowley.

Provide opportunity for students to work with ideas and extend their perception beyond the context of the common reading experience.

Examples

Having read in twelfth grade English "No Man Is an Island" by John Donne, the seventeenth-century poet-philosopher, students should be given opportunity to perceive the contemporary significance of this philosophy as expressed by Ernest Hemingway in *For Whom the Bell Tolls,* by Edna St. Vincent Millay in "There Are No Islands Anymore" and by the Hindu philosopher, Minoo Musani, in the chapter "No Man Is an Island" in his book, *The Growing Human Family.*

Having read in twelfth grade English Emerson's essay, "Self-Reliance" students should be given opportunity to see examples of this personal dimension portrayed by: Washington in Bryce Burle's *Morning of a Hero,* Charles Lindberg in *We,* Eddie Rickenbacher in *We Thought We Heard the Angels Sing,* Lawrence of Arabia in *Seven Pillars of Wisdom,* Winston Churchill in *The War Years,* Althea Gibson in *I Always Wanted To Be Somebody,* Elizabeth Blackwell in Nina Baker's *First Woman Doctor,* or Karana in Scott O'Dell's *Island of the Blue Dolphins.*

Provide opportunity for students after being introduced to novels, myths, legends, biographies, essays, plays, short stories, and poems, to explore, to read, and to enjoy other examples of that particular literary type.

Example

Having but a limited sampling of biography available in the ninth grade literature anthology, the English teacher and the librarian can develop cooperatively a library based unit to provide opportunity for students to become conversant with a varied selection of quality biography appropriate to their individual interests (See Table IX). This biography unit can well serve as a model for designing other library-support units for each of the types of literature listed above (See Appendix O).

TABLE IX

Subject:	English.
Grade:	Nine.
Library-Based Unit:	Biography.

PARTIAL UNIT OUTLINE

I. Objectives:

To acquaint students with biography and autobiography as literary forms.
To acquaint students with accomplished authors skilled in the writing of biography.
To acquaint students with biographical classics.
To develop students' ability to evaluate merits of biography by employing the art of literary criticism.
To develop through reading and guided discussion the students' ability to appreciate biography as a valuable source of information.
To employ biography as a medium for integrating English with other subject areas: art, music, physical education, science, and social studies.
To employ biography as a catalyst for developing students' self-awareness, self-perspective, social consciousness, and value judgments.
To encourage students to read biography with perception and pleasure.

II. Criteria to be used in judging biographies:

Adequacy of presentation	Excellence of style
Authenticity of detail	Fulfillment of purpose
Balance of pattern	Permanence of significance
Cohesiveness of structure	Stimulant to further reading
Completeness of incident	Vividness of impression
Comprehensiveness of inclusion	

III. Basic terminology to be introduced:

Authenticity
Autobiography
Bias
Biographee
Biographer
Biographical novel
Biography
Charisma
Chronological order
Chronology
Collective biography
Comprehensiveness
Empathy
Eulogy

Excellence of style
First person narration
Flashback
Fulfillment of purpose
Impression
Individual biography
Narrative style
Pivotal event
Primary source
Pulitzer Prize
Readability
Sketch
Vividness of impression

IV. Basic autobiographies to be introduced:

Autobiography—Benjamin Franklin
Story of My Life—Helen Keller
Up From Slavery—Booker T. Washington

V. Basic Pultizer Prize winners to be introduced:

Andrew Jackson—Marquis James
Paul Revere—Esther Forbes
Profiles of Courage—John F. Kennedy
The Raven—Marquis James

VI. Basic biographers to be introduced:

Biographer	Area of specialization
Jeanette Eaton	Biographies of historical figures
David Ewen	Biographies of musicians
Dorris Shannon Garst	Biographies from the wild and wooly West
Shirley Graham	Biographies of Negro leaders, patriots, scientists
Clara Judson	Biographies of humanitarians and historical personages
May McNeer	Biographies of humanitarians, religious and political leaders
Elizabeth Ripley	Biographies of artists
Gene Schoor	Biographies of athletes
Marguerite Vance	Biographies of famous women
Virginia Woolf	Biography of the Brownings

VII. Procedure:

Students are introduced to the unit by the classroom teacher;
Terminology is introduced and discussed;
Plan for reading, reporting, discussing, evaluating, and summarizing the unit is explored;
Biography Reading Summary Report form is distributed and explained;
A composite Biography Reading Summary Report is made by the class (See Example VII);
Students are introduced to the basic autobiographies, Pulitzer Prize winners, and biographies by the librarian;
Students are free to read as many basics as they wish;
Teacher and librarian share the summary discussion with the class.

VIII. Discussion guides to be employed in summarizing class criticism of biographies:

What purposes motivate the writing of biography?

Can a biographer create a false image unintentionally?

Does a biographer have the right to incorporate dialog into a factual biography?

What primary sources are commonly used by biographers?

Are footnotes as well as bibliographies essential?

What sources are of a biased nature?

Can any man be objective in recounting what he has not experienced directly?

Is truth stranger than fiction?

What is meant by a biographer creating an image larger than life?

Does a biographer break faith with the reader if he only presents the positive and not the negative aspects of the biographee?

What is the danger of the clay feet approach to writing or reading biography?

Is man ever trapped in a web of fate?

Is man the captain of his soul?

Does adversity make the man?

Is time necessary for judging the true significance of a public figure?

What are basic human values?

What is your opinion of Benjamin Franklin's checklist of virtues?

VIRTUES LISTED BY BENJAMIN FRANKLIN

1. *Temperance.* Eat not to dullness; drink not to elevation.
2. *Silence.* Speak not but what may benefit others or yourself; avoid trifling conversation.
3. *Order.* Let all your things have their places; let each part of your business have its time.
4. *Resolution.* Resolve to perform what you ought; perform without fail what you resolve.
5. *Frugality.* Make no expense but to do good to others or yourself; that is, waste nothing.
6. *Industry.* Lose no time; be always employed in something useful; cut off all unnecessary actions.
7. *Sincerity.* Use no hurtful deceit; think innocently and justly; and, if you speak, speak accordingly.
8. *Justice.* Wrong none by doing injuries or omitting the benefits that are your duty.
9. *Moderation.* Avoid extremes; forbear resenting injuries, so much as you think they deserve.
10. *Cleanliness.* Tolerate no uncleanliness in body, clothes, or habitation.
11. *Tranquility.* Be not disturbed at trifles or at accidents common or unavoidable.
12. *Chastity .* . . . . . .
13. *Humility.* Imitate Jesus and Socrates.

What would you include in a checklist of qualifications for a worth while person?

Measure the caliber of your biographee on the profile chart and determine his quality point rating (See Table X).

EXAMPLE V

BIOGRAPHY READING SUMMARY REPORT

Student_____Date_____

Biography read: _____

Author_____

Title_____

Publisher_____Copyright date_____

1. Please check the appropriate category:
   _____ Individual biography
   _____ Collective biography
   _____ Autobiography
   _____ Biographical novel

2. Comment on the style and literary quality of the book you have read.

3. In what field or fields has the biographee made a contribution?

4. Critically evaluate the biographee's
   character:

   personality:

   sense of values:

   contribution to society:

5. To what extent could you share with the biographee his problems, disappointments, achievements, successes?

TABLE X

BIOGRAPHEE PROFILE

RATING SCALE

Common sense	0	5	10
Compassion	0	5	10
Courage	0	5	10
Creativity	0	5	10
Curiosity	0	5	10
Dedication to ideals	0	5	10

Determination	0	5	10
Drive	0	5	10
Emotional stability	0	5	10
Empathy	0	5	10
Foresight	0	5	10
Generosity	0	5	10
Giftedness	0	5	10
Honesty	0	5	10
Idealism	0	5	10
Imagination	0	5	10
Integrity	0	5	10
Introspection	0	5	10
Inventiveness	0	5	10
Love of God	0	5	10
Patriotism	0	5	10
Purpose	0	5	10
Rationality	0	5	10
Respect for law	0	5	10
Self-criticism	0	5	10
Self-discipline	0	5	10
Self-lessness	0	5	10
Sense of humor	0	5	10
Sense of justice	0	5	10
Sense of values	0	5	10
Sensitivity	0	5	10
Sobriety	0	5	10
Social consciousness	0	5	10
Stick-to-itiveness	0	5	10

CRITERIA FOR EVALUATING LITERATURE

A particularly fine set of criteria for evaluating children's literature is offered by Charlotte Huck and Doris Kuhn and can well serve to strengthen selection on both the elementary and secondary levels:

GUIDES FOR EVALUATING CHILDREN'S LITERATURE[101]

BEFORE READING

What kind of book is this?
What does the reader anticipate from:
  Title
  Dust jacket illustration
  Size of print
  Illustrations
  Chapter headings
  Opening page?
For what age range is this book appropriate?
Does the book appear to be for either boys or girls?

PLOT

Does the book tell a good story? Will children enjoy it?
Is the plot original and fresh?
Is it plausible and credible?
  Is there preparation for the events?
  Is there a logical series of happenings?
  Is there a basis of cause and effect in the happenings?
Is there an identifiable climax?
How do events build to a climax?
Is the plot well constructed?

SETTING

Where does the story take place?
How does the author indicate the time?
How does the setting affect the action, characters, or theme?
Does the story transcend the setting and have universal implications?

THEME

Does the story have a theme?
Is the theme worth imparting to children?
Does the theme emerge naturally from the story or is it stated too obviously?
Does the theme overpower the story?
Does it avoid moralizing?

CHARACTERIZATION

How does the author reveal characters?
  Through narration?
  In conversation?
  By thoughts of others?
  By thoughts of the character?
  Through action?
Are the characters convincing and credible?
Do we see their strengths and their weaknesses?
Does the author avoid stereotyping?

[101] Huck, Charlotte E. and Doris Young Kuhn. Op. cit., pp. 17-18.

Is the behavior of the characters consistent with their age and background?
Is there any character development or growth?
Has the author shown the causes of character behavior or development?

STYLE

Is the style of writing appropriate to the subject?
Is the style straightforward or figurative?
Is the dialogue natural and suited to the characters?
Does the author balance narration and dialogue?
What are the main characteristics of the sentence patterns?
How did the author create a mood? Is the overall impression one of mystery, gloom, evil, joy, security?
What symbols has the author used to communicate meaning?
Is the point of view from which the story is told appropriate to the purpose of the book?

FORMAT

Do the illustrations enhance the story?
Are the illustrations consistent with the story?

LITERARY CRITICISM

There are a variety of approaches employed in teaching literature: by historical period, by author, by theme, by topic, by genre, by region. Recently a new approach has come into vogue and has won wide favor especially at the senior high school level, i.e., the critical analysis of literature. Criticism as used here "is the endeavor to find, to know, to love, to recommend not only the best, but all the good that has been known and written in the world."[102] In guiding the student, teacher and librarian can offer the following criteria for determining the quality of a literary work: "realism, interest, success in accomplishment of intension, appropriateness of media, clarity of thought and language, originality and imagination, and avoidance of triteness, sentimentality, and monotony."[103] Since the meaningful practice of criticism requires materials available in quantity and variety to allow depth experience in analytical criticism, the school library is essential for the adequate support and development of an English literature program employing the technique of critical analysis.

INTEREST SAFEGUARDS

Traditionally English classes have been less than enjoyable. Even though interest is recognized as the strongest factor predicating success in the language arts, student interest in English is frighteningly lacking.

> Surveys of the school subject preferences of children usually reveal that language class is rated the favorite by one in ten, but as the least liked by about three in ten. Within the specifics of the language course the item most frequently listed as the least preferred is book reporting. It is probably safe to assume that book

[102] Burton, William H. et al. Op. cit., p. 350.
[103] Ibid., p. 351.

reporting has not been a very popular activity with many children.[104]

Decrying the traditional malpractice of killing thoroughly student interest in reading literature, Robert Pooley addressed the following to English teachers:[105]

> In literature we have forced unready youth through selections unsuited to their abilities and experiences and in the name of literary appreciation have created attitudes of dislike and contempt for good literature. By a combination of misplaced zeal and unhappy procedures we have succeeded in making English for the great mass of students the most disliked subject in the curriculum.

If the aim of English teaching is "to increase the pupils' ability and *desire* to understand and appreciate literature" then impersonal, prescribed, restrictive book lists and required formal written and oral book reports should be as scarce as the saber-tooth tiger.

Since student interest in literature can be lessened if not destroyed by an overly demanding written report, Paul Anderson suggests that teachers devise checklists or reaction sheets which will maximize thinking and minimize writing (See Examples VI and VII). The inventive teacher can devise myriad ways to discover student reading perception. The Biography Reading Summary Form and the Biographee Profile Rating Scale included in the basic design of the ninth grade Biography Unit are examples of report forms devised to encourage student thought and to sharpen student perception without inflicting the undue penalty of excessive writing (See Table IX).

TRENDS TO BE DISCOURAGED IN TEACHING LITERATURE

The Harvard Report, *General Education in a Free Society,* stated that nothing less than the best practicable literature is good enough for school study. This Report listed the following prevailing trends that needed to be discouraged in the study of literature:[106]

> Stress on factual content as divorced from design.
> Emphasis on literary history, on generalizations as to periods, tendencies and ready-made valuations—in place of deeper familiarity with the texts.
> Strained correlation with civics, social studies.
> Overambitious technical analysis of structure, plot, figurative language, prosody, genre.
> Use of critical terms (Romanticism, Realism, Classical, Sentimental) as tags, coming between the reader and the work.
> Didacticism: lessons in behavior too closely sought.

---

104 Anderson, Paul S. *Language Skills in Elementary Education.* New York: Macmillan, 1964. p. 290.
105 Pooley, Robert C. "The Professional Status of the Teacher of English." *English Journal,* vol. XLVIII, September, 1959. p. 311.
106 *General Education in a Free Society.* Op. cit., pp. 110-111.

Superficial reading of too much, with no close knowledge of either
the content or its import.
Lack of any aids to the understanding of what is being read.
Indifference to or ignorance of techniques of literature.
Avoidance of critical terms and appraisals when the student is ready
for them.
Irresponsible attitude to the implication of what is being read.

EXAMPLE VI

READ FOR FUN*

NAME _____ DATE _____

BOOK TITLE _____

MAIN CHARACTER _____

_____

_____

People who like

_____ animal stories
_____ stories about children
_____ stories about _____

_____

_____ adventure stories
_____ funny stories
_____ exciting stories

_____

will like this book.

Did you enjoy this book?_____

It was

_____ easy to read.
_____ hard to read.
_____ just right.

The Harvard Report recommended that when literature was being selected
the following points should be taken into consideration:[107]

The limits of available time to be kept in mind. Less to be studied
rather than more. Omissions to be planned, not settled by the
accident of shortage of time.
Old and new writing to be proportioned with regard to a two-way
traffic between:
The new as more immediate and leading to the more remote.
The old as explaining the tradition on which more difficult modern writing depends.

* Anderson, Paul S. *Language Skills in Elementary Education.* New York: Macmillan,
1966. p. 292.
[107] Ibid., p. 111.

The values of American and English literature and of other literature in translation to be balanced.

Texts for classroom study to be supplemented by less difficult books for outside reading. Guidance to be provided since a chief end sought is extensive private reading.

Emphasis on mere *number* of books read or book reports made to be questioned.

EXAMPLE VII

BIOGRAPHY READING SUMMARY*

TITLE _____

AUTHOR _____ NUMBER OF PAGES _____

ILLUSTRATOR _____

The biographer (one who writes about a real person) tells the following childhood incident in the life of his subject:

_____

_____

_____

_____

The subject of the biography is:

_____

The following people were important in helping this real person to grow into a famous adult:

_____

_____

A problem which this person has to overcome was:

_____

This person overcame his problem in this way:

_____

This person had the following characteristics which I admire:

_____

I think the most exciting adventure which this person had was:

_____

_____

_____

* Anderson, Paul S. *Language Skills in Elementary Education*. New York: Macmillan, 1966. p. 295.

Proper liberty to be secured for teachers in choosing the texts they
    can handle best—with enough organization to prevent unde-
    sirable duplication.
Historical sequence to be followed only if illuminating to the lit-
    erature read.

THE LIBRARIAN AND THE LITERATURE PROGRAM

The librarian working as a cooperating member of a teaching team can
provide a wealth of literary resources which will meet the needs of the developmental literature program while meeting the needs, interests, goals,
abilities, reading disabilities, and progress rate of the individual student. A
literature program with high student appeal must be reflective of student
interest and ability. It is recommended that the school librarian employ an
interest inventory to gain insight into the reading interests of each student
(See Appendix J). It is the responsibility of the librarian to see that appropriate literary experiences are made available to all students. If the English
teacher will but plan with the librarian, each common reading experience
offered in the classroom can be enriched, reinforced and extended through
the use of resources uniquely suited to the developmental needs of the literature program and uniquely reflective of student interests.

LISTENING

The child in today's world lives in a noise polluted atmosphere. At an early
age the child learns to close his ears and his mind to the cacophony of his
environment. When the child comes to kindergarten he already is a veteran
in the art of only hearing what he wishes to hear; he is an expert in "tuning
out" his environment. Teaching the child to hear with discrimination and
discernment, in other words, to listen, is a necessary part of the English
language arts program.

Listening should be a vital component of the English language arts curriculum, yet traditionally we have neglected to teach students *how* to listen.
A survey conducted by Paul Rankin in the Detroit Public Schools showed
the following disparity between the amount of time actually spent in listening in a school day and the disproportionate amount of instructional time
spent on learning how to listen.[108]

THE SCHOOL DAY		
% of School Day Spent in:		% of Formal Instruction Directed to:
42%	Listening	8%
15%	Reading	52%
32%	Speaking	10%
11%	Writing	30%

Listening is too important a communication tool to be relegated to an area
of little or no teaching concern. Provision should be made within the

108 Rankin, Paul T. "The Importance of Listening Ability." *English Journal*. Chicago:
University of Chicago Press, vol. 17, October 1929. p. 629.

framework of course design to teach and to reinforce listening skills. The listening experiences outlined in Table XI and Checklist IX should be incorporated into the developmental, on going teaching and learning program both in the classroom and in the library.

TABLE XI

CLASSROOM EXPERIENCES IN LISTENING*

Kindergarten And Lower Elementary Grades

1. Discussing reasons for working to improve listening.
2. Setting standards for good listening habits by teacher and pupils and having pupils illustrate these standards with attractive posters using animal and flower ideas.
3. Increasing teacher awareness of need for giving clearly defined directions and expecting children to listen so that repetition will not be necessary.
4. Having the pupil repeat the teacher's question as part of the answer.
5. Listening for strange sounds and trying to imagine what is happening, then investigating and checking mental picture.
6. Selecting children to walk, jump, run, and so forth, while others close their eyes and guess what is happening.
7. Listening for sounds in home, in school, and on "listening" walks.
8. Drawing pictures of city sounds and country sounds.
9. Children's interpretation of the emotions in people's voices in various situations.
10. Comparing sounds—loud vs. quiet sounds, far away vs. near sounds, country vs. city sounds.
11. Listening to next note on a piano to tell whether it is lower or higher than the one just played.
12. Identifying a song played on the piano by hearing a phrase or two from the middle or end of it.
13. Reading to the class carefully selected poems and finger plays that are short, easily understood, and preferably humorous, and asking the pupils for rhyming words.
14. Reading animal stories and poems and asking the children to imitate the sound of the animal as it is mentioned in the story or poem.
15. Listening for repetitive endings of poems and having the pupils say them in unison.
16. Reading sentences with one word too many and asking the pupils what the extra word is.
17. Reading a poem and having the children choose the picture which illustrates the ending of the poem.
18. Reading a story and asking the pupils to draw answers to two or three questions about it.
19. Listening to a story and placing pictures in order of the main events.
20. Reading a paragraph or story to the class and having the pupils decide on a title for it.

AT THE UPPER ELEMENTARY LEVEL

1. Formulating by pupils and teachers of standards for good listening and using them for constant evaluation of listening habits.

* Curriculum Development Council for Southern New Jersey. *Teaching Study Skills: A Handbook for Teachers and Administrators of Grades K-12.* Glassboro, New Jersey: Glassboro State College, 1965. p. 15-16.

2. Keeping records of scores made on listening tests, both teacher made and standardized.
3. Working for better listening to directions in specific lessons in social studies and arithmetic, taught in such a way that only oral direction had to be followed.
4. Conducting classes during which the teacher, after advance warning, does not repeat directions.
5. Noting and eliminating noisy distractions.
6. Reading a paragraph and asking pupils to distinguish between the significant and the unimportant information.
7. Playing listening games.
8. Reading part of a story and asking pupils what they think will happen next.
9. Reporting by groups on different news broadcasts and comparing various points of view.
10. Analyzing commercials heard on radio and TV for shaded meanings.
11. Discussing the ways the advertiser tries to get one to think as he wants him to think without making really false statements.
12. Listening to short stories, answering questions based on the stories and discussing wrong responses.
13. Listening to poems of varied kinds and discussing the imagery created by them.
14. Listening for musical instruments on records.
15. Choosing the exact word to describe a sound: e.g., "the crackling embers," "a deafening roar."

FOR JUNIOR AND SENIOR HIGH SCHOOL

1. Following oral directions through use of short drills in number exercises, which ask the pupils to listen to several numbers and then write a specific number which is called for, such as the number included which was under 10, divisible equally by 5, etc.
2. Taping class discussions and having pupils evaluate their discussions.
3. Listening to tape of a political speech or editorial to determine the speaker's cause, party or prejudices, and to pick out propaganda—words or loaded expressions.
4. Listening to many different types of paragraphs read to the class for various items such as description, sensory words, relationship of one sentence to the next, punctuation for emphasis, etc.
5. Giving assignments orally only.
6. Reading a story and questioning for detail.
7. In dramatics, listening to the proper reading of lines with attention to pronunciation, inflection, and expression, followed by immediate limitation.

CHECKLIST IX

CHECKLIST FOR TEACHER EVALUATION OF
INDIVIDUAL STUDENT'S LISTENING SKILLS*

KINDERGARTEN AND LOWER ELEMENTARY GRADES

The child is able to:

_____1. Put main events of a story in sequence by use of pictures.
_____2. Sit quietly and listen without interruption during discussions, conversations, story telling, and music appreciation.
_____3. Differentiate between fact and fiction.
_____4. Follow directions for class movements, games, fire and air raid drills, and assignments in various subject matter areas.

* Ibid., p. 14.

_____5. Recognize and accept ways of speaking which differ from the manner of speaking to which he is accustomed.

_____6. Interpret what he hears in terms of his experiences.

_____7. Remember important things that have been said and repeat them when asked.

LATE ELEMENTARY GRADES

The pupil is able to:

_____1. Disregard distractions.

_____2. Sort out what is important to remember.

_____3. Do some note taking.

_____4. Use context clues to increase comprehension of unfamiliar words.

_____5. Begin to recognize when ideas are not well supported with evidence.

_____6. Think ahead and anticipate what is coming next.

_____7. Recognize the effect of the speaker's voice.

JUNIOR AND SENIOR HIGH SCHOOL

The student is able to:

_____1. Discern what has *not* been said as well as what *has* been said.

_____2. Summarize, noting central and supporting ideas.

_____3. Note prejudices and emotion laden words and ideas.

_____4. Take well organized notes.

_____5. Detect the way the speaker uses his voice and gestures, as well as words, to influence the listener.

_____6. Question such words as 'always-never'—'either-or' when used by the speaker.

_____7. Evaluate the way supporting evidence substantiates the speaker's generalizations.

LIBRARIAN TEACHES LISTENING

The school librarian has a dynamic role to play in teaching students to listen attentively with purpose, profit, discernment, appreciation, challenge and delight. Among the first listening experiences children have in their beginning school days is hearing the librarian read or tell stories. The librarian employs storytelling as a teaching tool uniquely designed to train children to listen, to recall, to retell. Here again interest is a strong motivational factor conditioning children to build receptivity to learning to listen. Children love to hear a story, and this inherent pleasure makes storytelling an ideal motivational device for the teaching of attentive and retentive listening.

LITERARY RECORDINGS

The library on all levels should provide quality literary recordings for student use in the library, in the classroom, and above all, at home. Recorded stories, poems, essays, plays, speeches, and other literary experiences give a fighting chance to the student with reading disabilities. Our commitment to provide each student with an educational program uniquely designed to meet his personal needs and interests requires a realistic approach to media management, i.e., what can the student use with profit, satisfaction and challenge? Media essential to the intellectual, cultural, social, and moral growth of a student should be readily available. There should be no barrier raised because of the traditional saber-tooth reluctance to circulate reference and audiovisual media for home use. If we believe that our responsibility as librarians is to provide all resources essential for student self-realization and self-development, then no learning experience can be denied the student because of a circulation restriction based on media format.

SPEAKING

The library has a significant role to play in supporting the formal speech program. While the teacher of speech has the special responsibility for teaching the mechanics of speech, the school librarian has the special responsibility of providing significant speech content. It is important that the librarian respect the needs of the formal speech program for:

> The ability to use the spoken word to accurately communicate thought or express feeling is the most significant skill developed by individuals in the highly complex social organization of modern life.[109]

The National Council for the Social Studies outlined the following general guides to provide continuity in a developmental speech program:[110]

TABLE XII

GENERAL GUIDES TO CONTINUITY
IN SPEAKING EXPERIENCES

FIVE- TO SEVEN-YEAR-OLDS

Discussion: Topics of immediate moment. Not much individual preparation. Teacher responsible as group leader in application of discussion skills.

Reporting: Begins with sharing of stories, personal experiences, objects brought from home, and the like. Ordering of content done quite spontaneously, without extensive individual preparation. Teacher (librarian) immediately available to assist, in ways sought by the reporter, in giving of the talk.

Interviewing: Largely cooperative group interviewing of persons invited to the classroom. Questions to be asked planned by children and teacher in advance. Teacher's role that of seeing that various children have an opportunity to participate, cuing the visitor to questions of special interest, and in introducing and closing the interview.

Dramatics: Almost entirely dramatic play and creative dramatics. Acting done spontaneously, with free interpretations.

109 Russell, David H. and Elizabeth Russell. "Listening and Speaking" in Anderson, Verna D., et al. *Readings in the Language Arts.* New York: Macmillan, 1964. p. 45.
110 Carpenter, Helen McCracken, ed. *Skill Development in Social Studies.* Thirty-third Yearbook. Washington, D.C.: National Council for the Social Studies, 1963. pp. 139-140.

Discussion: Topics of increasingly more precise dimensions. Direct attention to the nature of the discussion. More student responsibility in the use of discussion skills. Individual preparation for many of the discussion sessions. Teacher's role that of participant and of observer of needs for further teaching. Some beginnings of panel discussion, under teacher (librarian) guidance, may be introduced.

Reporting: Topics individually explored and ordered. Introduction of simple note-taking in preparation for reporting. Preparation of report and accompanying notes done individually with such teacher assistance as reporter and teacher cooperatively agreed on. During reporting and follow-up question or discussion period, reporter takes major responsibility for control of the situation. Teacher's (librarian's) role during the reporting largely that of astute listener and accessor of what needs further to be taught about reporting skills.

Interviewing: Introduction of individual interviewing, with continuation of group interviews. Understandings of nature and evaluation of interviews introduced. Use of results of individual interviews in reporting sessions. Consideration of interview skills as used in the mass media.

Dramatics: Largely creative dramatics; occasional experiences with scenes or sections from well-written plays. Some original playwriting. Attention by the teacher to the student's creation of character, his contributions to the action and dialogue, and his ability to contribute to the mood of the dramatization.

Discussion: Broad exploration of topic under consideration. More precise self-evaluation by the student of his contribution to discussion and his behavior as a discussant. Increased assumption by students of responsibility as discussion leader or moderator. Increased use of panel discussion, with greater discernment concerning the nature and procedures of panel discussion and concerning the roles of discussant, moderator, and audience member.

Reporting: Skillful in selection and ordering of topic or problem. Considerable independence in note-taking and in preparing for the style of the report or talk to be given. Quite independent control in the reporting situation itself with regard to language, speech, and social skills.

Interviewing: More individual interviews and reporting, with precision, the results of the interviewing done. Increasing skill in assessing interviews presented on radio or television.

Dramatics: Continued use of creative dramatics, individual, or group playwriting, and interpretation of scenes, episodes, and one-act plays. Depth of characterization, in acting and in comprehending interactions among characters, in portraying plot and action. Authenticity of the spirit of the play sensitively comprehended.

During these years, when youth are maturing rapidly, the instructional activities take on the tone of what will be lived as adults. Work on speaking skills in such activities as discussion, reporting, interviewing, and dramatics cannot appear in any sense childish; but the skills of speaking already quite well developed must be maintained, and those not so well developed must be strengthened. By this time, in discussion, interviewing, and reporting, semantic differences should be understood by the student; analysis of propaganda and methods of persuasion should be given consideration by him; and self-evaluation of his own effectiveness and efficiency in speaking abilities should be developing maturely. Involvement in speaking situations beyond the classroom will by this time have so increased that participation in whole-school and community enterprises calling for skillful speaking will be expected.

The librarian has many opportunities to integrate speaking activities with subject development. Frequently a speech activity will be based entirely on the utilization of library resources. For example, the library-based speech unit, The Speech Potential of a Ponderable Quote (See Table XIII) requires the availability of specialized library tools and reference sources as well as librarian orientation, instruction and guidance in how to use them efficiently and effectively.

TABLE XIII

Subject: English.
    examples to be utilized in class discussion.
Course: Speech.
Unit: The Speech Potential of a Ponderable Quote.
Grade: Twelve.
Goal: To provide an opportunity for each student to perceive and to appreciate the intellectual challenge and stimulus of a succinct, terse, thought-provoking quotation.
Objectives: To provide an opportunity for each student to discover the speech potential of a "quotable quote."

    To provide an opportunity for each student to reinforce and extend his knowledge of standard reference tools for identifying quotations.

    To provide an opportunity for each student to read and to discover within the context of his reading statements worthy of being quoted.

    To provide an opportunity for each student to go back to the original source from which a quotation has been abstracted and to place it in context for validation of meaning.

    To provide an opportunity for each student to deal with ideas common to several subjects.

    To provide an opportunity for each student in a speech experience to incorporate his own special interest or concern.

    To provide an opportunity for each student to express his own beliefs, concerns, and convictions in a logical, reasoned, cohesive, balanced pattern of intelligent thought.
    To provide an opportunity for each student to express his ideas orally in an effective, creative, and convincing manner.

Procedure:

The speech teacher in anticipation of this unit has, with the cooperation of librarian and other fellow teachers, compiled a basic list of quotations to serve as

The class reviews the cardinal principles governing the design, structure, development and presentation of a speech of substance and significance.

The class analyzes and evaluates the thought potential of a quotation employed as a focal or pivotal point in a speech.

The class discusses the various ways a speaker employs quotes to bolster an argument, to refute a statement, to catch attention, to introduce an idea, to accentuate a point, to underscore a plea, to appeal to the emotions, to place an idea in focus, to summarize a discussion.

The class examines, discusses, and experiments with quotations from the basic list.

The class in a scheduled visit to the library is introduced by the librarian to a variety of resources of special value in their search for quotations.

The class in a series of scheduled visits works in the library gaining background to be utilized in a speech employing quotations as pivotal or focal points.

The class presents the speeches, and the librarian and several other teachers serve as jurors determining the degree of excellence achieved.

Basic List of Quotations for Class Analysis:

"Adversity causes some men to break; others to break records." William Arthur Ward

"As a man thinketh, so is he." Bible

"Books are the poor man's university." Anonymous

"Don't be an agnostic. Be *something*." Robert Frost

"Drive with care. The life you save may be your own." National Safety Council

"Effective knowledge is that which includes knowledge of the limitations of one's knowledge." S. I. Hayakawa

"Every man has a right to his opinion, but no man has a right to be wrong in his facts." Bernard Baruch

"Fear is the darkroom where negatives are developed." E. L.

"Fiction is fact, rearranged and changed with a purpose." Thomas Wolfe

"For the triumph of evil, it is only necessary for good men to do nothing." Anonymous

"For time and the world do not stand still. Change is the law of life. And those who look only to the past are certain to miss the future." John F. Kennedy

"The frustrating thing is that the key to success doesn't always fit your ignition." Roger C. Meyer

"Genius is one percent inspiration and ninety-nine percent perspiration." Thomas Edison

"Hats off to the past; Coats off to the future." Anonymous

"He who neglects the past is condemned to repeat it." George Santayana

"If you want people to notice your faults, start giving advice." Kelly Stephens

"In general those who have nothing to say contrive to spend the longest time in doing it." James Russell Lowell

"In our new twilight of power, there is no quick path to a light switch." Adlai Stevenson

"Opportunity knocks but once, but temptation leans on the doorbell." Western Livestock Journal

"Paradoxically, science has given man a choice between destroying himself and enjoying for the first time in his history ample food, clothing, shelter, as well as ample hours to play, to meditate and to explore beyond undreamed horizons." J. N. Hook

"The political life of a nation is only a superficial part of its being; in order to learn its inner life—the source of its actions—we must penetrate to its very soul by way of its literature, its philosophy, and its art, where the ideas, the passions, and the dreams of its people are reflected." Romain Rolland

"Prejudice is never easy unless it can pass itself off for reason." William Haslitt

"Real freedom is won through self-government, not through self-expression." Roy L. Smith

"A skillful politician is one who can stand up and rock the boat and make you believe he is the only one who can save you from the storm." Roger Allen

"Some people reach the top of the ladder only to find it is leaning against the wrong wall." Calgary Herald

"Some people see things as they are and ask why. I dream things that never were and ask why not." George Bernard Shaw as quoted by Robert Kennedy

"To be free, a man must be capable of basing his choices and action on understandings which he himself achieves and on values which he examines for himself." Educational Policies Commission

"Virtue is a kind of health, beauty and good habit of the soul." Plato

"We fear things in proportion to our ignorance of them." Livy

"We judge ourselves by what we feel capable of doing, while others judge us by what we have already done." Walling Keith

"We must learn that the art of progress is to preserve order amid change and to preserve change amid order." Alfred North Whitehead

"When a true genius appears in the world, you may know him by this sign, that the dunces are all in confederacy against him." Jonathan Swift

"When bad men combine, the good must associate, else they will fall, one by one, an unpitied sacrifice in a contemptible struggle." Edmund Burke

"The world is not interested in the storms you have encountered, but did you bring in the ship." Anonymous

Quotation Tools to Be Introduced in This Unit:
Adams, Franklin P. *FPA's Book of Quotations.* New York: Funk, 1952.
Bartlett, John. *A Complete Concordance or Verbal Index to Words, Phrases and Passages in the Dramatic Works of Shakespeare* . . . New York: Macmillan, 1966.
———. *Familiar Quotations.* 13th ed. rev. New York: Little, 1955.
Bohle, Bruce. *Home Book of American Quotations.* New York: Dodd, 1967.
Braude, Jacob M. *Lifetime Speaker's Encyclopedia.* 2 vols. Englewood Cliffs, New Jersey: Prentice-Hall, 1962.
Evans, Bergen. *Dictionary of Quotations.* New York: Delacorte Press, 1968.
Hurd, Charles. *Words That Inspire: A Treasury of Great American Quotations.* Chicago: J. C. Ferguson, 1964.
Hyman, Robin. *The Quotation Dictionary.* New York: Macmillan, 1965.
Magill, Frank N. *Magill's Quotations in Context.* New York: Harper, 1965.

Mencken, H. L. *A New Dictionary of Quotations on Historical Principles from Ancient and Modern Sources.* New York: Alfred A. Knopf, 1942.

Mersaud, Joseph. *A Guide to the Use of Bartlett's Familiar Quotations.* 2nd ed. Boston: Little, 1964.

Miller, Madeleine and J. Lane Miller. *Harper's Bible Dictionary.* New York: Harper, 1961.

Oxford Dictionary of Quotations. 2nd ed. New York: Oxford University, 1959.

Peterson, Houston. *A Treasury of the World's Great Speeches.* New York: Simon, 1954.

The Reference Shelf Series. New York: H. W. Wilson, 1954 to date.

Roberts, Kate L. *Hoyt's New Cyclopedia of Practical Quotations.* 2nd ed. rev. New York: Funk, 1940.

Stevenson, Burton. *Home Book of Quotations.* 9th rev. ed. New York: Dodd, 1964.

————. *Home Book of Shakespeare Quotations.* New York: Scribner, 1966.

————. *Macmillan Book of Proverbs . . .* New York: Macmillan, 1965.

Wallis, Charles. *Speaker's Resources from Contemporary Literature.* New York: Harper, 1965.

WRITING

Writing is a common component of each of the aforementioned areas of the language arts. The development and refinement of the mechanics and skill of written communication are the special responsibility of the classroom teacher. This responsibility, however, is shared by the librarian, for he must provide the student with the substance or content appropriate for significant written communication.

NATIONAL COUNCIL OF TEACHERS OF ENGLISH ADVISES AGAINST "LIBRARY RESEARCH PAPER"

In 1963 The National Council of Teachers of English published the report, *High School-College Articulation of English.*[111] This report summarizes the recommendations made by 116 colleges (total enrollment of 570,000) when asked by the NCTE what degree of language proficiency they expected of incoming freshmen. One startling discovery was made—colleges do *not* approve of the traditional "library paper" assigned in high schools. Fewer than 10% considered such an assignment significant. Nearly a third of the colleges made the point that the student's time could better be spent on a number of short papers written in the classroom under the direction and observation of the English teacher. One college professor damned the "library paper" by describing it as "a river of quoted brilliance, dammed occasionally by a student-produced sandbar."[112]

The NCTE report makes the following recommendations for upgrading the teaching of high school writing:[113]

> Much of the writing should be done in class so that the teacher can supervise each step in the composition process and so that the student can develop fluency in writing under class conditions.
>
> Much of the writing should be short paragraphs, short themes, and essay tests.

---

[111] Committee on High School-College Articulation. *High School-College Articulation of English.* Champaign, Illinois: National Council of Teachers of English, 1963.

[112] Ibid., p. 5.

[113] Ibid., p. 5.

The subjects should be almost always nonpersonal . . .

Subjects of . . . themes narrow: in four hundred words even the brightest . . . can't do justice to "The Role of Democracy in Today's World."

When making a writing assignment . . . keep two principles in mind:

We should make sure that the student is aware of the rhetorical points that we are trying to make with the assignment.

We should make sure that we have the student write for an audience—real or imagined—against which we can gauge the effectiveness of his work.

THE ENGLISH LABORATORY

The NCTE publishes a number of journals, handbooks, monographs, resource units, etc., worthy of the attention of English teachers. The Council acts as a distribution agent not only for its own publications but also for a large number of commercially prepared books, pamphlets, filmstrips, art and study prints, maps, charts, and recordings. A librarian concerned with building a professional library collection or an English language laboratory (See Figure VI) collection will find the NCTE publications checklist, *Resources for the Teaching of English,* to be invaluable. Each item included in the comprehensive NCTE checklist has been field tested, evaluated and recommended by classroom teachers. The checklist is revised annually and distributed on request free of charge.*

A QUALITY LANGUAGE ARTS PROGRAM REQUIRES THE SUPPORT OF A QUALITY LIBRARY PROGRAM

A quality, optimum English program demands the ready accessibility of an appropriate library collection and the concerned guidance of a competent teacher-librarian. The library capable of supporting the implementation of a quality, optimum language arts curriculum provides not only significant ideas but ample opportunity for each student to practice working intelligently with these ideas. Today's school library serves as a learning laboratory where the students come as members of the English class, as members of a group, or as individuals to practice and to refine their communication skills. Library resources are the "content" of the language arts program; they are the media which supply the "messages" to be communicated through student reading, writing, speaking, and listening.

THE LIBRARIAN NURTURES STUDENT INTEREST

The librarian has a unique role to play in capitalizing on interest generated in the English classroom. Each English unit is a possible source for creating student interest in further viewing, further listening, further reading. It is the librarian's special privilege to keep that interest alive, to provide a constant flow of resources that will continue to stimulate, to challenge, and to satisfy. Long after formal class activities have been culminated a student will continue to pursue a learning interest providing

* *Resources for the Teaching of English.* Distributed by The National Council of Teachers of English, 508 South Sixth Street, Champaign, Illinois.

appropriate materials are available. Such student interest can be nurtured and sustained by the timely suggestion of additional reading, viewing, and listening experiences which will also delight.

The librarian has the rare opportunity to see the teaching goals and objectives actualized. For example, a constant goal of the English program is to develop student interest in recreational and associative pleasure reading. Such a goal cannot be achieved without suitable resources. It is the librarian's rare privilege to see this goal attained, for long after a biography, a play, a legend, or a novel has been read in class the student may well continue to read additional biographies, plays, legends, or novels on his own. It is not uncommon for a junior high school student who was introduced to *Treasure Island* in eighth grade to continue to search for a hearty pirate story in ninth grade. Nor is it uncommon for the student in high school to continue to read biographies long after his initial introduction to biography in ninth grade.

THE LIBRARIAN AND ENGLISH COURSE PLANNING

It is the special function of the librarian to suggest possible interdisciplinary interaction and integration when serving as a member of an English curriculum study committee. For example, the ninth grade Biography unit (See Table IX) includes appropriate biographies of minorities, scientists, humanitarians, patriots, politicians, religious leaders, artists, musicians, and athletes. It was the librarian's unique knowledge of the contents of the library collection which made it possible for this particular unit to incorporate such a wide variety of informational biography having so high a degree of reader appeal, and literary merit.

It is also the special responsibility of the librarian to suggest integrating English learning activities within the course framework of other curricular areas. It is becoming increasingly common for social studies and natural sciences to incorporate language arts teaching and learning experiences as an integral component of basic course design (See Figure VIII). For example, the fused library-based teaching unit, Transportation (See Table XIV), devotes four of seven objectives to the language arts:

> To provide an opportunity for the students to become acquainted with mythological and legendary heroes associated with man's conquest of land, sea, and air.
> To provide an opportunity for the students to become conversant with recreational reading experiences associated with the field of transportation.
> To provide the opportunity for the students to become aware of the impact of transportation terms on our vocabulary.
> To provide an opportunity for the students to apply and to refine the study skills of organizing and communicating ideas within a context of utility.

THE LIBRARY AND THE ENGLISH PROGRAM

A program designed to develop accuracy and comprehension in reading, clarity and fluency in speaking, correctness and effectiveness in writing, attentiveness and awareness in listening requires the services and the resources of the school library.

> The interdependence of teachers and librarians is becoming more clearly recognized—the status of the librarian (will) have to be changed from that of a cataloger to *teacher–librarian* or counselor. She will have to become acquainted with our courses of study, will have to learn something about teaching library skills and do everything possible to make the library a beehive of wholesome and worthwhile activity.[114]

Reading, writing, speaking, and listening are skills vital to each student's function as a learner, as a citizen, and as a human being. Library resources are the tools essential to the teacher in his teaching and to the student in his practice of the art and science of communication. It is, therefore, imperative that the teacher of English and the school librarian see that there be no static in the school's intercom when planning the English program. Direct communication between English teacher and librarian is essential for adequacy both in the design and in the implementation of the language arts program.

[114] Mersand, Joseph as quoted in J. N. Hook. Op. cit., p. 62.

7 The School Library As an Integral Part of the Social Studies Program

Those who cannot remember the past are condemned to repeat it. *
*Libraries are the keepers of our history and our culture. But they
are not merely storehouses of the relics of the past, but meeting
places for people and ideas, vital partners in our system of education.* **

The social studies program is designed to enable the youth of our nation to perceive and to value their unique heritage as human beings, as members of the society of man, and as citizens of the United States. The goal of the social studies program is to develop citizens who will view their world and its problems with dispassionate objectivity and will set about solving both their personal and social problems in a reasoned, rational, constructive manner. The social studies program carries the weight of the school's serious obligation to prepare our future citizens to live their lives in enlightened commitment to the American ideal.

The social studies curriculum draws on eight separate but related disciplines: anthropology, economics, geography, history, philosophy, political science, social psychology, and sociology (See Figure VII). The content of the social studies program embraces the study of man and his relationships to his social and physical environments.

Among the appreciations, attitudes, and understandings to be fostered and developed through the social studies program are the following:[115]

1. To learn the historical method of establishing facts;
2. To appreciate the contributions of the past;
3. To provide some perspective for looking at the modern world;
4. To be aware of the nature of one's social environment;
5. To understand the interdependence of peoples;

* Santayana, George. *The Life of Reason or The Phases of Human Progress.* 2nd ed. New York: Scribner's, 1922. vol. 1, p. 284.
** Cohen, Wilbur J. Chairman, President's Committee on Libraries. "Letter to the President." October 3, 1968.
115 Cartwright, William H. and Richard L. Watson, Jr., eds. *Interpreting and Teaching American History.* Thirty-First Yearbook. National Council for the Social Studies, 1961. pp. 339-341.

FIGURE VII

SOCIAL STUDIES CONTENT INCLUDES BASIC CONCEPTS
FROM MANY OF THE SOCIAL SCIENCES*

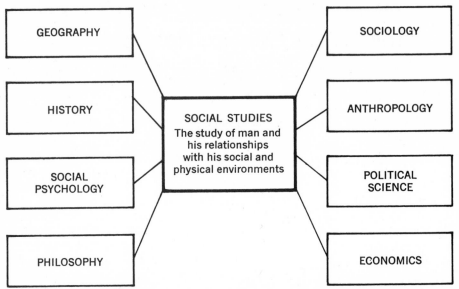

The social studies draw subject matter from the social sciences, are a specific and important part of the elementary school curriculum, acquaint the child with his social and physical environments, and have a unique responsibility to help pupils learn those understandings, attitudes, and skills which are necessary for democratic citizenship.

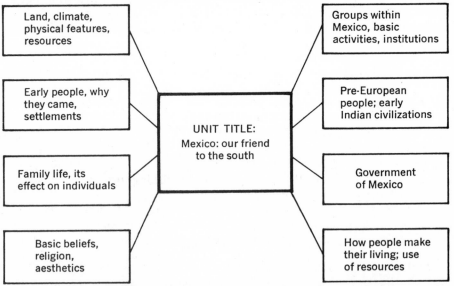

This diagram parallels the one above and shows how the various social sciences might contribute to a specific unit topic.

* Jarolimek, John. Op. cit., p. 4.

6. To comprehend historical allusions in everyday reading;
7. To understand that the past has had a great influence on our present patterns of living;
8. To develop intelligent patriotism;
9. To understand that continuity and change characterize progress;
10. To understand that change is an inevitable part of life;
11. To acquire a lasting interest in history;
12. To develop a sense of time, and relationship between time and place;
13. To have the vicarious experience of reliving the events of history;
14. To understand that history was made by common folk as well as those of high degree;
15. To use facts constructively in creative thinking;
16. To understand something of the motives which led people to act as they did;
17. To develop belief and action in democracy as a way of life;
18. To understand that history is being made continuously;
19. To realize the magnitude of the changes in the world in the last few years.

In order to facilitate building these appreciations, attitudes, and understandings the following skills and habits must be developed:

1. To read content material with understanding;
2. To read history with feeling;
3. To identify and organize major and minor ideas for outlining and summarizing;
4. To secure and use information from many sources;
5. To read pictures, maps, globes, graphs, charts, etc., for information;
6. To express ideas orally and in writing;
7. To plan, carry out, and evaluate activities;
8. To develop ability in associational reading where one combines his own experiences and purposes with the material read, criticizes the selection, finds illustrations of or exceptions to the author's statements, suggests further research or classroom activities, or in other ways responds independently of the subject matter.

The following objectives for the teaching of social studies were defined by the Detroit Board of Education in 1961:[116]

GENERAL OBJECTIVES

Objectives form one important basis of curriculum construction. Objectives represent the goals that are to be achieved through the curriculum and grow directly out of the educational philosophy of the school and the community.

[116] Board of Education. *A Program of Social Studies Instruction, Grades 1-12.* Detroit, Michigan: Detroit Board of Education, 1961. pp. 7-8.

The general goal of the social studies program is to develop citizens who can effectively participate in our American republican democracy. These future citizens need to learn how to carry on the free society they have inherited.

As previously indicated, history, geography, sociology, economics, and civics make up the content field of the social studies. In Detroit, the social studies program is begun in grade 1B and is systematically developed each year through grade 12A, with emphasis on either history, geography, civics, sociology, or economics depending upon the readiness of the pupils for the concepts to be learned in the different areas.

CONTRIBUTORY OBJECTIVES

To develop an understanding of the basic principles of our American society as set forth in the Constitution of the United States and primary writings regarding our American traditions, such as government by the consent of the governed, preservation of the rights of property and of personal liberty, and the responsibility of every citizen to support and defend our country.

To develop an understanding of existing institutions through a study of social relationships in the home, school, community, state, nation, and the world.

To develop the skills, knowledges, and attitudes necessary for efficiency as a member of society.

To develop a knowledge of persons, places, events, and ideas to which allusion is commonly made in newspapers, literature, radio, television, and conversation.

To develop ability in reflective and scientific thinking for use in the solution of social problems.

To create an understanding of the interdependence of men and nations, and through such understanding to develop the broader social-mindedness essential to human progress and well-being.

To develop in children such qualities of character as social mindedness, open-mindedness, tolerance, adaptability, loyalty to ideals, unselfishness, cooperativeness, respect for the rights of others, and respect for legally constituted authority.

To develop a sense of individual obligation to participate in activities that improve society.

To develop intellectual curiosity, a love for reading and thinking in the field of social studies, which will assure an adult interest and efficiency in public affairs and hence keep the individual abreast of the times in a rapidly changing world.

To understand and appreciate the long struggle for human freedom and why it requires eternal vigilance to maintain that freedom.

In order to implement the teaching of the social studies program, the librarian needs to build his understanding of the basic purposes of the program. John Michaelis has identified the following as being the *major purposes* of a social studies program:[117]

117 Michaelis, John U. Op. cit., pp. 14-17.

INFORMATION, CONCEPTS, AND GENERALIZATIONS

A dominant purpose is to develop understanding of the information, concepts, and generalizations derived from the social sciences with special reference to the following:

The geographic, economic, political, historical, and social factors of greatest importance in the past, the present, and the emerging future;

The impact of science, technology, education, and values on man's changing ways of living;

The interaction of people with their environment, man's use of resources, the effects of weather and climate, man's adaptation to and modification of the environment, and time, distance, and space relationships;

The similarities and differences in ways of meeting basic human needs here and now and in earlier times and places;

The growing interdependence characteristic of our times at home and throughout the world;

The contributions of individuals and many cultural groups to man's changing cultural heritage;

The role of the home, school, church, government, and other social institutions in human affairs;

The powerful influence of cultural values on man's ways of thinking, believing, and acting;

The operation of basic human activities or social functions such as transportation, communication, government, education, production, distribution and consumption of goods and services, conservation, and esthetic and religious expression;

The democratic beliefs that are important in our way of life: respect for the worth of each individual; maintenance of rights and freedoms under law; freedom of speech, religion, press, assembly, and inquiry; acceptance of responsibilities related to freedom; equality of justice and opportunity for all; use of intelligence to solve problems; faith in the ability of men to govern themselves; government by consent of the governed; majority rule with minority protection; personal sacrifice for the common good; separation of church and state; cooperation with others to secure world peace.

SKILLS AND ABILITIES

The skills and abilities included in statements of the purposes of the social studies may be summarized as follows:

Utilizing instructional resources such as textbooks, library materials, community resources, and audio-visual materials.

Locating, gathering, appraising, summarizing, and reporting information.

Interviewing, listening, and observing to gather ideas.

Reading and studying independently.

Interpreting and making maps, graphs, tables, time lines, and other graphic materials.

Interpreting sequences of events, time periods, chronology, and trends.

Organizing information from several sources and presenting it in oral, written, or graphic form.

Using problem solving, critical thinking, and creative thinking abilities.

Identifying and defining problems, issues, and standards.

Formulating hypotheses, generalizations, and plans of action.

Distinguishing facts from opinions, relevant from irrelevant information, means from ends, primary from secondary sources, and conclusions from supporting evidence.

Using criteria to make choices, weigh alternative plans of action, and appraise progress toward individual and group goals.

Detecting errors of thinking, unstated assumptions, unwarranted assertions, and the use of propaganda techniques.

Comparing ways of living, points of view, means of solving problems, and modes of expressing ideas.

Working as a member of groups.

Making plans for group work.

Assuming the role of leader or follower as needed to carry out group plans.

Adhering to group standards and using parliamentary procedures.

Evaluating individual and group efforts to achieve common goals.

ATTITUDES, APPRECIATIONS, AND BEHAVIOR PATTERNS

Learning experiences in the social studies contribute to the development of attitudes, appreciations, and behavior patterns that are consistent with democratic beliefs, enable the individual to meet changing conditions, and are helpful in both individual and group action. The following are examples of attitudes and appreciations being stressed at the present time:

Appreciation of the American heritage, democratic ideals, human freedoms, and the brotherhood of man;

Respect for self, and for others regardless of race, creed, economic status, or national origin;

Attitudes of open-mindedness, responsibleness, cooperativeness, concern for others, and creativeness;

High regard for the home, school, church, government, and other institutions that are important in our way of life;

Enlightened loyalty and patriotism based on devotion to one's country and clear understanding of current problems;

Appreciation of the contributions of others here and now and in early times and faraway places;

Appreciation of the many rights, responsibilities, and privileges accorded citizens in a democracy in contrast to those in totalitarian regimes;

Appreciation of the importance of moral, ethical, and spiritual values in human affairs;

A willingness to act in ways conducive to the general welfare and human progress.

Also being stressed are democratic behavior patterns characteristic of the individual who:

Keeps informed on issues and problems, studies them, and works with others to solve them;

Uses democratic processes in solving problems, working with others, making decisions, and carrying out plans of action;

Assumes responsibility for carrying out individual tasks and group obligations;

Respects constituted authority, the law, and lawful procedures for making changes;

Works with other individuals and with groups to improve individual and group welfare;

Examines critically the actions of individuals and agencies entrusted with public responsibilities;

Participates in socio-civic activities and renders service essential to the functioning of democracy;

Helps to carry out such principles as equality of opportunity for all and special privilege for none;

Evaluates his own actions and the efforts of others to further democratic beliefs;

Defends constitutional rights and democratic ideals.

CRITICAL THINKING

The social studies program structures into its teaching program learning experiences which are designed expressly to teach students how to think critically and reflectively with objectivity and integrity. "Critical thinking is used when a person seeks to differentiate truth from falsehood, fact from fiction. This activity, by its very nature, entails 'a combination of knowledge, skepticism, faith, common sense, and intelligent guessing.' "[118] The process of critical thinking includes:

1. Identification of the issue or problem.
2. Gathering, organizing, and evaluating relevant data.
3. Analysis of the issue or the problem.
4. Formulating and testing hypotheses.
5. Drawing warranted conclusions.
6. Testing conclusions.

LIBRARY RESOURCES

Library resources and informed guidance in the use of these resources are necessary to the development of a study skills program. "Reflective thought does not take peace in a vacuum; it occurs within the context of value judgments."[119] Students "do not learn to think critically by thinking critical thoughts about nothing in particular."[120]

Library media are the teaching and learning resources essential for the adequate support of the social studies program.

[118] Carpenter, Helen McCracken, ed. Op. cit., p. 36.
[119] Ibid., p. 32.
[120] Ibid., p. 36.

(Library resources) provide the foundation of research or information getting activities and are central elements of a good social studies program. Discussions, summaries, constructions, dramatics, writing and reporting are quite meaningless unless they have been preceded by some type of research activity. The effectiveness of social studies activities, therefore, is related directly to the teacher's ability to select and use instructional materials wisely.

PRINCIPLES TO GUIDE MEDIA SELECTION AND USE

1. In the selection of any instructional resource, the goals of learning should be uppermost in the mind of the teacher. The particular resource or material selected should be the one which will move the children in the direction of those goals most effectively: In short, instructional aids, materials, and resources are used to achieve specific purposes.
2. The greater the number of sensory perceptions which are made possible through the use of a resource, the greater is the likelihood that it will be effective. A trip to the bakery where the young child can see and hear the production process as well as smell, touch, and taste the newly baked bread is likely to be more effective than reading about the bakery in the classroom.
3. Instructional materials must be suited to the developmental level of the child. Younger children need many more concrete and firsthand experiences than older children since they are not able to profit from vicarious experiences to the same extent as older children. Primary grade children, for example, might make and use a layout on the classroom floor which represents the school yard or the immediate neighborhood, while middle- and upper-grade children are capable of using conventional wall maps.
4. The selection and use of instructional materials should take into full account the wide range of intellectual and achievement differences in children within the classroom. In the case of reading material, there needs to be a wide range in the reading difficulty of the material as well as in the difficulty of the content presented. The types of materials and resources available should cover the full range of abstraction from those which involve direct, concrete, firsthand experiences to those which are completely abstract.
5. Instructional materials need to be carefully evaluated before, during, and after they have been used. It is not a good policy to use any and all materials simply because they are available. The quality of the material or resource should be a primary consideration in deciding upon its use. Maps which are out of date, films which are of poor quality, pictures which are inaccurate, or field trips which are poorly guided, for example, might better not be used at all.
6. The maximum value of any instructional resource requires skillful use on the part of the teacher. No instructional material is entirely self-teaching—all of them require a teacher to set the stage for learning to take place. A first-rate textbook in the hands of an unimaginative teacher can be devastating to the social studies

program. The same book used by another teacher can become one of the most valuable resources to the class. Materials of the instruction can be no better than the teachers who use them.[121]

PROBLEMS APPROACH

The problem solving approach is employed to provide students with practice in learning how to analyze, how to evaluate, how to organize, and how to communicate information. Leonard Kenworthy in his *Guide to Social Studies Teaching* gives the following outline to guide teachers and librarians in teaching students how to solve problems in a logical manner:

1. Defining the problem.
   a. Encountering the problem.
   b. Selecting the problem.
   c. Wording the problem.
   d. Setting up tentative solutions.
2. Working on the problem.
   a. Recalling known information.
   b. Determining the need for more information.
   c. Locating sources of information.
   d. Analyzing and interpreting information.
3. Drawing a conclusion.
   a. Stating possible conclusions.
   b. Determining the most reliable and logical conclusion.
   c. Reaching a conclusion.
4. Carrying out a conclusion.
   a. Acting on a conclusion.
   b. Reconsidering the conclusion.[122]

PRIMARY SOURCE MATERIALS

The teacher of history has a unique opportunity to train students in the art of critical thinking while they utilize primary source materials to build their knowledge of the historical past. It is now a common practice to base entire history courses on the use of primary source materials rather than on the use of the traditional text. The tools the student uses in building his understanding are critical analysis, evaluation, and synthesis. The raw materials from which his knowledge is gained are: diaries, journals, letters, autobiographies, speeches, debates, newspapers, songs, photographs, cartoons, official documents, records, etc. President Kennedy enjoyed delving into documents from America's past. He said, "Documents are the primary sources of history; they are the means by which later generations draw close to historical events and enter into the thoughts, fears and hopes of the past."[123] The use of source materials offer an exciting challenge to the student to participate actively in interpreting history from the records of the past. In his use of primary source material, critical thinking skills are the instruments employed by the student as he prods, questions, relates, sub-

[121] Jarolimek, John. Op. cit., pp. 94-95.
[122] Kenworthy, Leonard S. *Guide to Social Studies Teaching in Secondary Schools*. Belmont, California: Wadsworth, 1962. p. 298.
[123] *National Archives Accessions*. No. 57, June, 1963. p. 33.

stantiates or discredits, learns to compare, contrast and formulate valid conclusions (See Checklist X).

CHECKLIST X

CHECKLIST OF CRITICAL THINKING SKILLS
TO BE DEVELOPED THROUGH THE USE OF PRIMARY SOURCE MATERIALS*

_____ Analyzing and evaluating evidence
_____ Anticipating outcomes
_____ Applying historical method
_____ Appraising validity of arguments
_____ Appraising validity of evidence
_____ Arranging facts, events, and ideas in sequence
_____ Associating similar ideas and experiences
_____ Classifying or categorizing ideas
_____ Comparing or contrasting ideas
_____ Detecting inconsistencies
_____ Determining adequacy of evidence
_____ Determining validity of statements
_____ Differentiating between inductive and deductive reasoning
_____ Differentiating between objective and subjective reasoning
_____ Discovering causal relationships
_____ Discovering hidden meanings
_____ Discovering thought and action patterns
_____ Distinguishing between fact and fiction
_____ Distinguishing between fact and opinion
_____ Distinguishing between fact and propaganda
_____ Drawing inferences and making generalizations
_____ Drawing valid conclusions
_____ Establishing sequence patterns
_____ Evaluating and reacting to ideas in the light of the author's purpose
_____ Evaluating attitudes and motives
_____ Evaluating definitive statements
_____ Evaluating summary statements
_____ Evaluating authenticity of sources
_____ Evaluating reliability of sources
_____ Expressing ideas
_____ Finding evidence to prove or disprove a generalization
_____ Formulating hypotheses
_____ Identifying bias
_____ Identifying main and subordinate themes or ideas
_____ Interpreting graphic and pictorial information
_____ Interpreting idiomatic and figurative language
_____ Interpreting implied ideas
_____ Judging reasonableness and relevancy of testimony
_____ Judging writer's and speaker's competence
_____ Making valid generalizations
_____ Making valid judgments
_____ Organizing evidence in systematic order

* Davies, Ruth A. and Vernon W. Metz. *A Guide to the Use of Primary Sources in Teaching and Interpreting American History*. Pittsburgh, Pennsylvania: North Hills School District, 1967. pp. 21-23.

FIGURE VIII

FORMS OF CURRICULAR ORGANIZATION*

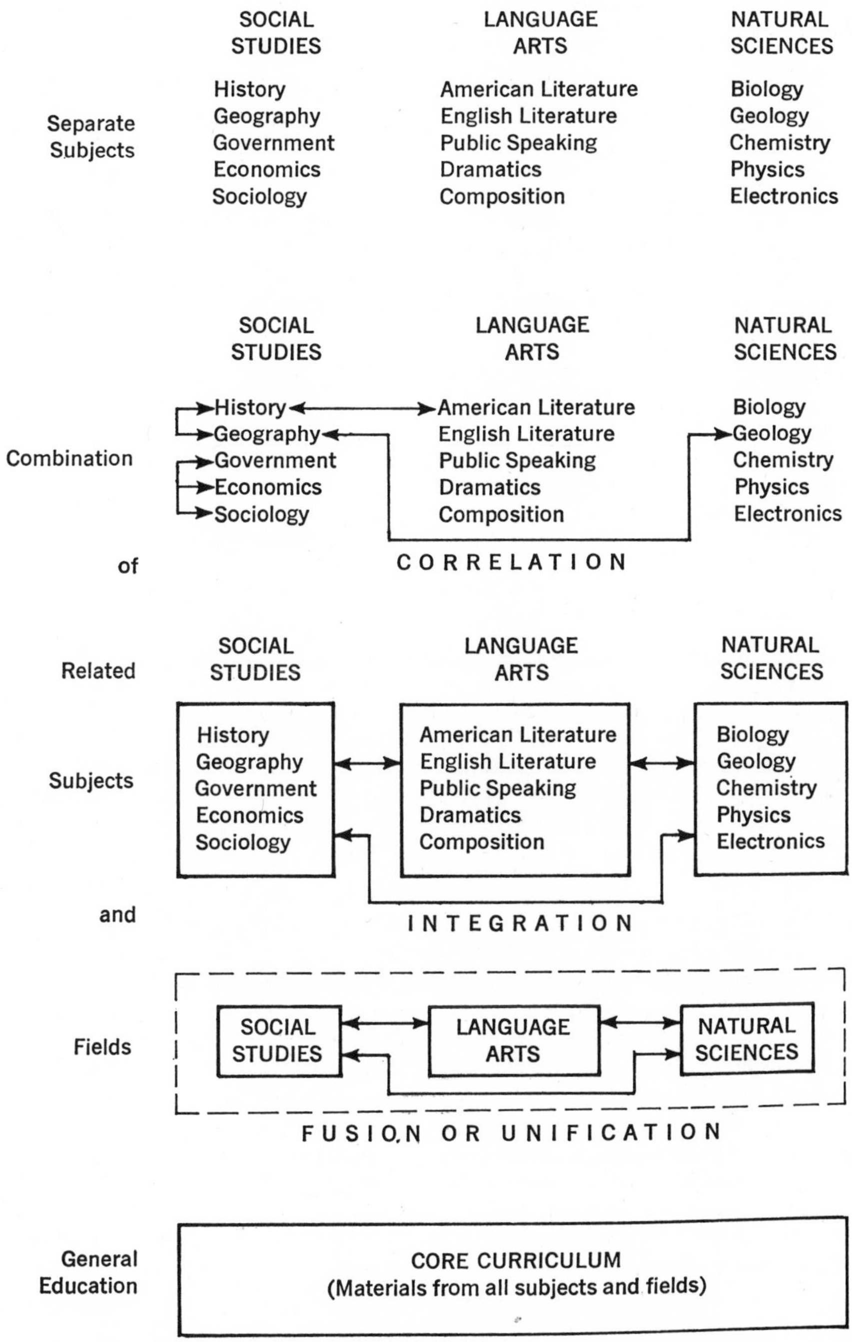

	SOCIAL STUDIES	LANGUAGE ARTS	NATURAL SCIENCES
Separate Subjects	History Geography Government Economics Sociology	American Literature English Literature Public Speaking Dramatics Composition	Biology Geology Chemistry Physics Electronics

	SOCIAL STUDIES	LANGUAGE ARTS	NATURAL SCIENCES
Combination	History Geography Government Economics Sociology	American Literature English Literature Public Speaking Dramatics Composition	Biology Geology Chemistry Physics Electronics

of   C O R R E L A T I O N

	SOCIAL STUDIES	LANGUAGE ARTS	NATURAL SCIENCES
Related Subjects	History Geography Government Economics Sociology	American Literature English Literature Public Speaking Dramatics Composition	Biology Geology Chemistry Physics Electronics

and   I N T E G R A T I O N

Fields | SOCIAL STUDIES | | LANGUAGE ARTS | | NATURAL SCIENCES |

F U S I O N   O R   U N I F I C A T I O N

General Education	CORE CURRICULUM (Materials from all subjects and fields)

* Wesley, Edgar B. and Stanley P. Wronski. *Teaching Social Studies in High Schools.* 5th ed. Boston, Massachusetts: Heath, 1964. p. 107.

_____ Organizing ideas in logical pattern
_____ Organizing notes around key ideas or questions
_____ Perceiving relationships
_____ Predicting outcomes
_____ Questioning immutability of the printed word and of statistics
_____ Reaching tentative conclusions
_____ Recognizing emotional coloration
_____ Recognizing propaganda and its purpose in a given context
_____ Relating the past to the present in the study of change and continuity
_____ Seeking for association between a particular episode and others connected with it
_____ Selecting evidence pertinent to an argument
_____ Selecting main ideas and supporting facts
_____ Suspending judgment where a conclusion is not warranted
_____ Synthesizing findings into an accurate and readable account
_____ Understanding abstract concepts

TABLE XIV

A FUSED LIBRARY-BASED TEACHING UNIT

Topic: Transportation.
Grade Level: Eight.
Subject Integration: Language Arts, Mathematics, Science, Social Studies.

I. Objectives

   1. To provide an opportunity for the students to become conversant with the historical, social, economic, and cultural significance of transportation.
   2. To provide an opportunity for the students to become conversant with occupational opportunities in the field of transportation.
   3. To provide an opportunity for the students to understand the scientific principles underlying the mechanics of various modes of transportation.
   4. To provide an opportunity for the students to become acquainted with mythological and legendary heroes associated with man's conquest of land, sea, and air.
   5. To provide an opportunity for the students to become conversant with recreational reading experiences associated with the field of transportation.
   6. To provide the opportunity for the student to become aware of the impact of transportation terms on our vocabulary.
   7. To provide an opportunity for the students to apply and to refine the study skills of organizing and communicating ideas within a context of utility.

II. Content

   A. Transportation—Air
      General

Aerospace industry	Rockets
Air mail	Science of flight
Air passenger service	Social significance
Aircraft engines	Solid fuels
Ballooning	Space medicine
Da Vinci's helicopter	Space nutrition
Economic significance	Space suits
History of flight	Space vehicles
Jet propulsion	Supersonic aircraft
Manned space flight	Unidentified flying objects

Modes of travel
Occupations
Problems of space flight

United States Army Air Force
United States Navy Air Force
Vehicles of the future

Aids to Air and Space Transportation

Aerospace training program
Airports and floating airfields
Launch vehicles

Radar
Research
Space stations

Biography

Aldren, Buzz
Anders, William
Armstrong, Neal
Borman, Frank
Carpenter, Scott
Collins, Michael
Cooper, Leroy
Earhart, Amelia
Gagarin, Yuri

Glenn, John
Goddard, Robert
Grissom, Virgil
Langley, Samuel
Lindberg, Charles
Lovell, James
Montgolfier, Jacques and Joseph
Rickenbacker, Eddie
Wright, Orville and Wilbur

Mythological Heroes

Daedalus
Icarus

Mercury
Pegasus

Impact on Contemporary Vocabulary

B. Transportation—Land

Beasts of Burden

Buffalo
Camel
Caribou
Dog
Elephant

Horse
Llama
Mule
Ox
Reindeer

Vehicular—Road and Rail
General

Automotive industry
Bicycles
Caterpillar tractors
Commercial vehicles
Economic significance
Fuels
Gas, diesel, and atomic engines
History of wheeled vehicles
Hydraulic transmission

Impact on history
Impact on industry
Impact on manners and customs
Locomotive industry
Modes of travel
Occupations
Self-propelled vehicles
Social significance
Vehicles of the future

Aids to Land Transportation

Alcan Highway
Bridges
Byways, highways, and thruways
Gasoline industry
Highway planning, financing, and construction

Historic roads
Pan American Highway
Road maps and travel guides
Rubber industry
Steel industry
Tunnels

Biography

Diesel, Rudolph
Duryea, Charles
Ford, Henry
Hill, James

Pullman, George
Trevithick, Richard
Westinghouse, George

Legendary Heroes
    Casey Jones   John Henry
    Jesse James

Impact on Contemporary Vocabulary

C. Transportation—Water
General

Atomic submarines	Occupations
Cargoes on Great Lakes	Pleasure craft
Clipper ships	Seas as highways
Economic significance	Ship building
History of water transportation	Ships in World War II
Hydrofoils	Ships that made U. S. history
Impact on history	Social significance
Impact on industry	Steamboat development
Impact on manners and customs	Tankers
Luxury liners	Warships
Merchant marine	Whalers
Nuclear power	

Aids to Water Transportation

Canals	Navigation instruments
Coast and geodetic surveys	Panama Canal
Coast Guard	Pennsylvania Canal
Electronic instruments	Radar
Erie Canal	St. Lawrence Seaway
Famous harbors	Sonar
Influence of rivers	Suez Canal
Lighthouses	

Biography

Ericson, John	Lindenthal, Gustav
Fitch, John	Masefield, John
Fulton, Robert	Melville, Herman
Goethals, George	Nordhoff, Charles
Hall, James	Rickover, Hyman
Heyerdahl, Thor	Roebling, Augustus
Holland, Clifford	Roebling, John
Holland, John	Stevens, John
Lesseps, Ferdinand de	

Legendary Heroes

Captain Kidd	Mike Fink
Grace Darling	Ol' Stormalong

Impact on Contemporary Vocabulary

TOPIC CHECKLIST FOR UNIT DEVELOPMENT

Continuity, unity, balance, and adequacy of course coverage must be planned to guard topic inclusion from costly omissions. It is recommended practice that social studies teachers and librarians working cooperatively develop topic inclusion checklists to guarantee uniform excellence in unit designs (See Checklist XI). Such checklists are invaluable in directing the building of balanced units in a course such as world cultures. Guaranteeing uniform parallel coverage for *all* cultures guards against providing a depth study for familiar cultures while offering but cursory coverage for unfamiliar cultures—a common tendency which defeats the purpose of a world cultures course.

CHECKLIST XI

TOPIC CHECKLIST TO UNIFY AND COORDINATE UNIT DEVELOPMENT

Subject: Social Studies.
Grade: Ten.
Course: World Cultures.

I. Agriculture

Markets	Products
Methods of farming	Statistics
Problems	

II. Arts and crafts

Dance	Painting
Folk art	Pottery
Jewelry	Sculpture
Metal work	Weaving

III. Commerce, business, banking

Balance of trade	Occupations
Currency	Problems
Exports	Statistics
Imports	

IV. Communication

Language	Methods
Mass media	Statistics

V. Education

History	Public schools
Literacy	Statistics
Private schools	Universities and colleges

VI. Architecture

Art galleries	Music halls, opera houses
Cathedrals, churches, temples	National shrines
Houses	Palaces, governmental offices
Libraries	Theaters
Museums	

VII. Famous people

Actors	Inventors
Architects	Jurists
Artists	Military leaders
Authors	Musicians
Doctors	Philosophers
Dramatists	Poets
Engineers	Religious leaders
Explorers	Rulers, government leaders
Geographers	Scientists
Heroes	Sculptors
Historians	Statesmen
Humanitarians	Teachers

VIII. Geography

Area	Physical features
Climate	Political divisions
Description	Statistics
Neighboring nations	

IX. Government

Description	Relationship with the United States
Membership in the United Nations	

X. Health and medicine

Hospitals	Research
Problems	Standards
Progress	Statistics

XI. History

Chronology	Events
Contribution to civilization	

XII. Holidays and festivals

National	Religious

XIII. Literature

Drama	Novels
Essays	Philosophy
Journalism	Poetry
Legends and folklore	

XIV. Manners and customs

Burial	Home furnishings
Costume	Marriage
Family life	Mores
Food	Place of women

XV. Manufacturing and industry

Markets	Products
Methods	Statistics
Problems	

XVI. Military strength

Alliances	Statistics
Organization	

XVII. Music

Composed	National anthem
Folk	

XVIII. National symbols

Flag	Seal

XIX. Natural resources

Animals	Soil
Minerals	Statistics
Plants	Water

XX. Population

Emigration and immigration	Statistics
Problems	

XXI.   Recreation and sports
       Importance   Kinds

XXII. Religion
       Importance   Statistics
       Sects

XXIII. Science and technology
       Achievements   Level of attainment
       Inventions

XXIV. Social classes
       Description   Standard of living
       Problems   Statistics

XXV.   Transportation
       Kinds   Statistics
       Problems

XXVI. World importance and contribution
       Past   Present
       Potential

TEACHER AND LIBRARIAN COOPERATIVELY SOLVE A TEACHING PROBLEM

Frequently the classroom teacher will ask the librarian for help in meeting special class needs: for example, the eighth grade teacher faced with teaching a class of 30 exceptionally bright students who thought they already knew more than they needed to know about American history. As each new unit was taught, the class refused to put forth effort. The teacher hit upon the idea of using a pretest to introduce the upcoming unit, "Civil War and Reconstruction." She asked for the librarian's help in structuring this pretest. Together the teacher and librarian identified 60 people whose biographies could well serve as content for the study of the Civil War (See Example VIII).

The teacher invited the librarian to come to the classroom to introduce the unit. The librarian distributed the pretest, gave the directions, conducted the discussion following the marking of the test, and alerted the students to the various primary source materials available for their use. The students were shocked to discover how many of these people they did not know—out of a possible 60 (all names on the list should have been marked *yes*) the highest number known to any student was 25; the majority could not identify 20! The pretest was more than a motivational device. It was a means of orienting the students to the unit and to the biographies essential for adequate understanding of the Civil War and Reconstruction. The students for the first time in that school year had a challenge in history class, for they discovered how much they did not know and yet needed to know. The history teacher, discovering that the pretest was an effective method of challenging the gifted, continued to employ a pretest as an introduction for subsequent units and asked for the librarian's help in structuring each pretest.

EXAMPLE VIII

UNIT PRETEST: THE CIVIL WAR AND RECONSTRUCTION*

Subject: Social Studies
Grade level: Eight

Name_____   Number indicated YES_____

                                           Number indicated NO_____

    After you have studied this list of famous Americans, please write "yes" or "no" before each name to indicate whether or not the person was involved directly or indirectly with the events of the Civil War.

_____ Louisa May Alcott		_____ Oliver Wendell Holmes, Jr.
_____ Clara Barton		_____ Julia Ward Howe
_____ August Bondi		_____ Sam Houston
_____ John Wilkes Booth		_____ "Stonewall" Jackson
_____ Belle Boyd		_____ Andrew Johnson
_____ Matthew Brady		_____ Robert E. Lee
_____ John Brown		_____ Abraham Lincoln
_____ Bill Cody		_____ Thaddeus Lowe
_____ Stephen Crane		_____ James Russell Lowell
_____ George Cook		_____ George McClellan
_____ George Custer		_____ George Meade
_____ Jefferson Davis		_____ John Hunt Morgan
_____ Varina Howell Davis		_____ John Mosby
_____ Dorothy Dix		_____ Samuel Mudd
_____ Abner Doubleday		_____ James Pettigru
_____ Stephen A. Douglas		_____ Joseph Pulitzer
_____ Frederick Douglass		_____ Edmund Ross
_____ Daniel Emmett		_____ Dred Scott
_____ John Ericsson		_____ Philip Sheridan
_____ Edward Everett		_____ William T. Sherman
_____ David Farragut		_____ Edwin Stanton
_____ Nathan B. Forrest		_____ Harriet Beecher Stowe
_____ Barbara Frietchie		_____ James E. B. Stuart
_____ William Lloyd Garrison		_____ Charles Sumner
_____ Ulysses S. Grant		_____ Roger Taney
_____ Rose O'Neil Greenhow		_____ Harriet Tubman
_____ William Gregg		_____ Molly Tynes
_____ Horace Greeley		_____ Lewis Wallace
_____ Cornelia Hancock		_____ Walt Whitman
_____ John Hay		_____ Brigham Young

LITERATURE INTEGRATION WITH SOCIAL STUDIES PROGRAM

The teacher of social studies, the teacher of reading and/or literature, and the librarian share a joint responsibility for integrating literature with the teaching of social studies content. "Of all the subjects not traditionally included under the social studies, none is more intimately affiliated with them than literature." Literature is employed in social studies teaching

---

* This pretest was developed cooperatively by classroom teacher and school librarian to create and sustain student interest in discovering who these people were and why they were significant.

"to heighten interest, deepen understanding, create moods and atmosphere, portray the diverse ways of living and thinking among people in various cultures, stimulate imagination, give colorful backgrounds, promote more complete identification with others, give a warm feeling for the problems of others, improve attitudes toward others, build appreciations for the contributions of others, provoke creativity, and give vivid impressions of ways of living being studied in various units."[124]

John Michaelis warns the teacher of social studies not to sacrifice the student's enjoyment of literature for the sake of obtaining a detailed report of what he has read. He recommends that the teacher keep the following points in mind when incorporating literature into the social studies program[125] (See Chapter Six):

1. Enjoy it, don't dissect it; analyze it only if analysis increases enjoyment.
2. Share it, don't ask questions; don't give tests on it or evaluate it as is done with factual materials.
3. Approach it to have fun, not to study it as is done in work-type materials.
4. Be aware of fiction and fantasy; don't teach them as facts.
5. Let the children discover values, moods, and meanings; don't moralize or struggle to develop certain points of real interest to yourself.
6. Let children memorize their favorites.
7. Use varied techniques and activities to share and enjoy literary selections in the social studies, such as those in the following list:

Card files of favorite poems and stories	Oral reading by children and teacher
Choral reading	Programs and pageants
Dramatization	Puppets and marionettes
Filmstrips	Radio and TV programs
Independent reading	Recordings (disc and tape)
Motion pictures	Sharing creative writing
	Storytelling

THE SOCIAL STUDIES LABORATORY COLLECTION

The librarian shares with the social studies faculty the responsibility of selecting resources for inclusion not only in the district professional library but especially in the social studies building laboratory. In the search for social studies laboratory materials, a high priority must be given to the publications of the National Council for the Social Studies, a department of the NEA.* This Council publishes yearbooks, bulletins, curriculum handbooks, and a "How To Do It" series dealing with specific problems of classroom procedure. The Yearbooks are published annually and are devoted to "an inclusive scholarly review of research, experience, and opinion concern-

---

* National Council for the Social Studies. 1201 Sixteenth Street, N.W., Washington, D.C. 20036.
124 Michaelis, John U. Op. cit., p. 529.
125 Ibid., pp. 529-530.

ing a single topic;" for example, the 33rd yearbook is devoted completely to a comprehensive treatment of study skills development (See Appendix L). Bulletins are issued with a frequency of from one to three a year; each is "devoted to practical classroom aids for the social studies teacher." Each of the 12 Curriculum Handbooks "contain specific suggestions for courses of study in the social studies." The "How To Do It" series numbers 22 pamphlets containing "illustrations and concrete suggestions on method" among which are: *How To Use a Motion Picture, How To Use a Textbook, How To Use a Bulletin Board, How To Use Group Discussion, How To Handle Controversial Issues.*

When searching for print and non-print resources to support teaching about foreign cultures, the librarian and the teacher will find invaluable the U.S. Chamber of Commerce handbook, *Guide to Foreign Information Sources,** revised annually, and sold by the Chamber at a cost of 25¢. In addition to suggesting sources of information, this *Guide* also includes a section on "Organizations and Services Relating to Areas of the World with References on Employment Abroad."

VITALIZING THE SOCIAL STUDIES PROGRAM

The teacher of social studies and the librarian share the responsibility of providing each student with meaningful experiences uniquely compatible with his own special needs. The emphasis in contemporary social studies teaching must shift from "subject" to "learner centered" experiences (See Figure V, and Tables IV, XV). The common concern of the social studies teacher and the librarian is to provide learning experiences commensurate with the needs of the student not only as a learner, but as a person, as a human being, and as a citizen. It is imperative that each student be given opportunity to see clearly his importance as a contributing member of society.

> The education of citizens for a free society is a task for all segments of the social order, but the schools are charged with a larger and special share. And, within the school, the social studies as school subjects have been assigned as one of their unique contributions some special responsibility in citizenship education. . . . *Unless we change the things we have been doing, we are dooming future generations to a life less rich, less free, less personally satisfying than even the modest lives most of us have today.*[126]
>
> To the extent that the school fails to provide an opportunity for every individual whom it touches and serves to develop his fullest potential; to prepare for a full personal life; and to acquire the skills and understanding essential for participating intelligently and effectively in government, in economic enterprise, and in the total life of the community and the nation, the school will have fallen short of its high purpose.[127]

* United States Chamber of Commerce. 1615 H Street, N.W., Washington, D.C. 20006.
[126] Grambs, Jean D. "The Challenge to the Social Studies" in *Citizenship and a Free Society: Education for the Future* edited by Franklin Patterson. Thirtieth Yearbook. Washington, D.C.: National Council for the Social Studies. National Education Association, 1960. p. 274.
[127] Commission on Imperatives in Education. *Imperatives in Education.* Washington, D.C.: American Association of School Administrators, 1966. p. 92.

The hope of vitalizing social studies teaching rests on the ready availability of appropriate instructional resources containing significant learning experiences compatible with the individual student's capabilities and needs. Individualization depends upon personalizing and customizing learner programs which, in turn, demand face to face communication between teacher and librarian. Working cooperatively the teacher and the librarian can provide learning experiences which will widen, deepen, and intensify the educational experience. Working in isolation neither teacher nor librarian can bring the same high degree of dynamic effectiveness to the teaching and learning program. Integrating the services and the resources of the school library with developmental on going social studies programs is an innovative teaching approach designed to raise the social studies program from subject centered impersonal teaching to learner centered personalized teaching.

TABLE XV

CHARACTERISTIC DIFFERENCES IN EMPHASIS BETWEEN
THE SUBJECT AND EXPERIENCE CURRICULUMS*

SUBJECT CURRICULUM	EXPERIENCE CURRICULUM
1. Centered in *subjects*.	1. Centered in *learners*.
2. Emphasis upon teaching subject matter.	2. Emphasis upon promoting the all-around growth of the learners.
3. Subject matter selected and organized *before* the teaching situation.	3. Subject matter selected and organized cooperatively by all learners *during* the learning situation.
4. Controlled by the teacher or someone representing authority external to the learning situation.	4. Controlled and directed cooperatively by learners (pupils, teachers, parents, supervisors, principals, and others) in the learning situation.
5. Emphasis upon teaching facts, imparting information requiring knowledge for its own sake or for possible future use.	5. Emphasis upon meanings which will function immediately in improving living.
6. Emphasis upon teaching specific habits and skills as separate and isolated aspects of learning.	6. Emphasis upon building habits and skills as integral parts of larger experiences.
7. Emphasis upon improving the methods of teaching subject matter of specific subjects.	7. Emphasis upon understanding and improving through use of the process of learning.
8. Emphasis upon uniformity of exposures to learning situations and, insofar as possible, uniformity of learning results.	8. Emphasis upon variability in exposures to learning situations and variability in the results expected and achieved.
9. Education as conforming to the patterns set by the curriculum and its various associated instruments.	9. Education as aiding each child to build a socially creative individuality.
10. Education considered as schooling.	10. Education considered as a continuous intelligent process of growth.

* Hopkins, L. Thomas. *Interaction: The Democratic Process*. Boston: D.C. Heath, 1941. p. 20.

8 The School Library as an Integral Part of the Science and Mathematics Programs

What science contributes to the national purpose is measured by what it adds to the sum of human knowledge; science serves the nation by serving humanity. *

Today we must learn more, learn it faster, remember it better, and use it more effectively. The professional school librarian is needed to see that these goals are realized. **

Change is the one constant in our contemporary world. In large measure the degree and kind of change is influenced by man's ever increasing scientific and technological "know-how."[128] Science both creates and controls change: science is the force that keeps change from becoming disruptive and destructive. Science brings order to change by channeling it within a frame of purposefulness and functional utility. Change without this order is chaos. The major responsibility of today's science program is to teach students to deal with change intelligently and competently, but also with integrity, confidence, and emotional stability.

> Science is by definition oriented to the future; it is characterized
> by change and progress . . . Young people should be equipped for
> lifelong learning and in a way that they can travel upon their own
> —an education that is geared to change and which trains for intel-
> lectual self-direction. Young people must be qualified to deal with
> ideas not yet born and with discoveries not yet made.[129]

DEVELOPING SCIENTIFIC LITERACY

The task of selecting content for the science program is overwhelming. The science faculty must practice their scientific ability when determining what

* Barry, Commoner et al. "Science and Human Welfare." *Science,* vol. 132, July 8, 1960. p. 69.
** Dale, Edgar. Op. cit., p. 134.
128 Hurd, Paul DeHart. *Science Teaching for a Changing World.* Chicago, Illinois: Scott, Foresman, 1963.
129 Editors of *Education U.S.A.* Op. cit., p. 24.

should be studied today in the light of what will have permanent value tomorrow. Selecting what will have lasting significance is no easy task, for man's proliferation of knowledge is accelerating constantly. It has been estimated that by the year 2000, man's fund of knowledge will be at least 100 times what it was in 1900. There are no fewer than 50,000 technical and scientific periodicals—exclusive of monographs and books—publishing the results of at least 1,000,000 research studies each year. "This means that every month of the year journals publish approximately 100,000 research studies reporting new ideas or data and refining the old."[130] New scientific knowledge has increased since the time of Newton by a factor of 1,000,000. "Never has man needed to know so much—just to be ignorant"[131] (See Figure I).

Because we live in a science-oriented society, schools must structure their programs upon two operational principles:[132]

> Modern science teaching must be for the citizen, not just the future scientist.
> Students should learn to accept and explore the ever-changing, rather than be handicapped with memorizing "unchangeable laws."

Since science permeates the totality of our very existence, it is imperative that we teach for scientific literacy.

> A scientifically literate citizen is essential to safeguard the national security, to assure advance in basic science, and to maintain our standard of living. Because of the pace of science in the culture of our times and its impact on the personal lives of people, it becomes imperative that science have a prominent place in the educational enterprise at every teaching level.[133]

GOALS OF THE MODERN SCIENCE PROGRAM

In addition to fostering the development of scientific literacy the following desirable goals give direction to current science curriculum programming:[134]

> Provide a logical and integrated picture of contemporary science: the theories, models, and generalizations that show the unity of science.
> Illustrate the diverse processes that are used to produce the conclusions of science and which show the limitations of these methods: the ways of inquiry and the structure of scientific knowledge.
> Enable the student to reach at some point the shadow of the frontier: to experience the meaning of "we just don't know" and to become sensitive to the *progress* of science.

130 Conner, Forrest E. and William J. Ellena. Op. cit., p. iii.
131 Hurd, Paul DeHart. Op. cit., p. 6.
132 Editors of *Education U.S.A.* Op. cit., p. 21.
133 National Science Teachers Association. *Planning for Excellence in High School Science.* Washington, D.C.: National Science Teachers Association, 1961. p. 19.
134 Editors of *Education U.S.A.* Op. cit., p. 23.

Implementing these three goals requires that the school recognize the need to give *all* students:[135]

> A knowledge of how scientists think and work.
>
> A knowledge of major "conceptual schemes" of science.
>
> An appreciation of the role of science in our society.
>
> Adequate information for making career decisions related to science.
>
> A continued interest in reading and learning about new developments in science.

The actualization of each of these goals requires the availability of library resources.

NEW DEFINITION OF SCIENCE

The very definition of *science* has undergone a basic change. Traditionally science was defined as an established body of facts explaining natural phenomena. This definition emphasized "content" that was static. The new concept of science is far from static:

> *Science, then, is a human enterprise including the on-going process of seeking explanations and understanding of the natural world, and also including that which the process produces—man's storehouse of knowledge. Science is process and product.*[136]

This definition places science in the position of being permanently *open-ended*. Far from limiting science to content alone, this interpretation views science as an *activity*. Today's science curriculum stresses activity or *process* as well as content or *product*. Content will change, become out-dated and obsolete; process will remain functionally valid, permanently useful.

ABILITIES AND SKILLS

The modern science program stresses abilities and skills which are both functional and mental. Functional skills and abilities include observing, recording, measuring, pouring, weighing, and reporting; mental abilities and skills include problem solving and critical thinking. Through the modern science program the student learns how to:[137]

> Make careful and complete plans for solving problems.
>
> Develop theories, and to make and test predictions on the basis of these theories.
>
> Find or devise experiments that will solve problems or answer questions.
>
> Predict the outcome of an experiment, and offer reasons to justify the prediction.
>
> Perform experiments involving simple cause-and-effect relationships, and to describe or explain satisfactorily what happened.

[135] Conner, Forrest E. and William J. Ellena. Op. cit., p. 257.
[136] National Science Teachers Association. Op. cit., p. 15.
[137] Victor, Edward. *Science for the Elementary School.* New York: Macmillan, 1965. pp. 25-26.

Plan and execute experiments carefully.

Make accurate measurements and readings.

Manipulate science equipment satisfactorily.

Observe and describe similarities and differences in experimental behavior, and in objects and their characteristics.

Distinguish between pertinent and irrelevant observations and information.

Make valid and reliable comparisons.

Make quantitative as well as qualitative observations.

Organize and classify observations.

Explain phenomena on the basis of truth and logic, rather than on the basis of superstition and wishful thinking.

Distinguish fact from fantasy.

Apply previously learned concepts to interpret new phenomena.

Predict what will happen when conditions are changed.

Where experimentation is impossible or unfeasible, to determine other appropriate methods of investigation.

Distinguish between science books that are read for fun and those that are read for reliable information.

Use the table of contents, index, and glossary of science texts and references.

Read science content with understanding.

Abstract major concepts and understandings from the science content in texts and references.

Read and interpret simple charts, tables, and graphs.

Organize observations or reading into effective oral or written reports.

Develop the verbal and written skills of communication used by scientists.

Participate actively in group discussion.

Stay close to the topic being discussed.

Formulate clear and intelligent questions.

Report clearly, concisely, and accurately.

Listen intelligently.

Work together, in small or large groups.

Cooperate with others when planning an investigation.

Persevere in projects that are undertaken.

SCIENTIFIC ATTITUDES

The modern science curriculum is designed to foster the following scientific attitudes:[138]

Open mindedness.

Willingness to change one's mind in the light of new evidence.

Willingness to allow others to question and challenge one's ideas.

Suspended judgment, which is the reservation of decisions until all the available evidence has been collected.

Reluctance to generalize on the basis of one experiment or limited evidence.

[138] Ibid., p. 26.

Respect for the ideas, opinions, and ways of life of others.

Awareness that there is a difference between facts and opinions.

Unwillingness to accept statements as facts unless they are backed by sufficient proof.

Reluctance to allow decisions to be affected by personal likes or dislikes, anger, fear, and ignorance.

Unwillingness to compromise with the truth.

Development of the habit of explaining things in a scientific manner.

Desirability of checking thinking by doing experiments or consulting reliable books and people.

Going to reliable sources for evidence.

Awareness that sometimes printed matter is not accurate or correct.

Willingness to cooperate.

Curiosity about the world in which we live.

Unwillingness to believe in superstitions.

Awareness that truth itself never changes, but that our concept of what is true continues to change as our knowledge increases.

APPRECIATIONS

The modern science program provides opportunity for the children to appreciate the functional utility and impact of science on everyday living. The following are examples of appreciations developed through an adequate modern science program.[139]

The role science plays in our daily lives.

The many ways that science can be used to explain the environment around us.

The impact of science and technology on our civilization.

The influence of science upon man's way of thinking, his relations with others, his religion, and his social responsibility.

The role that problem solving and critical thinking can play in our personal habits, attitudes, and relationships.

The concept that science is the result of human endeavor and flourishes best when there is intellectual freedom.

The constant striving of scientists to know more about the world.

The contributions of scientists to the world we live in.

The tools and techniques of science.

The orderliness of nature and of natural laws.

The ever-changing nature of science.

The beauty in nature.

SCIENCE CURRICULUM CRITERIA

The emphasis in teaching science has shifted from "massive doses of facts without conceptual order, without unity, without showing how these facts were arrived at, and without developing a feeling for the intellectual methods that won them from nature"[140] to a selected group of conceptual schemes fundamental to an adequate understanding and appreciation of sci-

139 Ibid., p. 27.
140 Hurd, Paul DeHart. Op. cit., pp. 7-8.

ence and the process of science. Likewise the teaching of science has become a continuous process beginning in kindergarten and extending in sequential progression through grade 12.

A good science program:

Is strongly structured.

Is balanced in selection of concepts which are developed in spiral progression.

Is geared to the students' developmental needs.

Carries its responsibility to the future.

Develops scientific literacy.

Nurtures rational attitudes that are essential to reasoned and constructive behavior.

Gives students personal insight into as well as respect for orderliness in thinking and behavior.

Encourages learning from many experiences and sources.

Increases the student's understanding and appreciation of the beauty and the vastness of the creation of the universe.

TEACHING SCIENCE TO DEVELOP PROBLEM SOLVING SKILLS

The obligation of the modern science program extends beyond knowledge of science content to including learning how to learn.

> The first objective of any education, over and beyond the pleasure it may give, is that it serves the future. Knowledge, to be of greatest value, must be usable beyond the context in which it was learned.
>
> For several years now attempts have been made to develop courses in science to meet the "immediate needs" of children and young people. The developments of curricula for a rapidly changing society demand that what is learned be more durable than this. *Learning in every course must also count for the rest of the student's life.*
>
> There is too much to know and too much demanded of one today to be able to afford learning which has only temporary or immediate use—learning that will wither into obsolescence before the student finishes school.
>
> But even durability is not enough, for most of the knowledge that young people will need in their lifetime has not yet been announced or discovered. *This means that we need to provide students with an entrance into this knowledge in a way that they can travel on their own.*[141]

The science program to be effective and to meet its obligation to the future must prepare the students to think critically, analytically, reflectively, creatively, with disciplined imagination.

The teacher of science must devise teaching and learning experiences for the express purpose of giving the students guided practice in critical think-

141 Ibid., pp. 8-9.

ing. The following abilities rightfully can be developed as integral components of science classroom and library supported teaching and learning programs:

A person may be said to think critically to the degree that he exhibits the following skills and attitudes:

RECOGNIZES AND DEFINES PROBLEMS. He is sensitive to problem situations; he recognizes and makes explicit the nature of any difficulty which blocks his attainment of a desired goal; he locates the crucial aspects of the problem; he defines key terms and issues; he breaks complex problems into workable parts.

FORMULATES ADEQUATE HYPOTHESES. He approaches problems in a flexible manner; he formulates or recognizes feasible hypotheses; he is skillful in establishing an appropriate "solution model."

MAKES PERTINENT SELECTIONS. He is aware of the need for facts, for evidence; he is adept at devising methods for obtaining and judging evidence; he is able to keep a problem clearly in mind; he consistently discriminates between relevant and irrelevant assumptions, materials techniques, and issues; he distinguishes between reliable and unreliable information; he exhibits good judgment.

DRAWS VALID CONCLUSIONS. He is rational; he makes reasonable generalizations from specific data (induction); he applies judiciously the canons of logic (deduction); he recognizes the influence of emotions and values; he suspends judgment; he is cautious in asserting the generality of a conclusion because he is aware of the limited data supporting the generalization; he extends the scope of his generalizations only as he discovers additional supporting data.

APPLIES CONCLUSIONS. He grasps the general principles which relate to a problem; he is apt in applying these generalizations whenever they are appropriate; he is capable of decisions, of action consistent with his conclusions.[142]

THE SCHOOL LIBRARY PROVIDES CONTENT FOR AND PRACTICE IN CRITICAL THINKING

Developing student understanding of the process of science requires extended practice in problem solving. The librarian shares with the science teacher the responsibility for teaching the student how to solve problems scientifically. The checklist of problem solving practices listed in Checklist XII can well serve as an orientation guide to teacher and to librarian as cooperatively they design problem solving experiments requiring library resources for adequate solution.

Library resources are essential if problem solving is to take place within a context of purpose, utility, and significance. Since science content cannot be limited to textbook or classroom collection if adequacy of understanding is to be developed, the library must become a laboratory for building and practicing scientific literacy. It is in the library as well as in the science classroom and science laboratory that students learn to utilize their critical thinking skills within a context of functional utility.

142 Burton, William H. et al. Op. cit., p. 426.

The necessity of providing library resources and services to maximize the effectiveness of science teaching and learning is attested to in numerous contemporary writings on science teaching. Thomas Aylesworth in his handbook, *Planning for Effective Science Teaching,* states:[143]

> We must all teach the students . . . the language of science.
> We must teach them to read in science, to develop vocabulary in science, to speak about science. We must teach them to listen to science, write about science and use the *library* for science work.

Forrest E. Conner and William J. Ellena predicate their hope for individualizing science teaching and learning on the availability of library resources:[144]

> Science teachers and curriculum planners are recognizing that concept development is a personal thing and more apt to occur in science when there is personal involvement in scientific inquiry or problem solving. Therefore, we see more and more opportunities for the student to observe scientific phenomena in his own way and to work at his own pace . . .
> Because learning is an individual process, emphasis on learning produces a trend toward more individualized instruction. Ideally the laboratory and the *library* become centers of learning.
>
> To provide for true individualization of instruction, science topics and activities are being selected from a wide variety of curriculum resources. The selection of teaching-learning materials and related facilities and equipment is increasingly broad, and all elements must be carefully chosen.
> An emerging point of view on textbooks, for example, is that a science textbook is a teaching aid, not a course of study. Most modern textbooks . . . lack much current material that a student should learn. Paperback books are helping to provide a wide range of materials from which to choose for classroom work and for supplementary and enrichment reading. To some extent, they also contain material that is more current than that found in textbooks. Therefore, science programs are being supported by *increasingly large libraries,* both collections in the school library and special collections for immediate use in the science room.

Glenn O. Blough and Julius Schwartz highlight in their textbook, *Elementary School Science and How to Teach It,* the absolute necessity of employing library resources to support the science program.[145]

> An important skill for the teacher to develop is that of getting into the book (textbook) when necessary and getting out of it when

---

143 Aylesworth, Thomas G. *Planning for Effective Science Teaching.* Special reprint permission granted by *Current Science,* published by American Education Publications/A Xerox Co. Columbus, Ohio: 1964. p. 15.
144 Conner, Forrest E. and William J. Ellena. Op. cit., pp. 257-258.
145 Blough, Glenn O. and Julius Schwartz. *Elementary School Science and How to Teach It.* New York: Holt, 1964. p. 10.

not. It is getting stuck in the book that is bad . . . (supplementary books) often supply the exact material needed and should be relied on *heavily* for their contribution to the science program.

There is much to be said in favor of a library of trade (supplementary) books in addition to the basic text or texts:

(1) They meet the needs of *individual* children.
(2) They permit the pursuit of a topic in depth.
(3) They develop the habit of using many sources.
(4) They permit pupils to work independently.
(5) They may serve with special effectiveness the pupils who have reading difficulty.

The American Association for the Advancement of Science publishes two book lists of science and mathematics resources for elementary and secondary school libraries. These two lists are evidence of the AAAS concern for school library support of the science program. The AAAS SCIENCE BOOK LIST FOR YOUNG ADULTS[146] contains an annotated list of 1,376 science and mathematics titles useful for students in grades nine through twelve. The AAAS SCIENCE BOOK LIST FOR CHILDREN[147] contains annotations of 1,291 titles for pupils in grades one through eight. The AAAS compiles and distributes these book lists to carry science teaching and science learning beyond the limitations of the text.[148]

No longer is it desirable to limit science instruction to a single textbook which the student accepts as immutable fact, or to a single laboratory manual in which the student repeats classic exercises yielding known results, labels outline diagrams, etc. Instead, the sciences and mathematics are being presented as dynamic, outgoing, open-ended processes. The instructional materials communicate to and involve the student in the excitement of bibliographic research, experimentation, testing, discovery, and rational evaluation—processes that have characterized the march of science and technology during the entire course of human progress.

Collateral reading and reference work form an integral part of these curricula. This collateral reading is considered so important that, where there are gaps in the published literature, special materials are being produced under the auspices of some curriculum study groups . . .

Librarians often ask how many science and mathematics books a good high school library should own . . . Considering the importance of science, mathematics, and technical vocational instruction in the curricula of modern secondary schools, it is believed that a minimum of 20 per cent of the total book collection in the library should be in the pure, in the medical, and in the engineering sciences . . .

Modern science instruction includes the use of motion pictures,

146 *The AAAS Science Book List for Young Adults.* Washington, D.C.: American Association for the Advancement of Science, 1964.
147 *The AAAS Science Book List for Children.* Washington, D.C.: American Association for the Advancement of Science, 1963.
148 *The AAAS Science Book List for Young Adults.* Op. cit., pp. viii-ix.

filmstrips, recordings, programmed learning, and other nonbook materials. Many school libraries, in fact, are now called "instructional materials centers."

CHECKLIST XII

CHECKLIST OF PROBLEM SOLVING PRACTICES
RECOMMENDED FOR SCIENCE TEACHER USE*

A. SENSING AND DEFINING PROBLEMS

To what extent do you:

_____ Help pupils sense situations involving personal and social problems?

_____ Help pupils recognize specific problems in those situations?

_____ Help pupils in isolating the single major idea of a problem?

_____ Help pupils state problems as definite and concise questions?

_____ Help pupils pick out and define the key words as a means of getting a better understanding of the problem?

_____ Help pupils evaluate problems in terms of personal and social needs?

_____ Help pupils to be aware of the exact meaning of word-groups and shades of meaning of words in problems involving the expression of ideas?

_____ Present overview lessons to raise significant problems?

_____ Permit pupils to discuss possible problems for study?

_____ Encourage personal interviews about problems of individual interest?

B. COLLECTING EVIDENCE ON PROBLEMS

To what extent do you:

_____ Provide a wide variety of sources of information?

_____ Help pupils develop skill in using reference sources?

_____ Help pupils develop skill in note taking?

_____ Help pupils develop skill in using reading aids in books?

_____ Help pupils evaluate information pertinent to the problem?

_____ Provide laboratory demonstrations for collecting evidence on a problem?

_____ Provide controlled experiments for collecting evidence on a problem?

_____ Help pupils develop skill in interviewing to secure evidence on a problem?

_____ Provide for using the resources of the community in securing evidence on a problem?

_____ Provide for using visual aids in securing evidence on a problem?

_____ Evaluate the pupils' ability for collecting evidence on a problem as carefully as you evaluate their knowledge of facts?

C. ORGANIZING EVIDENCE ON PROBLEMS

To what extent do you:

_____ Help pupils develop skill in arranging data?

_____ Help pupils develop skill in making graphs of data?

_____ Help pupils make use of deductive reasoning in areas best suited?

_____ Provide opportunity for pupils to make summaries of data?

_____ Help pupils distinguish relevant from irrelevant data?

_____ Provide opportunity for pupils to make outlines of data?

_____ Evaluate the pupils' ability to organize evidence on a problem as carefully as you evaluate their knowledge of facts?

* Burton, William H. et al. Op. cit., pp. 430-432.

D. INTERPRETING EVIDENCE ON PROBLEMS

To what extent do you:

_____ Help pupils select the important ideas related to the problem?

_____ Help pupils identify the different relationships which may exist between the important ideas?

_____ Help pupils see the consistencies and weaknesses in data?

_____ Help pupils state relationships as generalizations which may serve as hypotheses?

_____ Evaluate the pupils' ability for interpreting evidence as carefully as you evaluate their knowledge of facts?

E. SELECTING AND TESTING HYPOTHESES

To what extent do you:

_____ Help pupils judge the significance or pertinency of data?

_____ Help pupils check hypotheses with recognized authorities?

_____ Help pupils make inferences from facts and observations?

_____ Help pupils devise controlled experiments suitable for testing hypotheses?

_____ Help pupils recognize and formulate assumptions basic to a given hypothesis?

_____ Help pupils recheck data for possible errors in interpretation?

_____ Evaluate the pupils' ability for selecting and testing hypotheses as carefully as you evaluate their knowledge of facts?

F. FORMULATING CONCLUSIONS

To what extent do you:

_____ Help pupils formulate conclusions on the basis of tested evidence?

_____ Help pupils evaluate their conclusions in the light of the assumptions they set up for the problem?

_____ Help pupils apply their conclusions to new situations?

_____ Evaluate the pupils' ability to formulate conclusions as carefully as you evaluate their knowledge of facts?

SCIENCE RESOURCE KITS

Because resources beyond the textbook and classroom library are essential to develop depth, breadth and adequacy of scientific knowledge, it is recommended practice that book and nonreading media appropriate for classroom development of basic concepts be organized into resource teaching kits. A variety of commercially prepared kits is available which, if they coincide with the local science course of study, can make a valuable contribution by enriching science teaching. In order to assure the availability of supporting media uniquely applicable to local science courses of study, many districts have built their own science teaching kits.

Many schools with well-organized science programs make their own kits. These kits differ from the commercial kits in that there are many homemade kits, each containing a variety of materials designed to teach concepts in only one topic or area of science. In this way there would be kits on sound, light, color, expansion and contraction, magnets, electromagnets, electricity, weather, the earth and sun, earth science, and so forth. Often suggested activities, together with instructions, are included in the kit. Sometimes, for those teachers who are inexperienced in science, a list of equipment is also enclosed, accompanied by drawings or pictures of special equipment with which the teacher might be unfamiliar . . .

The chief advantage of these homemade kits is that their contents can be geared to the objectives of the school science program and to the suggested activities that are a part of the program.[149]

In Los Angeles, California, 600 kits are available upon request to any classroom teacher. In San Angelo, California, a series of science kits has been devised to:

provide equipment, library books, and filmstrips for areas being taught. Coordinated by the science supervisor, the units are rotated in six-week periods. Thus, each teacher has access to more than 450 items of equipment, 300 library books, and some 250 filmstrips to teach science.[150]

SELECTING RESOURCES—A SHARED RESPONSIBILITY

The school librarian, the science supervisor, the curriculum director and the classroom teacher all have an important role to play in selecting materials to be included in the school library, in the science classroom collection, in teaching kits, and in the science laboratory collection. Whether the book, the filmstrip, the recording, or the model are to be used in the library, the classroom, the laboratory, or in the student's home, evaluating the educational validity of resources demands the competence of those particularly versed in the specialized field of scientific knowledge. Therefore, science media selection is a shared responsibility.

LITERARY-BASED SCIENCE UNITS

The necessity of providing library resources to compensate for the limitations of the textbook frequently results in science teacher and librarian designing cooperatively a library-based science unit. A science unit with the comprehensive coverage found in the library-based unit, "Exploring Our Universe" (See Table XVI) could never be offered if teacher and students were restricted to science classroom or science textbook. The science teacher relies on the library and its resources to bring depth of concept development and breadth of topic coverage as well as to provide learning experiences and activities compatible with individual student interest and needs.

TABLE XVI

OUTLINE OF TOPICS FOR LIBRARY INVESTIGATION

Subject: Science.
Grade: Nine.
Library-based Unit: Exploring Our Universe.

  I. Building historical perspective
      A. Investigating historical concepts of the universe
          Ancient world   Renaissance
          Middle Ages   Modern world

[149] Victor, Edward. Op. cit., p. 217.
[150] National Science Teachers Association. *New Developments in Elementary School Science.* Washington, D.C.: National Science Teachers Association, 1963. p. 34.

B. Becoming acquainted with early astronomers

Thales 640–546 B.C	Giordano Bruno 1548–1600 A.D.
Pythagoras ?–572 B.C	Galileo Galilei 1564–1642 A.D.
Meton ?–432 B.C.	Johann Kepler 1571–1630 A.D.
Aristotle 384–322 B.C.	Hans Lippershey ?–1619 A.D.
Aristarchus 310–230 B.C.	Christian Huygens 1629–1695 A.D.
Archimedes 287–212 B.C.	James Gregory 1638–1675 A.D.
Hipparchus 160–125 B.C.	Isaac Newton 1642–1727 A.D.
Ptolemy ?–150 A.D.	Olaus Roemer 1644–1710 A.D.
Nicolaus Copernicus 1473–	Edmund Halley 1656–1742 A.D.
1540 A.D.	William Herschel 1738–1822 A.D.
Tyco Brahe 1546–1601 A.D.	

II. Exploring the solar system

A. Discovering the characteristics of the sun

Atmosphere	Prominences
Composition and surface	Size
Color	Solar time
Corona	Speed
Description	Storms
Distance from earth and other	Sunspots
planets	Temperature
Energy	Volume
Gravity	
Influence on earth and	
other planets	

B. Discovering the characteristics of the planets

Mercury

Atmosphere	Possibility of life
Composition and surface	Size
Day	Speed
Description	Surface gravity
Distance from sun, earth and	Symbol
other planets	Temperature
Orbit	Year
Phases	

Venus

Atmosphere	Possibility of life
Composition and surface	Size
Day	Speed
Description	Surface gravity
Distance from sun, earth and	Symbol
other planets	Temperature
Orbit	Year
Phases	

Earth

Atmosphere	Seasons
Axis	Shape
Creation theories	Size
Day	Speed
Distance from the sun and	Surface gravity
other planets	Symbol
Orbit	Temperature

Rotation   Weight
Satellites   Year

Mars

Atmosphere   Phases
Canals   Possibility of life
Composition and surface   Size
Day   Speed
Description   Surface gravity
Distance from sun, earth, and   Symbol
  other planets   Temperature
Orbit   Year

Jupiter

Atmosphere   Radio noise
Composition and surface   Roemer light velocity theory
Day   Satellites
Description   Size
Distance from earth and   Speed
  other planets   Surface gravity
Orbit   Symbol
Phases   Temperature
Possibility of life   Year

Saturn

Atmosphere   Possibility of life
Composition and surface   Size
Day   Speed
Description   Surface gravity
Distance from sun, earth, and   Symbol
  other planets   Temperature
Orbit   Year
Phases

Uranus

Atmosphere   Possibility of life
Composition and surface   Satellites
Day   Size
Description   Speed
Distance from sun, earth, and   Surface gravity
  other planets   Symbol
Orbit   Temperature
Phases   Year

Neptune

Atmosphere   Possibility of life
Composition and surface   Size
Day   Speed
Description   Surface gravity
Distance from sun, earth, and   Symbol
  other planets   Temperature
Orbit   Year
Phases

Pluto

Atmosphere   Possibility of life
Composition and surface   Size

Day	Speed
Description	Surface gravity
Distance from sun, earth, and other planets	Symbol
Orbit	Temperature
Phases	Year

III.   Charting the solar system

    A.   Utilizing symbols to indicate planets

    B.   Indicating

Distance from earth in miles	Length of day
Distance from sun in miles	Length of year
Speed in orbit	Moons
Diameter in miles	Atmosphere

IV.   Discovering the characteristics of the moon

    A.   Determining

Atmosphere	Light
Composition and surface	Orbit
Craters	Phases
Day	Tides
Description	Time
Distance from sun, earth, and other planets	Temperature

    B.   Exploring the moon

V.   Discovering the characteristics of stars

    A.   Determining

Brightest	Multiple stars
Composition and surface	Nearest stars
Distance from earth	Sideral time
Double stars	Spiral nebulae
Galaxies	Star clusters
Magnitudes	Temperature
Measuring star distances	Variable stars

    B.   Making a star map

VI.   Exploring space

    A.   Becoming conversant with

Cosmic radiation	Messages from space
Escape from the earth	Missiles
Exploring planets	Principles of space travel
Flying saucers	Problems of space travel
History of man's interest in space	Space biology
International Geophysical Year	Space medicine
Ion engine	Space nutrition
Journey to the moon	Space pathology
Living in space	Space scientists
Lunar base	Space vocations

    B.   Training for space exploration

    C.   Training for space habitation

VII. Probing for facts

A. Using instruments

Astro-camera	Refracting telescope
Binoculars	Spectrograph
Radio telescope	Spectroscope
Reflecting telescope	Zeiss Projection Instrument

B. Using observatories

Allegheny, Pittsburgh, Pennsylvania
Dominion, Victoria, British Columbia
Greenwich, Greenwich, England
Harvard, Cambridge, Massachusetts
Lick, Mount Hamilton, California
Mount Wilson, Pasadena, California
Naval, Washington, District of Columbia
Palomar, Mount Palomar, California
Yerkes, Williams Bay, Wisconsin

C. Visiting planetaria

Adler, Chicago, Illinois
Buhl, Pittsburgh, Pennsylvania
Cleveland, Cleveland, Ohio
Fels, Philadelphia, Pennsylvania
Griffith, Los Angeles, California
Hayden, New York, New York
Morrison, San Francisco, California

VIII. Becoming acquainted with modern astronomers

John Brashear	Maria Mitchell
George Hale	Simon Newcomb
Karl Jansky	Fred Whipple
Percival Lowell	

IX. Exploring astronomy and space as possible areas for earning a living

A. Identifying job possibilities
B. Determining

Advantages	Element of risk
Compensation	Personal qualifications
Disadvantages	Physical qualifications
Educational qualifications	Social significance

THE MODERN MATHEMATICS PROGRAM

Innovation, renovation, change and challenge characterize today's mathematics program. The redesign, restructure, and retooling of the mathematics teaching program have been the direct result of man's pushing back and beyond the frontiers of mathematical knowledge. "The changes in mathematics in progress at the present time are so extensive, so far-reaching in their implications, and so profound that they can be described only as revolutionary."[151] This mathematics revolution has been brought about by two factors: the ever increasing tempo of mathematical research and the impact of automation. The twentieth century has become the

[151] Price, G. Baley. "Progress in Mathematics and Its Implications for the Schools" in *The Revolution in School Mathematics: A Challenge for Administrators and Teachers.* Washington, D.C.: National Council of Teachers of Mathematics, 1961. p. 1.

"golden age of mathematics, since more mathematics, and more profound mathematics, has been created in this period than during all the rest of history."[152]

The automatic digital computing machine has made it possible for calculations to go beyond the limitations of human capacity, space and time.

> . . . computations which were formerly completely impossible can now be made quickly and efficiently. Consider again the launching of a guided missile. The computing machine remains on the ground, but radar supplies information to it about the flight of the missile. The computing machine makes the necessary calculations and through a radar connection, sets the controls in the missile. The flight of the missile can be influenced only during the period the engine is in operation, a period which is usually not more than two or three minutes. No group of human computers could possibly receive the data, make the necessary calculations, and transmit the results back to the missile in so few seconds. The electronic digital computer handles the problem with ease.[153]

Through research, automation and computerization man has gained new insights into the social, scientific, technological and economic functions and applications of mathematics. Modern mathematical programs have been organized by our schools to incorporate into the teaching and learning enterprise those fundamental experiences which will equip students for mathematical literacy in the contemporary, functional meaning of the term.

GOALS BASIC TO MATHEMATICS EDUCATION

The following are goals basic to a mathematics program of excellence:[154]

1. To develop a knowledge and understanding of mathematical principles and practices.
2. To develop an understanding of the structure of mathematics and the nature of proof.
3. To develop skill in the use of problem-solving techniques and computational procedures.
4. To develop an appreciation of the applications of mathematics and its importance in society.
5. To develop a self-sufficiency and independence of thought leading to independent progress.
6. To develop the ability to receive and impart mathematical ideas by both the written and the spoken word.
7. To develop interest, curiosity, and appreciation about mathematical ideas and their significance.

STRONGLY STRUCTURED PROGRAMS

"Today's mathematics program should provide a sequential, integrated curriculum which stresses a knowledge of structure and pattern of mathematics

---

152 Ibid., p. 1.
153 Ibid., pp. 4-5.
154 Pennsylvania Bureau of General and Academic Education. *Mathematics Education in Pennsylvania*. Harrisburg, Pennsylvania: Department of Public Instruction, 1967. unpaged.

as well as computational ability, and provides differentiated challenge for students with varying needs and levels of ability."[155]

BASIC PRINCIPLES

In designing the mathematics program the following principles should guide the selection of teaching and learning experiences:[156]

1. Because every child has his own rate and his own ways of learning and growing, mathematical experiences in number, measurement, and form should be considered on every grade level in terms appropriate to the individual needs, abilities, and interest of each child. Implied in this is opportunity for individualized growth and for a curriculum which provides for continuity in understanding mathematics, for recurrence of opportunities in order to sharpen or broaden concepts, and for practice necessary to produce proficiency in using mathematics.
2. Because certain characteristics seem to be exhibited by children of similar chronological ages, a sequence of major experiences seems pertinent to each grade level. Allowance must be made within each group, however, for individual needs, interests, and abilities if all children are to be challenged to grow.
3. Because mathematics pervades all areas of living, opportunities for development of mathematical understanding pervade all areas of the curriculum.
4. Mathematics gets its meaning from the environment, and understanding mathematics develops greater understanding of the environment. Therefore, children should be given many opportunities to explore mathematical situations, relationships, and possibilities in the environment. An understanding of mathematics occurs only in the mind of the individual; concepts are developed and broadened from many meaningful experiences. Since the quality of thought is revealed in speech and action, the teacher must give each child many opportunities to express and clarify in a variety of ways his understanding of mathematics.

One of the most important contemporary statements of mathematical purposes, principles, and goals is the bulletin *Goals for School Mathematics, The Report of the Cambridge Conference on School Mathematics.*[157] Irving Adler has summarized 12 of the guiding principles set forth in the Cambridge Report as follows:[158]

1. Beginning with the earliest grades there should be a parallel and integrated development of algebra and geometry.
2. Teach for understanding, not merely for manipulative skill.

[155] Ibid.
[156] Grossnickle, Foster E. et al. *Discovering Meanings in Elementary School Mathematics.* 5th edition. New York: Holt, 1968. pp. 11-12.
[157] *Goals for School Mathematics, The Report of the Cambridge Conference on School Mathematics.* Boston, Massachusetts: Educational Services, 1963.
[158] Adler, Irving. "The Cambridge Report: Blueprint or Fantasy?" in *The Arithmetic Teacher*, March 1966, 13:185-186.

3. The first approach to each topic should be intuitive. Use many approaches to illuminate the topics from many sides. Provide experience in the manipulation of physical objects as the basis for abstract learning.

4. Pay serious attention to the development of suitable problem material. In particular, provide the children with problems that give them opportunities to explore and make discoveries that are within their reach.

5. Replace drill for drill's sake by the use of past learnings in new, meaningful situations.

6. Use the spiral approach, in which the same subject arises at different times with increasing degrees of complexity and rigor.

7. Make fuller use of the historical background of a topic to develop an appreciation of how it arose and why it is studied.

8. Many significant mathematical topics can be approached through exciting games, tricks or puzzles. Exploit the recreational aspects of mathematics, especially in the lower grades.

9. Use supplementary pamphlets for individual work by the student who is ready to pursue a topic more broadly and deeply.

10. Show how mathematics is applied in the physical sciences or to other studies of the real world. But keep in mind that many important applications are internal, that is, they are applications to mathematics itself. . . .

11. Aim to develop a growing awareness of the nature of logical reasoning. . . .

12. In the development of postulational thinking avoid excessive delicacy and austerity. If proofs are too long and seem to be only laborious ways of arriving at what seems obvious to the student the deductive method is not likely to look either attractive or powerful.

LIBRARY SUPPORT ESSENTIAL

The necessity of providing instructional media beyond the textbook and conventional classroom resources is stressed as being imperative by authorities in the field of mathematics teaching. For example:

> To support a new program each school system must acquire an adequate *library* of reference material for students and teachers . . . There is much new material that can be read independently by students, and it is necessary that they learn how to use the *library* in the study of mathematics. This type of training is very important in developing the ability of students to do independent work. The *library* is also very helpful to teachers, particularly while they are studying the new programs.[159]

> The resources of the *library* should be used continually to enrich the work in mathematics. *The library is the heart of an enrichment program for the superior learner with special interest in*

159 Ferguson, W. Eugene. "Implementing the New Mathematics Program in Your School" in *The Revolution in School Mathematics: A Challenge for Administrators and Teachers,* Op. cit., p. 47.

mathematics. These students are likely to browse widely among available printed materials of all kinds, seeking information they desire on all matters of interest. Independent reading and study is a high type of learning that should be encouraged and facilitated by having available a well-selected variety of printed materials, including general books, reference books, magazines, bulletins, schedules, and the like.[160]

The Pennsylvania Department of Public Instruction makes the following recommendation:[161]

Much use should be made of diverse teaching aids to provide realism and motivation; an emphasis should be placed on applications of mathematics and interrelationships with other disciplines, particularly the sciences; and there should be extensive use of the laboratory approach . . .

The following learning aids are recommended:

1. Reading materials: books, pamphlets, periodicals, programmed topics, and texts of mathematics.
2. Audio-visual equipment: overhead, slide, movie, and opaque projectors, tapes, tape recorders, projectuals.
3. Manipulative materials: models, charts, boards, cards, discs, games, symbols.
4. Measuring instruments: sextant, level, spherometer, balances, calipers, transit.
5. Construction materials: cardboard, plastic, metals, wood, tools.
6. Computing devices: Napier's rods, desk calculator, computer, abacus, slide rule.

ENRICHED UNITS AND DIFFERENTIATED INSTRUCTION

Instructional resource support of the modern mathematics program is so valued by the National Council of Teachers of Mathematics that it has devoted its entire twenty-seventh[162] and its entire twenty-eighth[163] yearbooks to an exploration of enrichment resources and procedures.

Enrichment is the most widely accepted practice for providing learning experiences for the talented child. . . .

Inherent in the idea of enrichment are the concepts of *breadth* and *depth*. Breadth implies that the enrichment material will be broader in scope than that which occurs in the standard textbook program but that it will be *related* and *continuous with* this program, and *appropriate* for elementary (and secondary) school children. . . .

160 Grossnickle, Foster E. et al. Op. cit., p. 440.
161 Pennsylvania Bureau of General and Academic Education. Op. cit., unpaged.
162 *Enrichment Mathematics for the Grades.* Twenty-Seventh Yearbook. Washington, D.C.: National Council of Teachers of Mathematics. 1963.
163 *Enrichment Mathematics for the Grades.* Twenty-Eighth Yearbook. Washington, D.C.: National Council of Teachers of Mathematics. 1964.

Whereas the concept of breadth is concerned with the introduction of *new but related* topics, the concept of depth is concerned with developing new insights into what is *presently* taught. Jung says that depth in the learning, or fuller utilization of content, involves emphasis upon development of inventiveness and reflective thinking. It is best developed by:

1. Confronting the student with challenging problems—but problems within his power of comprehension.
2. Leading him from the very beginning to see the futility of thought without dependable data.
3. Maturing him in those methods of disciplined thought which have been found to facilitate the work of mathematicians.
4. Providing opportunity to discover and to find original solutions.
5. Steadily encouraging him to new levels of creative thinking.

It should be noted that the concepts of breadth and depth are not mutually exclusive. On the contrary, the outcomes of depth-in-learning can be achieved as well through topics that are new, but appropriate and related, as through topics that are part of the present programs. Enrichment, whether through breadth within appropriate topics, or through depth, or through both, is the richest reservoir of content and experiences for talented children in elementary (and secondary) school mathematics.[164]

Consistent checking of the publications of the National Council of Teachers of Mathematics is imperative if the librarian is to keep conversant with trends and materials in mathematics.

The librarian and the mathematics teacher cooperatively can bring depth and breadth to the mathematics program by building learning experiences which are significant, appropriate and related but are not possible if the class be limited to the information contained in the textbook and to the resources of the classroom. Frequently library-based units are designed and structured cooperatively by mathematics teacher and librarian to provide learning experiences possible only through the use of library resources. The unit, "Money, Interest, Banking, and Investments" (See Table XVII) offers such a diversity of topic inclusion that it would be impossible to teach so comprehensive a unit without the support of an adequate library collection.

The necessity of teaching mathematics in a differentiated manner in order to encourage students to "new levels of creative thinking" requires teacher willingness to preplan with the librarian for the timely availability of appropriate resources.

Power in mathematics is developed not by disorganized random experiences, however interesting they may be, but by confronting children with challenging questions and problems that are within their power of comprehension. Children should be given many opportunities to discover informal solutions and generalizations. They should be led to see the necessity of dependable data as a basis of thinking and action, and they should become familiar with

[164] *Enrichment Mathematics for the Grades.* Twenty-Seventh Yearbook. Op. cit., pp. 26-27.

the ways in which reliable information can be gathered. They should have experiences that will gradually develop in them the methods of logical, systematic, disciplined thought that facilitate all mathematical work and lead to creative thinking.

By differentiated instruction we mean making adjustments of class organization, curriculum, methods, and materials so as to adapt instruction as far as is practical to the wide range of differences in mental ability, achievement, interests and needs that exist in almost all classes, even in classes in mathematics for superior learners. Under such circumstances the teacher must make a special effort to meet the needs of individual pupils and to enrich the work for all of the more able children, especially those who seem to have unusual ability in mathematics. . . . Differentiated goals and instruction are practical procedures that can be used in any classroom, regardless of the ability level of the children.[165]

A media support program capable of meeting the developmental needs of the mathematics program and the personal and educational needs of the student is the result of careful, competent teacher planning with the librarian. Just as "it is becoming increasingly evident that there is no place in curriculum for accidental or incidental science projects conducted just for the sake of 'doing something scientific,' "[166] so it is increasingly evident that there is no place in the curriculum for accidental or incidental mathematics projects, conducted under the guise of "enrichment."

TABLE XVII

LIST OF TOPICS FOR LIBRARY INVESTIGATION

Subject: Mathematics.
Grade: Eight.
Library-based Unit: MONEY, INTEREST, BANKING, AND INVESTMENTS

1. Bank draft	16. Coin collecting as a hobby
2. Bank holiday	17. Consumer credit
3. Bankruptcy	18. Counterfeiting
4. Barter	19. Credit buying
5. "Bear" market	20. Credit cards
6. Better Business Bureau	21. Credit union
7. Blue chip issues	22. Debtors' prison
8. British Mint	23. Deficit financing
9. "Bull" market	24. Dow-Jones average
10. Bullion	25. Foreign currency
11. Business index	26. Foreign exchange
12. Capital investment	27. Gold reserve
13. Cashier's check	28. Gold standard
14. Certified public accountant	29. Graphs: history, construction interpretation
15. Check credit	

[165] Grossnickle, Foster E. et al. Op. cit., pp. 434-435.
[166] Conner, Forrest E. and William J. Ellena. Op. cit., p. 261.

30. Gross national product
31. Hard money
32. History of banking
33. History of money
34. History of the stock exchange
35. History of United States currency
36. How a bank operates
37. How the stock exchange operates
38. Legal tender
39. Money orders
40. Mutual funds
41. Personal loan
42. Printing paper money
43. Purchasing power of the current dollar
44. Rates of interest
45. Silver certificates
46. Statistics: interpretation, verification, use
47. Stock broker
48. Telegraphing money
49. Ticker tape
50. Travelers checks
51. Types of bonds
52. Types of stocks
53. Usury
54. Wall Street
55. Wall Street Journal
56. World Bank

CHALLENGING THE GIFTED

The mathematically talented student is entitled to a mathematics program compatible with his special mathematics capabilities. The librarian and the mathematics teacher in today's school must realize that

> . . . the program that is good and necessary for the average child is not a sufficient program for the talented child. Further the program that is balanced for the average child may indeed be an *unbalanced* program for the talented. Or stated otherwise, it may well be that the program that leans heavily toward the mathematical point of view, and would therefore be an unbalanced one for the average child, may be very appropriate for the talented child. Since it is characteristic of talented children to see relationships and make generalizations more quickly than average children and since these characteristics are important in mathematics learning, it would seem reasonable to provide a program that capitalizes these abilities.[167]

Talent is not identical with measured intelligence (I.Q.). Many children with above average intelligence are not mathematically talented. Just as it is unrealistic to expect each student with an above average I.Q. to be a talented artist or a gifted musician so it is unrealistic and grossly unfair to expect each student with an above average I.Q. to be capable of gifted performance in all academic subjects. The teacher and librarian wishing to identify the mathematically talented child should be guided by the following list of characteristics attributed to the mathematically gifted:[168]

1. Sensitivity to, awareness of, and curiosity regarding the quantitative aspect of things within the environment.
2. Quickness in perceiving, comprehending, understanding, and dealing effectively with quantity and the quantitative aspect of things within the environment.
3. Ability to think and work abstractly and symbolically when dealing with quantity and quantitative ideas.

[167] *Enrichment Mathematics for the Grades.* Twenty-Seventh Yearbook. Op. cit., p. 25.
[168] Ibid., pp. 28-29.

4. Ability to communicate quantitative ideas effectively to others, both orally and in writing; and to readily receive and assimilate quantitative ideas in the same way.
5. Ability to perceive mathematical patterns, structures, relationships, and inter-relationships.
6. Ability to think and perform in quantitative situations in a flexible rather than in a stereotype manner: with insight, imagination, creativity, originality, self-direction, independence, eagerness, concentration, and persistence.
7. Ability to think and reason analytically and deductively; ability to think and reason inductively, and to generalize.
8. Ability to transfer learning to new or novel "untaught" quantitative situations.
9. Ability to apply mathematical learning to social situations, to other curriculum areas, and the like.
10. Ability to remember and retain that which has been learned.

The librarian and the teacher must not confuse creative thinking ability in mathematics with measured intelligence or the I.Q. Creative thinking ability in mathematics as in science or in any other subject area is closely related to subject matter achievement and interest. There is no set pattern of subject interest common to students with high measured intelligence; talent and creativity are not indicated by an I.Q. When planning enrichment mathematics experiences the teacher and the librarian should relate difficulty of mathematics performance demanded with demonstrated mathematics ability and interest, not with an intelligence quotient.

Programmed instruction is an effective way to challenge the mathematically gifted learner. When commercially prepared programs commensurate with individual student ability and interest are not available, the school librarian and the teacher can design and structure learning programs to meet these student needs. The following Pittman guide (See Chapter Five for an explanation of the Pittman method of media programming) was developed to enable a talented sixth grader to delve more deeply into the realm of Roman numerals.

EXAMPLE IX

THE PITTMAN LEARNING GUIDE—ROMAN NUMERALS

Card 1

Mathematics
Grade 6
Topic: Learning To Use Roman Numerals

Sub-topic 1: How did the Romans write their numbers 1 through 1,000?

SOURCE A—
Lauber, Patricia. *The Story of Numbers*. Random House. 1961. pp. 46-53.

or

SOURCE B—
The New Book of Knowledge. vol. 16. Grolier. pp. 309-310.

or

SOURCE C—
The Reader's Digest Almanac. Reader's Digest. Check the Index for Roman Numerals.

or

SOURCE D—
The World Almanac. Doubleday. Check the Index for Roman Numerals.

Sub-topic 2: How did the Romans add numbers?

SOURCE—
Simon, Leonard. *The Day the Numbers Disappeared.* McGraw-Hill. 1963. p. 37.

Card 2

Sub-topic 3: How did the Romans subtract numbers?

SOURCE—
Simon, Leonard. *The Day the Numbers Disappeared.* McGraw-Hill. 1963. p. 37.

Sub-topic 4: How did the Romans multiply numbers?

SOURCE—
Highland, Esther. *The How and Why Wonder Book of Mathematics.* Grosset & Dunlap. 1961. p. 31.

Optional Activity 1: Review what you have learned about Roman numerals by using the Cyclo-teacher* with the following:

Cycle M46—sides 1 and 2
Cycle M47—sides 1 and 2
Cycle M48—sides 1 and 2

Optional Activity 2: Prepare a transparency or a poster showing Roman numerals for:

1	100	4,000	25,000	1,000,000
10	1,000	5,000	50,000	5,000,000
50	2,000	10,000	100,000	10,000,000

Card 3

Optional Activity 2: SOURCE—
The World Book. vol. 16. Field Enterprises. p. 395.

Optional Activity 3: Make a series of flash cards to be used in testing your class's ability to interpret Roman numerals.

Optional Activity 4: Place on transparencies problems in addition, subtraction and multiplication using Roman numerals you wish to present to your class.

Optional Activity 5: The Statue of Liberty holds in her left hand a tablet on which the date July IV, MDCCLXXVI is written. Can you translate that date into arabic numerals? Do you know why this date is significant?

---

* The cyclo-teacher is a self instructional teaching machine with programmed cycles for each of the disciplines on the elementary and junior high school level. This machine and its accompanying cycles are only sold by Field Educational Publications, Inc., 609 Mission Street, San Francisco, California 94105.

LIBRARY SUPPORT IMPERATIVE FOR SCIENCE AND MATHEMATICS PROGRAMS OF EXCELLENCE

The planned integration of library resources and services is imperative for the implementation of science and mathematics programs of excellence. It is upon the timely availability of appropriate knowledge building and knowledge extending media that depth and breadth of scientific and mathematical literacy depends. Library support of these two academic areas is an effective means of capitalizing on student interest and of nurturing special ability. Library resources are both the way and the means of individualizing and personalizing the science and mathematics programs. It is in the library that all students—the below average, the average, and the above average—should find resources and guidance which will enable them to learn in their own way and at their own special rate. It is in the school library where the student can rely on the concerned guidance of a special resource teacher to help him discover materials uniquely compatible with his personal needs and abilities whether his need be for information or recreation, acceleration or remediation.

The science and mathematics collection in today's school library should be as divergent as the students themselves. Here the student should find resources of an informational and of a recreational nature; here he should expect to find resources to match his own private quest either for knowledge or for relaxation. Here he will find background information on the history of science and mathematics, biographies of scientists and mathematicians, and comprehensive handbooks of science and mathematics experiments and projects. Here he should find not only science fact but science fiction; not only mathematical guides to computation but mathematical "brain teasers" and "nuts to crack." Here he should find not only printed resources but audiovisual "software" and "hardware" as well. Here he should find basic scientific and mathematical instruments available for his use. Here he should discover that *all* of the resources, instruments and equipment can be borrowed for home use as well as for use at school.

Since adequacy of understanding and optimum individual achievement are our educational goals, schools can no longer defend restricting the use of library resources to the school itself. How can educators defend requiring students to return to the school to utilize resources? Resources are *ideas* not *things*. How can an educator in conscience restrict the circulation and dissemination of ideas? Why should the student be required to return to the school at night or on weekends to utilize resources that are easily portable? It is neither logical nor humane to restrict library resources to in-school use. Student time and energy are in too short supply to permit the needless wasting or dissipation of either.

In today's school library it should be common practice to have available for home use all library resources, equipment and instruments. *All* library instructional materials should circulate be they book, pamphlet, chart, study print, record, tape, slide, filmstrip, model, object, instrument, or kit. If cost of these resources be thought too high to permit the circulation, then it is imperative that we reassess our values and realign our priorities to match our educational goals and objectives with our practices. What school district hesitates to equip each football player with an outfit costing $200 or more knowing full well it will be ripped, torn and rolled in the mud! What school hesitates to purchase multiple footballs though each one cost approximately the same as a functional inexpensive microscope, spectroscope or telescope? A school with sincere concern for the quality of its science and mathematics programs will provide ample resources for the students on the elementary and secondary levels to extend their scientific and mathematical understanding beyond the confines of their classroom, their library, and their school.

THE SCHOOL LIBRARY—SCIENCE AND MATHEMATICS LEARNING LABORATORY

The claim of the modern science and mathematics programs to educational excellence goes far beyond the redesigned and restructured courses of study. Course content is only one of several fundamental changes. Two other basic changes essential for educational excellence are new patterns of instruction and new teacher attitude toward learning. The new emphasis in instruction is on direct participation of each student in the science and math learning process. Learning is the focus of teacher attention not instruction per se. Likewise, the locus of teacher concern is on individual student achievement rather than class attainment. Teacher emphasis has shifted away from the class to the individual and from memorization to functional application with utility the proof of learning. The modern school library is the science and mathematics learning laboratory where the student comes as a member of a class, of a group or as an individual to build and to practice scientific and mathematical literacy (See Figure IX) in an information permeated environment conducive to optimum individual student "perceiving, behaving and becoming" scientifically and mathematically literate.

FIGURE IX
BLUEPRINT FOR LITERACY

L̲ ibrary functioning as a learning laboratory

I̲ ndividualizes instruction and expedites learning.

T̲ eachers and librarians planning and working together as a team

E̲ xtend knowledge beyond classroom and subject boundaries.

R̲ eading, viewing, and listening with purpose and direction in the library

A̲ pplies critical thinking skills in a context of meaningful utility.

C̲ ompetent, purposeful, constructive application of knowledge is the

Y̲ ardstick for measuring the educational effectiveness of the school library

program.

9 The School Library as an Integral Part of the Guidance Program

*We believe in the dignity and worth of the individual and it is our unshakeable purpose to protect and preserve that dignity. We believe that every person should be enabled to achieve the best that is in him.**

In a democracy the caliber of each individual citizen is of paramount importance, since each citizen is free to participate in decisions affecting all (See Chapter One). Our concern as educators is to prepare our children and youth to live intelligent, purposeful, constructive, creative, healthy, happy lives. The basic tenet underlying our educational design is to nurture and encourage the positive development of each student's personality as well as to encourage the optimum development of his intellect. Since education looks "to the nature of man and to the good of society" our schools are obligated to provide ample opportunity for each student "to perceive, to behave, to become" a creative, compassionate, thinking human being capable of making a positive contribution as a member of our free society.

The constant goal of American education is to encourage each student to learn how to think in an intelligently reasoned, rational, constructive behavior pattern. Unfortunately man is not born a reasonable creature. Man is born with the same emotions, drives, and instincts common to the caveman. Mankind's long, tortuous struggle to achieve control over his nature and to channel his energies and drives into constructive action is in essence the history of civilization. The battle to retain control over man's emotions and thereby remain civilized is never won—each new generation must refight the battle. Organized general education is the tool society has developed and employs to civilize its young citizens. The problem challenging those who teach is, how to seize the imagination of the young so they will be committed to the ideal of personal excellence. Our greatest challenge is that of devising methods and means of teaching our young people to think intelligently and creatively within a context of positive value judgments. The degree to which we as educators are successful in thus civilizing our youth will determine the fate of democracy itself.

All who teach share the concern of the guidance counselors to enable each student to build a positive attitude toward himself as an individual, as a

* Gardner, John W. Op. cit., p. 156.

student, as a worker, and as a contributing member of a family, a school, a church, a community, a nation and a world. The shocking increase in crime in our society gives cause for alarm. In the period from 1960 to 1967 crime increased 88% while the population increased but 10%.[169] Decency fails to appeal to far too many of our youth. In large segments of our population we have not developed a positive attitude toward self and toward society. The seriousness of meeting immediately and competently the stern demands of our times requires that we recognize the inadequacies of our past attempts and begin at once to provide an innovative guidance program which will capture the imagination of each child. We must incorporate within the framework of our teaching ample experiences from the affective area of learning. For as a man thinketh so is he!

PURPOSE OF FORMAL GUIDANCE PROGRAM

The educational goal of enabling and encouraging each student to achieve self-perspective, self-understanding, self-realization, self-development, self-fulfillment and self-respect requires an organized, formal, on-going guidance program. "The objective of all educational guidance should be to stimulate the individual to make the most of his potentialities."[170] The American School Counselor Association has developed the following rationale to guide the thinking and action of those concerned with meeting the needs of students:[171]

THE PUPIL

Each pupil is a unique ind⸱⸱⸱⸱ual. His behavior is purposeful and represents his attempt to develop in society as he perceives it.
Each pupil has a right to acceptance as a human being, regardless of the nature and results of his behavior, beliefs, and inherent characteristics.
Each pupil has a right to individual self-development and self-fulfillment. The extent and nature of self-fulfillment is directly a function of the extent to which the individual possess real and informed personal freedom.
Each pupil has a right to self-direction as well as responsibility for making decisions and living with the consequence of these decisions.

THE SCHOOL

The school in a democracy has as its basic purpose the education and development of all pupils for individual fulfillment.
The primary method of the school is group instruction. The school counselor contributes to the school's attempt to educate all children by providing services which directly support instruction and those responsible for it. The school counselor also contributes to the total psycho-social development of pupils by providing direct non-instructional services to them.

169 *U.S. News and World Report.* May 20, 1968. p. 50.
170 *Pursuit of Excellence.* Op. cit., p. 30.
171 American School Counselor Association. *Statement of Policy for Secondary School Counselors.* . . . Washington, D.C.: American Personnel and Guidance Association, 1964. pp. 3-4.

Because the school is a democratic institution using group objectives and methods, and because learning, maturing and self-realization are inevitably individual processes, a paradox or conflict for the student is implicit within our educational structure. Therefore, the school counselor recognizes such conflict as a natural part of the educative process in a democracy and sees the mediation of this conflict as a very important part of his role.

SOCIETY

Change and the potential for change are inherent in a democratic society. Thus, the individual who is to live with personal satisfaction and who is to achieve self-fulfillment in a democratic society must understand not only the nature by which he as an individual can best adapt to change and best adapt change to himself.

A democratic society provides a great many resources and opportunities for development to individuals during their life span. Each individual needs the competence to distinguish and select these resources and opportunities most appropriate for him.

The strength and health of a democratic society is ultimately dependent upon the contributions each of its members makes to others. If in a democratic society each individual is to be free to decide for himself the contributions he will attempt to make, then it is essential that each individual have substantial self-understanding and personal perspective on which he can base his decisions.

TYPES OF GUIDANCE

The formal guidance program encompasses personal guidance, social guidance, educational guidance, and vocational guidance. Each faculty member shares with the guidance department its responsibility for implementing all phases of the guidance program. No goal of the school's educational endeavor is of greater significance or of greater challenge than that of encouraging and enabling each student to become a fully actualized, creative, self-motivated and self-disciplined person. To achieve this goal the guidance program must permeate the totality of the educational plan and endeavor; each teacher must hold authentic concern and respect for the individuality and potential promise of each student.

PERSONAL GUIDANCE

While each student is a unique individual he shares with other human beings the five basic needs or drives common to all:[172] physiological needs; safety and security needs; love needs; esteem needs; self-actualization needs. These needs are of hierarchical relationship—the fulfillment of any given category rests on the fulfillment of prior needs. If the child is hungry, insecure, unwanted and unloved he will have little concern for things of the mind. This psychological fact brings into sharp focus our need to be concerned for devising ways and means of compensating for a child's environ-

[172] Commission on Imperatives in Education. Op. cit., pp. 79-80.

mental disadvantages. Project Head Start* is an example of a Federally funded program designed to administer to the child's physiological, security and love needs before attempting to teach him to learn.

Each teacher must develop his own self-perspective in viewing his importance to a child's development of the concept of "self." The child's search for "self" is an on-going, life-long accumulative process—each teacher and each life experience has an impact value that is sure to leave its mark. The child's search for identity becomes the youth's search for identity which becomes in turn the adult's search for identity. Each stage in the development of "self" reflects contemporary experiences whether they be of a positive or of a negative quality. The stature of a child's concept of "self" is a composite of all of his experiences in his many worlds—at home, at school, at church, at play. The school has a vital role to play in off-setting the negative aspects of the child's environment at home and in the community as well as in building a positive attitude toward himself as a learner, as a citizen, and as a human being.

The "self" image of the child in large measure is set by the climate in the classroom, the laboratory, the school library, the gymnasium, the auditorium. Each student has the right in a democratic society to expect and to receive authentic concern and respect for his individuality. Such concern transcends things of an academic nature and encompasses things of the mind, the spirit, the heart, and the soul. The teacher of excellence is concerned not only with the intellectual development of the student but also with his cultural, social, moral, and spiritual development as well. Unfortunately, the Supreme Court decision outlawing the saying of prayers in a public school has been misinterpreted by some to mean that schools are no longer to be concerned with things of an ethical, moral, or spiritual nature. This is contrary to fact; in a democracy we must be concerned with the quality and the caliber of each citizen, for freedom becomes license when removed fom a context of shared responsibility for continued decency. It behooves each teacher to focus the attention of the student on permanent ethical, moral, and spiritual values so that these values will become an integral part of the student's stream of consciousness, a basis for shaping and directing his thought and his action.

> . . . responsibility must be related most clearly to freedom of action. The consequences of mistake must never be too costly or freedom defeats itself and dire consequences may come to the individual and to all of those with whom he is associated. This is the delicate balance that parents and teachers and school administrators must maintain as they give constructive directions to the actions of those who look to them with confidence for guidance.
>
> The person who is free is well informed. There is nothing more effective in releasing the human spirit from the bondage of superstition, apprehensions, and fear than knowledge and understanding. And there is nothing that builds in people the power to resist

---

* Project Head Start is the Office of Economic Opportunity's program to give pre-school children from disadvantaged backgrounds, and their families, a comprehensive program of education, medical care, social services and nutritional help which they need.

the forces which would dwarf their personalities, blemish their characters, instill in them low standards of ethical conduct, and deny them freedom more than knowledge and understanding.[173]

It is imperative that those who teach re-examine their commitment to preserve, strengthen and safe-guard the American way of life. Consistently throughout our history decency and moral fortitude have been an integral part of the American ideal. Today we are faced with reassessing the value of continued commitment to basic decency. Our responsibility as educators extends beyond the cognitive area into the affective area of learning.

How can the moral fabric of society be strengthened? How can students be taught the true meaning of freedom and responsibility? There is, of course, no one body of content, no cluster of experience, no tried and true procedure that will accomplish this end, but it may be helpful to teachers and administrators—indeed, to everyone—to call attention to a few possibilities.

Let students be concerned with that which makes men free—not that all knowledge does not in some measure serve this end—beginning with that which directly and at the moment effects this purpose, be it a circumstance on the playground, a situation in the management of the school, or some incident in literature or history within their range of comprehension. (To achieve this requires an effective library program.)

Let an honest curiosity be cultivated in all students. Let them be inquisitive about everything about them and explore everything that is singular and rare. See that no restraining bounds in books or in subjects are imposed; and if there be eminent people, momentous events, or notable places in the school neighborhood, make them a part of their program of studies.

Let them be curious in their search for reasons why this or that happened or a particular procedure was followed, but let them be seasoned to submit to truth whenever they have found it.

Let them thoroughly sift through everything they read or each parcel of information that comes to their attention and seek more than one authority for substantiation of a fact or truth. An individual with a free and open mind knows full well that an assertion made by even an eminent man or woman is not necessarily true.

Let them put whatever they have learned into a hundred different forms to see if they rightly comprehend it and have made it their very own.

Let them put every lesson they have learned into practice whenever and wherever possible so that they learn at an early age the subtle art of transposing learning into living.

---

[173] Ibid., p. 65.

Let them have their turns in discussion and discourse, parry with ideas, learn to discern, learn to discriminate and to choose, taste strange new fruits of learning, and try their wings while they can be guided.

Let them laugh and play and strive to excel their companions in ability and vigor, for the youthful spirit that is bridled and curbed and that does not have a chance to try and prove its strength is soon dull and stagnant—more fitted for subjugation than for probing into new domains.

Let them avoid vain and childish pretensions to being more accomplished than they really are.

Let them discover and acknowledge their errors and misconceptions wherever they exist, knowing that as such shortcomings are fully recognized by themselves, new measures of strength and stature and new dimensions of freedom are added to their lives.

Let them drink deeply of the satisfaction that comes from work well done; let them know that work is not a curse.

Let them develop a sense of freedom and responsibility by living it, by helping to shape the standards that will guide their present and future actions.

Let them know that he who acts unjustly not only wrongs himself but harms others.[174]

VOCATIONAL GUIDANCE

All who teach share with the guidance counselor the responsibility for planning and implementing an effective formal vocational guidance program. Every opportunity should be taken by counselor, teacher, and librarian[175] to integrate vocational awareness into the fabric of the teaching and learning program. Each course of study (academic and nonacademic) should be scrutinized to discover appropriate vocational integration opportunities. Beginning in the primary grades and continuing throughout his school career each child should be encouraged to ask himself "What can I be?"

Often vocational information is a natural component of a teaching program. For example, the first grade beginning reader series, "I Want To Be"* combines learning about occupations while building social studies concepts and providing practice of reading skills. The series includes 36 occupations from such diverse fields as: doctor, lawyer, telephone operator, carpenter, teacher, scientist, newspaper reporter, space pilot, restaurant owner, baseball player, musician, homemaker, and zoo keeper. This series is typical of the type of library resources having multiple teaching values—they are not only reading skill builders but social and vocational awareness builders as well.

Through the planned integration of library resources with teaching pro-

---

* "I Want To Be" Series. Chicago, Illinois: Children's Press, 1956–1962.

174 Ibid., pp. 67-68.

175 American Association of School Librarians. Op. cit., pp. 20, 82.

grams many opportunities can be provided to build and extend student knowledge of vocations. For example, in social studies a unit on transportation offers opportunity for the student to become acquainted with a wide variety of occupations possible in the field of transportation (See Table XIV). A science unit such as "Exploring Our Universe" (Table XVI) offers an excellent opportunity for students to become acquainted with the space vocational spectrum.

In addition to acquainting students with all types and kinds of vocational possibilities the responsibility of the school extends to enabling and encouraging each student to appraise his own capabilities when exploring the requirements of any vocation. It is imperative that guidance counselors, teachers, and librarians deal with students in an honest, humane and realistic manner when helping each to equate his potentialities with the demands of any vocation. Personalizing the student's understanding of job requirements and demands is basic to preparing the student to deal realistically with his own future as a wage earner. It is not logical nor is it kind to have a student set his heart on being an astronaut when he knows he lacks the physical equilibrium to stand on a ten foot ladder!

The school is a testing ground for measuring a student's vocational potentialities. Here the student should learn how to measure his own capabilities against the demands of a vocation. Here he should be taught how to investigate the requirements of a vocation under the headings of: physical requirements; mental requirements; emotional requirements; academic requirements; training requirements; persistence requirements; skill requirements; monetary requirements.

Having identified the specific requirements he should then be encouraged to measure his own abilities, disabilities, and potentialities against the requirements of the vocation. It is imperative that the vocational guidance program provide young people with a process of self-evaluation to help them make intelligent choices.[176]

> To help each student to come to know himself, to study the world of work and of job opportunities, to gain experience in matching himself with job possibilities, to discern whether he has the ability to profit from the training involved, and to master the mechanics of getting and holding a job is a clear purpose of the school. A major goal of institutions of learning at all levels is to prepare properly motivated and highly skilled workers enthusiastically devoting a major part of their time, effort, and thought to productive work. This all important end cannot and must not be left to chance or be merely an incident by-product of the educative process. The school must not only see this as a major purpose, it must be willing to do something about it. The requirements are:
>
>   1. A more direct focus of curriculum upon vocational objectives.
>   2. Opportunity for young people to know themselves.
>   3. Expert counseling.
>   4. Appropriate school maintained records.

176 Commission on Imperatives in Education. Op. cit., pp. 32-33.

We do the student no favor by perpetuating the false belief that anyone is equally capable of doing everything in a democracy. Man is not created equal in physical and emotional stamina, in mental and creative potential, in stick-to-itiveness, in drive. Our responsibility is to encourage and to enable each student to aspire to the highest of which he is capable and then to help him see clearly how to set about preparing himself to accomplish his goal. Education is a means of enabling each young citizen to build self-awareness and self-understanding to the degree that he will temper childlike dreaming with mature facing of reality.

In *Schools for the 60's* the NEA Project on Instruction focused attention on the need for schools to develop each student's vocational competence and flexibility.[177]

> Competence in basic understandings and skills is still the best contribution of the elementary schools to future workers, but the schools can also help students learn about the world of work. Depending upon the students and upon associated factors in the community, the public high schools should provide some direct or preparatory vocational experience in some of the following ways:
>   1. College bound students need opportunities that provide initial preparation for their life's work. For example, it is becoming increasingly difficult for a student to pursue a collegiate course of study in science and engineering unless he has given special attention to the study of mathematics at the secondary school level.
>   2. Students who do not plan to continue their formal schooling beyond the secondary level should receive some direct vocational education before graduation. This training should relate to the new industries and skills the economy requires, rather than the outmoded trades perpetuated in some present-day vocational courses.
>   3. Students among the disadvantaged or culturally deprived need school programs that stress basic skills, relate school experience to work experience and on-the-job training, and help to make up for cultural deficiencies. It is important, however, that these students not be treated intellectually as second-class citizens. The great challenge here is a two-fold one: first, to develop a program meaningful to these young people, a task which needs much study in depth and which must be tailor made, in many respects, to each community; second, to relate the school program to employment opportunities.
>   4. Students who are mentally or physically handicapped should have special opportunities for education.
>   5. Every secondary school in the United States with a school population of more than 250 to 300 students should have at least one staff member who is competent in vocational guidance, a recommendation made by James B. Conant and seconded here.

[177] National Education Association. Project on Instruction. Op. cit., pp. 112-113.

The Special Commission of the National Association of School Administrators appointed to identify the imperatives in contemporary education identified the preparation of people for the world of work to be one of the nine basic imperatives.

> In the past the average employed individual changed jobs at least three times during his lifetime. Some leading economists and industrialists predict that in the future a person may need to change his *vocation* three times during his working years.[178]

The student must be prepared to expect and to anticipate a number of possible occupational changes. It is part of his educational training to understand the changing vocation scene and to see the necessity of meeting vocational change with emotional balance and personal fortitude.

THE LIBRARY AND THE GUIDANCE PROGRAM

The librarian has limitless opportunity to guide individual students in their quest for self-understanding, self-realization, self-development, and self-fulfillment. Frequently the librarian has the opportunity to help students come to grips with personal, social, recreational, educational, and vocational problems such as the following:

PERSONAL QUEST

Defining possible vocational interests
Determining one's own personality quotient
Dressing effectively on a limited budget
Earning a merit badge in Scouting
Finding a weight-watchers diet
Gaining self-confidence
Getting acquainted with one's own family
Learning how to care for children
Learning how to introduce a guest speaker at assembly
Learning the techniques and rules for portrait painting
Learning to paint with oils
Learning to plan menus
Learning to play a guitar
Learning to style hair
Overcoming shyness
Passing a driver's test
Planning a vacation
Publishing a poem, essay, short story, etc.
Redecorating a room
Solving a grooming problem
Solving a personal problem
Training a pet

SOCIAL QUEST

Brushing up on manners
Dressing for a formal occasion
Making favors for a formal dinner
Planning a wedding reception
Presiding at a club meeting
Selecting a name for a new club
Setting a table for a banquet
Writing a constitution for a church youth group
Writing a formal "thank you" note
Writing invitations to a formal tea

[178] Grossnickle, Foster E. et al. Op. cit., p. 4.

RECREATIONAL QUEST

Building a stereo
Building a swimming pool
Choosing a hobby
Customizing a car
Decorating for a party
Designing a costume for a party
Designing stage sets
Determining the value of a rare coin or stamp
Equipping a dark-room
Identifying an insect, flower, bird, etc.
Learning to bowl
Learning to square dance
Making a record cabinet
Making posters for a dance
Planning a "pep" assembly
Reading for pleasure
Selecting a skit for a club initiation
Selecting an art print to borrow for home decorating
Selecting games for a Scouting jamboree
Selecting records for home or school listening

EDUCATIONAL QUEST

Learning how to study
Making a science fair project
Making a star map
Planning a layout for a graphic arts project
Preparing a debate
Preparing for civil service exams
Preparing for college exams
Proving a theory
Reading for background information
Reviewing for a test
Searching for a suitable speech or theme topic
Selecting a biography, play, short story, etc. for study and criticism
Selecting a college, junior college, or business school
Setting up a science demonstration
Studying a musical score

VOCATIONAL QUEST

Comparing costs of various colleges
Determining job possibilities in a field of special interest
Determining job possibilities in various geographic areas
Determining on-the-job training opportunities in industry
Determining the requirements for admittance to a college, a
business school, a junior college
Discovering the advantages and disadvantages of a given occupation or profession
Exploring kinds of job opportunities in a given field
Preparing for an interview
Reading vocational fiction

GUIDANCE LABORATORY

The guidance counselor needs a special professional laboratory collection right at hand as he plans with students, parents, faculty, and members of the community. He needs college catalogs, vocational and occupational monographs and pamphlets, personal guidance resources readily available for use when the need arises. The librarian and the counselor working together can select materials of a general nature to be housed in the school library and materials of a specialized guidance nature to be housed in the guidance laboratory.

THE SCHOOL LIBRARY AS
A HUMANIZING AGENCY

No phase of the library program is of greater significance than working directly with students in their search for self-understanding, self-perspective, self-respect, self-realization, and self-fulfillment. The librarian can gain authentic concern for the personal as well as the educational development of each student if he will but ask himself this question, "Have I made it possible for students to go home from school each day having tasted of success and thereby having gained increased self-respect and educational satisfaction?" It is the affirmative answer to this question which validates the librarian's claim to professional educational status and respect.

10 The School Library as an Integral Part of the Study Skills Program

*Before coming to college I had been taught to comprehend but not to interpret, to summarize but not to extend. A Stephens College Senior**

A planned developmental study skills program is an integral part of an educational program of excellence. Since skills are the tools for productive learning, effective thinking, and intelligent action, the skills program is a common concern of all who teach. The real test of the effectiveness of the study skills program will come when the student of today intelligently applies his skills as he solves the problems he meets in the future. The aim of the school is to bring the student's skill development to the level where he can solve creatively and effectively the problems he will meet throughout his lifetime. "Perhaps much of what the pupil learns in the social studies will wear thin or become obsolete but skills learned in school continue to be functional indefinitely, or for as long as they are needed. Skills are the most permanent of learnings."[179]

CENTRAL PURPOSE OF EDUCATION

The Educational Policies Commission identified the single, cohesive purpose of education to be the development of each student's ability to think rationally:[180]

> The purpose which runs through and strengthens all other educational purposes—the common thread of education—is the development of the ability to think. This is the central purpose to which the school must be oriented if it is to accomplish either its traditional tasks or those newly accentuated by recent changes in the world. To say that it is central is not to say that it is the sole purpose or in all circumstances the most important purpose, but

* Johnson, B. Lamar and Eloise Lindstrom, eds. *The Librarian and the Teacher in General Education: A Report of Library-Instructional Activities at Stephens College.* Chicago: American Library Association, 1948. p. 40.

179 Carpenter, Helen McCracken, ed. Op. cit., p. 33.

180 Educational Policies Commission. *The Central Purpose of American Education.* Washington, D.C.: National Education Association, 1961. p. 12.

that it must be a pervasive concern in the work of the school. Many agencies contribute to achieving educational objectives, but this particular objective will not be generally attained unless the school focuses on it. In this context, therefore, the development of every student's rational powers must be recognized as centrally important.

Reiterating the necessity for schools to prepare students for rational thinking and rational behavior, the NEA Project on Instruction stated:

> Education is a process of changing behavior—behavior in the broad sense of thinking, feeling, and acting. As a result of education, students should acquire ideas they did not have, skills they did not possess, interests broader and more mature than they had known, ways of thinking more effective than they had employed. From this viewpoint, educational objectives may be stated in terms of behavioral change, and the responsibilities of the schools may be differentiated from those of other educative agencies.[181]

RATIONALE FOR A DEVELOPMENTAL SKILLS PROGRAM

Skills are thinking tools essential for self-initiated learning and self-directed problem solving.

> Without an adequate command of skills, it is doubtful that students can gain the insights concerning their society or develop the habits of intellectual and social behavior that constitute the ultimate goals of the . . . (educational) program. Skills are tools for learning, both in and out of school. The student who develops a command of . . . skills during his school years and carries these skills into the adult years has laid a firm basis for continued learning throughout his life.[182]

Learning how to think, learning how to learn, learning how to solve problems is training preparatory to effective citizenship.

Developing citizens who are functionally literate is the goal of education in our free society. A skills program designed to educate citizens for functional literacy provides for the progressive, sequential teaching and learning of skills beginning in kindergarten and extending through grade 12. An effective skills program requires the planned use of teaching and learning resources appropriate for developing specific skills and subskills at each grade level. The library shares this responsibility for teaching skills and for providing resources to expedite the teaching and learning of skills.

A PLANNED SKILLS PROGRAM

An effective study skills program is planned for the timely integration of skills with content development. An effective study skills program is an

181 National Education Association. Project on Instruction. Op. cit., pp. 8-9.
182 Carpenter, Helen McCracken, ed. Op. cit., p. 310.

important part of the total instructional effort. The incidental or un-planned teaching of skills will not develop a high level of skills proficiency.

> Skills are the tools which the learner uses in his pursuit of con-ceptual learning . . . The skills, therefore, cannot and should not be taught apart from a content framework. Pupils do not learn to think critically by thinking critical thoughts about nothing in par-ticular. Skills have no meaning if they are divorced from content. While skills are developed through the use of carefully selected teaching processes which will foster their growth, they are inti-mately related to the content of the program.[183]

In the saber-tooth tiger days study skills were unheard of. The closest ap-proach to learning how to learn was a series of formal lessons taught by the librarian on how to use reference tools. These lessons were unrelated to any part of an on-going developmental curricular program; they were practice devoid of educational need, tie-in, purpose, and significance. Be-cause they were taught in isolation from functional utility, they were abor-tive—accomplishing little save a feeling of relief on the part of student and librarian when the ordeal was over. There are no library skills per se—only study skills. All study skills are the shared province and joint responsibility of all who teach and should be an integral part of the planned, on-going classroom teaching and learning program (See Appendix L, N).

GUIDING PRINCIPLES

In the planned program for skill development opportunities should be pro-vided in each unit for the students "to define problems and issues, raise questions, search for and relate information, organize and reorganize ideas, propose and test hypotheses, express thoughts and feelings in original ways, and make critical appraisals of proposals, procedures, and plans of ac-tion."[184] The following principles guide the development of a functional study skills program:

> The skill should be taught functionally, in the context of a topic of study, rather than as a separate exercise.

> The learner must understand the meaning and purpose of the skill, and have motivation for developing it.

> The learner should be carefully supervised in his first attempts to apply the skill, so that he will form correct habits from the begin-ning.

> The learner needs repeated opportunities to practice the skill, with immediate evaluation so that he knows where he has succeeded or failed in his performance.

> The learner needs individual help, through diagnostic measures and follow-up exercises, since not all members of any group learn at exactly the same rate or retain equal amounts of what they have learned.

[183] Ibid., p. 32.
[184] Michaelis, John U. Op. cit., p. 8.

Skill instruction should be presented at increasing levels of difficulty, moving from the simple to the more complex; the resulting growth in skills should be cumulative as the learner moves through school, with each level of instruction building on and reinforcing what has been taught previously.

Students should be helped, at each stage, to generalize the skills, by applying them in many and varied situations; in this way, maximum transfer of learning can be achieved.

The program of instruction should be sufficiently flexible to allow skills to be taught as they are needed by the learner; many skills should be developed concurrently.[185]

DESIGNING A STUDY SKILLS PROGRAM

The following operational guides will facilitate designing and developing a study skills program at the district or school building level:

I. Continuity in learning how to learn requires a scientifically planned and a scientifically developed study skills program. The development of a study skills program for the district and for each school is a shared responsibility of *all* who teach.

> No longer valid to refer to study skills as "library skills"; they are thinking and learning skills.

> No longer valid to relegate the teaching of skills to a formal skills program taught in isolation from the teaching and learning program.

> No longer valid to teach a skill and then fail to reteach and reinforce it.

When designing and structuring a district or a school study skills program:

> View the program in its entirety, K–12 (See Appendix L).

> Determine what needs to be taught, what needs to be learned—these are the basic or fundamental skills.

> Determine when each skill can best be taught.

> Assign priorities to each phase of the program.

> Design specific teaching and specific learning strategies and activities to teach or reinforce each fundamental skill.

> Integrate skill teaching with curriculum development.

> Order the teaching of each skill in a logical sequence unit by unit, experience by experience.

> Provide ample skill practice in meaningful context.

185 Carpenter, Helen McCracken, ed., Op. cit., pp. 311-312.

II. The major concern of the library staff is to determine the library's function and role in implementing the study skills program.

> Must identify skills uniquely dependent on library experience and resources.

> Must determine when and how to introduce, re-introduce, or reinforce each skill.

> Must design specific teaching and learning experiences necessary for the introduction and practice of each skill.

> Must identify and provide resources essential for teaching and learning of specific skills.

> Must develop guides and activities for the practice of specific skills.

> Must design testing and evaluating techniques and procedures to determine the effectiveness of each phase of the developmental skills program.

> Must cooperatively redesign the program to correct inadequacies.

> Must be alert to skill development and integration possibilities in each new textbook, unit, teacher's plan, or course of study.

Since the librarian is responsible for teaching students how to learn, he must be conversant with the principles of teaching children how to learn to think (See Tables XVIII, XIX, XX). Proficiency in teaching students how to work productively in the library is to be expected of any professionally trained librarian. As stated in the 1960 *Standards* the librarian must, "Help children and young people to become *skillful* and *discriminating* users of libraries and of printed and audio-visual materials." [186]

TABLE XVIII

GENERAL PRINCIPLES FOR GUIDANCE
OF CHILDREN'S THINKING*

1. The development of the abilities and skills in thinking should be thought of as a goal of the total school program and not as the outcome of special subjects or projects. The processes of thinking may be generalized and verbalized with older learners, but on lower levels there must be permitted considerable free, personalized, spontaneous procedure.
2. Occasions for thinking will occur most frequently when teachers encourage pupils to raise questions of their own, to evaluate statements by teacher and classmates, to "talk back" as necessary.
   Adult authority and demands for conformity reduce the creativity, the critical judgment children use.

* Burton, William H. et al. Op. cit., pp. 342-343.
[186] American Association of School Librarians. Op. cit., p. 9.

Encouragement to present personal problems without fear will stimulate thinking. Admonitions to "think" or "think hard" and other exhortations do not produce thinking.

3. Evidence exists showing that teaching can assist in the development of inquisitiveness, experimentation, and creative production. The problem-solving process can be aided by teaching organized to that end.

4. Occasions calling for thinking must be real to the children, must deal with their purposes and activities, and must be sufficiently diversified to stimulate flexibility and creativity. Imposed or isolated situations are not effective.

5. Occasions for thinking must be related to the learner's maturity, experiential background, readiness.

6. *The materials and processes must be within the understanding of the learner, must be available, must be found and identified with reasonable ease.**

7. The formal processes of thinking cannot be imposed; they must be discovered and developed by the learner. Balance between conformity and spontaneity will merge at first through the learner's own experiences and may be aided later by direct instruction.

8. A wide range of individual differences in all aspects of the thinking processes must be accepted.

9. Varied attacks on problem solving and thinking generally are more effective than following one more-or-less set pattern. Varied experiences are more effective than repetitive experience.

10. Emphasis should be chiefly on developing understanding of the processes and reasons for correctness and not solely on correct response.

11. Assistance should be given not through supplying the right facts, processes, or answer, but through questions and suggested alternatives, calling attention to factors hitherto unnoticed.
Testing solutions in action is one of the best suggested aids and is a cure for verbalizing without sufficient backing.

12. Children need to observe and read widely, but stuffing them with subject matter does not produce thinking.

13. Thinking is affected by numerous factors: motivation, set, social-class mores, peer-group values, teacher personality, the situation, learner's own emotional nature (insecurity, cocksureness, perfectionism, complacency, satisfaction with mediocre work), and own personality factors.

14. Children need time for "thinking it over" (or, with older learners, contemplation); they must search their background, recall similar situations and decisions. They cannot be hurried to immediate decisions.

15. Inability to solve problems in a given area may be caused by weakness in some given aspect of the process, not the total movement: unfamiliar vocabulary, insufficient reading skill, weakness in computation, poor definition of terms and language usage generally, and others. Learners need aid in identifying subsidiary causes of error.

TABLE XIX

SOME GUIDELINES FOR TEACHERS IN DEVELOPING THE SKILLS
OF CRITICAL THINKING AND PROBLEM SOLVING**

1. Critical thinking is one aspect of the total thinking process; its development is based, in large part, upon the more generalized thinking process which is the concern of the teacher.

2. Effective thinking and the effective solution of problems is in part dependent

* Italization for emphasis.
** Michaelis, John U., ed. Op. cit., p. 174.

upon the ability of the child to reconstruct parts of many experiences into a new thought unit, a "concept."

3. The development of concepts, and their use in the solution of problems, appears to be highly dependent upon the ability of pupils to verbalize these re-formed or re-grouped experiences.

4. The development of verbal facility in pupils is one of the most important tasks facing the teacher.

5. A problem must be recognized as such by an individual pupil.

6. Problem solving involves five rather broad steps: identification of the problem; comparison of the present problem with previous experiences; formulation of a tentative solution; testing the tentative solution; and acceptance or rejection of the solution.

    The solution of problems in the classroom should be continually approached through this procedure in order that pupils may have the opportunity to develop the habit of such an approach.

7. Pupils need to be challenged; however, they need to know that their inevitable failures will be met with understanding on the part of the teacher and of their peers. (The teachers should be continually aware of the danger of developing anxiety in pupils.)

8. The teacher should be aware of the importance of the sequence in the development of the study skills so that careful guidance may be given to pupils at all times.

TABLE XX
PATTERNS OF CRITICAL THINKING*

How may a teacher tell when a student has learned to think critically? Here are some things which such a student does:

1. Recognizes when a problem or issue exists.
2. Identifies and defines a central issue clearly.
3. Recognizes underlying assumptions.
4. Determines the relative significance of questions related to an issue.
5. Suggests a number of possible solutions to a problem.
6. Identifies sources that may be utilized to gather information on a topic.
7. Seeks information from a wide variety of sources, including books, periodicals, audio-visual materials, and resource persons.
8. Makes use of what has already been learned.
9. Considers the position and degree of authority of sources employed.
10. Recognizes the kinds of data which are relevant to a problem.
11. Distinguishes between statements of fact and statements of opinion.
12. Interprets trends revealed by statistical data in graphs, charts, and tables.
13. Recognizes biased statements and common propaganda techniques.
14. Spots words and phrases that can mean different things to different people.
15. Distinguishes between verifiable and unverifiable data.
16. Determines the recency and adequacy of information pertaining to an issue or topic.
17. Detects errors and inconsistencies in data.
18. Arranges data in an orderly and logical sequence.
19. Presents data clearly and without distortion.
20. Determines whether facts support a generalization.
21. Recognizes when data are inadequate for reaching a conclusion.
22. Considers all of the evidence before generalizing and drawing conclusions.
23. Recognizes the tentative nature of conclusions.

* Curriculum Development Council for Southern New Jersey. Op. cit., p. 26.

24. Re-evaluates conclusions in terms of the completeness and reliability of data and the consistency in arguments advanced to support the conclusions.
25. Applies generalizations and conclusions drawn to new, day-to-day situations.

ASSIGNMENTS AND STUDY SKILLS

Special mention must be made of the importance of the teacher's assignment in a developmental study skill program. The assignment is "the key to teaching and learning . . . (and) largely determines what pupils do and how they do it; hence it determines the results achieved."[187]

The quality of the assignment directly influences the success or failure of the learning endeavor. "Evidence . . . shows that vague, indefinite assignments that lack the power to motivate are common causes of children's failure to learn."[188]

Poor assignments are evidence of a serious teacher disability.

> Two serious obstacles to good assignment technique seem to reside within the teacher and can be cured only by the teacher. These are unwillingness to take the necessary time and unwillingness to exert the very real effort demanded. The assignment, too, often slighted, is an important part of teaching procedure. It requires time for pondering, for critical study, for written organization, for tryout, for discussion with others. It requires systematic and continuous effort. Good assignments simply cannot be "dashed off."[189]

The following difficulties are inherent in constructing assignments:[190]

> Finding provocative and convincing connections between subject and life needs or interests.
> Producing clear and definite statement of objectives.
> Providing appropriate and challenging study guides and aids.
> Making sure all pupils understand objectives and methods of procedures (know what to do).
> Providing adequate variations in requirements to fit range of differences in the group.
> Gauging difficulty of requirements and time necessary for accomplishment by different levels of ability.
> Avoiding extremes of too much or too little.
> Providing continuity.
> Ensuring correlation with other subjects and other activities.
> Providing means of evaluating pupil progress and achievement.

CHECKLIST XIII

DETERMINING FEASIBILITY OF ASSIGNMENTS

_____ *Is this assignment educationally significant and worthy of the student's attention?*
> There is too much needing to be taught and too much needing to be learned ever to permit or excuse the teaching of trivia such as "What

187 Burton, William H. Op. cit., p. 289.
188 Ibid., p. 290.
189 Ibid., p. 294.
190 Ibid., pp. 294-295.

was the color of Shakespeare's eyes?" Nor is there ever an excuse for misleading assignments such as requiring students to locate on a world map the "Islets of Langerhans" (endocrine glands) or including in a unit on sheep ranching the topic "steel wool."

_____ *Is this assignment designed to create and sustain interest in learning?*
A reasonable, significant, interesting assignment that can be translated readily into foreseeable patterns of action is a strong motivational factor. Seeing purpose and promise of achievement in an assignment are powerful interest sustainers.

_____ *Is this assignment an out-growth of the unit goals and objectives?*
Relevance of assignments to unit goals and objectives keeps learning activities congruent with the purpose and design of the unit. Peripheral topic inclusion not only dissipates time and energy but dissipates student interest as well.

_____ *Is this assignment essential and timely to the task at hand?*
Recency, frequency, and utility are important factors in encouraging learning. It is poor teaching technique to make any assignment whose significance or relevance is not readily perceived by the student. It is an exercise in total frustration if the student does not perceive clearly the utility and the relevance of an assigned task. Idea linkage is impossible if the first link in the chain of understanding is missing.

_____ *Is this assignment suitable to the maturity level of the students?*
Utter confusion arises when an assignment demands background experience or mental sophistication beyond the years the students have lived. A sense of bewilderment overwhelms any student, even the most gifted, when an assignment is incomprehensible. Who could defend assigning a third grader the research topic, "Discuss the separation of church and state"?

_____ *Is this assignment reasonable and justifiable in the light of both time and effort required?*
Nothing is more damaging to student receptivity to learning than to have an unreasonable time limitation imposed when he is being assigned a significant learning task. This is an example of interest "overkill." If the task is worth doing, a reasonable amount of time must be alloted for the completion of the task.

_____ *Is this assignment differentiated to meet adequately the varying capabilities of the class?*
Since each student is a unique learner, mass assignments are unrealistic and pedagogically indefensible. What is a challenge and a satisfaction to one student may well be a frustrating, dead-end experience to another. How could all students in a tenth grade world history class where reading abilities range from fifth to twelfth grade be expected to read with understanding Machiavelli's *The Prince?*

_____ *Is this assignment humane in the light of the students' cultural, social, economic, and personal backgrounds?*
In the scheme of teaching no phase of responsibility requires greater sensitivity on the part of the teacher than sensing what is *not* appropriate for any given class, group, or individual. Who could excuse a teacher's assigning as a topic for class discussion, "What I got for Christmas," when he knows that some students received nothing? In this realm alone if in no other the teacher will not be replaced by the machine, for in this area the teacher must think with his heart as well as with his mind!

_____ *Is this assignment defensible in the light of the ready availability of appropriate supporting resources in sufficient quantity?*

The teacher breaks faith with the student when he bases an assignment on too little available material or on non-existent material. There is nothing more destructive of student interest than to be given an impossible task. Assignments requiring supporting resources that are not available readily cannot be justified by any teacher. A teacher who is the least bit introspective can well understand the negative effect of impossible assignments if he will but recall his own frustrations and feeling of resentment when as a student he was given an impossible assignment or a meaningless task. The burden of proof in finding required support materials should rest with the teacher, not with the student (See Appendix N).

_____ *Is the assignment stated clearly so it can be translated easily into action patterns and learning strategies?*

Even the most gifted and avid learner loses interest when he cannot translate an assignment into specific avenues to be followed in building and communicating understanding. Impossible assignments like "Trace the historic development and impact of man's capacity to think individually and collectively throughout the history of mankind" or "Write a documented research paper on the sociological, political, and anthropological aspects of the Caribbean lands" never can be completed. The student is never able to proceed past the assignment itself.

_____ *Is the assignment dependent on the utilization of new learning skills, new reference tools and techniques?*

The teacher has the obligation to foresee the skills necessary for the completion of an assigned task. A competent teacher plans to equip the students to work intelligently and efficiently by introducing or having the librarian introduce the skills and techniques essential to building the skill level of performance demanded by each assignment.

The librarian's contribution to facilitating the development of the student's ability to read, to write, to think, and to act with competence is of vital importance. Thinking skills prepare the future citizen for intelligent participation in political, economic, social, and personal decision making. In our complex society it is imperative that the student of today be prepared to solve adequately the problems of tomorrow. In large measure study skills are the most permanent and most useful of all learnings; facts will change, but how to deal efficiently, effectively, creatively, and honestly with facts will not change. The librarian shares the responsibility of all who teach to equip future citizens to function in an informed, effective, efficient, and constructive manner. This responsibility is of vast import for:

> The mastery of these skills . . . raises the student from an amateur reader, listener, observer of life, and citizen of his community seeing life as a miscellaneous parade, to a person who can select from the confusion of life and knowledge that information which serves his purposes and who can bring it to bear on his many tasks. From just an onlooker he becomes a participant in determining the direction of events round about him.[191]

[191] Carpenter, Helen McCracken, ed. Op. cit., p. 77.

11 Evaluating the Effectiveness of the School Library Program

*Policy makers, school administrators, and the entire teaching staff must continuously examine the extent to which the ongoing media program meets local needs and established and accepted standards.**

The democratic concern for educational excellence necessitates continuous reappraisal of the total educational endeavor. "We must develop a philosophy and a technique of continuous reappraisal and innovation."[192] Educational quality is neither permanent nor absolute. Quality, because it is directly related to the capability of the school program to meet the emergent needs of contemporary society, is both relative and transitory. An educational program of excellence five years ago may be only mediocre today and inferior next year if it lacks the capability of keeping pace with the changing and emerging needs of society and of the individual in society. Excellence in any educational endeavor is never static, never permanent, never won.

PURPOSE OF EVALUATION

Evaluation is the method educators employ when judging the degree of excellence latent in or being achieved by any educational plan, procedure, resource or product. Just as the quantity and quality of gold are determined both by its being weighed and by its being tested by acid, so is the quantity and the quality of an educational enterprise assayed by its being objectively "weighed" on the scales of established standards and by its being critically appraised by the acid test of functional excellence in practice. In any professional evaluation there must be a sincere respect for the truth and seriousness of purpose which preclude ignoring or minimizing the educational dross and highlighting or maximizing the educational gold. The professional educator must keep faith with the purpose of evaluation—the improvement of instruction.

* Wisconsin Department of Public Instruction. *Elements of an Effective Audiovisual Program: A Handbook for Wisconsin Educators.* Madison, Wisconsin: State Department of Public Instruction, 1966.
192 President's Commission on National Goals. Op. cit., p. 99.

DEFINITION OF TERMS

Precise use of terms is a necessary and effective means of bringing objectivity to a discussion of evaluative techniques and procedures (See Appendix C). Each of the following basic terms has been abstracted from the *Dictionary of Education*.[193]

> CHECKLIST. A prepared list of items that may relate to a person, procedure, institution, building, etc., used for purposes of observation and/or evaluation, and on which one may show by a check mark or other simple method the presence, absence, or frequency or occurrence of each item on the list (See Figures X, XII, and Table XXI).
>
> CRITERION, CRITERIA, pl. A standard, norm, or judgment selected as a basis for quantitative and qualitative comparison.
>
> EVALUATIVE CRITERIA. (1) The standards against which a person or group or a procedure may be checked; (2) the factors considered by an accrediting agency in analyzing the status of an educational institution to determine whether it shall be accredited.
>
> EVALUATIVE METHOD. The procedure in a study that has evaluation as its chief purpose and that in most cases includes some definite fact finding, through observation, and that involves the careful description of aspects to be evaluated, a statement of purpose, frame of reference, and criteria for the evaluation, and the degrees or terms that are to be employed in recording judgments.
>
> INVENTORY. In the field of evaluation, a test or checklist used to determine the subject's or examinee's ability, achievement, aptitude, interest, or likes, generally in a limited area (See Appendix J).
>
> RATING SCALE. A device used in evaluating products, attitudes, or other characteristics of instructors or learners (See Figures XI, XII and Appendix G).
>
> SCHOOL SURVEY. A study or evaluation of a school, a school system, or any part thereof; may be fact finding, or may indicate the strong and weak features as judged by definite criteria; *commonly concluded with suggestions for needed changes and/or recommendations for more desirable practices.*
>
> STANDARD. (1) A goal or objective or criterion of education expressed either numerically as a statistical average or philosophically as an ideal of excellence; (2) any criterion by which things are judged.

CRITERIA FOR DETERMINING EVALUATIVE EXCELLENCE

The American Association of School Administrators in joint enterprise with the National School Boards Association has identified the following twelve criteria as being basic for judging evaluative excellence:

[193] Good, Carter V., ed. *Dictionary of Education.* 2nd ed. New York: McGraw-Hill, 1959.

Evaluation should be based on stated objectives.

Evaluation should be based on intimate and comprehensive knowledge of the community.

Evaluation should be a continuous activity.

Evaluation should be comprehensive.

Evaluation should be a cooperative process involving many people.

Evaluation should identify strengths as well as deficiencies.

Evaluation should involve many measuring instruments.

Evaluation should be based on knowledge of children and youth.

Evaluation requires the board to look at itself.

Evaluation should appraise existing practices affecting the staff.

Evaluation is based on the belief that what people think makes a difference.

Evaluation should culminate in self-improvement.[194]

EVALUATIVE CRITERIA

The most commonly used evaluative instruments for schools on the secondary level are *Evaluative Criteria* [195] (Senior High School) and *Evaluative criteria for Junior High Schools.** Both of these instruments are published by the National Study of Secondary School Evaluation. This organization originally known as the Cooperative Study of Secondary School Standards has taken the responsibility since 1933 for preparing evaluative criteria to be used to:

Determine the characteristics of a good secondary school.

Find practical means and methods to evaluate the effectiveness of a school in terms of its objectives.

Determine the means and processes by which a good school develops into a better one.

Devise ways by which regional associations can stimulate and assist secondary schools to continuous growth.

The *Evaluative Criteria* and *Criteria for Evaluating Junior High Schools* are instruments designed for internal-external evaluation. The general procedure is for the school to conduct a self evaluation preparatory to an external evaluation by a guest committee of educators. Frequently as long as a year is spent by the faculty in self-study and self-appraisal. School librarians by the nature of their faculty status are required to serve on various evaluative teams and to take an active part in all phases of the school's evaluation of the over-all educational program.

During faculty analysis and evaluation of the quality of the educational program four questions are kept constantly in the foreground of each teacher's thinking as he quests for truth:

* National Study of Secondary School Evaluation. *Evaluative Criteria for Junior High Schools*. 2nd ed. National Study of Secondary School Evaluation. Distributed by the American Council on Education. 1970.

194 Harris, Lewis E. and Clyde B. Moore. *Keys to Quality*. Quest for Quality Series. Booklet No. 14. Washington, D. C.: American Association of School Administrators, 1960. pp. 7-8.

195 National Study of Secondary School Evaluation. *Evaluative Criteria*. 4th ed. Washington, D. C.: National Study of Secondary School Evaluation. Distributed by the American Council on Education. 1969.

What are our directional goals and basic philosophy?
What experiences should we provide in the light of our directional
goals and basic philosophy?
What evidence of progress or retrogression do we find in evidence?
What remedial, rennovative, and innovative action should we un-
dertake to strengthen noted weaknesses and to increase the educational effectiveness and efficiency of the total program?

A number of instruments for evaluating educational programs include
the school library within the framework and basic design of the evaluation
guide. For example:

ELEMENTARY SCHOOLS

Arizona State Department of Public Instruction. *Evaluative Criteria for the
Elementary Schools of Arizona.* Phoenix, Arizona: State Department of Public Instruction, 1951.

Arkansas State Department of Education. *Guide for the Study of the Elementary School.* Little Rock, Arkansas: State Department of Education,
1951.

Boston University. *Elementary Evaluative Criteria.* Boston, Massachusetts:
Boston University, 1953.

Colorado State Department of Education. *Self-evaluation of Elementary
Schools in Colorado.* Denver, Colorado: State Department of Education,
1956.

Nebraska State Department of Education. *A Guide for Evaluating and Improving Nebraska Elementary Schools.* Lincoln, Nebraska: State Department
of Education, 1955.

Oklahoma Curriculum Improvement Commission, State Department of Public Instruction. *Evaluation Manual for Elementary Schools.* Oklahoma City,
Oklahoma: State Department of Public Instruction, 1958.

Pennsylvania Department of Public Instruction. *Faculty Self Study in the
Elementary School.* 2nd edition. Harrisburg, Pennsylvania: State Department of Public Instruction, 1965.

Southern Association's Cooperative Study in Elementary Education. *Cooperative Program in Elementary Education of the Southern Association of
Colleges and Secondary Schools.* Austin, Texas: Texas Education Agency,
1960.

Texas Education Agency. *Principles and Standards for Accrediting Elementary and Secondary Schools.* Austin, Texas: Texas Education Agency, 1967.

SECONDARY SCHOOLS

Connecticut State Department of Education. *An Assessment Guide for Use
in Junior High Schools.* Hartford, Connecticut: State Department of Education, 1960.

National Study of Secondary School Evaluation. *Evaluative Criteria.* 4th
edition. Washington, District of Columbia: National Study of Secondary
School Evaluation. Distributed by the American Council on Education.
1969.

National Study of Secondary School Evaluation. *Evaluative Criteria for*

Junior High Schools. 2nd edition. Washington, District of Columbia: National Study of Secondary School Evaluation. Distributed by the American Council on Education. 1970.

Texas Education Agency. *Principles and Standards for Accrediting Elementary and Secondary Schools.* Austin, Texas: Texas Education Agency, 1967.

The Texas Study of Secondary Education, University of Texas. *Research Study No. 21, Criteria for Evaluating Junior High Schools.* Austin, Texas: University of Texas, 1959.

SCHOOL LIBRARY EVALUATION—A NECESSITY

It is imperative that a policy of continuous appraisal be instituted to determine the quality of a library program by relating its function to developmental needs of the current educational program and to the personal and educational needs of today's student body.

> ... The effectiveness of the library program and of instructional resources is measured by the extent to which they meet the changing needs of students, teachers, and the total instructional program. Evaluation, therefore, is a continuous procedure.[196]
> ... teaching and learning resources and services are never static. Through continuous evaluation they are always changing to meet new demands of students and the school's instructional program.[197]

Frances Henne, crusader for innovative excellence in school librarianship, has prepared a more than adequate overview of the history, purpose, procedures, and tools of school library evaluation. Dr. Henne's observations on evaluation provide school librarians with a philosophic approach to practical, objective, professional self-study—required reading for all who would gain insight into intelligent school library evaluation. She recommends that:

> ... evaluations, whether self-survey or conducted by outside specialists, involve not only the school librarians but also the administration, faculty, and, not infrequently, students and parents. The pattern of having some person or persons "blow in, blow off, and blow out," although not unknown in the annals of school library evaluation, has little, if anything, to commend it. Under any circumstances evaluations should be constructive in design and intent, with the primary purpose of working with and assisting the school and the librarians to effect improvements in the library benefiting students and teachers.[198]

The following planning guides, rating scales, inventories, surveys, and checklists are representative of the various devices employed by a state, a county, a district, or a school seeking to evaluate the effectiveness and efficiency of its library program.

[196] *The School Library Program and Instructional Resources.* Bulletin 640. Austin, Texas: Texas Education Agency, 1964. p. 34.

[197] *The School Library Program and Instructional Resources 1965–66: Standards and Guidelines for Texas Schools.* Bulletin 659. Austin, Texas: Texas Education Agency, 1965. p. vi.

[198] Henne, Frances. "School Libraries" in *Library Surveys* edited by Maurice F. Tauber and Irene R. Stephens. New York: Columbia University Press. 1967. p. 194.

SCHOOL LIBRARY EVALUATIVE AND
ACTION PLANNING INSTRUMENTS

American Association of School Librarians: School Library Development Project. *Individual School Guide for Planning School Library Development.* Chicago, American Association of School Librarians, 1962.

―――― *Planning School Library Development.* Report by Mary Frances Kennon and Leila Ann Doyle. Chicago, American Library Association, 1962.

―――― *School District Guide for Planning School Library Development.* Chicago, American Association of School Librarians, 1962.

Boula, James A. "Guidelines for Instructional Materials" in *Illinois Journal of Education.* October, 1963. pp. 2-3 (See Figure X).

Fulton, W. R. *Evaluative Checklist: An Instrument for Self-rating an Educational Media Program in School Systems.* Washington, District of Columbia: Department of Audiovisual Instruction, National Education Association, 1965 (See Appendix G).

Gaver, Mary. *The Accessibility of Learning Materials, a Rating Scale.* East Brunswick, New Jersey: ssh press, 1962.

Gaver, Mary and Marian Scott. *Evaluating Library Resources for Elementary School Libraries.* East Brunswick, New Jersey: ssh press, 1962.

Henne, Frances et al. *A Planning Guide for the High School Library Program.* Chicago, Illinois: American Library Association, 1951.

International Paper Company. *How to Get the School Library Your Chid Needs.* New York: International Paper Company, 1965 (See Checklist XIV).

Kansas State Department of Public Instruction. *Evaluating the School Library.* Topeka, Kansas: State Department of Public Instruction, 1964.

Michigan Curriculum Program assisted by the Michigan Library Association. *Mr. Administrator: What Is Your Library Service Profile?* Lansing, Michigan: Michigan State Library, 1960 (See Figure XI).

National Study of Secondary School Evaluation. *Evaluative Criteria.* 4th edition. Washington, District of Columbia: National Study of Secondary School Evaluation. Distributed by the American Council on Education, 1969. "Instructional Materials Services—Library and Audio-Visual" sold as a separate booklet.

―――― *Evaluative Criteria for Junior High Schools.* 2nd edition. Washington, District of Columbia: National Study of Secondary School Evaluation. Distributed by the American Council on Education, 1970. "Instructional Materials Services—Library and Audio-Visual" sold as a separate booklet.

Nevada Department of Public Instruction. *Suggested Aims for School Library Development in Nevada.* Carson City, Nevada: State Department of Public Instruction, 1963. "Library Development Checklist" pp. 12-15.

New York Library Association. School Libraries Section. *Evaluating the School Library: Suggestions for Studying the School Library in Action.* New York: New York Library Association, 1962. (See following pages for abstract of this guide).

North Carolina State Department of Public Instruction. *Checklist for the*

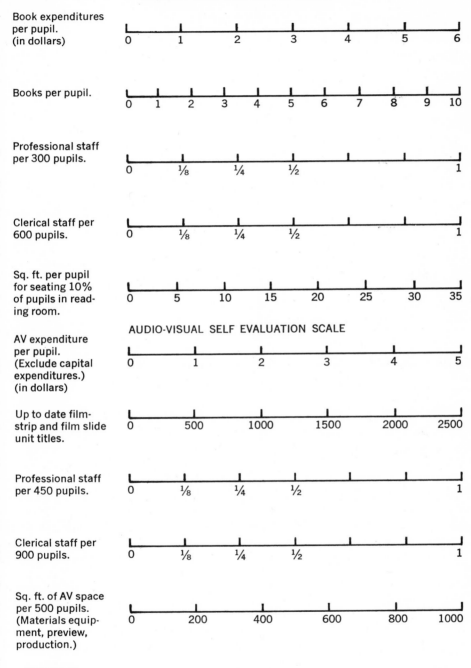

FIGURE X

NOTE: This instrument can be updated to reflect the current standards by changing the quantitative indicators to match new AASL-DAVI recommendations.

* Boula, James A. "Guidelines for Instructional Materials" in *Illinois Journal of Education.* October, 1963. p. 3.

PROGRESS CHART

	STAFF	SIZE OF CENTRAL LIBRARY	OTHER LIBRARY MATERIALS	ANNUAL AMOUNT SPENT ON LIBRARY BOOKS	NUMBER OF BOOKS	SCHOOL ENROLLMENT
WHERE YOU NOW STAND						
WHERE YOU SHOULD BE						
1969-70						
1970-71						
1971-72						
1972-73						

* International Paper Company. *How to Get the School Library Your Child Needs*. New York: International Paper Company, 1965. p. 1-B.

FIND YOUR SCHOOL LIBRARY SERVICE PROFILE

Your School Library	1	2	3	4
Personnel				
Materials				
Organization				
Room and Equip.				
Budget				
Instruction				

Good — Fair — Poor

SEE HOW YOUR LIBRARY RATES

1. Find the item in each of the six sections which most nearly applies to your library.
2. Check this item in the proper box on the chart.
3. Draw a line connecting these checks.

PROFILE POINTS

A. Personnel
1. One full time librarian per 300 students with clerical help.
2. One full time librarian per 500 students with clerical help.
3. One part-time teacher-librarian.
4. Library is a teacher's extra-curricular activity.

B. Materials
1. More than ten books per pupil plus fifty magazine titles, plus reference books, plus audio-visual materials.
2. Seven books per pupil plus twenty-five magazine titles, plus up-to-date reference books.
3. Five books per pupil plus sets of encyclopedias.
4. Sample texts and a set of encyclopedias.

C. Organization
1. Books and other library materials completely classified and cataloged with adequate charging system for all materials.
2. Only books classified and simple catalog maintained, plus simple charging system.
3. Books not classified but shelved in some organized manner, simple charging system.
4. Books not organized, no charging system.

D. Room and Equipment
1. Well equipped library to seat 10%-20% of enrollment (not more than 100 in one room), work room with running water, conference rooms and room for preparation and use of audio-visual materials.
2. Library seating largest sized class, catalog case, charging desk, work space with running water.
3. Library room, but too small to seat one entire class group.
4. Book cases in a classroom or study hall, or book storage room.

E. Library Budget
1. More than $4.00 per pupil annually for printed materials after the library collection is up to standard. Encyclopedias replaced every five years from an extra allotment. Additional budget for audio-visual materials, supplies, etc.
2. Less than $4.00 per pupil per year for all library materials, supplies, and equipment.
3. $2.00 per pupil per year for library purposes.
4. $1.00 or less per pupil per year for library purposes.

F. Library Instruction
1. Program of library instruction for all students worked out in cooperation with classroom teachers and public library. Evaluation and follow-up activities are planned.
2. A number of scheduled lessons in library use are given to all students.
3. Individual help given on request is the only instruction offered.
4. Library hours and rules are posted.

NOW YOU KNOW—

If your profile is GOOD, keep moving ahead toward superior service.
If your profile is FAIR, you need to concentrate on your library program.
If your profile is POOR, you need help at once.

FIGURE XI

* Michigan Curriculum Program assisted by the Michigan Library Association. *Mr. Administrator: What Is Your Library Service Profile?* Lansing, Michigan: Michigan State Library, 1960.

Library Quarters. Raleigh, North Carolina: State Department of Public Instruction, 1963.

Pennsylvania Department of Public Instruction. *The School Instructional Materials Center and the Curriculum: The Library Audio-Visual Center*. Curriculum Development Series No. 5. Harrisburg, Pennsylvania: State Department of Public Instruction, 1962. pp. 28-34.

Scholl, Joyce B. *Find Your School Media Center Service Profile*. Harrisburg, Pennsylvania: Division of School Libraries, Pennsylvania Department of Public Instruction, 1969 (See Figure XII).

Southern Association of Colleges and Schools. Committee on Elementary Education. *Evaluating the Elementary School Library Program*. Atlanta, Georgia: Southern Association of Colleges and Schools, 1964.

Washington State Superintendent of Public Instruction. *School Library and Audio-Visual Survey*. Olympia, Washington: State Department of Public Instruction, 1964.

SCHOOL LIBRARY EVALUATION—PROCEDURE

The school library section of the New York Library Association published in 1962 a most effective guide to be utilized in determining the educational effectiveness and promise of a school library program. Since this guide, *Evaluating the School Library: Suggestions for Studying the School Library in Action,* is so comprehensive in its treatment of the need, purpose, plan, procedure, and significance of school library evaluation it is worthy of more than cursory attention. Therefore, the following abstracts are included here for administrator, supervisor, teacher, and librarian consideration:

EVALUATING THE SCHOOL LIBRARY[199]

Discussions of school library essentials and school library standards point to school library evaluation as a basis for the further development of school libraries and as a means of improving school library programs. These suggestions and questions are presented as possible aids to superintendents, principals, and school librarians who have had some experience in school library evaluation as well as to those who have not previously measured the resources, the use, or the influence of a school library.

School libraries have many functions. They are centers for books and other materials of learning. They are reading centers and reference centers. They are teaching, guidance, and service agencies. They should support the entire curriculum and exert an integrating influence in the school. For these reasons it is difficult, though important, to make a simple outline for evaluation.

It is evident that each school should make its own outline and plan because, if its library is functioning in relation to its pupils, its objectives and its curriculum, its approach to evaluation should be distinctive, creative and constructive.

[199] New York Library Association. School Libraries Section. Op. cit.

WHY EVALUATE THE SCHOOL LIBRARY PROGRAM?

1. To recognize and interpret its accomplishments.
2. To determine its need.
3. To plan its future.

WHO PARTICIPATES IN SCHOOL LIBRARY EVALUATION?

These groups are essential:

1. The librarian and the library staff—those directly responsible for library organization, library administration, library teaching and library service.
2. The members of the school, the pupils, and the teachers, including the librarians—those who use the library and those who cooperate in library planning and library teaching.
3. The principal, the superintendent of schools, and the board of education—those who are responsible for school supervision and school administration, and for the interpretation and support of the library.

Studies made by the librarian or by the librarian and the principal or by the librarian and a committee of teachers working under the direction of the principal should result in significant conclusions. Self-evaluation is always necessary, but the challenge of taking a fresh look at the library in introducing it to a visitor or of learning how it impresses someone who is not closely related to the detail of its operation is refreshing, and often helpful.

WHAT IS TO BE EVALUATED?

1. Library essentials. An appropriate, up to date, adequate book collection, the other library materials, the organization of library materials, the card catalog, the library's quarters, the plans for library teaching, reading guidance, and library service, and/or the librarian and the library staff.
2. The administration of the library, the school's plan for making the library accessible and useful to the pupils, the appearance, order, and atmosphere of the library, the participation of the faculty in library administration, in library teaching, and in encouraging the use of the library.
3. The use of the library by pupils and teachers for school courses, school activities, and personal interests.
4. The library's contribution to teaching and learning, the library as a resource for dealing with individual differences in ability and interest, the library as a socializing influence, the part played by the library in improving the quality of teaching, library publicity and public relations, and the interpretation of the school library to the pupils, the faculty, and the community.
5. The adequacy and size of the professional staff, the clerical staff, the book collection, the library's quarters, and the budget for the enrollment and the program.

FIRST STEPS? OR, PLANNING BEFORE ACTION

1. Recognize that it is practical to prepare for an evaluation by becoming familiar with one or two plans or outlines proposed for school or school library evaluation (See Appendix G).
2. Realize that evaluating is a time taking process, and decide to set aside a specific amount of time for the job.
3. Decide what to evaluate.
4. Make plans for the writing of the summary report or reports.

WHAT ARE THE METHODS OF EVALUATION?

1. Observe the school library in action when school is in session and either before or after school.
2. Notice the best developments and practices. Seek essential information.
3. Make a brief, written record of general impressions of activities, accomplishments, and needs based on observations in the library, in classrooms, and elsewhere in the school.
4. Find out how the library's objectives compare with the school's objectives, and to what extent the library supports the school program.
5. Study the school library's records and reports. Use statistical information—as well as opinions.
6. Compare library resources, organization, facilities, teaching programs and use with the recommendations of established standards for school libraries.
7. Compare this library with school libraries in similar communities, libraries of similar age, which have similar objectives and resources.
8. Study the library as a whole or such features of the library as the library instruction program, the effect of the library on the pupils, the use of the library by school departments, the role of the librarian as teacher and as advisor.
9. Ask again "What does the library accomplish?"

HOW USE THE EVALUATION?

1. A brief, written report—on good values, needs, problems, questions.
2. Discussion of the findings by the librarian, the principal, and the superintendent.
3. Consider what improvements can be made with present resources and what additional resources are needed.
4. Decision as to interpretation to other individuals or groups.
5. Developing a plan for action.
6. Implementation of the plan.
7. Provision for a follow-up study.

HOW DO YOU LOOK AT YOUR SCHOOL LIBRARY?

Does it project an image of books in repose or a picture of education in action?

Is it ever changing, growing and becoming, or is it the same every day?

USING LIBRARY STANDARDS AS EVALUATIVE CRITERIA

The library profession has taken a leadership role in providing standards of both a quantitative and of a qualitative nature. These standards should be employed when a school district or a building library staff wish to design a self-evaluation instrument. The Michigan Curriculum Program assisted by the Michigan Library Association developed in 1960 a checklist and library profile rating device to encourage Michigan school librarians to measure their library program, collection, personnel, and facilities against the *1960 AASL Standards for School Library Programs (See Figure XI)*. Mrs. Joyce B. Scholl* has modified this device (See Figure XII) to reflect the *1969 AASL-DAVI Standards for School Media Programs*. Each of the aforementioned evaluation instruments can be similarly updated to reflect emerging standards.

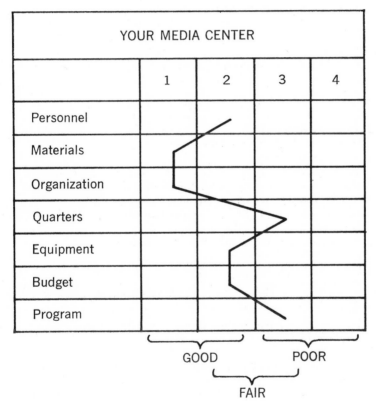

FIGURE XII

FIND YOUR SCHOOL MEDIA CENTER SERVICE PROFILE**

* Adapted by Joyce B. Scholl, Advisor, Western Area Branch Division of School Libraries, Pa. Dept. Public Inst. from "Mr. Administrator: What Is Your Library Service Profile?" revised. Michigan State Library. Lansing, Michigan. 1960.
** School Library Development Advisor, Western Area Branch of the Pennsylvania Division of School Libraries.

YOU WILL DISCOVER THAT—

If your profile is *good,* keep moving ahead toward superior service
If your profile is *fair,* you need to concentrate on your library program.
If your profile is *poor,* you need help at once.

USING THE *1969 STANDARDS FOR SCHOOL MEDIA PROGRAMS* *

PROFILE POINTS
   A. PERSONNEL.
      1. One full time media specialist plus one full time technician and one full time media aide per 250 students.
      2. One full time media specialist plus one full time media aide per 250 students.
      3. One full time media specialist per 250 students.
      4. Less than one full time media specialist per 250 students.
   B. MATERIALS.
      1. 20 or more books per pupil plus 36 or more pieces of non book media per pupil.
      2. Ten books per pupil plus 18 pieces of non book media per pupil.
      3. Five books per pupil plus 9 pieces of non book media per pupil.
      4. Fewer than 5 books per pupil.
   C. ORGANIZATION.
      1. All print media classified and cataloged and all non print media cataloged, with changing procedure systematized for all media and facilitating equipment.
      2. Only books classified and cataloged with charging system.
      3. Media not classified but organized in some orderly manner with simple charging system.
      4. Media not organized, no charging system.
   D. QUARTERS.
      1. Space to seat 15 percent of student enrollment at 40 square feet per student plus reception, large group instruction, conference, office, work, storage, production, and professional materials areas.
      2. Space to seat largest class plus reception, conference, office, work and storage areas.
      3. Space to seat largest class, plus work and storage areas.
      4. Space insufficient to seat largest class.
   E. EQUIPMENT.
      1. Shelving and cabinet storage to accommodate with growth allowance entire media collection, furniture to implement all media center activities, plus hardware to activate all media.
      2. Shelving and cabinet storage to accommodate media collection, furniture to implement some media center activities, plus hardware to activate some media.
      3. Some shelving and cabinet storage, some implementing furniture.
      4. Shelving, seating.
   F. BUDGET.
      1. Six percent of the district average per pupil operational cost (for average daily attendance) for media center purposes other than original installation, salaries, plant maintenance.
      2. Four percent of the district average per pupil operational cost (for aver-

* American Association of School Librarians and the Department of Audiovisual Instruction. *Standards for School Media Programs.* Chicago, Illinois: ALA and Washington, D. C.: National Education Association, 1969.

age daily attendance) for media center purposes other than original installation, salaries, plant maintenance.
3. Two percent of the district average per pupil operational cost (for average
daily attendance) for media center purposes other than original installation,
salaries, plant maintenance.
4. One percent of the district average per pupil operational cost (for average
daily attendance) for media center purposes other than original installation, salaries, plant maintenance.

G. PROGRAM.
1. The media center program functioning as an integral supporting component of the total educational program: voluntary recreational reading plus
planned informational curriculum support actively presented for all students and faculty on an open schedule.
2. Recreational reading and curriculum support programs available to students and faculty on an open schedule.
3. Recreational reading and reference use available to students and faculty.
4. Study halls scheduled into media centers.

SEE HOW YOUR LIBRARY RATES
1. Find the item in each of the seven sections which most nearly applies to your
library.
2. Check this item in the proper box on the chart.
3. Draw a line connecting these checks.

YOUR MEDIA CENTER				
	1	2	3	4
Personnel				
Materials				
Organization				
Quarters				
Equipment				
Budget				
Program				

GOOD   POOR

FAIR

EVALUATING THE PROFESSIONAL EXCELLENCE OF THE LIBRARIAN

Just as the quality of the teacher is the key to the quality of the educational program so is the professional quality of the librarian the key to the degree of educational excellence to be achieved by the library program.

> Love of learning, curiosity, self-discipline, intellectual honesty, the capacity to think clearly—these and all the other consequences of a good education cannot be insured by skillful administrative devices. *The quality of the teacher is the key to good education.*[200]

The librarian with a sincere commitment to actualizing the ideal of the school library as a source and a force for educational excellence will welcome the opportunity to appraise his own proficiency as a teacher. Numerous rating devices are available such as the list developed by Leonard S. Kenworthy (See Table XXI) which will be useful to the school librarian in determining his own professional self-evaluation.

TABLE XXI
CHARACTERISTICS OF AN EFFECTIVE TEACHER*

CONTENT:

_____ You have knowledge in depth of subject content;
_____ You have something to communicate;
_____ You are capable of sorting out your knowledge under the headings: vital, crucial, important;
_____ Your knowledge is functional.

CONFIDENCE:

_____ You have confidence in yourself and in the pupils;
_____ You know your strength and your weaknesses;
_____ You realize that there is far more to know than you know but this does not worry you;
_____ You are able to help others because you are confident in your ability and knowledge;
_____ You value others, because you value yourself.

CARING:

_____ You care a great deal about individuals and about society;
_____ You enjoy children individually and in groups;
_____ You are genuinely concerned for the welfare of people;
_____ You have faith in adolescents.

COMMUNICATION:

_____ You can communicate knowledge, confidence, and a sense of caring;
_____ You can stimulate children to want to learn;
_____ You can make big ideas and generalizations concrete and clear to learners.

CREATIVITY:

_____ You have imagination, or creativity;
_____ You are dynamic in your teaching;
_____ You use a variety of devices to create and sustain interest.

* Abstracted with adaptations from Kenworthy, Leonard S. Op. cit., pp. 355-368.
[200] President's Commission on National Goals. Op. cit., p. 82.

CURIOSITY:

_____ You are never satisfied with the knowledge you possess;
_____ You are never content with the methodology you have developed;
_____ You are never complacent about your teaching;
_____ You are eager to probe new ideas and extend your own horizons as as well as those of your pupils;
_____ You possess what the poet calls "divine discontent."

COMMITMENT:

_____ You are never satisfied with knowledge for knowledge's sake;
_____ You want knowledge to serve a useful purpose;
_____ You want knowledge to be useful, to help pupils and society attain higher standards of living and thinking;
_____ You have beliefs—carefully examined beliefs that have universal application—and hold these beliefs firmly but re-examine them in the light of new knowledge and new experiences;
_____ You are committed to the democratic life—at its best.

CATALYTIC POWER:

_____ You have the power to excite others, to stimulate them, to urge them to greater effort, to allay their fears, and to make them proud of themselves.

A PLAN FOR ACTION

The real value accrued from any evaluative endeavor lies in the corrective action that results from the findings. Having completed the evaluation of the educational program or of the library program immediate action should be taken to put the recommendations into an operational master plan for improvement. This master plan should outline objectively in specific detail the exact procedure to be followed in upgrading the educational or library program by strengthening noted weaknesses and by putting into operation recommended innovations and changes. This master plan should provide target dates and priorities for both immediate and long range action (See Checklist XIV). It is reasonable to develop the master plan on a three, four, or five year basis designating for the first year those concerns of the greatest significance, for the second year those concerns of the next greatest significance and so on. Such an on-going developmental plan for consistent upgrading of a district school library program should provide for all phases of the program: district school library coordinator and staff, district instructional materials center, district professional library, district centralized ordering and processing service (See Appendix K) as well as providing libraries in each district school which meet the AASL-DAVI standards for personnel, budget, collection, facilities, and program (See Figure XII).

The success of any educational evaluative endeavor is determined by the ability of the educational staff—teachers, librarians, supervisors, administrators—to relate specific program needs to specific program modifications, rennovations and innovations. Such a task demands the cooperative efforts of an educational team of workers who share the vision of educational excellence and who are competent to translate the vision of excellence into concrete operational designs. Such a team requires the efforts of a visionary librarian who can dream constructively within the framework of creative innovation.

12 The School Library Supervisor

*Good administrators use sound judgment based on sound philosophy.**

*Creative teachers ... need creative supervision.*** **

The terms "supervision" and "supervisor" have a historical connotation which has caused them to be anathema to teachers in the past. To many these words automatically call to the foreground of memory a picture of authoritarian dictatorship. Unfortunately the misconception of the purpose and function of supervision inherited from the past continues to persist in the minds of teachers today.

SUPERVISION—HISTORICAL ROLE

When teachers only needed a high school diploma to be certified to teach, the supervisor was appointed to show teachers how to teach. Supervision began as a source of on the job training. There was not too much concern over the teacher's lack of subject knowledge—the textbook was expected to provide course content. It was only in the field of methodology where the teacher was judged in need of training. In order to provide professional knowhow district and county supervisors made their rounds evaluating the effectiveness of the teacher and making recommendations for his improvement.

SABER-TOOTH SUPERVISION

Unfortunately the constructive contribution of the countless many fine supervisors has been forgotten. The overwhelming flood of anecdotal accounts told and retold about the blatantly incompetent supervisor has obliterated the contribution of the competent supervisor from the teacher's historical memory. There are innumerable stories told about supervisors who had little concern for things of the mind; their major concern was for things of a housekeeping nature. They judged a teacher's competency on whether or not the window shades were even; whether or not the blackboard

* Pullen, Thomas G., Jr. *Increasing Your Administrative Skills in Dealing with the Instructional Program.* By George B. Brain. Englewood Cliffs, New Jersey: Prentice-Hall, 1966. Foreword. p. 6.
** E. Paul Torrance. *Education and the Creative Potential.* Minneapolis, Minnesota: University of Minnesota Press, 1963. p. 11.

was washed and the erasers dusted; whether or not lights were burned unnecessarily; whether or not the classroom was maintained at a proper temperature (no mean trick when the room was heated by a pot bellied stove or by a furnace lacking a thermostatic control); whether or not every nubbin of chalk and every smidgin of paper were used; whether or not the teacher remembered to remove the bucket from under the leak in the roof the minute the rain had stopped. This type of vindictive, negative supervision led to the coining of the term "snoopervision." It was the kind of destructive supervision which caused teacher frustration and fear.

In the past the power of the supervisor was absolute—he held the teacher's professional life in his hands. It was upon the recommendation of the supervisor that a teacher's hope for reappointment and salary increase depended. For in the saber-tooth tiger days a salary scale and tenure were not the rule. A teaching contract was for but one year—renewal was by board action. Each year the board decided who would be fired, who would be rehired, and what salary each would be paid. In large measure the recommendation of the supervisor determined the decision of the board. Because the supervisor held the job and salary future of the teacher in his hands he came to be feared as a collector of professional scalps.

CONTEMPORARY CONCEPT OF SUPERVISION

The traditional need for the supervisor to teach the teacher how to teach is long since past. Certification requirements have been upgraded to preclude the necessity of supervision based on methodology. The contemporary concept of supervision is a far cry from "snoopervision." The term as used in contemporary education means:

> All efforts of designated school officials directed toward providing *leadership* to teachers and other educational workers in the *improvement of instruction;* involves the stimulation of professional growth and development of teachers, the selection and revision of objectives, materials of instruction, and methods of teaching, and the evaluation of instruction.[201]

The function of supervision in today's educational endeavor has nothing in common with authoritarian dictatorship. The constant operational goal of modern supervision is improvement of instruction. Therefore, the major responsibility of the supervisor is to provide competent, constructive *leadership* and *guidance* to the educational staff. Today's supervisor does *not* dictate change, does *not* berate teachers, does *not* hire or fire teachers; his function is to inspire, to guide, to lead, to coordinate the efforts of the entire staff as they all work toward a common goal which is mutually understood and mutually respected.

EDUCATIONAL FUNCTION OF THE SUPERVISOR

Supervision is valued by a competent teacher as "an expert technical service primarily aimed at *studying* and *improving cooperatively* all factors which affect child growth and development."[202] The focus of emphasis in construc-

[201] Good, Carter V., ed. Op. cit.
[202] Burton, William H. and Leo J. Brueckner. *Supervision Is a Social Process.* 3rd edition. New York: Appleton-Century-Crofts, Educational Division, Meredith Corp. 1955. p. 11.

tive supervision is on shared responsibility in improving the educational program; the supervisor is an agent for constructive, timely, necessary, intelligent, creative change. It is the special province of the supervisor to anticipate the necessity for change and then to facilitate and expedite group action in understanding and in planning to implement the necessary changes. The object of educational supervision "is to provide leadership in *studying, planning, organizing, coordination and evaluating* of the school programs and in the handling of the problem areas that materialize in the schools."[203] Today's supervisor is not an arm chair general but an active member of an educational task force faced with the responsibility of liberating the children from each educational experience of traditional mediocrity and of winning for all children an educational program of innovative excellence. The leadership role as conceived in modern education "is goal centered, value oriented, communicative, catalytic, energizing, initiatory, and/or creative; the leader is understanding, perceptive, communicative and accepted; what he does or what happens within groups identifies, clarifies, strengthens, supports, suggests new alternatives, alters relationships and arrangements, provides new structure or means of operation, creates new understandings, motivates, provides new perspective and conceptualization."[204]

TASKS ASSIGNED TO SUPERVISORS

The educational tasks or imperative accomplishments ascribed to supervision in today's schools include:[205]

Task I. TO HELP THE PEOPLE OF THE SCHOOL COMMUNITY DEFINE THEIR EDUCATIONAL GOALS AND OBJECTIVES.
Kinds of action needed to accomplish this:
Seek clarification of values held for education;
Seek a rational basis for agreement on operational goals and the means of achieving them;
Seek a rational basis for agreement on the role of the school as one of the educating agencies of the community.

Task II. TO FACILITATE THE TEACHING-LEARNING PROCESS—DEVELOP GREATER EFFECTIVENESS IN TEACHING.
Kinds of action needed to accomplish this:
Provide for continual clarification and mutual acceptance of the educational goals and the means for achieving these;
Employ an adequate concept of change;
Make the learning process the focus of all organizational effort;
Make adequate provision for institutional as well as individual change.

Task III. TO BUILD A PRODUCTIVE ORGANIZATIONAL UNIT.
Kinds of action needed to accomplish this:
Propose and seek agreement on organizational structure which

[203] Burnham, Reba M. and Martha L. King. *Supervision in Action*. Washington, D.C.: Association for Supervision and Curriculum Development, 1961. pp. 31-32. Reprinted with permission.
[204] National Educational Association. *Leadership for Improving Instruction*. Washington, D.C.: National Educational Association, 1960. p. 27.
[205] Abstracted from Ibid., pp. 29-51.

defines the functional working relationship required of all staff
members to achieve the school's goals;

Seek clarification and mutual acceptance of the roles of individuals and subgroups;

Clarify the authority—responsibility—power relationships among
individuals and subgroups;

Make adequate provisions for communication throughout the
school and with other agencies of the community;

Provide adequately for continuous appraisal (See Chapter
Eleven).

Task IV. TO CREATE A CLIMATE FOR GROWTH AND THE EMERGENCE
OF LEADERSHIP.

Conditions necessary to accomplish this:

Teachers (and librarians) must feel that the climate of the school
situation in which they work is conducive to creativeness, experimentation and the expression of individual skill and talent;

Teachers (and librarians) who have difficulties in teaching must
feel free to ask for help;

Support must be given to ensure the integrity of the school program and those who are working to improve it;

Dependence must be placed upon emergent leadership;

Leaders are perceived as helpful;

Central office coordination supersedes central office control.

Task V. TO PROVIDE ADEQUATE RESOURCES FOR EFFECTIVE TEACHING.

Kinds of resources needed to accomplish this:

Professional knowledge and skill;

Human relations skills;

Organizational skills;

Conceptual skills;

Specialized services;

Resources external to the situation (consultants).

To accomplish the tasks as outlined above the following unique
responsibilities are assigned persons in an educational leadership
position:[206]

1. Official leaders are employed in the expectation that they will
   lead. For such people to operate only as arbitrators or facili-
   tators of group action is an abrogation of responsibility which
   may as frequently lead to a *laissez faire* situation as to productive democratic action.
2. Official leaders are responsible for identifying needs for curriculum change and instructional improvement, and for setting up
   arrangements to meet these needs. This includes responsibility
   for awakening an awareness in others of unperceived needs.
3. Official leaders are held by the community personally account-
   able for task accomplishment within the sphere of their responsibilities.
4. Official leaders must be capable of recognizing and utilizing all

[206] Ibid., p. 108.

resources available in promoting the welfare of children and youth. Such resources include the participative leadership potential that exists in all members of the school community.

5. Official leaders need to guard against the tendency to become isolated from those who occupy dissimilar roles. Status isolation of this kind seems to increase as the number of people in similar positions decreases.

CRITERIA FOR SUPERVISORY APPRAISAL

The Association for Supervision and Curriculum Development offers the following criteria for appraising the effectiveness of instructional leadership:[207]

I. EDUCATIONAL OBJECTIVES.

1. Individuals and groups are actively involved in defining and clarifying educational goals and objectives.
2. Agreement has been reached on the role of the school among the educational agencies of the community.
3. A common direction for the educational enterprise has been established, and cooperative effort directed to the achievement of these mutually held goals.
4. People with conflicting values and beliefs harmonize them sufficiently so that they are able to act cooperatively and with unity.
5. Individuals and groups with specialized interests have established a proper balance between such interests and the concerns of the larger community.

II. ROLE PERCEPTION.

1. The roles of individuals and subgroups in the total educational enterprise are clearly defined and are understood.
2. The functional working relationships of all staff members are clearly defined and are understood.
3. The role of specialized resource persons has been clearly defined cooperatively, and is understood by all members of the staff.
4. Individuals and groups clearly understand authority-responsibility-power relationships.
5. Persons able to conceptualize the total tasks of the school help others to perceive more clearly the relationship of their roles to the total educational enterprise.
6. Areas in which individuals and groups are free to operate are clearly defined and understood.
7. Teachers and noncertified personnel participate in making crucial rather than only the routine decisions.
8. Group discussions are held frequently to clarify purposes and roles. These discussions are initiated by official leaders.
9. Leadership emerges from the group at all levels of the school system's operation.
10. Status is achieved through group acceptance and demonstrated competence.

207 Ibid., pp. 164-168.

11. Official leaders are perceived by members of the groups they lead as being helpful.
12. Officially designated leaders of the staff bring special competencies and skills to the groups with which they work.
13. Leaders regularly examine possible sources of confusion in the conceptions held by others concerning the leaders' roles.
14. Leaders have achieved reasonable clarity and conviction concerning expectations of others regarding their roles.
15. Leaders are not expected to hold the same perceptions or to discharge responsibilities using identical means.
16. Leaders help all staff members to reassess their roles in terms of emerging evidence from the sciences undergirding education.
17. Leaders help individuals and groups to place problems or events in an ordered sequence according to importance.
18. Recognized leaders support the school program and members of the staff as they work to improve both.
19. The central administrative staff coordinates efforts for improvement of instruction rather than imposes its plan of activity on teachers.
20. The major function of the building principal is conceived to be that of providing instructional leadership for his staff.
21. Attention is given, insofar as possible, to the personality needs of every person in the school structure.

III. ORGANIZATIONAL STRUCTURE.

1. Rules of procedure are developed by the total staff working under the direction of the superintendent.
2. Rules of procedure are recorded and constantly tested in action to determine their effectiveness in achieving goals.
3. The organizational structure provides for development of procedures to carry policy agreements into action.
4. The organizational structure provides for functions which may be described as catalytic, coordinating, expediting, consulting, helping, appraising, and controlling.
5. The organizational structure is modified when this is essential to facilitate the teaching-learning process and not the reverse.
6. The organizational structure operates successfully in consolidating the gains made by individuals so that the entire staff is improved.
7. The organizational structure provides systematic and effective procedures for identifying and developing all individuals with leadership potential.

IV. GROUP ACTION AND MORALE.

1. Administrative officials encourage cooperative planning and deliberation by school staff and other groups.
2. Groups evidence movement toward mutually held goals, productivity in achieving these goals, and maintenance of group solidarity.

3. Individuals and subgroups evidence high morale as they work together.
4. Human relations skills are in evidence in all aspects of the school's functioning.
5. The staff acts rationally in resolving issues and in seeking solutions to problems.
6. Qualities that enhance interaction of persons in the group may be described in terms such as initiative, originality, communication, empathy, cooperation, understanding, cohesiveness, morale, productivity.
7. Decisions regarding program changes are cooperatively made on the basis of the most objective data obtainable.
8. The total staff is encouraged toward realizing its potential.
9. Teachers encountering teaching or other difficulties feel free to seek assistance.

V. EXPERIMENTATION.
1. The climate of the school situation is conducive to creativeness, experimentation, and expression of individual skill and talent.
2. Experimentation is regularly conducted to discover better ways of using the intelligence of people in solving the problems of the schools.
3. Hypotheses which have been established for improving practices are being tested in action.
4. New ideas which seem to the instructional staff and the patrons to have promise are tested by school workers to determine their effectiveness.
5. Individuals and groups are eager to explore or experiment with suggestions which are made by the group.
6. The staff uses knowledge and data effectively in solving problems and resolving issues.
7. Provision is made so that all staff members are constantly acquiring new skills, understanding, and attitudes.
8. Although most program decisions are made at the local school level, consideration is given to a system-wide framework of common purposes, philosophy, and scope that gives unity and guidance to individual schools and staff members.

VI. COMMUNICATION.
1. Channels of communication are effectively established for a regular flow of ideas to the center of control and from it to every interested person and group.
2. Much communication within the defined structure consists of face-to-face discussion, and sufficient staff is provided to make this possible.
3. Many ways are used to provide discussions related to school policies: system-wide and building staff meetings, open forums, neighborhood discussions, parent-teacher meetings, grade-parent meetings, student-parent forums, and total community groups.

4. Much communication within the schools and the school system is informal in nature.

5. All staff members are frequently informed regarding legal limitations placed upon the schools and the policies established by the local board. These policies should be available in written form.

VII. RESOURCES.

1. An effective structure or organization has been created so that available resources may be known to all and may be used wisely in improving instruction.

2. The organizational structure is such that individuals and groups are encouraged to reach out beyond known resources for imaginative and creative solutions to problems.

3. Resources from outside the group are used effectively to help clarify goals, resolve issues, catch new insights, and develop new skills.

4. Lay and professional resource persons in addition to the regularly employed staff are identified and used as needed for improving instruction and contributing to staff growth-in-service.

5. Specialized resource persons such as psychologists, guidance workers, physicians, nurses, and social workers are employed, and they assist in improving instruction.

6. Effective use is made of available instructional materials, and new resources are constantly sought and made available.

7. Funds are available so the individual school can secure inexpensive materials when they are needed instead of going through slow requisitioning processes.

8. The principal of the school and the teacher of the class are clearly seen as the agents through whom resources are related to learning situations for children.

VIII. EVALUATION.

1. Procedures have been established for evaluating the effectiveness of instructional leadership processes.

2. Administrators, teachers, specialized personnel, parents, and pupils all participate as appropriate in the appraisal processes.

IMPACT OF SUPERVISION ON THE INDIVIDUAL TEACHER

Supervision to be constructively effective must be personalized. "By personalizing is meant the meeting of another at a level and through a means which is central to the concerns, interests, ideas and modes of thinking and feeling of another."[208] Supervision to be effective must be a person-to-person relationship even in an enterprise involving a number of people. The value of the supervisor lies in his capacity to generate in each participant (regard-

[208] Berman, Louise M. and Mary Lou Usery. *Personalized Supervision: Sources and Insights.* Washington, D.C.: Association for Supervision and Curriculum Development, 1966. p. 1. Reprinted with permission.

less of the size of the group) a genuine concern for achieving a commonly accepted and a commonly respected goal. The effective supervisor is capable of selling fellow educators on a better instructional way of life.

BASIC TENETS OF SUPERVISION

The following tenets undergird the modern concept of educational supervision:[209]

Instructional supervision is a dynamic, growing process that is occupying an increasingly important role in the schools.

The purpose of supervision is to offer leadership in the improvement of educational experiences for children and youth.

Leadership is centered in a group, not in an individual.

The type and quality of supervision are affected by the situation, the organization, in which the supervision exists.

The climate of human relationships within the group and the degree to which members are committed to group goals influence the degree of change in practice.

The way in which individuals perceive the problems and the tasks inherent in the situation affects their behavior.

The actual role of supervision—and of instructional leaders—is a composite of all the expectations held for the role by the people associated with it.

A primary goal of supervisory leaders is to foster leadership in others.

SUPERVISION OF LIBRARY PROGRAM

The direct involvement of the school library in the teaching and learning endeavor demands a library program of uniform excellence throughout a school district. A district educational program of uniform excellence cannot tolerate nor excuse a library program of less than excellence. A library program of excellence requires an overall coordinated operational plan designed to provide library services, resources, and media usage patterns commensurate with the developmental needs of the educational program. A district library program of functional excellence requires the competence, the vision, the guidance, the leadership of a library supervisor or, as the term so frequently used synonymously, of a coordinator.

When there are two or more libraries in a district, it is recommended that a librarian be appointed library supervisor or coordinator;[210] this supervisor or coordinator to provide the leadership and direction necessary for planning, structuring, implementing, and evaluating a library program as a supporting educational agent for excellence.

The function of the library supervisor as outlined by the American Association of School Librarians encompasses the following:[211]

209 Burnham, Reba M. and Martha L. King. Op. cit., p. 32.

210 Pennsylvania Division of School Libraries. *A Guide for School Librarians.* Harrisburg, Pennsylvania: Department of Public Instruction, 1969.

211 American Association of School Libraries. Op. cit., pp. 43-45.

1. The school library supervisor serves as a consultant for and works with the chief school administrator in such matters as:
   a. The use of school library instruction, services, resources in implementing and enriching the total educational program.
   b. Methods for acquainting teachers with resource materials.
   c. Planning and evaluating school library programs.
   d. Staffing school libraries.
   e. Planning library budgets.
   f. Planning basic collections of materials in the schools.
   g. Planning library quarters.
   h. Developing central purchasing, processing, and organizational procedures for library materials.

2. The school library supervisor has responsibility for:
   a. Exerting leadership in creating an understanding of the role of the school library in curriculum development.
   b. Interpreting the functions and needs of the school libraries in the system.
   c. Administering the school library budget as provided by the board of education and superintendent of schools.
   d. Coordinating the program of library service and library instruction among the several schools.
   e. Providing for the cooperative evaluation and selection of materials by school librarians, teachers, and curriculum specialists.
   f. Directing the materials center.
   g. Directing the central acquisition and processing of materials.

3. The school library supervisor works closely with supervisors and staff members in other departments of the central school office, and continuously provides advisory and cooperative services by means of:
   a. Developing policies, procedures, and standards for the program of library services in the schools as related to phases of the educational program.
   b. Participating in curriculum study and evaluation, and recommending printed and other materials for resource units.
   c. Serving as consultant whenever needed.
   d. Contributing to the inservice training of teachers.
   e. Evaluating and recommending printed and audio-visual materials for purchase.
   f. Providing library statistics, records, reports, and research.

4. The school library supervisor provides guidance and leadership in professional growth for the librarians in the school system by means of:
   a. Giving advisory and consultant services, and having conferences with individual librarians about their library programs.
   b. Planning inservice education through meetings, workshops, and conferences.
   c. Encouraging librarians to participate with teachers, counselors, and others in solving problems of mutual concern.
   d. Preparing bulletins, newsletters, and other aids for transmit-

ting suggestions for library improvements and for circulating information about library developments.

e. Encouraging individual initiative in experimentation and research.

f. Promoting continuity of practice to assure uniformity of basic library procedures throughout the system, and at the same time encouraging continuous improvements and individual enterprise.

g. Making visits to the libraries in the schools.

h. Giving stimulation, evaluation, and sympathetic understanding to the school librarians.

5. The school library supervisor maintains a continuous program of evaluation by:

a. Analyzing and evaluating techniques and services in the school library programs and in the central office.

b. Measuring growth of the school libraries by local, state, and national standards.

c. Cooperating in national and state surveys.

d. Preparing reports and recommendations.

6. The school library supervisor maintains a program of good public relations by:

a. Cooperating with other libraries in the community in encouraging library use by pupils and adults.

b. Participating in civic projects relating to libraries, books, audio-visual materials, and reading, listening, and viewing.

c. Participating in professional education and library organizations, at local, state, and national levels.

d. Contributing to professional journals and publications.

e. Providing professional consultative service to individuals and community groups.

f. Interpreting school library service through all communication media.

The library supervisor shares with the building principal the responsibility for the integration of the library program with the classroom teaching and learning program. This is a joint administrative concern. It is the principal who sets the educational priorities for his faculty; it is the principal who encourages by his attitude the teachers to plan with the librarian for class, group, and individual student use of the library.

Instructional changes which call for significant new ways of using professional talent, drawing upon instructional resources, allocating physical facilities, scheduling instructional time or altering physical space—rearrangements of the structural elements of the institution—depend almost exclusively upon administrative initiative.

Authority is a critical element in the shaping of institutional decisions. Schools depend heavily upon administrative authority in decision-making. Consequently, the control center of the institution, as schools are managed today, is the administrator. He may not be—and frequently is not—the original source of interest in a new type of program, but unless he gives it his attention and actively promotes its use, it will not come into being.[212]

The following advice is given to the principal concerning his responsibility for developing a dynamic library program for his school by Dr. George B. Brain, Dean of the College of Education at Washington State University:[213]

The library program in your school will be a creative, dynamic one only if you (the principal) understand and discharge your obligations to it. You must:

1. Interpret the library program to teachers so that they see it in relation to the rest of the instructional program and also appreciate its interrelationship with each of the areas in the instructional program. Use inservice training to help your staff develop skills for diagnosis and to show them how diagnosis can serve as an aid to teaching. Correctly planned and executed by a principal whose educational philosophy recognizes the importance of the school library, this type of activity can lead to high staff morale, which in turn leads to a cohesiveness among the different departments in the instructional program, and, therefore, to a contribution to the individual student.

2. Select, or aid in selecting, the librarian with the same careful attention that you give to selecting a teacher.

3. Work with the librarian, applying the same principles of supervision that you use with the teaching staff. Include her in all curriculum planning activities within the school. Assume the responsibility to make her and the teaching staff aware of their interdependence.

4. Provide for the best possible library program. This involves planning so that the librarian (a) works with children in small groups and entire classes, both in the library and in classrooms, and (b) gives individual attention to pupils.

5. Involve the librarian in the school program by requiring that she attend all meetings at which the content of courses is discussed and by expecting her to assume committee assignments and extra-curricular duties. (But do not assign duties at the lunch hour or before or after school, because this will curtail the library service.)

6. Make the program feasible administratively (a) by providing time for teachers and the librarian to plan together, (b) by scheduling so that children have time to use the library, and (c) by seeing that rules and regulations encourage maximum use of the library by children and their teachers.

7. Provide for evaluation of the library and its services. One of

[212] From "Facts and Fallacies About New Media in Education" by Donald Ely, *Revolution in Teaching: New Theory, Technology, and Curricula,* edited by Alfred de Grazia and David A. Sohn. Copyright © 1962, 1964 by Metron, Inc. By permission of Bantam Books, Inc. P. 47.
[213] Brain, George B. *Increasing Your Administrative Skills in Dealing with the Instructional Program.* Englewood Cliffs, New Jersey: Prentice-Hall, 1966. pp. 52-53.

the best ways to provide for constant evaluation is to have a library evaluation committee (composed of staff members and the librarian) study the library and make recommendations concerning its improvement and use. Though much of the work can be done by others, you should serve as the core of this committee, for, without your support, improvements will not be made. More important, if you are a key person on this committee, you will be more aware of the needs of the library and more interested and sympathetic when funds are requested for improvements.

The school library supervisor provides leadership in determining what methods most effectively predict success in promoting teacher and student use of library resources and services. The final success of the program rests in the hands of each individual member of the library staff. Each librarian is of equal significance; each has a vital part to play in encouraging teachers and students to utilize the facilities, services and resources of the library as a natural supporting part of their teaching and learning program. Therefore, the competent school library supervisor organizes his library staff as a library team; encouraging each librarian to participate in all phases of the design, structure, and implementation of the library program. The school library supervisor takes to heart the following admonition:[214]

In assessing the competence of a professional person one does not measure his performance on "housekeeping" activities . . . . "Housekeeping" duties are often *necessary* conditions for performance, but are not critical. The critical or sufficient conditions of proficiency assessment are those that are defined as the essentials of a profession—a fund of abstract knowledge, kept up to date by constant study, applied by the practitioner to perform an essential public service better than one outside the professional group can perform it.

The library supervisor or coordinator is assigned the following imperative accomplishments:

Keeping educationally and professionally informed.

Alerting the administrative staff and the library staff to emerging concepts and patterns of recommended library service.

Representing the library staff and interpreting the library program in administrative counsels.

Designing media programs for consideration, criticism, refinement, and cooperative redesign by the library staff.

Supervising the organization and the operation of the district instructional materials center, the district centralized ordering and processing center, and the district professional library.

Planning new library facilities with the chief school administrator, the administrative staff, the architect, and the library staff.

[214] Macdonald, James B., ed. *Theories of Instruction*. Washington, D.C.: Association for Supervision and Curriculum Development, 1965. p. 67. Reprinted by permission.

Planning with the community library staff for a district climate of mutual respect and cooperation between the school and the public library.

"Selling" the library program to the community, i.e., articles in newspapers; speeches to community groups; talks to P.T.A.'s and mothers' clubs, etc.

Preparing annual and special reports for the administration and the school board.

Keeping conversant with new materials, equipment, processes, curricular developments, etc., and sharing this knowledge with the library staff.

Evaluating the strength and weakness of the district library program and assigning priorities and target dates for upgrading and strengthening each substandard aspect of that program.

Determining library staff assignment in consultation with the chief school administrator and/or director of teacher personnel and the librarians involved.

Participating in administrative policy and/or decision making meetings and alerting library staff to anticipated changes pertinent to them.

Preparing and presenting to the administrative staff the budget requirements for the district library program. (This budget proposal having been drawn up cooperatively by the library staff and the supervisor.)

Participating in district curriculum study, evaluation and revision and alerting the librarians to anticipated curriculum changes.

Foreseeing problems and planning strategy to avoid or solve them.

Translating curriculum changes into print and non-print media support needs and into budget requirement needs.

Preparing bid specifications, checking bids received, placing orders for furniture, equipment and supplies for each of the district individual building libraries.

Scheduling, planning and conducting library staff meetings.

Obtaining and distributing print and non-print materials for librarian evaluation.

Ordering or causing to be ordered all materials to be employed in the district library program and in the individual building libraries.

Serving as a materials consultant to the librarian; to the teacher or committee building a unit requiring the support of library resources.

Designing and/or having produced forms, checklists, schedules, evaluative criteria, etc. for use by library staff.

Organizing and implementing plans for pilot study programs for the testing of instructional media.

Proof of the leadership impact of the school library supervisor or coordinator was uncovered by Alice Lohrer in her national survey of instructional materials centers. Miss Lohrer reported:[215]

> In all types of schools where the materials program was functioning smoothly, staff members had know-how in administering the service. They knew children, materials, sources of selection, how to organize resources for use, and were more interested in providing services than in techniques. In such programs the invisible wall that is evident in other schools between the library and the audiovisual programs was nonexistent or had broken down. The needs of boys and girls rather than concern over media and devices took precedence in schools where librarians were developing effective programs of service. Working with teachers and experimenting with them in the use of mass media and in newer methods of teaching were also parts of such library programs. Openmindedness, cooperation, willingness to experiment and to learn were attitudes held by these school librarians. They had professional concern relating to the teaching functions of the school library program. *Programs that were under the direction and planning of city, town, or country school library supervisors or instructional materials coordinators seemed to function more smoothly and were developing more rapidly than was true in other school systems.*
>
> *Where there were supervisors or directors, another trend was noted which is not clearly represented in library literature. This is in the field of centralized processing for school libraries* (See Appendix K).

The professionally competent school library supervisor or coordinator will provide innovative, creative leadership in devising increasingly more effective and more efficient ways to facilitate the integration of the library program with the educational program while freeing the library staff from all tasks of an educationally nonproductive nature.

QUALIFICATIONS FOR A SCHOOL LIBRARY SUPERVISOR

The library supervisor who has at heart a personal concern for the library program will inspire his library staff to share his concern and to take an active part in constantly striving ever to better the program. In order to accomplish this the school library supervisor must possess: a sense of commitment, a sense of proportion, a sense of priorities, a sense of values, a sense of perception, a sense of justice, a sense of loyalty, a sense of emotional balance, a sense of humor, a sense of vision, and common sense in abun-

[215] Lohrer, Alice. "School Libraries as Instructional Materials Centers With Implications for Training: A Progress Report of This Study Under Title VII, National Defense Education Act." In *The School Library as a Materials Center: Educational Needs of Librarians and Teachers in Its Administration and Use.* Edited by Mary Helen Mahar. Washington, D.C.: U.S. Department of Health, Education, and Welfare, 1963. p. 14.

dance. In addition to being a "sense-able" person, the school library supervisor must be a:

Dynamic leader	Creative innovator
Competent educator	Idealistic realist
Knowledgeable librarian	Imaginative strategist
Gifted teacher	Practical philosopher
Media programming expert	Disciplined dreamer
Curriculum content specialist	Practicing humanist
Effective communicator	Persistent scholar
Efficient administrator	Avid reader.
Diagnostic technician	

In summation, the supervisor of school library service on the district, county, regional, or state level should possess the leadership qualities and the professional competencies and vision essential for developing a school library program commensurate with all the needs of an educational program of continued, ever increasing excellence and promise.

13 The School Library — A Laboratory for Learning

*"Ideals are like stars; you will not succeed in touching them with your hands. But like the seafaring man on the desert of waters, you choose them as your guides, and following them you will reach your destiny."**

CARL SCHURZ

THE SCHOOL LIBRARY
FORCE FOR LEARNING HOW TO THINK

The school library shares with the school its responsibility for teaching the student how to learn to think effectively, efficiently, and creatively with satisfaction and zest. Learning to learn in the library requires that the librarian function as a teacher actively guiding the student as he works with ideas, teaching him how to identify, analyze, select, group, and unify ideas into patterns of cohesive interrelatedness and significance (See Appendix N). The school library is the knowledge-building laboratory where today's student is encouraged to practice thinking within a context of need, purpose, and functional utility under the concerned and competent guidance of the librarian.

IMPERATIVE REQUISITES

Actualizing the promise to provide a quality, optimum educational experience for each student demands that the educational program be one of uniform excellence, planned and worked for, not left to chance or accident. The school library as an integral component of the educational program also must be planned, designed, and structured scientifically to synchronize with the developmental needs of the on-going teaching and learning program. Just as the "process of education" must be scientific in design and operation, so must the school library program.

To assure a district library program of uniform educational excellence the following are imperative:

> Administrative initiative, concern, respect, and backing in designing, structuring, and implementing the district library program.

* Schurz, Carl. Address. Faneuil Hall, Boston, Massachusetts. April 18, 1859. Bartlett, John. *Bartlett's Familiar Quotations.* 13th ed. rev. Boston, Massachusetts: Little, Brown, 1955. p. 644.

A district climate conducive to teacher respect for the educational significance of planned library usage.

A district library program designed and structured as an integral component of the total educational enterprise (See Appendix I).

A district library program reflective of the district educational philosophy, goals, objectives, and program.

A district program reflective of the standards in staff budget, facilities, media collection, and program (See Figure XII).

A district library coordinator (where there are two or more building libraries) to develop with the administration staff a district library master plan and then to provide the leadership and guidance in putting the master plan into operation.

A district library staff organized to function as a cooperative team, pooling energies, competencies, special knowledge, and sharing obligations and responsibilities.

A library staff in each library of sufficient number and specialized educational competence to fulfill effectively and efficiently the teaching obligation of the library (See Figure XII).

A media collection in each elementary and secondary school reflective of the developmental needs of the curriculum and of the personal and educational needs of the students and sufficient in quantity and quality to satisfy both (See Figure XII).

A district instructional materials center to augment and reinforce the media collections of the building libraries and subject laboratories.

A centralized district ordering and processing service to expedite the media acquisition service and to liberate building librarians from time consuming nonprofessonal responsibilities (See Appendix K).

A district professional library commensurate with the curriculum and faculty study and growth needs (See Checklist VI).

A policy of constant evaluation of the educational efficiency and effectiveness of the library program at both the building and district level (See Figures X, XI, XII).

A five year library developmental plan with specific target dates and priorities for strengthening building and district library service (See Checklist XIV).

THE IMAGE OF TODAY'S LIBRARIAN

Because the school library is involved directly in the teaching and learning enterprise, the quality of the librarian as a teacher is of the greatest importance. No longer can the school librarian anticipate service as a cataloger contentedly typing away in cloistered seclusion from the educational combat zone. School librarianship is no enterprise for the faint of heart, the timid

or the shy. Today's school librarian must be a teacher not only in preparation and certification but a competent teacher in function, attitude and
spirit. He must welcome the opportunity to be involved directly in the
school's battle to win for each student a meaningful, satisfying, challenging education. The school librarian aloof from and uninvolved with the educational battle is as vocationally anachronistic as the town crier and the
chimney sweep! Today's school librarian is a teacher not a librarian in the
narrow sense of a practitioner of library routines. Just as the classroom
teacher is an educator with special background in English, social studies,
music, art, etc., so the librarian is an educator with special background in
utilizing library resources and services to support the entire educational
program.

Today's school librarian serves in the triple capacity of educational
generalist, materials specialist, and media programming engineer.

As an educational generalist the school librarian must possess and demonstrate:

> Enthusiasm and respect for teaching and for learning;
> Zest for keeping informed as to the innovative trends in education;
> Perspective in viewing self as a teacher;
> Perspective in viewing the educational role of the school library as
> support agent to the total educational endeavor;
> Broad academic background and interests;
> Knowledge in depth of the educational program;
> Competence to relate the resources and services of the library to the
> total educational program;
> Authentic concern for the optimum achievement and self-realiza-
> tion of each student;
> Competence to plan and work cooperatively and effectively with
> administrators and fellow teachers for the purposeful, appropriate,
> productive use of library resources, facilities, and services.

As a materials specialist the school librarian must possess and demonstrate:

> Respect for all medium of knowledge regardless of format;
> Sensitivity to the educational potential of instructional media;
> Knowledge *in depth* of the content of the library's resources;
> Zest for keeping informed as to the latest media developments,
> trends, releases, productions, and concepts;
> Competence to search for, select, organize, balance, and administer
> a media collection which will effectively meet the developmental
> needs of the curriculum and the personal and educational needs
> of the students.

As a media programming engineer the school librarian must be competent to:

> Design media usage patterns reflective of teaching goals and com-
> mensurate with individual learner needs and potential;
> Design and produce or supervise production of instructional media
> to meet unique curricular development needs;

Relate specific resources to specific topic and/or concept development needs;

Determine when the use of a resource is: timely to topic and/or
concept development; suitable to class, group or individual student
interest, ability, and maturity level; educationally appropriate,
supportive, necessary, and significant;

Blueprint media usage sequence patterns to introduce, develop,
relate, and interrelate ideas in a logical, progressively sequential
order;

Personalize the services and resources of the library by designing
media usage programs commensurate with the developmental needs
of the curriculum and/or the educational and personal needs of the
students;

Implement with imagination and stamina all library strategies.

TODAY'S SCHOOL LIBRARIAN MUST BE A TEACHER

Repeatedly throughout these pages the point has been made that a quality
educational program demands the support of a quality library program.
Likewise, the point has been reiterated that the quality of the library program is in direct proportion to the degree of professional excellence attained and demonstrated by the school librarian. Direct involvement in the
teaching and learning program has changed the function of the library from
a materials storehouse to a learning laboratory and has changed the role of
the librarian from curator of things to energizer of thought and expediter
of learning. Therefore, today's school librarian must be a teacher in training, certification, attitude, self-image, service, and commitment.

In emphasizing that the school librarian must be a teacher, the author
has used the term in its generic sense; let the reader make no mistake as to
intent. It is imperative that the reader—be he administrator, school board
member, guidance counselor, department chairman, teacher-in-training,
teacher-in-service, librarian-in-training, librarian-in-service, or layman—perceive clearly the professional role of the librarian as direct participant in
the educational endeavor:

> The librarian of today and tomorrow must have many technical
> and professional skills, but above all he must have skill with
> people. He is a teacher whose subject is learning itself.[216]

Since the school librarian is a teacher, he must possess the same high degree
of professional competence demanded in a free society of all who would
teach. "The alertness, commitment, and creative skill of the individual
teacher are both the foundation stone and the capstone of the teaching-
learning experience."[217] Teaching, therefore, is no job for the less than
able, for one suffering from poverty of the mind or of the spirit!

Just as it is grossly unfair to encourage the student to dream of a vocation for which he is unsuited, so is it grossly unfair to minimize the demands
and the requirements of a profession in order to paint a glamorous picture.

216 Knight, Douglas M. "Foreword." *Library Services for the Nation's Needs: Toward
Fulfillment of a National Policy—Report of the National Advisory Commission on Libraries,* July, 1968. Washington, D.C.: National Advisory Commission on Libraries, 1968.
217 National Education Association. *Joint Project on the Individual and the School.* Op.
cit., p. 13.

It is not the purpose of this book to solve the manpower shortage by enticing the less than able into school librarianship. Rather, it is the mission of this book by sharply focusing the true image of the school librarian, to attract to the profession only those willing and competent to translate the standards of excellence from blueprint to actuality.

If the reader cherishes in his mind the picture of the librarian reading in cloistered seclusion far removed from the turmoil of the classroom, he has missed the message of this book. Being a school librarian in the functional sense of the term is a rigorous, demanding, energy and time consuming job. One's work is never done; time is a constant taskmaster: this book must be read, this filmstrip previewed, this curriculum meeting attended, this resource unit structured, this teacher's request answered, this state report studied, this budget form completed, this student's special needs met, this speech class scheduled, this learning program developed, this study skill transparency designed, etc.

A school librarian of true professional stature expects to work hard and sees the reason for expending maximum effort to achieve a library program of educational excellence. Such a librarian does not come to librarianship because of disenchantment with teaching, does not use the school library as a fire escape from the purgatory of the classroom. Such a librarian is not a member of a happiness cult but is a realist in professional expectation, knowing full well that "happiness . . . consists of moments. A teacher cannot expect an endless series of joy filled hours, success after success. A reasonable goal may be one or two moments a day—on the average . . ."[218] Such a librarian is not an unrealistic dreamer but a clear eyed idealist welcoming the chance to participate in the radical shifts and swift changes of the contemporary educational world, changes that require boldness, vision, and hard work.

THERE WILL BE DAYS—

The pressures of everyday teaching—the multitude of sheer numbers, the complexity and regularity of problems, the perversity of human nature, the vastness of the enterprise, the remoteness of policy shapers—can make even the most dedicated and competent teacher feel overwhelmed. This is the malaise which traps the unwary into becoming self-pitying, chronic complainers. It is imperative that school librarians as teachers keep their perspective, maintain their professional equilibrium, and discipline their introspection by looking beyond the annoyances, frustrations, and disappointments to the ultimate purpose and goal of education in maintaining and strengthening our free society. They do not work in vain!

ELAN—THE HIGHEST DEGREE OF COMMITMENT

To strive, to survive, to achieve, the librarian must have the highest degree of professional commitment to the ideal of excellence. Max Lerner uses the word, *elan,* to dramatize this highest degree of professional commitment demanded of those who would teach.

> What I mean by *elan* is a feeling of commitment and of being on fire, a sense of mission, a sense that there are things worth dying and living for.

[218] Hook, J. N. Op. cit., p. 461.

When I talk of *elan,* I am talking really of maintaining the dream and the vision without which the whole structure of free world power will become blind and ultimately collapse.

If you look back at the history of the rise and fall of civilizations you will find, I think, that civilizations also have died of two things. They died of rigidity, as Ortega y Gasset has suggested: of a kind of arteriosclerosis of their master institutions. But they have also died because of a failure of nerve. . . .

We need to understand some of these causes of the death of civilizations if we are to understand also what it is that a nation lives of. I would say it lives of its dreams and visions, but also of a lively sense of danger and resolve. . . . The problem is whether, not just in war but in peace, not just for military power and destruction but for the purposes of a peaceful society, we can again have our lives "touched with fire."[219]

To be a school librarian of competence requires a commitment to the ideal of service characterized by the word and the spirit of *elan!*

CHALLENGE OF THE 70'S

The goal of the 60's was to establish school libraries in all schools and to stock those libraries with sufficient resources to support the educational program. In large measure because of professional vision and leadership, public concern, administrative backing, increased school board awareness, and federal funding, this goal is in sight.

The challenge of the 70's is to man school libraries with sufficient efficient professional and paraprofessional personnel to power adequately the school library educational support program. The time of truth is at hand: given adequate facilities, resources, and staff, can today's librarians demonstrate in practice the theory that the school library is a vitalizing source and a dynamic force for educational excellence?

The onus of proof falls squarely on the shoulders of each librarian. The quality of the library program reflects directly the professional quality of the library staff. Today's school librarian holds in his hands the hope of the school library's attaining full educational stature, status, and respect. It is the librarian who customizes, personalizes, and humanizes the services of the school library. It is the school librarian who is the energizing force powering the library's educational support program. It is the school librarian who must utilize library resources wisely, creatively, and compassionately so that learning will be more lastingly significant, more permanently meaningful, and more personally satisfying. This is a grave responsibility. It is also a rewarding challenge, for the extent to which today's children and youth "will be creative, informed, knowledgeable, and within their own years, wise,"[220] will depend in large measure on the avail-

[219] Lerner, Max. "Humanist Goals" in *Education: An Instrument of National Goals.* New York: McGraw-Hill, 1962. pp. 105-107.
[220] American Association of School Librarians. Op. cit., p. 4.

ability of appropriate resources and on the availability of professionally competent librarians.

The challenge of the 70's is to demonstrate in action that the school librarian is a teacher—a mediating source and force for educational excellence.

APPENDIX A

Basic Background Readings

EXCERPTS FROM: GENERAL EDUCATION IN A FREE SOCIETY: A REPORT OF THE HARVARD COMMITTEE*

. . . The primary concern of American education today is not the development of the "good life" in young gentlemen born to the purple. It is the infusion of the liberal and humane tradition into our entire educational system. Our purpose is to cultivate in the largest possible number of our future citizens an appreciation of both the responsibilities and the benefits which come to them because they are Americans and are free. . . .

Such a concept of general education is the imperative need of the American educational system. It alone can give cohesion to our efforts and guide the contribution of your youth to the nation's future. (pp. xiii-xv)

General education, as education for an informed responsible life in our society, has chiefly to do with . . . the question of common standards and common purposes. Taken as a whole, education seeks to do two things: help young persons fulfill the unique, particular functions in life which it is in them to fulfill, and fit them so far as it can for those common spheres which, as citizens and heirs of a joint culture, they will share with others. (p. 4)

. . . The hope of the American school system, indeed of our society, is precisely that it can pursue two goals simultaneously: give scope to ability and raise the average. . . . (p. 35)

* *General Education in a Free Society: A Report of the Harvard Committee.* Cambridge, Mass.: Harvard University Press, 1945.

. . . The school is a civilizing place in the fundamental sense of giving young people the tools on which any civilization depends. . . . (p. 36)

. . . To the belief in man's dignity must be added the recognition of his duty to his fellow men. Dignity does not rest on any man as being separate from all other beings, which he in any case cannot be, but springs from his common humanity and exists positively as he makes the common good his own. . . . It is impossible to escape the realization that our society, like any society, rests on common beliefs and that a major task of education is to perpetuate them. (pp. 46-47)

This conclusion raises one of the most fundamental problems of education, indeed of society itself: how to reconcile this necessity for common belief with the equally obvious necessity for new and independent insights leading to change. . . . The true task of education is . . . so to reconcile the sense of pattern and direction deriving from heritage with the sense of experiment and innovation deriving from science that they may exist fruitfully together. . . . (p. 47)

Democracy is the view that not only the few but that all are free, in that everyone governs his own life and shares in the responsibility for the management of the community. This being the case, it follows that all human beings stand in need of an ampler and rounder education. The task of modern democracy is to preserve the ancient ideal of liberal education and to extend it as far as possible to all the members of the community. . . . To believe in the equality of human beings is to believe that the good life, and the education which trains the citizen for the good life, are equally the privilege of all. And these are the touchstones of the liberated man: first, is he free; that is to say, is he able to judge and plan for himself, so that he can truly govern himself? In order to do this, his must be a mind capable of self-criticism; he must lead that self-examined life which according to Socrates is alone worthy of a free man. Thus he will possess inner freedom as well as social freedom. Second, is he universal in his motives and sympathies? For the civilized man is a citizen of the entire universe; he has overcome provincialism, he is objective, and is a "spectator of all time and all existence." Surely these two are the very aims of democracy itself. (pp. 52-53)

. . . The problem of general education is one of combining fixity of aim with diversity in application. It is not a question of providing a general education which will be uniform through the same classes of all schools and colleges all over the country, even were such a thing possible in our decentralized system. It is rather to adapt general education to the needs and intentions of different groups and, so far as possible, to carry its spirit into special education. The effectiveness of teaching has always largely depended on this willingness to adapt a central unvarying purpose to varying outlooks. Such adaptation is as much in the interest of the quick as of the slow, of the bookish as of the unbookish, and is the necessary protection of each. What is wanted, then, is a general education capable at once of taking on many different forms and yet of representing in all its forms the common knowledge and the common values on which a free society depends. (pp. 57-58)

. . . education looks both to the nature of knowledge and to the good of man in society. It is to the latter aspect that we shall now turn our attention

—more particularly to the traits and characteristics of mind fostered by education.

By characteristics we mean aims so important as to prescribe how general education should be carried out and which abilities should be sought above all others in every part of it. These abilities, in our opinion, are: *to think effectively, to communicate thought, to make revelant judgments, to discriminate among values.* They are not in practice separable and are not to be developed in isolation. Each is an indispensable coexistent functions of a sanely growing mind. . . . (pp. 64-65)

Human personality cannot . . . be broken up into distinct parts of traits. Education must look to the whole man. It has been wisely said that education aims at the good man, the good citizen, and the useful man. . . . the fruit of education is intelligence in action. The aim is mastery of life; and since living is an art, wisdom is the indispensable means to this end. (pp. 74-75)

. . . It is important to realize that the ideal of a free society involves a twofold value, the value of freedom and that of society. Democracy is a community of free men. We are apt sometimes to stress freedom—the power of individual choice and the right to think for oneself—without taking sufficient account of the obligations to cooperate with our fellow men; democracy must represent an adjustment between the values of freedom and social living. (p. 76)

. . . Democracy is the attempt to combine liberty with loyalty, each limiting the other, and also each reinforcing the other. (p. 77)

. . . The main upshot of all that has been said until now is so simple that any statement of it sounds almost absurdly flat. It is that, as Americans, we are necessarily both one and many, both a people following the same road to a joint future and a set of individuals following scattered roads as gifts and circumstances dictate. But though flat and truistic this double fact is the foundation of this report. Simple in itself, it is far from simple in its consequences. It means that, though common aims must bind together the whole educational system, there exists no one body of knowledge, no single system of instruction equally valid for every part of it. (p. 79)

. . . within a generation the problem of how best to meet this immense range of talent and need has grown up, like the fabled beanstalk, to overshadow virtually every other education problem. It is in truth at the heart of any attempt to achieve education for democracy. (p. 81)

. . . equal opportunity does not mean identical provisions for all. Rather, it means access for all to those avenues of education which match their gifts and interests. . . . Here we are back at what was called earlier the main task of our educational system: to nurture ability while raising the average. (p. 86)

. . . *How can general education be so adapted to different ages and, above all, differing abilities and outlooks, so that it can appeal deeply to each, yet remain in goal and essential teaching the same for all?* The answer to this question, it seems not too much to say, is the key to anything like complete democracy. (p. 93)

EXCERPTS FROM: THE PURSUIT OF EXCELLENCE: EDUCATION AND THE FUTURE OF AMERICA*

There is no more searching or difficult problem for a free people than to identify, nurture and wisely use its own talents. Indeed, on its ability to solve this problem rests, at least in part, its fate as a free people. For a free society cannot commandeer talent: it must be true to its own vision of individual liberty. And yet at a time when we face problems of desperate gravity and complexity an undiscovered talent, a wasted skill, a misplaced ability is a threat to the capacity of a free people to survive.

But there is another and deeper reason why a free nation must cultivate its own human potential: such a task reflects the very purposes for which a free society exists. If our nation seeks to strengthen the opportunities for free men to develop their individual capacities and to inspire creative effort, our aim is as importantly that of widening and deepening the life purposes of our citizens as it is to add to the success of our national effort. A free society nurtures the individual not alone for the contribution he may make to the social effort, but also and primarily for the sake of the contribution he may make to his own realization and development.

Hence a free nation's search for talent is always a critical aspect of its national existence. (p. v)

The greatness of a nation may be manifested in many ways—in its purposes, its courage, its moral responsibility, its cultural and scientific eminence, the tenor of its daily life. But ultimately the source of its greatness is in the individuals who constitute the living substance of the nation.

A concern for the realization of individual potentialities is deeply rooted in our moral heritage, our political philosophy, and the texture of our daily customs. . . . We believe that man—by virtue of his humanity—should live in the light of reason, exercise moral responsibility, and be free to develop to the full the talents that are in him. (p. 1)

. . . in its deepest sense our concern for human excellence is a reflection of our ideal of the overriding importance of human dignity. It is not a means but an end. It expresses our notion of what constitutes a good life and our ultimate values. (pp. 1-2)

Every democracy *must* encourage high individual performance. If it does not, it closes itself off from the main springs of its dynamism and talent and imagination, and the traditional democratic invitation to the individual to realize his full potentialities becomes meaningless.

. . . men are unequal in their native capacities and their motivations, and therefore in their attainments. In elaborating our national views of equality, the most widely accepted means of dealing with this problem has been to emphasize *equality of opportunity*. The great advantage of the conception of equality of opportunity is that it candidly recognizes differences in endowment and motivation and accepts the certainty of differences in achievement. By allowing free play to these differences, it preserves the

* *The Pursuit of Excellence: Education and the Future of America.* ("America at Mid-Century Series," Special Studies Project Report V, Rockefeller Brothers Fund.) Garden City, N.Y.: Doubleday, 1958.

freedom to excel which counts for so much in terms of individual aspirations, and has produced so much of man's greatness.

Having committed ourselves to equality of opportunity we must strive incessantly to make it a reality in our society. . . .

With respect to the pursuit of excellence there are several considerations that we must keep firmly in mind. First, we must not make the mistake of adopting a narrow or constricting view of excellence. *Our conception of excellence must embrace many kinds of achievement at many levels . . .*

Second, we must not assume that native capacity is the sole ingredient in superior performance. Excellence . . . is a product of ability and motivation and character. And the more one observes high performance in the dust and heat of daily life, the more one is likely to be impressed with the contribution made by the latter two ingredients.

Finally, we must recognize that judgments of differences in talent are not judgments of differences in human worth.

To sum up, it is possible for us to cultivate the ideal of excellence while retaining the moral values of equality. Whether we shall succeed in doing so is perhaps the fundamental issue in the development of our human resources. A challenge must be recognized before it can be met. Our society will have passed an important milestone of maturity when those who are the most enthusiastic proponents of a democratic way of life are also the most vigorous proponents of excellence. (pp. 16-17)

. . . We must recognize that in many areas our educational facilities are poor and our educational effort slovenly. (p. 19)

. . . The fateful question is not whether we have done well, or whether we are doing better than we have done in the past, but whether we are meeting the stern demands and unparalleled opportunities of the times. And the answer is that we are *not*.

Not only must our educators handle a huge increase in the number of students, they must offer higher quality of education. From time to time one still hears arguments over *quantity* versus *quality* education. Behind such arguments is the assumption that a society can choose to educate a few people exceedingly well, but that it cannot do both. But a modern society such as ours cannot choose to do one or the other. It has no choice but to do both. Our kind of society calls for the maximum development of individual potentialities *at all levels*.

Fortunately the demand to educate everyone up to the level of his ability and the demand for excellence in education are not incompatible. We must honor both goals. We must seek excellence in a context of concern for all. (p. 22)

. . . By insisting that *equality* means an exactly similar exposure to education, regardless of the variations in interest and capacity of the student, we are in fact inflicting a subtle but serious form of inequality upon our young people. We are limiting the development of individual excellence in exchange for a uniformity of external treatment. . . . Because many educators reject the idea of grouping by ability, the ablest students are often exposed to educational programs whose content is too thin and whose pace is too slow to challenge their abilities.

No educational system can be better than its teachers. Yet we face severe problems both in the supply of teachers at all levels and in their quality. (pp. 22-23)

. . . We can be certain that there will never be enough teachers with the extraordinary human gifts which make for inspiring teaching. We must therefore utilize our superior teachers more effectively. (p. 25)

. . . It is important to accept the desirability of a rigorous reappraisal of present patterns and courageous experimentation with new patterns. This must include a candid weighing of essentials and non-essentials in the curriculum; more flexible and imaginative approaches to the problem of class size; and—at the level of higher education—the trying out of approaches which place more responsibility on the student for his own education. (p. 31)

. . . we must modernize and improve the quality of the courses themselves. Virtually every subject in the curriculum would profit by a lively reform movement. (p. 27)

Any educational system is, among other things, a great sorting out process. One of the most important goals is to identify and guide able students and to challenge each student to develop his capacities to the utmost. (pp. 28-29)

If we are really serious about equality of opportunity, we shall be serious about individual differences, because what constitutes opportunity for one man is a stone wall for the next. If we are to do justice to the individual we must seek for him the level and kind of education which will open *his* eyes, stimulate *his* mind and unlock *his* potentialities. We should seek to develop many educational patterns—each geared to the particular capacities of the student for whom it is designed.

But though the educational pattern may differ, the goals remain the same for all: enabling each young person to go as far as his aptitude will permit in fundamental knowledge and skills, and motivating him to continue his own self-development to the full along similar lines. (p. 32)

Unused talents lead to personal frustration but they also deprive a society of the mainspring of its vitality. To realize our ideal of maximum personal development, it is not only essential that we inspire our people to the best that is in them but it is also essential to give them an opportunity to exercise that best. A society must learn to regard every instance of a misuse of talent as an injustice to the individual and injury to itself. And it must cultivate the ideal and the exercise of excellence by every means at its disposal. (p. 35)

Excellent performance is a blend of talent and motive, of ability fused with zeal. Aptitude without aspiration is lifeless and inert.

And that is only part of the story. When ability is brought to life by aspiration, there is no further question of the ends to which these gifts are applied. We do not wish to nurture the man of great talent and evil purpose. Not only does high performance take place in a context of values and purpose but if it is to be worth fostering, the values and purposes must be worthy of our allegiance. (p. 45)

. . . there should be a general recognition that development of the individual's potentialities occurs in a context of values. Education is not just a mechanical process for communication to the young of certain skills and information. It springs from our most deeply rooted convictions. And if it is to have vitality both teachers and students must be infused with the values which have shaped the system.

No inspired and inspiring education can go forward without powerful undergirding by the deepest values of our society. The students are there in the first place because generations of Americans have been profoundly committed to a republican form of government and to equality of opportunity. They benefit by a tradition of intellectual freedom because generations of ardent and stubborn men and women nourished that tradition in Western Civilization. Their education is based upon the notion of the dignity and the worth of the individual because those values are rooted in religious and philosophical heritage. They are preparing themselves for a world in which, as Thornton Wilder said, "every good and excellent thing . . . stands moment by moment on the razor edge of danger and must be fought for." They are preparing themselves for a world which has always been shaped and always will be shaped by societies which have placed at the service of their most cherished values a firmness of purpose, discipline, energy, and devotion.

We do not wish to impose upon students a rigidly defined set of values. Each student is free to vary the nature of his commitment. But this freedom must be understood in its true light. We believe that the individual should be free and morally responsible; the two are inseparable. The fact that we tolerate differing values must not be confused with moral neutrality. Such tolerance must be built upon a base of moral commitment; otherwise it degenerates into a flaccid indifference, purged of all belief and devotion.

In short, we will wish to allow wide latitude in the choice of values, but we must assume that education is a process that should be infused with meaning and purpose; that everyone will have deeply held beliefs; that every young American will wish to serve the values which have nurtured him and made possible his education and his freedom as an individual. (pp. 48-49)

EXCERPTS FROM: GOALS FOR AMERICANS*

The paramount goal of the United States was set long ago. It is to guard the rights of the individual, to ensure his development, and to enlarge his opportunity. . . .

The way to preserve freedom is to live it. Our enduring aim is to build a nation and help build a world in which every human being shall be free to develop his capacities to the fullest. (p. 1)

This Report . . . . is directed to the citizens of this country, each of whom sets his own goals and seeks to realize them in his life, through private groups, and through various levels of government. Choices are hard,

* The Report of the President's Commission on National Goals, from *Goals for Americans* © 1960 by the American Assembly, Columbia University, New York. Reprinted by permission of Prentice-Hall, Inc., Englewood Cliffs, N.J.

and costs heavy. They demand subordination of lesser goals to the greater. But the rewards are beyond calculation, for the future of our nation depends on the result. (p. 2)

The status of the individual must remain our primary concern. All our institutions—political, social, and economic—must further enhance the dignity of the citizen, promote the maximum development of his capabilities, stimulate their responsible exercise, and widen the range and effectiveness of opportunities for individual choice.

From this concern springs our purpose to achieve equal treatment of men and women, to enlarge their incentives and to expand their opportunities for self-development and self-expression. (p. 3)

Democracy gives reality to our striving for equality. It is the expression of individual self-respect; it clears the way for individual initiative, exercise of responsibility, and use of varied talents. It is basic to the peaceful adjustment of differences of opinion. It must not be curtailed out of impatience to find quick solutions. (p. 5)

The development of the individual and the nation demand that education at every level and in every discipline be strengthened and its effectiveness enhanced. New teaching techniques must continue to be developed. The increase in population and the growing complexity of the world add urgency.

Greater resources—private, corporate, municipal, state, and federal—must be mobilized. A higher proportion of the gross national product must be devoted to educational purposes. This is at once an investment in the individual, in the democratic process, in the growth of the economy, and in the stature of the United States. (p. 6)

There must be more and better teachers, enlarged facilities, and changes in curricula and methods. . . . Above all, schooling should fit the varying capacities of individuals: every student should be stimulated to work to his utmost; authentic concern for excellence is imperative. (p. 7)

The very deepest goals for Americans relate to the spiritual health of our people. The right of every individual to seek God and the wellsprings of truth, each in his own way, is infinitely precious. We must continue to guarantee it, and we must exercise it, for ours is a spiritually-based society. Our material achievements in fact represent a triumph of the spirit of man in the mastery of his material environment.

The major domestic goals of equality and education depend overwhelmingly on individual attitudes and actions.

It is the responsibility of men and women in every walk of life to maintain the highest standards of integrity. (p. 22)

. . . Our goals will be attained and our way of life preserved if enough Americans take the national interest sufficiently into account in day-by-day decisions.

Above all, Americans must demonstrate in every aspect of their lives the fallacy of a purely selfish attitude—the materialistic ethic. Indifference to poverty and disease is inexcusable in a society dedicated to the dignity of the individual; so also is indifference to values other than material comfort and national power. Our faith is that man lives, not by bread alone, but by self-respect, by regard for other men, by convictions of right and wrong, by strong religious faith.

Man has never been an island unto himself. The shores of his concern have expanded from his neighborhood to his nation, and from his nation to his world. Free men have always known the necessity for responsibility. A basic goal for each American is to achieve a sense of responsibility as broad as his world-wide concerns and as compelling as the dangers and opportunities he confronts. (p. 23)

. . . Nothing can impair the influence of the United States with the uncommitted peoples as denials of equality before the law and equality of opportunity. (p. 39)

The basic natural resource of the United States is its people. It follows inescapably that the first national goal to be pursued—at all levels, federal, state, local, and private—should be the development of each individual to his fullest potential. No limits are known to the degree to which, by the expenditure of adequate time, energy, skill, and money, the human mind can be developed at various levels of ability.

This goal touches the foundations of democracy. From the first it was realized that popular government required an educated citizenry. The declaration in the Northwest Ordinance of 1787 is classic: "Religion, morality, and knowledge being necessary to good government and the happiness of mankind, schools and the means of education shall forever be encouraged." What was necessary then is doubly essential today.

The political necessity for the fullest, most competent, and most continuous education should be obvious. When any citizen, for whatever reason, is deprived of this development, it is a denial of one of his unalienable rights. It is a threat to the rights and wellbeing of the rest of us. It is a subtraction from the viability of our democracy. Every incompetent citizen is a menace to the freedom of all. (p. 53)

Political strength, economic growth, security of the nation unite in demanding personal development. Social considerations make the same demand. An underdeveloped citizen—physically, mentally, morally—is not an energizer but a burden upon society.

The effectiveness of democracy—the most rewarding and most difficult form of government—rests not alone upon knowledge and judgment but upon character. Only the morally mature individual will be determined to do away with slums, end corruption, and help lift the load from the poverty-stricken at home and abroad. Only through moral sensitiveness can there be escape from the smugness that wealth and comfort breed. Moral sense resists avarice and self-seeking. It stimulates that concern for his fellowmen by which society escapes disintegration, while giving the individual maximum play for his talents, tastes, and interests. (p. 55)

There is no such thing as "mass education." Every use of the phrase is a denial of a vital reality; education is a wholly individual process. The life of the mind—despite all pressures to invade it—remains a private life. It occurs in each person uniquely. We do democracy no service in seeking to inhibit thought—free, wide-ranging, hazardous.

. . . there must be vastly more concern to develop schools devoted to growth. It is not enough to pass child labor laws and compulsory attendance laws to keep young people off the labor market and immure them in buildings. The need is for challenge and stimulation.

If we make effective self-discipline in freedom the chief educational goal of the sixties, we shall bring a fresh perspective to all our tasks. It would be a clean break with the materialistic of determinism of the Soviets. It would establish the moral stance of the United States before the world. It would give us a vastly more efficient society. (p. 56)

. . . a society such as ours, dedicated to the worth of the individual, committed to the nurture of free, rational and responsible men and women, has special reasons for valuing education. Our deepest convictions impel us to foster individual fulfillment. We wish each one to achieve the promise that is in him. We wish each one to be worthy of a free society, and capable of strengthening a free society.

Education is essential not only to individual fulfillment but to the vitality of our national life. The vigor of our free institutions depends upon educated men and women at every level of the society. And at this moment in history, free institutions are on trial.

Ultimately, education serves all of our purposes—liberty, justice and all our other aims—but the one it serves most directly is equality of opportunity. We promise such equality, and education is the instrument by which we hope to make good the promise. It is the high road of individual opportunity, the great avenue that all may travel. That is why we must renew our efforts to remove barriers to education that still exist for disadvantaged individuals—barriers of poverty, of prejudice and of ignorance. The fulfillment of the individual must not be dependent on his color, religion, economic status or place of residence.

Our devotion to equality does not ignore the fact that individuals differ greatly in their talents and motivations. It simply asserts that each should be enabled to develop to the full, in his own style and to his own limit. Each is worthy of respect as a human being. This means that there must be diverse programs within the educational system to take care of the diversity of individuals; and that each of these programs should be accorded respect and stature. (p. 81)

Love of learning, curiosity, self-discipline, intellectual honesty, the capacity to think clearly—these and all other consequences of a good education cannot be insured by skillful administrative devices. The quality of the teacher is the key to good education. (p. 82)

In dealing with students, the first goal is equality of opportunity. (p. 83)

. . . each child should be dealt with in terms of his own abilities. Every child should have the benefit of an educational program designed to suit his capacities and to develop him to the limit of his potentialities—whatever that limit may be. None should be required to fit a pace and pattern of education designed for children of other capacities.

In dealing with children of differing potentialities, we must remember that all are worthy of respect as human beings. . . .

To urge an adequate program for the gifted youngsters is not to recommend favoritism. They do not need more attention than other children—in some situations they may even need less. They need a different *kind* of attention.

Attempts to identify children of unusual potentialities should begin when schooling begins. When a child's family and neighborhood background are culturally impoverished, the school may be the only channel through which his gifts can be nourished: the sooner they are discovered the better.

Children of high academic talent, most of whom will have to devote more years to education than the average youngster, should be given the opportunity to move more rapidly. There should be various forms of grouping by ability from the earliest years of school; and every effort should be made in and out of school to provide enrichment for the gifted student. (pp. 84-85)

By 1970 the teaching of every subject from the elementary grades through high school should have received intensive reappraisal by teams composed of (a) the best minds in the subject-matter field, (b) curriculum specialists, and (c) the most experienced elementary or secondary school teachers of the subject. (p. 86)

All the organizational arrangements, all the methods and procedures that characterize American education today were originally devised to help us accomplish our purposes. If they no longer help us, we must revise them. The arrangements and methods must serve us and not control us. (p. 88)

If we really believe in individual fulfillment, our concern for education will reach far beyond the formal system. We shall expect people to continue to learn and grow in and out of school, in every possible circumstance, and at every stage of their lives. (p. 94)

. . . We must develop a philosophy and a technique of continuous reappraisal and innovation. (p. 99)

This report deals with concrete, practical measures. But all the arrangements will fail unless they are in the service of an authentic concern for excellence. We must raise standards in every phase of our national life. Education is no exception. We must do a better job. And the concern for educational quality must be widely shared. . . .

American education can be as good as the American people want it to be. And no better.

And in striving for excellence, we must never forget that American education has a clear mission to accomplish with every single child who walks into the school. Modern life has pressed some urgent and sharply defined tasks on education, tasks of producing certain specially needed kinds of educated talent. For the sake of our future we had better succeed in these tasks—but they cannot and should not crowd out the great basic goals of our educational system: to foster individual fulfillment and to nurture free, rational and responsible men and women without whom our kind of society cannot endure. Our schools must prepare *all* young people, whatever their talents, for the serious business of being free men and women. (p. 100)

APPENDIX B

Job Description:
What School Librarians Do*

Major functions of school librarians:

I. Administrative functions:
    Planning the library program.
    Implementing the library program.
    Planning library quarters.
    Selecting and arranging library furniture and equipment.
    Scheduling, training and supervising clerical staff.
    Scheduling the use of the library by classes and by groups.
    Preparing and administering the library budget.
    Planning with the administrative staff for the integration of the library
    program with the educational program.
    Relating the building library program to the district library program.
    Programming for student and teacher use of library resources.
    Preparing statistical, financial, and progress reports.
    Organizing and supervising the circulation of library materials.
    Publicizing the services and resources of the library.
    Coordinating the services of school and public libraries.
    Cooperating with school and community organizations.
    Participating in evaluating and implementing the district library pro-
    gram.
    Evaluating the building library program, services, and materials in
    terms of adequacy in meeting curricular needs, student needs, com-
    munity needs, and state and national standards.

* Division of School Libraries. *A Guide for School Librarians.* Harrisburg, Pennsylvania:
Department of Public Instruction, 1969.

Participating actively in library and other educational and professional associations on the local, regional, state and national level.

II. Educational functions:

Becoming conversant with all aspects of the educational program: courses of study, textbooks, manuals, workbooks, resource units, teacher-made study guides and plans, and pilot projects.

Becoming conversant with individual student needs, interests, goals, abilities, and progress rate.

Actively planning with individual teachers and groups of teachers to integrate library service, guidance, and materials with the classroom teaching program.

Providing library service, guidance, and resources which will customize and personalize teaching.

Providing library service, guidance, and resources which will individualize learning.

Sharing with classroom teachers the responsibility for designing and implementing a functional study skills program.

Participating in classroom planning, reporting, and culminating activities to build librarian's knowledge of class needs, interests, and abilities.

Participating in departmental and faculty meetings.

Participating in curriculum study and revision.

Keeping conversant with current educational research, trends, methods, and materials.

Providing materials for the professional growth of the faculty.

Creating and maintaining atmosphere conducive to effective library use.

III. Technical functions:

Establishing routines and procedures for selecting, ordering, processing, organizing, and circulating materials.

Maintaining accurate records of library holdings.

Weeding obsolete and worn materials from the collection.

Supervising the clerical routines necessary for the smooth operation of the library.

APPENDIX C

Terminology*

"The aboriginal logical sin, from which flows most bad intellectual consequences, is failure to define." John Dewey**

ABILITY. A generalized power to carry on an integrated complex of related activities. Burton, William H. p. 98.

ACCULTURATION. Greater capability for pupils of a minority group to assimilate and to adapt to the general cultural patterns of the community. Putnam, John. p. 176.

AFFECTIVE DOMAIN. Educational objectives which describe changes in interest, attitudes, and values, and the development of appreciations and adequate adjustment. Bloom, Benjamin. p. 7.

AIMS. A statement of what the school system is attempting to do to meet the needs and interests of its patrons in accordance with its educational philosophy. Putnam, John. p. 124.

ANALYSIS. The breakdown of a communication into its constituent elements or parts such that the relative hierarchy of ideas is made clear and/or the relations between the ideas expressed are made explicit. Bloom, Benjamin. p. 205.

APPLICATION. The use of abstractions in particular and concrete situations. The abstractions may be in the form of general ideas, rules of procedures, or generalized methods. The abstractions may also be technical principles, ideas, and theories which must be remembered and applied. Bloom, Benjamin. p. 205.

APPRECIATIONS AND ATTITUDES. A greater awareness of the value and signifi-

---

* Definition sources are identified at the end of the terminology listing.
** Dewey, John. *How We Think*. rev. ed. Boston, Mass.: D.C. Heath, 1933. p. 160.

cance of aspects of the subject-matter area (including aesthetic appreciations), and a greater readiness to respond in a mature manner to phenomenons related to the area. Putnam, John. p. 176.

APPROPRIATE BEHAVIOR. Patterns of acting, thinking, and feeling which are more consistent with those of selected cultural groups to which the pupils belong, consistent especially with the norms and standards set to govern pupil behavior within the school. Putnam, John. p. 177.

ARTICULATION. The relationship and interdependence existing among the different elements of the educational program; the degree to which the interlocking and interrelation of the successive levels of the educational system facilitate continuous and efficient educational progress of pupils. Good, Carter. pp. 39-40.

ATTITUDE. A predisposition to react in a certain way to objects, persons, or ideas. It may be conscious and willful, or subconscious; it may be rational or irrational. Attitudes are related to knowledge, although by no means entirely so . . . Attitudes have to deal mainly with feelings and emotions, in short, with affective processes. Jarolimek, John. p. 60.

AUDIO. Of or pertaining to sound. Specifically a sound recording. Loosely, any part or all of the complex of sound equipment, facilities, and personnel. Department of Audiovisual Instruction. p. 36.

AUDIOVISUAL MEDIA. Nonprint instructional materials designed to teach through the eye and/or ear such as disc and tape recordings, motion pictures, filmstrips, slides, and study prints. Davies, Ruth.

AUTO-INSTRUCTIONAL DEVICES. Systems and machines for individual instruction including individual reading pacers, individual viewing and listening equipment, language laboratories, programmed printed materials, and the true teaching machine . . . which presents verbal and pictorial programs in various ways, electronic, and mechanical, so that the individual responds and is informed of errors and progress. Department of Audiovisual Instruction. p. 37.

BASAL READER. A textbook, usually part of a graded series, used for instruction in reading; there are four types: literary, story, factual, and learn-to-study. Synonym: basic reader. Good, Carter. p. 442.

BRANCH. In programmed instruction, a point of choice at which students are sent to alternative items depending on their responses to the particular item. Department of Audiovisual Instruction. p. 38.

CARREL, CARRELL. An individual study station designed to minimize distraction and to facilitate independent student learning; also referred to as a "Quest Space" or "Q Space." Davies, Ruth.

CHECKLIST. A prepared list of items that may be related to a person, procedure, institution, building, etc. used for purposes of observation and/or evaluation, and on which one may show by a check mark or other simple method the presence, absence, or frequency of occurrence of each item on the list. Good, Carter. p. 88.

COGNITION. The act of gaining knowledge or becoming acquainted with an object through personal experience; knowledge that extends beyond mere awareness. Good, Carter. p. 107.

COGNITIVE DOMAIN. Educational objectives which deal with recall or recognition of knowledge and the development of intellectual abilities and skills. Bloom, Benjamin. p. 7.

COMMUNITY RESOURCES. The facilities, agencies, businesses, and persons outside the schools in the community that may be used, or are used by the schools for their educative values, e.g., theaters, parks, playgrounds, libraries, art galleries, museums, zoos, planetariums, botanic gardens, universities, churches, Boy Scouts, service clubs, social-service agencies, industries, and individuals, including representatives of various occupational groups, cultural groups, and civic organizations. Putnam, John. p. 139.

COMPREHENSION. The lowest level of understanding. It refers to a type of understanding or apprehension such that the individual knows what is being communicated and can make use of the material or idea being communicated without necessarily relating it to other material or seeing its fullest implications. Bloom, Benjamin. p. 204.

CONCEPT. Any object of awareness together with its significance or meaning; anything one can think about that can be distinguished from other things. A general meaning, an idea, or a property that can be predicted of two or more individual items. Knowledge that is not directly perceived through the senses but is the result of the manipulation of sensory impressions. . . . A concept requires both abstraction and generalization—the first to isolate the property, the second to recognize that it may be ascribed to several objects. Department of Audiovisual Instruction. p. 42.

CONTENT. The substance of a teaching or learning resource; a unit or course of study, a teaching or learning program or plan. Davies, Ruth.

CONTINUITY. The planned, ordered progression of learning experiences designed to build understanding in a cohesive, unified, inter-related sequence, K–12. Synonym: vertical articulation. Davies, Ruth.

COORDINATOR see LIBRARY COORDINATOR OR SUPERVISOR.

COURSE. An organization of subject matter and related learning experiences provided for the instruction of pupils on a regular or systematic basis, usually for a predetermined period of time. Putnam, John. p. 64.

CREATIVITY. The ability to or the quality of producing something new, unique, original, not-before-existent. A creative act finds a new unity in the variety of nature, sees a likeness among items not thought of before. Burton, William. p. 394.

CROSS-MEDIA APPROACH, MULTI-MEDIA APPROACH. Methodology based on the principle that a variety of audiovisual media and experiences correlated with other instructional materials overlap and reinforce the value of each other. Some of the material may be used to motivate interest, others, to communicate basic facts; still others, to clear up misconceptions and deepen understanding. Department of Audiovisual Instruction. p. 44.

CURRICULUM. The instructional activities planned and provided for pupils by the school or school system. The curriculum . . . is the planned interaction of pupils with instructional content, instructional resources, and instructional processes for the attainment of predetermined educational objectives. Putnam, John. p. 3.

DEVELOPMENTAL TASKS. Those basic learnings, competencies, tasks, and adjustments in which the individual must become proficient if his behavior is to fall within the limits of social acceptance and/or if he is to carry on a way of life which does not deviate sharply from other individuals in society. Jarolimek, John. p. 50.

EVALUATION. The making of judgments about the value . . . of ideas, works, solutions, methods, material, etc. It involves the use of criteria as well as standards for appraising the extent to which particulars are accurate, effective, economical, or satisfying. The judgments may be either quantitative or qualitative. Bloom, Benjamin. p. 185.

EXPEDITE. To speed on its way; to foresee and avoid obstacles or hinderances and there-by save time. Davies, Ruth.

FACILITATE. To provide the guidance and the resources requisite to expediting teaching or learning. Davies, Ruth.

FACT. Any act, event, circumstance, or existence which comes to pass. It is determined by measuring, counting, identifying, or by describing through consistent use of agreed upon definitions of terms. Burton, William H. p. 99.

FUNDAMENTAL. An idea that has wide as well as powerful applicability. Bruner, Jerome. p. 18.

GENERALIZATION. An inclusive statement of a relationship, trend, or tendency. Based on detailed facts, it provides a basis for interpreting additional facts which fit the general category. Wesley, Edgar. p. 613.

GOALS. The statement of the long-range, directional purposes which will guide the school in its educational planning to meet the needs of the students. Davies, Ruth.

HEAD LIBRARIAN. The member of a library staff delegated the responsibility for administering and directing a building library program. Davies, Ruth.

IMPLEMENTATION. To facilitate, expedite, or actualize the accomplishment of an educational plan, goal, or objective. Davies, Ruth.

IMPLODE. To burst inward causing a tidal wave in the learner's stream of consciousness. Davies, Ruth.

INDIVIDUALIZED INSTRUCTION. The manner in which instruction is individualized, including the use of procedures, materials, and equipment such as independent study, tutoring, small groups, programmed instruction, and assignments of differing quantities and types of school work given to one or more pupils according to individual needs, interests, and abilities. Putnam, John. pp. 215-216.

IN-SERVICE EDUCATION. A planned program of continuous learning which provides opportunities for growth through formal and informal on-the-job experiences for *all* professional personnel. Fleming, Robert S. p. 599.

INSTRUCTION. The activities dealing directly with the teaching of pupils and with improving the quality of teaching. The purpose of instruction is to enhance learning. Curriculum is what is taught; instruction is how it is taught. Putnam, John. p. 3.

INSTRUCTIONAL AIDS. Devices which assist an instructor in the teaching-learning process by simply presenting supporting or supplementary material. . . . They are not self-supporting. Department of Audiovisual Instruction. p. 54.

INSTRUCTIONAL MATERIALS. The whole range of media through which teachers and pupils communicate. Shores, Louis. p. 3.

INSTRUCTIONAL PROCESSES. The nature, appropriateness, and variety of the media of instruction, methods of instruction, and teaching procedures. Putnam, John. p. 140.

INSTRUCTIONAL PROGRAM. The totality of the curriculum and its implementation in a school system or school. Putnam, John. p. 3.

INTERPRETATION. The explanation or summarization of a communication. Whereas translation involves an objective part-for-part rendering of a communication, interpretation involves a re-ordering, rearrangement, or a new view of the material. Bloom, Benjamin. p. 205.

KIT. A collection of pertinent materials gathered and integrated into an instructional unit; e.g., a textbook, filmstrip, and a tape recording integrated into one basic unit. Department of Audiovisual Instruction. p. 55.

KNOWLEDGE. The recall of specifics and universals, the recall of methods and processes, or the recall of a pattern, structure, or setting. Bloom, Benjamin. p. 201.

LIBRARY-BASED UNIT. A unit designed to be taught in its entirety through the utilization of library resources, facilities, and guidance; each phase of the designing, teaching, and evaluating of a library based unit is a shared responsibility of classroom teacher and librarian. Davies, Ruth.

LIBRARY COORDINATOR OR SUPERVISOR. The librarian delegated the administrative authority and responsibility for developing and implementing a district, county, regional, or state program of library service. Davies, Ruth.

LISTENING. Hearing with discrimination and discernment. Davies, Ruth.

LITERACY. The ability to read, write, and compute at the level of performance expected of an "average" sixth grade pupil in order to become better able to meet adult responsibilities. Putnam, John. p. 178.

LITERACY, FUNCTIONAL. The ability to read, to write, to think, and to act with competence. Davies, Ruth.

MASS MEDIA. The instruments of communication that reach large numbers of people at once with a common message: books, magazines, television, radio, motion pictures, etc. Department of Audiovisual Instruction. p. 58.

MEDIA MANAGEMENT. Systematizing the organization and utilization of instructional media to assure easy accessibility and ready availability of all support media appropriate for each teaching or learning quest. Davies, Ruth.

MEDIA PROGRAMMING. Blueprinting a media usage sequence plan to build understanding in logical progression. Davies, Ruth.

MEDIATING AGENT. A means of conveying, extending, or reinforcing knowledge; a teaching resource. Davies, Ruth.

MEDIUM, pl. MEDIA. A vehicle for conveying information; an agent for communicating ideas. Davies, Ruth.

MESSAGE. The information to be transmitted; the content, the meaning. Department of Audiovisual Instruction. p. 24.

METHODS. A planned systematic procedure of dealing with the presentation of facts and concepts by a communicant. Department of Audiovisual Instruction. p. 59.

METHODS OF INSTRUCTION. Procedures utilized by the teacher and/or student in instruction, e.g., demonstration, discussion, experimentation, lecture, practice, problem solving, and seminar. Putnam, John. p. 139.

MULTI-MEDIA APPROACH see CROSS MEDIA APPROACH.

NONREADING MATERIAL. A broad classification to indicate those materials which depend more heavily upon sight and sound to convey meaning than upon the interpretation of printed words. Jarolimek, John. p. 105.

OBJECTIVES. Explicit formulations of the ways in which students are expected to be changed by the educational process. That is, the ways in which they will change in their thinking, their feelings, and their actions. Bloom, Benjamin. p. 26.

PERSONAL SATISFACTION. A sense of reward and pleasure resulting from involvement in an activity and/or from enjoyment of the product or results of the activity. Putnam, John. p. 178.

PERSONALIZING. The meeting of another at a level and through a means which is central to the concerns, interests, ideas, and modes of thinking and feeling of another. Berman, Louise M. p. 1.

PHILOSOPHY. The carefully developed statement expressing the ideals the school system attempts to realize in its practices. Putnam, John. p. 123.

PILOT STUDY. A preliminary study conducted in an operational environment to test and determine the effectiveness and value of techniques, procedures, methods, and/or materials. Davies, Ruth.

POLICIES. A statement of judgments, derived from a system of values and an assessment of situational factors, operating within the school system as a general plan for guiding decisions about how to attain desired educational aims and objectives. Putnam, John. p. 124.

PROFESSION. A calling requiring specialized knowledge and often long and intensive preparation including instruction in the skills and methods as well as the scientific, historical, or scholarly principles underlying such skills and methods, maintaining by force of organization or concerted opinion high standards of achievement and conduct, and committing its members to continued study and a kind of work which has for its prime purpose the rendering of public service. Webster. p. 1811.

PROGRAM. A sequence of carefully constructed items leading the student to mastery of a subject with minimal error. Department of Audiovisual Instruction. p. 64.

READINESS. A willingness, desire, and ability to participate in activities related to the subject matter area, depending on the necessary level of pupils' physical, mental, and emotional maturity. Putnam, John. p. 178.

RESOURCE. An agent for communicating meaning; a rich deposit of information. Davies, Ruth.

SCHOOL LIBRARIAN. A certified teacher possessing knowledge in depth of media content with specialized training in curriculum support techniques, in the selection, organization, and utilization of media, and in the design and development of customized teaching and learning strategies; vested with the professional responsibility of programming for the most efficient use of media to expedite teaching and to facilitate learning. The school librarian serves in the triple capacity of teacher, media programming engineer, and curriculum expediter. Davies, Ruth.

SCHOOL LIBRARY. A learning laboratory providing all types and kinds of instructional media essential for the optimum support of the educational program, providing opportunity for each student to work with ideas intelligently, intensively, extensively, while being competently guided in an environment conducive to maximal learning. Davies, Ruth.

SCOPE. A term used in curriculum building to denote the comprehensiveness, breadth, variety, and extent of learning experiences to be provided. It has to do with what is to be included in the program in terms of the range of subject matter and experiences pupils are to have. Jarolimek, John. p. 33.

SEARCH (SEEKING MATERIAL). The operation to determine whether certain information is in storage, the manner in which it is organized, and where it is located. As information is stored in a wider diversity of forms, the problem of search becomes increasingly complex. Another complicating factor is the need to include in the search procedure such considerations as the character of the audience for which the message is designed and the task it proposes to do. Department of Audiovisual Instruction. p. 70.

SELF-UNDERSTANDING. Greater understanding of one's abilities, interests, environmental factors, and educational needs. Putnam, John. p. 179.

SEQUENCE. A series of scenes, items, or experiences directly related by subject or by underlying thought. Department of Audiovisual Instruction. p. 70.

SKILL. Facility in performance of any given response; it is a relatively fixed, relatively automatic response to similar and recurring situations. Skills may be either mental or motor. Burton, William H. p. 99.

STRATEGY. An action plan calculated to expedite and facilitate learning from introduction to completion of a given task or topic. Davies, Ruth.

SUPERVISION. All efforts of designated school officials directed toward providing leadership to teachers and other educational workers in the improvement of instruction; involves the stimulation of professional growth and development of teachers, the selection and revision of objectives, materials of instruction, and methods of teaching, and the evaluation of instruction. Good, Carter V. p. 346.

SYSTEMS APPROACH. The programmed use of media in a pre-determined, structured pattern designed to build understanding of a given topic, concept, process, experiment, etc., in a logical, balanced progression or sequence. Davies, Ruth.

TEACHING LABORATORY. A teacher-study-work-planning center equipped with materials and machines essential for the development and implementation of effective, creative teaching programs. Davies, Ruth.

TEAM TEACHING. The sharing by several or more teachers of the responsibility for teaching a given class. Each member of a teaching team has certain unique functions; all participate in planning, scheduling, and evaluating the team activities. Davies, Ruth.

TRUMP PLAN. A system of instruction . . . . or of curricular organization in which the methods of teaching, student groupings, scheduling, and teacher and pupil activities adjust to the purposes and content of instruction. It utilizes three basic learning structures: large group instruction, small group instruction, and individual instruction. Department of Audiovisual Instruction. p. 81.

VERTICAL ARTICULATION see CONTINUITY.

DEFINITION SOURCES

Berman, Louise M. and Mary Lou Usery. *Personalized Supervision: Sources and Insights.* Washington, D.C.: Association for Supervision and Curriculum Development, 1966.

Bloom, Benjamin S., ed. *Taxonomy of Educational Objectives: The Classification of Educational Goals, Handbook I, Cognitive Domain.* New York: David McKay, 1956.

Bruner, Jerome S. *The Process of Education.* Cambridge, Massachusetts: Harvard University Press, 1960.

Burton, William H. *The Guidance of Learning Activities: A Summary of the Principles of Teaching Based on the Growth of the Learner.* 3rd edition. New York: Appleton-Century-Crofts, 1962.

Department of Audiovisual Instruction. "The Changing Role of the Audiovisual Process in Education: A Definition and a Glossary of Related Terms." *AV Communication Review.* vol. II, no. 1. January-February, 1963.

Fleming, Robert S., ed. *Curriculum for Today's Boys and Girls.* Columbus, Ohio: Charles E. Merrill, 1963.

Good, Carter V., ed. *Dictionary of Education.* 2nd edition. New York: McGraw-Hill, 1956.

Jarolimek, John. *Social Studies in Elementary Education.* 2nd edition. New York: Macmillan, 1963.

Putnam, John F. and W. Dale Chismore, eds. *Standard Terminology for Instruction in State and Local School Systems: An Analysis of Instructional Content, Resources, and Processes.* Washington, D.C.: United States Department of Health, Education and Welfare, 1967.

Shores, Louis. *Instructional Materials: An Introduction for Teachers.* New York: Ronald Press, 1960.

Webster's Third International Dictionary of the English Language. New York: Merriam-Webster, 1961.

Wesley, Edgar B. and Stanley P. Wronski. *Teaching Social Studies in High Schools.* 5th edition. Boston, Massachusetts: Heath, 1964.

Sample Resource Unit:
The Civil War and Reconstruction*

OBJECTIVES

This unit should make progress toward the development of the following:

UNDERSTANDINGS

1. The Civil War was a result of complex economic, social, and political pressures, not of any single cause.
2. Political parties attempt to compromise differences among sections of the country.
3. The supremacy of the national government was established in a long, costly war.
4. Periods of crisis sharply test political leadership and a constitutional form of government.
5. The influence of cultural continuity makes it difficult to effect abrupt changes in men's institutions.
6. Severe treatment of defeated peoples tends to arouse bitter and lasting feelings.
7. There are no easy solutions to social problems.

SKILLS AND ABILITIES

1. Evaluating sources of information.
2. Taking notes on reading.
3. Adjusting the rate and method of reading to material and purpose.
4. Presenting ideas orally.
5. Relating different types of phenomena among map patterns.
6. Using pivotal dates to understand time relationships among events.

* Developed by Genevieve P. Zito, University of Minnesota High School. In Fraser, Dorothy McClure and Edith West. *Social Studies in Secondary Schools: Curriculum and Methods.* New York: Ronald Press, 1961. pp. 431-446.

ATTITUDES AND HABITS
1. An interest in history and historical materials.
2. The habit of evaluating sources of information.
3. A desire to understand other people's points of view.
4. Skepticism of easy solutions.

OUTLINE OF CONTENT

I. The Civil War and its aftermath resulted in repercussions which are still felt today.
  A. Many of today's civil rights problems date back to the Reconstruction period.
  B. The Civil War and Reconstruction had marked effects upon our political parties.
  C. The War and its aftermath left the South with serious economic problems, some of which have not yet been solved.
II. There was no single cause of the Civil War; it resulted from complex political, economic, and social pressures.
  A. The United States had not achieved national unity by 1860.
    1. The federal-state relationship remained unresolved.
      a. The authority of the federal government had been challenged repeatedly since 1789.
      b. Two divergent views of the constitutional relationship between the central government and the states developed.
    2. Economy and society varied in the North, the South, and the West.
      a. Many and significant changes marked the life of the Northwest section.
        (1) Economy was diversified.
        (2) Society was mobile, changing, and growing.
      b. Southern economy and society were relatively stable and static.
        (1) The economy was dominated by the plantation system.
          (a) The South was chiefly an exporting area for staples and an importing area for manufactured goods.
          (b) Four million slaves (1860) provided the labor to run the large and small plantations.
          (c) The majority of Southerners were not large planters.
          (d) Although the South was essentially agricultural, small industry was profitable in strategic areas.
        (2) The planter aristocracy controlled the social and political as well as the economic life of the South.
      c. Frontier settlement was a dominant concern in this era.
        (1) Extension into new lands was pushed by two conflicting groups: the small farmers and the larger planters.
          (a) The plantation system expanded through Louisiana, Texas, and Missouri.
          (b) Small farming expanded beyond the Northwest Territory into the plains area.
          (c) Improved modes of transportation spurred on settlement.

(d) As settlement increased, the clash between the conflicting groups became increasingly serious.

(2) The frontier gave men the chance to start anew and to build a new place in society.

(3) Religious and social reformers had a profound influence in the frontier area.

B. The struggle between the North and the South for control of the central government developed from 1820–1860.

1. Until 1850 a balance of power was maintained.

a. Control of the West was determined by compromises.

(1) The Missouri Compromise applied to territory acquired from France in 1803.

(2) The desire for the annexation of Texas was matched by the acquisition of Oregon.

(3) The Compromise of 1850 was an attempt to solve the struggle for land acquired from Mexico.

b. Political parties attempted to compromise the sectional differences.

(1) The Democrats tried to please supporters by arranging platforms and candidates to cater to all sections.

(2) The Whigs, led by Clay, attempted to secure compromises which would satisfy both the Northern and Southern elements in the party.

2. After 1850 compromise gave way step by step to bitter controversies and war.

a. The Compromise of 1850 proved unworkable. Agitation increased both in the North and in the South. Some Northern states refused to obey the fugitive slave law.

b. The Kansas-Nebraska Act broke the Missouri Compromise and reopened the issue for the Louisiana purchase area.

(1) Kansas became the site of armed clash between the slaveholders and the free-soilers.

(2) The Republican Party united Western and Northern groups against the Southerners' desire for extension of slavery in the territory.

(3) Propaganda by radicals on both sides increased.

c. The Supreme Court in the Dred Scott decision declared the Missouri Compromise void, and made slavery legal in the territories.

d. John Brown's raid encouraged more agitation on both sides.

e. The election of 1860 created a crisis in politics.

f. The Southern states seceded and established their own government.

C. The causes of the war continue to be a fertile field for historical interpretation.

1. Some historians have believed that slavery was the fundamental cause of the war.

2. Some historians have emphasized economic rivalry between sections as the cause of the war.

3. Some historians have presented a psychological interpretation

and have concluded that the war was the result of blunders on both sides.

4. Some historians have emphasized the states' rights or constitutional issue.

5. A number of historians have presented a broader political, economic, and social interpretation.

III. The supremacy of the national government was established in a long and costly war.

A. The strategy employed by the Blue and Gray forces was simple and direct.

1. The federal forces launched an offensive war with a threefold plan of attack: blockade of Southern ports, division of the Southern heartland, and capture of the Southern capital.

2. The South's strategy was mainly defensive, although the South did make attacks and raids into Union territory.

B. New kinds of warfare were introduced: ironclads, trenches, "total war," railroad raids, and so forth.

C. Problems behind the lines (such as finances, conscription, loyalty, diplomacy) increased as the war continued.

D. Superior Union resources and leadership led ultimately to the defeat of an exhausted South.

1. The Union capitalized on its strengths.

a. Federal armies were manned and supplied by a growing industry, an expanding population, and an improved transportation system.

b. The Union used its official status to prevent European recognition of the Confederacy.

c. Lincoln exerted forceful and effective leadership in centralizing the Union war effort.

2. The Confederacy overestimated its advantages and failed to unify its defense efforts.

a. European intervention was not forthcoming.

b. The upper border states as well as the Ohio Valley states remained loyal to the Union despite activities of Southern sympathizers.

c. Southern military forces, though ably led and trained, were poorly supplied, equipped, and coordinated.

d. Davis failed to convince states'-righters of the need for a centralized war effort.

E. The war was very costly in lives, property, and money.

IV. Periods of crisis sharply test political leadership and a constitutional form of government.

A. From 1850 to 1860, as the political parties were realigning, many politicians attempted to assume leadership.

B. Lincoln, faced with the secession crisis, actively engaged in the struggle to preserve the Union.

1. Lincoln exercised broad executive powers to organize and coordinate the war effort.

a. He used his "war powers" to justify executive assumption of congressional powers.

       b. He made frequent use of executive decrees to facilitate mobilization of the Union's strength.

       c. He often changed military leaders to guarantee success of the Union's attack.

       d. He used strong measures to suppress anti-Union activity in the North.

  2. As president, Lincoln realized the importance of his political position.

       a. He used patronage to control and appease his party.

       b. He signed into laws the aims of the party platform of 1860.

       c. He evaluated the effects of the war on public opinion at home and abroad.

          (1) The issuance of the Emancipation Proclamation was carefully timed.

          (2) His bid for re-election in 1864 as a Union party candidate was successful despite many difficulties.

  3. Lincoln kept a watchful eye on diplomacy to forestall European recognition of the Confederate government. He carefully weighed all diplomatic actions.

C. The need for security during the Civil War brought a challenge to civil liberties.

  1. Lincoln suspended the writ of habeas corpus and authorized military trials in non-war areas.

  2. A congressional investigating committee spurred on a government loyalty program.

  3. Loyalty oaths were required and widespread both in the North and in the South.

D. Although the supremacy of the national government was established by the war, effective national leadership was not present in the postwar era.

  1. Upon Lincoln's assassination, Johnson, a War Democrat from Tennessee, became president.

       a. Johnson, attempting to carry through Lincoln's plans for reconstruction, did not receive the support of the radical Republicans in control of Congress.

       b. Bitter political controversy over reconstruction led to the attempted impeachment of Johnson.

  2. The two-party system did not operate effectively in the Reconstruction period.

       a. The Democratic party, discredited by the war, was not able to compete successfully on a national level.

       b. The radical Republicans tried to prevent the resurgence of the Democratic party in the South through the Negro vote.

       c. The rise of political bosses increased and political corruption was rampant on all levels of government.

V. The federal government failed in its efforts to reconstruct the defeated South. In imposing abrupt changes in men's institutions, those in power did not consider the importance of cultural continuity.

A. Recreation of society and economy was the most pressing problem facing the nation after the war.

1. Destruction of life and property was evident throughout the defeated South.
2. The Negroes, newly freed by the Thirteenth Amendment, were handicapped socially and economically.
3. The political status of the Confederate states and citizens was in doubt.

B. Congressional reconstruction sought to change drastically Southern society.

1. The Congress refused to readmit the representatives of the Southern states reconstructed under the Lincoln-Johnson plan.
2. Military occupation of the Southern states was prescribed until the states developed governments acceptable to Congress.
3. New constitutions and governments were established, revolutionizing Southern political life.
   a. The traditional leaders were disenfranchised.
   b. The former slaves were made citizens, given the right to vote, and put into a position of leadership. Republicans campaigned actively for the Negro vote.
   c. To guarantee these reforms, the Fourteenth and Fifteenth Amendments had to be ratified.
   d. The Republican reconstruction governments were run by a coalition of carpetbaggers, scalawags, and freedmen under the protection of the federal army.
   e. Certain other reforms were made, such as tax supported schools, revised tax schedules, abolition of debtors' prisons.

C. White Southerners reacted with bitterness to military reconstruction. They strove to restore their former patterns of life.

1. They developed various means to restore themselves to a position of dominance in society.
   a. At first, they struck back violently through secret organizations like the Ku Klux Klan.
   b. Devices such as the grandfather clauses, poll taxes, white primaries, and literacy tests were used to keep the Negro from voting.
   c. Segregation of the races in all areas of life became a dominant trend. The Negro was once again placed in an inferior social and economic position.
2. They also tried to re-establish their economy.
   a. Production of staples continued to dominate the Southern economy, as sharecropping and tenant farming replaced the plantation system.
   b. Although transportation was improved and new industries such as cigarettes, textiles, and oil developed in the South, the economy remained essentially agrarian into the twentieth century.

VI. There are no easy solutions to social problems. Problems arising from the Civil War and Reconstruction era are still prevalent today.

A. The nation is still sharply divided on the civil rights issue. The race problem is one of the most crucial problems facing the country today.

B. Although sharecropping has been declining in recent years, it continues to be a serious social problem.
C. Although inroads have been made in the Democratic stronghold, the South has a predominantly one party system with all of its limitations.

TEACHING PROCEDURES

INITIATORY ACTIVITIES

1. Prepare a bulletin board display entitled "The Civil War Is Felt Today." Use pictures and newspaper headlines to illustrate effects. Ask for volunteers to keep the display up to date during the unit.
2. Use a magazine or newspaper article on a recent civil rights issue or on a recent election to initiate a discussion showing how these issues and others can be traced back to the Civil War period. Point out the need for finding out more about a period which has had such lasting effects upon American society.
3. Give a pretest to determine the extent to which students have misconceptions about the causes of the war, conditions of slavery, and other aspects of the era.
4. To determine the extent to which students have been influenced by legend, have them discuss the reasons why Lincoln has become such an important symbol in American life. Tape this discussion and replay it later in the unit. If a written activity is preferred, have each student write an essay on Lincoln as a symbol of American life. Have the students write reappraisals later.
5. Read aloud quotations from three or four historians, each representing a different interpretation of the Civil War. Have the class discuss these viewpoints. (Tape this discussion and replay it after the class has completed its study of causes of the war.) Point out the difficulties of historical interpretation, the role of bias, and so forth. Suggest that reading during the unit should help students decide which historian is most nearly right.
6. Give a pretest to discover the ability of students to evaluate sources of information. Discuss the results. Point out the need for evaluating sources in this unit by reading aloud passages from biased materials.
7. Since the Civil War period has been portrayed often in fictional materials, introduce several novels to the class for concurrent reading. Give students time to browse through the novels to create interest.
8. If biographies are preferred to fictional accounts, introduce the class to available books which cover this era. Put some of the book jackets on the bulletin board with excerpts from student reviews of past years under each. Have the students formulate questions to guide their reading. Describe the value of note-cards so that students can take proper notes as they read. Have the students serve as resource persons during class discussions which concern the personalities about whom they have read.
9. Have students read rapidly from different textbooks to gain an overview of the unit. For example, poor readers might use Gavian

and Hamm, average readers Canfield and Wilder or Todd and Curti, and better readers Bailey, or Carmen and Syrette. Before students begin reading, remind them that their reading rate should be different from that which they use when reading for detail. Ask each student to list the four or five topics he finds most interesting. Use these lists to help prepare a sheet of suggested activities for the class.

10. Have class members select individual and group activities to investigate as they study the causes of the Civil War. A number are suggested below in the approximate order in which they might be presented in order to develop the suggested outline of content. Before beginning work on the topics, discuss with the class ways of improving oral and written work. For example, have them use the criteria which they developed at the beginning of the year to evaluate progress on oral reports in the last unit and to identify specific things on which they should work. If students have not presented panels or debates previously, or if their presentations need improvement, take time to discuss methods of making such presentations effective. Have students working in groups prepare brief written progress reports every day or every other day.

DEVELOPMENTAL ACTIVITIES

11. Have students review the federal-state relationship prior to 1850. Discuss the challenges to federal authority, the divergent interpretations of the Constitution, and the implications of this conflict. Have students build a chart tracing challenges to the supreme law of the land. Include in the chart a column on the cause of discontent, one on the section of the country most involved, and one on the action taken by the federal government. Have students continue this chart during the unit.

12. Have a group of students find out how their state felt about the approaching Civil War and the part it played prior to the war. Advise them to check local resources.

13. Have a group of students make maps locating the farming areas, mercantile areas, manufacturing sites, and routes of transportation in the North for 1820, 1840, and 1860. These maps can be made individually or as overlays. The class can use these maps as it discusses significant economic changes of this period.

14. Have a student use an historical atlas or *Historical Statistics* to compare maps of population or population data for the period 1800–1860. Let him write a report analyzing his findings in terms of their implications for the struggle between the North and the South.

15. Suggest that a student pretend he is a pre-Civil War planter who visits New York in 1858. He can write a series of letters to his wife describing features of Northern life which differ from those in the South and the factors which worry him about Northern strength.

16. If nothing has been done on the reform movements of 1830–1860 in a previous unit, consider these here, possibly by an informal lecture. Emphasize the climate of opinion and the impact of the reform movements on Northern and Western society.

17. If students have been reading novels (see activity seven), hold a class discussion in which they present their findings in terms of the biases of the authors and the conflicting descriptions of Southern life.

18. Have the students compare and evaluate eyewitness accounts of prewar Southern life. Either prepare a dittoed series of eyewitness reports or have students read in the many collections of such materials. Discuss the findings concerning conditions of Southern life and the validity of witnesses.

19. If activities 17-18 have not been used, have a group of students present a symposium on the conditions of plantation life in the antebellum South. Review with students the purposes of a symposium and aid them in selecting the information and in organizing the report.

20. Hold a panel discussion on the Southern defense of slavery.

21. Delegate a student to present an oral report on the movement against slavery in the South.

22. Have a group of students make a series of maps. On one they can locate the areas of large plantations, sites of Southern industry, and districts where cotton, tobacco, and rice were grown. Have them make a plastic overlay map of per capita slaves in Southern districts and superimpose this map over the other.

23. Have a student construct a graph showing cotton and tobacco exports for 1800, 1820, 1840, and 1860 and explain the implications of the graph to the class.

24. Assign several students or the entire class to prepare papers evaluating the reasoning behind the statement: "Cotton is King, sir; the North can not make war on cotton and win!"

25. Delegate a student to construct a graph showing wheat and corn production by states in the years 1800, 1840, and 1860. Have him explain to the class the reasons for the shift in leadership among the states.

26. Have the class compare and evaluate dittoed excerpts from eyewitness accounts of life on the Northwestern and Southwestern frontiers. Contrast frontier conditions with life on the seacoast, North and South.

27. Use an opaque projector to show a series of maps and various territories which were prominent in the prewar controversies. Discuss the significance of different features of the areas. Display pictures of these areas on the bulletin board. Attach them by string to the appropriate locations on large outline maps of each area. Ask students to compare patterns of different phenomena in these areas in an attempt to generalize about their usefulness for production of crops in which slave labor could be employed. Get volunteers to use a book on historical geography to find out whether or not these hypotheses can be verified.

28. Have a group of students present a "You Are There" program on the Senate debate over the admission of Missouri in 1820.

29. The Compromise of 1850 produced one of the most stirring debates in American history. Have a group of students analyze the

roles played by Webster, Benton, Clay, Calhoun, and Houston in these debates and present their findings orally or in writing.

30. Have a student draw a series of cartoons, representing different viewpoints on some important event prior to the Civil War (for example, the Compromise of 1850 or the Dred Scott decision).

31. Assign students to present oral reports on the following questions: "How successful was the underground railroad?" "The fugitive slave law: did the North obey it?" "Who opposed the abolitionists in the North?"

32. Or, have a student write a paper on the ways in which Northern states obstructed efforts to enforce the fugitive slave law. Have him explain why this action was a threat to the federal union.

33. Have the class pretend that it is the Senate of 1854 which is considering the Kansas-Nebraska bill. Have each student choose a state to represent and determine what role a Senator from that state played in the original debate. The bill can be introduced, discussed, and voted upon.

34. Let a student imagine that he is a representative of the federal government and is investigating the clashes in Kansas. Have him prepare a written report of his findings.

35. Have students present oral reports on the following topics: "Founding of the Republican Party and Its Stand on Slavery," "Abolitionist Propaganda: Accounts of Slavery in the South," "Why Did the Supreme Court Decide That Dred Scott Was Still a Slave?"

36. Harriet Beecher Stowe's *Uncle Tom's Cabin* was one of the most effective pieces of propaganda produced in the Civil War era. Assign a student to read the novel and write a paper on its reception both at home and abroad.

37. Have a student write a series of letters concerning the Dred Scott decision to the editor of the *New York Times*. Include letters from a Republican, a Douglas Democrat, a Southern Democrat, and an abolitionist.

38. Have a student imagine that he is a reporter writing a series of articles on the Lincoln-Douglas debates.

39. Have a student find out what actually happened in the John Brown raid and why it caused such nationwide excitement and hysteria. Have him present his findings in a written report. Or have a group of students prepare an informal debate on the topic: "John Brown: Rabble-rouser or Martyr?"

40. Have groups of students prepare panels on the following topics: "Constitution: Provoker of the War?" "The West: Provoker of the War?" "Slavery: Provoker of the War?" and "Plantation Life *vs.* Industrialization: Provoker of the War?" Hold a culminating discussion on the causes of the war.

41. Or have a group of students debate the causes of the war under the following question: "Resolved, that slavery was the chief cause of the Civil War."

42. If activity five was used, replay the tape and ask students to examine their original viewpoints on causes of the war in the light of the knowledge they have acquired.

43. Have a group of students prepare a symposium on the fateful election of 1860. Or have the class discuss the election as an immediate cause of the war. In advance, have a student prepare charts analyzing the election results, popular and electoral. In addition, use a dittoed copy of the South Carolina Ordinance of Secession to show the Southern reaction to Lincoln's victory. Use this document in a reading exercise and as a review of the states' rights interpretation of the Constitution.

44. Have a group of students prepare a two page newspaper, complete with news items, editorials, background commentary, and fashion notes, for the day after Lincoln's election. Make the paper one for their local area. Have another group make a similar paper which might have appeared in a different section of the country.

45. Have a group of students dramatize events in Washington following South Carolina's Ordinance of Secession. They can use the pattern of "on-the-spot news broadcasts" used by radio and television reporters for modern political conventions.

46. Have a student make a map showing the areas in the Southern states which favored and opposed secession. Show this map along with the series prepared in activity 22 and have the class see what conclusions they can draw from the data.

47. Have a student prepare an oral report, trying to answer the following question: "Could Buchanan have arrested the approaching war?"

48. For a review, have the class choose the significant events, 1850–1860, and build a timeline to establish the pattern of these events. Have students evaluate the significance of these events and their relationships to one another. Also have the class build a chart comparing Northern and Southern strength in 1860, using the data already prepared in previous activities.

49. Introduce the section on the war by showing the Brady war photos which are available in book form, on slides, and on film. Other pictures are available in *Divided We Fought*.

50. Have students read textbook sections for the war years 1861–1865 to see the chronology of events. After the reading is completed, have them do an exercise in which they arrange the following events in chronological order: Emancipation Proclamation, Gettysburg, Lincoln's Assassination, Vicksburg, Antietam, Appomattox, Trent Affair, Sherman's March.

51. Have a committee prepare a two page newspaper for their home town for the day after the attack on Fort Sumter. Use the pattern suggested in activity 44. Students might include imaginary interviews with Lincoln and with Jefferson Davis.

52. Have a student prepare an overlay map for the map made in activity number 46. It should show the chief features of Union's attack. Have the student explain the reasons for choosing these lines of assault.

53. Divide the class into five or six groups, each one to investigate one of the major battles of the war. Have students read authoritative accounts as well as accounts by participants in the battles. Also have each group prepare a large scale map of the battle area. Have

each group leader present the findings of his group in an illustrated oral report.

54. Or have each of the five or six groups, investigate a significant war personality such as Lee, Grant, Jackson, Sherman, Farragut, or Morgan. Have students read primary accounts of these men as well as accounts in the *Dictionary of American Biography*. Have the group leaders report findings to the class.

55. Have a student read two or more viewpoints on some outstanding military figure of the period and write an analysis of his personality and of the competency and bias of the authors.

56. Assign a committee to add a chapter to a class booklet on "Our Town in American History." Suggest that they visit the local newspaper offices and county museums, and talk with people whose families have lived in the area since the Civil War. Suggest that they locate realia from the period. Have them prepare a display of materials, including replicas which they can make.

57. Have several students compare the reporting of key battles in Northern and Southern newspapers. They will find accounts in the *Confederate Reader* and in the *Union Reader*.

58. Have a student write a report based on firsthand accounts of life in the Northern and Southern armies.

59. Suggest that a student read and report on firsthand accounts of prison conditions in the North and in the South.

60. Ditto several pages of firsthand accounts of army life and discipline, draft riots, bounty-jumping, and prison conditions. Use the material in a discussion of the problem of manning the Union and the Confederate armies.

61. Have a student prepare a written report on the part played by the railroads in the war effort. Assign another student to prepare a report on advances in military and naval weapons and tactics.

62. Have a student give an oral report on: "Was the blockade the key to victory?" or "What were the effects of the blockade on Southern life?" Suggest that a student prepare charts on tonnage of items carried through the blockade.

63. Have a committee present a panel discussion: "Did England hold the balance of power in the War Between the States?"

64. Read aloud to the class Sherman's own account of his march through Georgia to motivate a discussion on the justification of his tactics.

65. Have a student use *Historical Statistics* and the *World Almanac* to prepare a chart comparing American casualties in the Revolution, the War of 1812, the Civil War, World War I, and World War II. Use this chart in a discussion of losses.

66. Have a panel or class discussion on the topic: "Why Did the North Win the War?" Use this discussion to: (1) bring together an appraisal of military leadership and strategy; (2) raise the question of the role political leadership played in the outcome of the war. Use the second point to lead into a discussion of the many problems facing the president in the Civil War.

67. If activity 66 is not used, discuss the problems facing the president in this crisis. Review the chief powers which the Constitution

grants the president of the United States, as well as the precedents set by past presidents facing crises.

68. Use an opaque projector to show students some of the cartoons in *Lincoln in Caricature.*

69. Have students prepare oral reports and debates on the topics: "Government by Edict: Use of Executive Decrees by Lincoln," "The Emancipation Proclamation: Lincoln a Politician or Humanitarian?" "What Were Lincoln's Views About Slavery?"

70. Have a student prepare a written report on the topic: "Why Was the Thirteenth Amendment Necessary to Free the Slaves?"

71. Have several students analyze certain aspects of the Lincoln legends in oral or written reports. Possible topics: "The Slave Market Story," "The Anne Rutledge Story," "Mary Todd Lincoln."

72. Have a student pretend to be a news commentator who analyzes the significance of the election of 1864.

73. Have a student present an oral report on: "Why was Andrew Johnson chosen as Lincoln's running mate in 1864?"

74. Have a committee prepare a "Hear It Now" program in which they interview Charles Francis Adams in London during the Civil War.

75. Have a group of students present a symposium on Northern opposition to the War.

76. Suggest that another group debate the topic: "Resolved, that the security of the nation justified Lincoln's restriction of civil liberties."

77. Have students write reports on such topics as: "How effective was the government loyalty program?" "An evaluation of the book, *Who Murdered Lincoln?*"

78. Have a class discussion in which students evaluate Lincoln's effectiveness in meeting the crisis which he faced. Discuss Lincoln's leadership in comparison with the Confederate leadership as a factor in the Union victory. If a tape was made as suggested in activity four, replay it and have students appraise their original ideas. If an essay was written, as suggested in activity four, have students do a written appraisal at this time. Compare the two sets of papers.

79. To introduce the section on reconstruction, use an opaque projector to show scenes of the South at the close of the war. In addition to the Brady photos, good illustrations are found in *The Desolate South.*

80. Following the pattern used in activity five, read aloud quotations from historians about the Reconstruction era. Discuss these viewpoints with the class, pointing out once again the problems of historical interpretation.

81. Have students read different accounts of the Reconstruction. Have some read the usual text treatments; have superior students read sections in the Amherst pamphlet, *Reconstruction in the South* or in standard works on the Reconstruction period. Have students take notes indicating which interpretation of the Reconstruction period is found in their reading. Have them prepare questions to aid in their notetaking.

82. Have a group of students consult the *Dictionary of American Biography* on the leading personalities of the Reconstruction era. See that they take careful notes on actions and attitudes toward reconstruction policies. Use these students as resource persons in class discussions of policies.

83. Have students read dittoed excerpts from Carl Schurz, John T. Trobridge, and Richard Taylor on conditions in the South after the war. Discuss the question of bias as well as the accuracy of the reports.

84. Or have a student read firsthand accounts of the destruction in the South after the war. Suggest he analyze three accounts and prepare a paper on his findings.

85. Have a group of students prepare a dramatic report of the opening session of Congress on December 4, 1865. Suggest they use "on-the-spot" interviews like those of present-day newscasters.

86. Have students make a chart comparing Johnson's plan for reconstruction with that of Congress. Discuss the ways in which the president and Congress tried to check one another in carrying out a reconstruction plan.

87. Have a symposium in which students consider the problems facing the newly freed slave as well as the attempts to adjust him to his new role in society.

88. Have a student read Booker T. Washington's *Up From Slavery* and in a written report, compare it with other firsthand accounts of the Negro in the South during Reconstruction.

89. Have a student give an oral report on the struggle over ratification of the Fourteenth Amendment. Suggest he include the 1866 congressional elections.

90. Discuss the motives of the Radicals in seeking Johnson's removal; then show the film of Johnson's impeachment. As a sequel to the movie, discuss the ways in which Congress attempted to control the Court in this era.

91. Have a student report on the role of the Ku Klux Klan during Reconstruction. Follow the report with a discussion of other means which the whites used to return to political control.

92. Have a student report on the disputed election of 1876 or on the South Carolina election of the same year.

93. Suggest that a student prepare a series of cartoons representing different viewpoints on the election of 1876.

94. Have a student prepare a graph on cotton exports in 1860, 1870, 1880, and 1890. Compare the chart with that made in activity 23.

CULMINATING ACTIVITIES

95. Have a summarizing discussion comparing conditions in 1880 with those in 1850 to see if the outcomes of the war had solved the problems giving rise to it. For example, compare economic and political balance between regions, status of the Negro in prewar and postwar days, and the effect of the war on acceptance of the Constitution as the supreme law of the land.

96. To review the time framework for this period, have a discussion

based upon the student made charts, graphs, and maps. Use 1860 as an illustrative pivotal date. Demonstrate differences before and after the date for certain economic phenomena which helped shape political events (for example, railroad construction, settlement of the west, industrial development, cotton production, wheat production, immigration). Using the same date, point out the relationship of events occurring throughout the world (for example, unification movement in Italy and Germany as compared with nationalist movement in the United States; the freeing of the serfs in Russia as compared with the rising democratic thought in the United States).

97. Have students interview Southerners and report on their analysis of the present-day attitude toward Congressional reconstruction.

98. Have a student prepare a map showing patterns of farm ownership in the South today. Ask the student to explain his findings to the class.

99. Have a student analyze the last four presidential elections and give a report on: (1) the strength of the Democratic party in the Southern states, and (2) the areas of decided Republican power. Discuss the findings and relate them to the Civil War and Reconstruction period.

100. Discuss current news articles which show the problems of racial attitudes and segregation in the United States today. Have a student prepare a map showing the density of Negro population throughout the nation today. Have another student report on the percentage of Negroes voting in the South. Ask for volunteers to form a follow-up committee to bring current news related to this unit to the attention of the class during the remainder of the year.

101. Give a unit test. Readminister the pretest on evaluating sources, or give a similar test. Discuss the results.

Growth Characteristics of Pupils*

PURPOSE:

To give the teacher an understanding of the developmental characteristics
of his pupils so that he can more effectively:
Plan and guide the learning experiences;
Adopt appropriate teaching techniques;
Plan instruction to meet individual differences.

APPROACH:

Reading Vertically: The teacher will note some important characteristics of
the children he is teaching.

Reading Horizontally: The teacher will note the developmental sequence
of certain characteristics, with growth from age group to age group
being continuous and gradual.

*The teacher must realize that because children develop at different rates
no child will exactly fit the pattern of his particular age level. The teacher
will wish, therefore, to study the characteristics of both older and younger
children so that he may see the extent of individual differences within his
class.*

GROUP I: PUPILS TO AGE 6

Muscular Development Incomplete But Improving.
Use large manipulative materials: clay, finger paints, large crayons,
and brushes, large blocks.

* *A Guide for Teaching Social Studies, Kindergarten Through Grade Seven.* Minneapolis
Public Schools: Minneapolis, Minnesota, 1957. Used by permission.

Visual Perception of Fine, Close Objects Not Yet Fully Developed; Eye-Hand Coordination Not Highly Developed.

Avoid activities requiring close vision.

Difficulty in Sitting Still: Preference for Running and Jumping.

Establish a flexible daily program which follows a general pattern of alternating physical activities with those of a more quiet nature.

Tendency to Remain Restless and Irritable When Tired, Rather Than to Seek Rest.

Watch for signs of fatigue and restlessness.

Provide frequent rest periods.

Short Attention Span.

Relate experiences to spontaneous interest of the children.

Plan all activities for short duration.

Vocabulary Span Very Limited.

Choose words carefully.

Develop meanings of new words through experiences.

Clear up misconceptions through planned experiences.

Largely Concerned With the Immediate Present and the Immediate World.

Utilize experiences related to child's immediate environment and community, such as home, school, store, and pets.

Increasing But Limited Knowledge of the World at Large; No Idea of Cultural Heritage.

Make use of opportunities to acquaint children with an expanding community, using such occasions as national holidays, visitors to the school, different family backgrounds, Junior Red Cross.

Little Concept of Time and Space.

Start to develop time concepts such as: today, yesterday, tomorrow, day of the week, clocks, and calendars.

Start to develop concepts of distance based on simple specific landmarks.

Imitation of Adults Natural.

Set appropriate examples of behavior.

Eager to Please Adults and Win Their Approval.

Find some way to praise each child.

Feelings of Both Dependence and Independence in Relations With Adults.

Recognize that each child sometimes may work independently and at other times is dependent on teacher for direction.

Sharing Not Common.

Encourage pupils to share experiences, ideas, and articles brought from home.

Difficulty in Respecting Property and Rights of Others.

Encourage pupils to take turns, to get permission when using property of others, and to use equipment carefully.

Develop consideration of others.

Enjoyment in Working and Playing With Others, Preferably in Small Groups.

Provide opportunity for children to work in small groups, with memberships changing from time to time.

Desire For Status With the Group and Fear of Being Left Out.

Provide each child with definite responsibilities in routine matters.

Help poorly adjusted children to capitalize on their special interests.

GROUP II: PUPILS, AGE 6 TO 9

Growth Slow and Steady With Small Muscles Developing; Physical Endurance Increasing.

Proceed gradually from large to small instructional materials but avoid very fine and detailed work.

Hand and Eye Coordination Developing; Far-Sightedness Diminishing.

Use blackboard often in preference to pencil and paper.

Guard against eye strain.

Tendency to Be Restless, Impulsive, and Boisterous Continued But Somewhat Diminished.

Vary classroom activities between the physical and mental.

Tendency to Tire Easily Without Recognizing Need For Rest.

Provide opportunities for relaxation.

Span of Attention Still Short But Increasing; Interest and Ability Important Factors.

Have children help plan work for the day and keep track of time allotments.

Work periods may increase in length.

Children able to carry on a unit over a period of weeks.

Girls Advanced Physically Ahead of Boys.

Boys and girls should play together but avoid competition between them.

Great Growths In Vocabulary But Yet Quite Restricted.

Develop understandings by use of concrete illustrations and experiences.

Eagerness To Learn About Community Expanded Beyond the Home and School.

Study the many processes and activities of community life.

Maturing, But Still Not Developed, Concepts of Time and Place.

Most learnings should be related to the here and now.

Introduce simple stories of the past and use various devices to bring out the concept of time.

Introduce concepts of direction and distance; use simple maps and introduce the globe.

Abstract Thinking Developing Slowly, But Some Attempts Made at Generalization.

Provide opportunities for children to summarize and evaluate their activities.

Failure To Distinguish Clearly Between Fact and Fancy.

Encourage creative activities.

Create interest in using reference material.

Desire For Adult Approval But Starting To Work Out Personal Ideas.

Encourage and help children to develop their own ideas.

Be a sympathetic listener.

Continued Lack of Respect For Property and Rights of Others.

Encourage care and conservation of property, private and public.

Guide in developing consideration of others.

Extremely Social, With Development of Greater Ability To Cooperate.

Let children participate in planning.

Guide planning for responsibilities to include all children.

Provide many opportunities for sharing information, treasures, and experiences.

Assuming and Following of Leadership In Small Groups; Entering Into Teamwork In Larger Groups.

Organize several groups; encourage participation by each child; be sure each child knows what he is to do.

Desire For Approval of Other Children.

Encourage children to make use of their special interests and abilities.

Help children select activities at which they can succeed.

Growth In Creative Expression.

Provide opportunities for creative work in rhythms, art, music, written expression, and dramatic play.

GROUP III: PUPILS, AGE 9 TO 11

Muscular Coordination Improving; Bodily Growth Rapid.

Provide instructional materials consistent with the pupils' stage of development.

Eye-Hand Coordination Developed.

Able to do detailed drawing and construction work.

Tendency To Become Over-Fatigued.

Provide for frequent short periods of relaxation.

Attention Span Increasing.

Work periods may be lengthened.

A unit may be of longer duration.

Girls Generally Physically Advanced Over Boys.

Avoid competition between girl groups and boy groups.

Growth In Vocabulary.

Develop the vocabulary of social studies; use concrete experience.

Interest In the Expanding Community Now Broadened To Include the World.

Make use of the growing interest in the ways that other peoples live to guide them to realize the common needs of people everywhere.

Interest In the Contribution of the Past To Our Present Living.

Cultivate this interest by stressing the narrative approach, the story of adventure rather than an analytical approach.

Concepts of Time and Chronology Still Not Mature; Beginning To See Some Sequence In Past Events.

Strengthen time concepts through use of various devices.

Make use of pupils' past experiences to enrich their concept of time.

Concept of Size and Location Emerging.

Give further experience in working with maps and globes.

More Discrimination Shown In Tasks Undertaken; Some Regard for Outcomes.

Encourage children to participate in planning work to be done.

Encourage acceptance of responsibility.

Guide pupils to evaluate progress of the work.

Eager To Attain Skills In Learning.

Skills experiences must be meaningful to the learner.

Provision must be made for an increasing range of individual differences in all skills.

Keen Interest In Reading; Eager To Use Reference Books.

Encourage wide reading.

Establish sound reference habits.

Establish Social Standards and Codes of Fair Play; Acceptance of Rules When Made By Group Participation.

Guide children in formulating own group standards of behavior, fair play, and sportsmanship.

Guard against making rules that are too strict.

Little Companionship Between Girls and Boys.

Recognize this tendency in group activity but encourage boys and girls to work together at times.

Critical of Self and Others, Including Adults.

Help children realize that all people make mistakes.

Give children guidance in making individual and group evaluation.

Hero Worship Common.

Introduce biographies.

Use hero worship as a motivation for building desirable attitudes and traits.

GROUP IV: PUPILS, AGE 11 TO 15

A Time For Rapid Growth and Great Physical Change; Surplus Energy Evident.

Expect restlessness and unusual behavior.

Provide varied activities with some allowance for pupils to move around.

Frequent Minor Illnesses and Short Absences From School.

Patience, understanding, and individual attention are necessary.

Flexible assignments and frequent reviews are suggested.

Tendency To Feel Awkward, Self-Conscious.

Be considerate rather than demanding when a student is embarrassed or upset.

Ease, rather than force, shy students into the spotlight.

Increased Concern for School, Community, and World Problems.

Provide for study of these problems through activities which will give children a chance to do something about them.

Greater Understanding of Concepts of Time and Place.

There is still need for systematic instruction in developing these concepts.

Gradual Increase in Reasoning Ability and In Handling Abstractions.

Provide much opportunity for experience in critical thinking in realistic problem solving.

Readiness To Accept Quick and Easy Conclusions With Overconfidence.

Encourage pupils to regard conclusions as tentative, subject to possible modification later.

Widening Range In Individual Differences In Reading Abilities and In Personal Interests.

Provide varied materials and activities to challenge all pupils.

Growing Interest In Physical Attractiveness and Personal Neatness.

Show value of good grooming in daily personal contacts.

Desire To Excel In Group Activities.

Provide group activities in which everyone may have some responsibility.

Desire To Talk and Argue Rather Than To Listen.

Develop techniques and skills in listening, analyzing, and summarizing what others have said.

Conflict Due To Desire for Independence; Half-Child, Half-Adult Status;
Desire for Privileges But Not for Responsibilities of Adulthood.

Lead pupils to see that privileges are accompanied by responsibilities.

Greater Insight Into Self; Increased Responsibility for Self-Direction.

Provide guidance in self-evaluation.

Status With Peers More Important Than Adult Approval.

Plan activities through which pupils can work together in achieving their goals.

Reluctance To Be Different From the Group Physically and Socially.

Lead pupils to realize that people differ in many respects just as they are similar, and that differences are normal.

Increased Awareness of Moral Codes, But Groups or Gangs Sometimes Un-
Democratic or In Conflict With Cultural Codes.

Stress the value of moral codes and democratic processes.

Emerging Companionship With Members of Opposite Sex.

Provide group activities in which boys and girls participate together.

Idealistic; Inclined Toward Hero Worship.

Use personalities from biographies and current news to provide examples worthy of imitation.

APPENDIX F

School Libraries as Instructional Materials Centers*

The American Association of School Librarians believes that the school library, in addition to doing its vital work of individual reading guidance and development of the school curriculum, should serve the school as a center for instructional materials. Instructional materials include books—the literature of children, young people and adults—other printed materials, films, recordings, and newer media developed to aid learning.

Teaching methods advocated by leaders in the field of curriculum development and now used in elementary and secondary education call for extensive and frequently combined use of traditional along with many new and different kinds of materials. Since these methods depend for their success upon a cross-media approach to learning, a convenient way of approaching instructional materials on a subject or problem basis must be immediately at hand in each school. Historically, libraries of all types have been established to provide convenient centers for books and reading and for locating ideas and information important to the communities they serve. The interest a modern school now has in finding and using good motion pictures, sound recordings, filmstrips, and other newer materials simply challenges and gives increased dimension to established library roles.

The school librarian has always encouraged development of appreciation for and ability to make good and continuing use of printed materials and library services. Taking into account individual differences of children and young people, the school library stimulates and guides each child in the selection and use of materials for the building of taste on appropriate levels

* This statement was passed by unanimous vote at the business meeting of the American Association of School Librarians during the American Library Association conference, Miami Beach, June 21, 1956. It is, therefore, an official statement of the American Association of School Librarians.

of maturity. Now in good library practice, the school library also helps both pupils and teachers to discover new materials of interest and to determine their values. It may provide these materials and the equipment needed for their use for both individual and classroom study and teaching.

The function of an instructional materials center is to locate, gather, provide and coordinate a school's materials for learning and the equipment required for use of these materials. Primary responsibility for administering such a center, producing new instructional materials, and supervising regular programs of in-service training for use of materials may be the province of librarians, or, it may be shared. In any case, trained school librarians must be ready to cooperate with others and themselves serve as coordinators, consultants, and supervisors of instructional materials service on each level of school administration—in the individual school building, for the city or county unit, for the state.

School librarians are normally educated as teachers and meet state requirements for regular teaching certificates. They must also receive special training in analysis, educational evaluation, selection, organization, systematic distribution and use of instructional materials. The professional education of school librarians should contribute this basic knowledge as well as provide understanding of fundamental learning processes, teaching methods, and the psychology of children and adolescents. Also, school librarians must be familiar with the history and current trends in development of school curricula.

In summary, the well-trained professional school librarian should anticipate service as both a teacher and as an instructional materials specialist. Where adequate funds and staff are available, the school library can serve as an efficient and economical means of coordinating the instructional materials and equipment needed for a given school program. It should always stand ready to provide informed guidance concerning selection and use of both printed and newer media.

A STATEMENT PREPARED BY THE JOINT AASL-ACRL-DAVI COMMITTEE*

The three professional organizations represented on the Joint Committee are the American Association of School Librarians and the Association of College and Research Libraries, both divisions of ALA, and the Department of Audio-Visual Instruction of the NEA. These organizations share a basic interest which is the maintenance of high educational standards and continued improvement of instruction in American schools, colleges, and universities.

In recent years, many new types of instructional materials and equipment have been developed, such as educational television programs, specialized training devices, and new projection materials. At the same time, more familiar media such as books, films, and recordings have been made increasingly effective through modern techniques of illustration, improved design, and new production processes. In addition to tangible media, the concept of "instructional materials" includes such community resources as individuals who can make a significant contribution and the use of first hand

* Approved in 1958 by the executive boards of the participating organizations.

experiences in the field. All instructional materials now available, and others yet to come, are needed to secure effective and efficient utilization of educational facilities and teaching personnel.

Each type of material has a unique contribution to make to the educational process. Some materials will be more effective in achieving one teaching or learning objective; others will serve another purpose better. There is no basic competition among instructional materials. The point is that in any situation the distinctive characteristics of each medum should be recognized and all appropriate materials should be used.

Because of the broad variety of media now available and the rapid increase of production within each medium, teachers are faced with a vast reservoir of instructional materials from which to choose. This means that teachers require more and more help from specialists to locate, evaluate, select, produce, and use instructional materials to best advantage. In order to provide such help specialists need to have a working knowledge of the entire range of media, the potential contributions each can make to learning, and effective methods of use.

The professional associations named in this statement, together with other professional organizations, such as those concerned with curriculum improvement and with educational television, are vitally concerned with study, development, and application of all types of instructional materials. They also have in common important responsibilities for recruitment, professional education, and certification of school, college and university staff members who now or in the future will serve as specialists in this field. The Committee agrees that certain knowledge and specific skills, as outlined below, are essential in the professional education of librarians, audio-visual specialists, and others who have a primary responsibility for instructional materials.

PREREQUISITES FOR ATTAINMENT OF PROFESSIONAL STATUS BY INSTRUCTIONAL MATERIALS SPECIALISTS

In light of the significance of instructional materials specialists to the total educational program, it is necessary that there be definition of responsibilities, of required competencies, and of the means by which these competencies can best be developed.

Under consideration here is the professionally competent instructional materials specialist at all levels. By "instructional materials specialists" is meant those individuals who, on a professional level, are directly responsible for a school, college, or university program of counsel, service, or in-service education for student and teacher use of instructional materials. The distinction between the optimum qualifications of the beginning professional worker and of the director of a system-wide program is essentially one of degree and not of kind.

Those personal characteristics and abilities necessary to be effective in working with people in a leadership role become of major importance when that role is one of improving teaching and learning. To fulfill this role is the primary responsibility of instructional materials specialists. Their province is the materials of learning and teaching. The challenge is that of developing increasingly effective use of all types of materials by teachers and students. The measure of their success is the quality of teaching and learning which results.

Looking ahead to the future, the Joint Committee believes that the knowledge and basic skills required for instructional materials specialists to do professional work in education, and the most likely sources of obtaining basic competencies, are as follows:

SUCCESSFUL TEACHING EXPERIENCE: Instructional materials specialists should first of all be experienced teachers. This experience may be acquired by years of classroom teaching, or, in the case of those who enter the profession without experience, through an organized internship program following the completion of their course work. It is essential that instructional materials specialists secure experience on curriculum committees and that they gain experience in guidance and supervision.

FOUNDATION AREAS: Instructional materials specialists should have course work in (a) educational administration and supervision; (b) principles of learning; (c) curriculum development; (d) guidance and counseling; and (e) mass communications. Furthermore they should demonstrate a working knowledge of research methods as applied to instructional materials.

SPECIALIZED AREAS: Instructional materials specialists should have course work and in-service experience in the following areas relating directly to the nature and effective use of materials: (a) analysis of instructional materials, their nature and content; (b) methods of selecting and evaluating materials, through study of individual media as well as through cross-media study by curriculum unit or grade level; (c) utilization of materials; (d) production of appropriate instructional materials, including laboratory work with specific media; and (e) processes for the organization and maintenance of materials and equipment.

The foregoing statement regarding instructional materials specialists and the preparation they require has important implications for many groups, including the students and teachers who are to be served, the professional associations concerned, and especially for those institutions of high education which have responsibility for recruitment and professional education of teachers, librarians, and audio-visual specialists. Whatever their titles may be, specialists in the materials of instruction, who have a broad view of the field, are needed to provide essential services for a modern program of education.

Evaluative Checklist: An Instrument For Self-Evaluating an Educational Media Program in School Systems*

INTRODUCTION

This Evaluative Checklist is based on the assumption that there are fundamental elements of an educational media program which will facilitate the improvement of instruction. The elements around which this Checklist was developed were assumed to be common to most educational media programs. These include: 1) administrators and teachers are committed to the proper use of educational media for instructional purposes, 2) educational media are an integral part of curriculum and instruction, 3) an educational media center is accessible to the faculty, 4) the physical facilities are conducive to proper use of educational media, 5) the media program is adequately financed, and 6) the staff is adequate and qualified to provide for the educational needs of all faculty members.

The status of an educational media program is not likely to be known without periodic evaluation. The use of this Checklist should greatly facilitate such an evaluation by providing useful guidelines for making judgments on program elements.

The term "educational media" as used in this instrument means all equipment and materials traditionally called "audio-visual materials" and all of the newer media such as television, overhead projectuals, and programmed materials. Likewise, the terms "media" and "educational media"

---

* W. R. Fulton, University of Oklahoma, Norman, Oklahoma. This instrument is a part of a study performed pursuant to a contract with the United States Office of Education, Department of Health, Education and Welfare, under the provisions of Title VII, Public Law 85-864. Printed and distributed by the Department of Audiovisual Instruction of the NEA without use of government funds as a service to the teaching profession.

are used interchangeably to mean both instructional equipment and instructional materials.

Before completing the Checklist, the evaluator may want to become familiar with the inventory of educational media and pertinent physical facilities of the program being evaluated. He may also want to study the criteria relating to the elements covered in the Checklist.

EVALUATIVE CHECKLIST

DIRECTIONS:

Mark *one* of the spaces at the left of the statement that most nearly represents the situation in your school system. If a statement accurately describes your school, mark the *middle space* to the left of that statement. If you feel that the situation at your school is below what is described, mark the *lower numbered space;* if above, mark the *higher numbered space.* In any case mark only *one* space.

EXAMPLE:

① ② ③   There is no full-time director of the media program.

④ ⑤ ⑥   There is a full-time director in charge of the media program.

⑦ ⑧ ⑨   There are a full-time director and a sufficient number of clerical and technical personnel.

I. SCHOOL SYSTEM EDUCATIONAL MEDIA SERVICES

CRITERIA

A school system should have a program of educational media services administered through a school media center, and building centers if such are needed, which provides teachers with an adequate supply of appropriate instructional materials.

The educational media center should be a separate service unit that operates at the same level as other major school services.

A school system should have clearly defined policies, procedures, and plans for its educational media program, including short-range, and long-range goals.

There should be a sufficient number of professional media staff members to administer the educational media program and to provide consultative services to teachers throughout the school system.

A. Commitment to the Media Program

① ② ③   The school's educational media program consists of services from a media center managed by clerical and technical staff members. The services are not well coordinated and no one person has been given administrative responsibility for system-wide media activities.

④ ⑤ ⑥   The school's educational media program consists of a media center with clerical and technical staff. The program is directed by a staff person who has some educational media training but not enough to qualify him as an educational media specialist.

He reports to the administrative officer in charge of instruction.

☐7 ☐8 ☐9 The school has an educational media program including an educational media center and necessary building media centers directed by an educational media specialist who reports directly to the administrative officer in charge of instruction. He is provided with facilities, finances, and staff essential in meeting the media needs of the instructional program.

B. Commitment to Educational Media as an Integral Part of Instruction

☐1 ☐2 ☐3 The school provides some educational media and services for teachers who request them, but teachers are not particularly encouraged to use the services.

☐4 ☐5 ☐6 A variety of educational media and services are generally available and some attempts are made to acquaint teachers with the services, and to encourage their use.

☐7 ☐8 ☐9 The school provides the quantity and variety of educational media and services needed by all buildings and encourages teachers to use media as integral parts of instruction.

C. Commitment to Providing Educational Media Facilities

☐1 ☐2 ☐3 Although some new and remodeled facilities provide for the use of some types of educational media, the school gives little attention to media utilization at the time buildings are planned.

☐4 ☐5 ☐6 The school provides most new and remodeled buildings with light control and other facilities necessary for the use of some types of educational media.

☐7 ☐8 ☐9 All new buildings are equipped for the greatest possible use of educational media and are designed to permit adaptation for new developments in media. Old buildings are being modified as fast as possible to provide for effective use of media.

D. Commitment to Financing the Educational Media Program

☐1 ☐2 ☐3 Finances for the educational media program are inadequate to provide the services that teachers need and are prepared to use. There are no written policies relative to allocations, income sources and charges against the budget.

☐4 ☐5 ☐6 maintain the status quo, but the current media services are not Finances for the educational media program are sufficient to sufficient to meet the instructional needs. Long-range curriculum plans do not include provisions for financing needed educational media services.

☐7 ☐8 ☐9 The educational media program is financed entirely from regularly appropriated school funds. The budget reflects to some degree long-range educational media plans and includes provisions for special media for unusual curriculum problems. The budget is prepared, presented, and defended by the director of the media services in the same manner as that of any other budget unit.

E. Commitment to Staffing the Educational Media Program

The responsibility for educational media services is assigned to

1 2 3   various staff members whose primary commitments are in other school jobs.

4 5 6   The responsibility for educational media services is delegated to a person who has had some training in educational media. He is provided with some clerical and technical assistance.

7 8 9   Leadership and consultative services are provided by an educational media specialist and a qualified professional staff. An adequate clerical and technical staff is also provided.

II. EDUCATIONAL MEDIA SERVICES— CURRICULUM AND INSTRUCTION

CRITERIA

A school system should engage in a continuous evaluation of its educational media program as it relates to the instructional program.

Continuous inservice education in the use of educational media should be carried on as a means of improving instruction.

The faculty and the professional media staff should cooperate in planning and developing the parts of the instructional program that make provisions for the use of educational media.

Professional educational media personnel should be readily available for consultation on all instructional problems where media are concerned.

A. Consultative Services in Educational Media Utilization

1 2 3   Educational media personnel render consultative assistance in the instructional application of educational media when they are asked to do so and are free from other duties.

4 5 6   Educational media personnel are usually available and are called on for consultative assistance in the use of educational media.

7 8 9   Educational media professional personnel work, as a part of their regular assignments, with teachers in analyzing teaching needs and in designing, selecting, and using educational media to meet these needs.

B. Inservice Education in Educational Media Utilization

1 2 3   Inservice education is left entirely to building instructional units and is limited to their own capabilities and such other resources as they can find.

4 5 6   Professional educational media staff members are available on request to assist teachers and supervisors in inservice education activities relative to the use of educational media.

7 8 9   Professional educational media staff members are involved in planning and conducting continuous inservice education activities concerned with the selection, development, production, and use of all types of educational media.

C. Faculty-Student Use of Educational Media

☐1 ☐2 ☐3 Only a few teachers make any use of educational media in their classrooms. Students rarely use media in class presentations.

☐4 ☐5 ☐6 Quite a few teachers make occasional use of educational media in their classrooms. Students occasionally use media in class presentations.

☐7 ☐8 ☐9 Most teachers use appropriate educational media in their classrooms. Students use appropriate media for individual and group study, as well as for class presentations.

D. Involvement of the Media Staff in Planning

☐1 ☐2 ☐3 The professional educational media staff is seldom involved with teachers in planning for the use of educational media.

☐4 ☐5 ☐6 The professional educational media staff is occasionally involved with teachers and supervisors in planning and producing materials for use in the instructional program.

☐7 ☐8 ☐9 The educational media specialist and his professional staff are usually involved with teachers, supervisors and other curriculum workers in planning for the use of and in experimenting with educational media in the instructional program. He is also regularly involved in decision making activities relating to the integration of educational media with the curriculum and instruction.

III. THE EDUCATIONAL MEDIA CENTER

CRITERIA

Educational media centers should be organized around the concept of offering a wide variety of services and media to all instructional and administrative units of a school system, with leadership, consultative help, and other services provided by professional media specialists and other media center personnel.

The instructional program should be supported by an adequate supply of educational media and a system of making them accessible to the faculty and students.

The educational media center should provide such media services as procurement, maintenance, and production of appropriate educational media to support the instructional program.

A. Location and Accessibility of Educational Media

☐1 ☐2 ☐3 The location of the school's educational media center is such that media are not accessible to most teachers. The school's educational media center is not supplemented by building centers where media are placed on long-term loan.

☐4 ☐5 ☐6 The location of the school's educational media center is such that media are not very accessible to teachers. The school's educational media center is supplemented by a few building centers that provide some media and services not available from the school media center, but merely duplicate others.

[7] [8] [9] The location of the school's educational media center and the presence of necessary building centers make media highly accessible to all instructional units. Both the school's and the buildings' educational media centers are adequately equipped to support a quality instructional program.

B. Dissemination of Media Information

[1] [2] [3] Information concerning educational media is seldom disseminated to prospective users, but there are no definite plans or channels for such dissemination.

[4] [5] [6] Information concerning educational media is disseminated to teachers and staff members on an occasional basis or when requested.

[7] [8] [9] Information concerning all educational media and programs is frequently disseminated to teachers and staff members as a matter of policy.

C. Availability of Educational Media

[1] [2] [3] The quantity of educational media is so limited that significant delays occur between requests for materials and their availability. Reservations must be made on a "first come, first served" basis, and the media must be picked up by the user.

[4] [5] [6] The quantity of educational media and the distribution system makes it possible for media to be delivered to teachers on relatively short notice.

[7] [8] [9] There is a sufficient quantity of educational media and an adequate distribution system to insure the delivery of all media to teachers on any day during the week in which they are requested.

D. Storage and Retrieval of Media

[1] [2] [3] Media storage facilities are available but are inadequate for some types of educational media, and personnel have difficulty in locating and retrieving specific items.

[4] [5] [6] The school's educational media center and all building centers have enough storage shelves and drawers for currently owned instructional materials. The retrieval system is adequate most of the time.

[7] [8] [9] Adequate storage space, including space for future expansion, is provided in the school's educational media center and in all building centers, with proper humidity control where needed. The school's educational media center has a master retrieval system for immediate location of all media.

E. Maintenance of Media

[1] [2] [3] Educational media are cleaned and repaired when complaints regarding their operable condition are made by users.

[4] [5] [6] Educational media are cleaned and repaired whenever the maintenance Staff has time to do so.

[7] [8] [9] All educational media are inspected after each usage and are cleaned and repaired on a regular basis or when inspection indicates the need.

F. Production of Media

[1] [2] [3] Limited production facilities are available for teachers to produce their own materials.

[4] [5] [6] Educational media personnel, as well as teachers, produce some educational materials, but the media staff is limited to the extent that all demands for production cannot be met.

[7] [8] [9] Educational media personnel, as well as teachers, produce a variety of educational media not otherwise available, and meet most production demands for such media as films, filmstrips, slides, graphics, and recordings.

IV. PHYSICAL FACILITIES FOR EDUCATIONAL MEDIA

CRITERIA

Each classroom should be designed for and provided with essential facilities for effective use of appropriate educational media of all kinds.

Each classroom should be equipped with full light control, electrical outlets, forced ventilation, and educational media storage space.

Classrooms should be equipped with permanently installed bulletin boards, chalkboards, projection screens, map rails, and storage facilities needed for the particular type of instruction conduced in each classroom.

A. Physical Facilities in Existing Classrooms

[1] [2] [3] A few classrooms have been modified for use of educational media. However, no systematic plans have been made to adapt all classrooms for the use of educational media, except that some departments have made such plans for their own classrooms.

[4] [5] [6] Some classrooms have been modified and equipped with such physical facilities as light control and electrical outlets and others are partially equipped. A plan for systematically equipping all classrooms is in operation.

[7] [8] [9] All classrooms have been modified and equipped for optimum use of all types of educational media.

B. Physical Facilities in New Classrooms

[1] [2] [3] Some new classrooms are provided with physical facilities such as light control and electrical outlets, but only in special cases are provisions made for the use of a wide variety of media.

[4] [5] [6] Most new classrooms are provided with physical facilities that make possible optimum use of educational media.

[7] [8] [9] All new classrooms are designed for and equipped with physical facilities that make possible optimum use of all types of educational media by faculty and students.

V. BUDGET AND FINANCE OF THE EDUCATIONAL MEDIA PROGRAM

CRITERION

Financing the educational media program should be based on both the school system's long-range goals and immediate educational needs. The budget should reflect a recognition of long-range goals, and be sufficient to support an adequate media program for optimum instructional improvement.

A. Reporting Financial Needs

[1] [2] [3] The financial needs of the educational media program are reported to the administrative officer in charge of instruction only when immediate expenditures are urgently needed.

[4] [5] [6] The financial needs of the educational media program are regularly reported to the administrative officer in charge of instruction.

[7] [8] [9] Regular reports reflecting the status and needs of the educational media program, including facts about inventory, facilities, level of utilization, and effectiveness of the media program, are made to the administrative officer in charge of instruction.

B. Basis for Budget Allocations

[1] [2] [3] The educational media budget is based on an arbitrary allotment of funds irrespective of need.

[4] [5] [6] The educational media budget is based almost entirely on immediate needs, though some consideration is given to long-range goals.

[7] [8] [9] The educational media budget is based on both the immediate needs and the long-range goals of the school and reflect clear-cut policies concerning allocations, income sources, and budget practices.

C. Development of Media Budget

[1] [2] [3] Each building instructional unit develops its own educational media budget without consulting an educational media specialist.

[4] [5] [6] The budget of the educational media program reflects the media needs of most building instructional units. However, some buildings have their own media budget which has no relationship to the educational media program.

[7] [8] [9] The budget of the educational media program reflects the media needs of the entire school system and is developed by the professional media staff in consultation with financial officers, principals and other school administrators.

VI. EDUCATIONAL MEDIA STAFF

CRITERION

> The educational media program should be directed by a well quali-
> fied full-time media specialist who is provided with sufficient pro-
> fessional, clerical, and technical staff to provide adequate media
> services to the entire school system.

A. School System Media Staff

[1] [2] [3] A staff person has been assigned to look after the media program. He performs more as a clerk and a technician than as a
professional media person.

[4] [5] [6] A professional media person with some special training is in
charge of the educational media program and has some professional, clerical, and technical assistance. He and his assistants
are primarily oriented toward the mechanical and technical
aspects of the program.

[7] [8] [9] The educational media program is directed by a well qualified
media specialist who is provided with sufficient professional,
clerical, and technical staff to provide adequate media services
from the school media center. Professional media staff members
are oriented toward curriculum and instruction.

B. Building Media Staff

[1] [2] [3] Some buildings have a teacher, a clerk, or someone else assigned to help obtain materials and care for equipment, but
no released time is granted from other jobs to coordinate media
activities in the building.

[4] [5] [6] Most buildings have a teacher, or a member of the professional
staff assigned to coordinate media activities, but he has not been
given sufficient released time from other school tasks, or enough
clerical and technical assistance to permit him to render media
services needed in the instructional program.

[7] [8] [9] A full-time professional educational media coordinator serves
each building. Buildings that do not have sufficient teachers
and media utilization to warrant a full-time coordinator share
his services. He is provided sufficient clerical and technical
assistance to supply all media services needed in the building.
He reports to the school's educational media director and works
closely with the media staff, supervisors, and other curriculum
workers.

PROFILE SHEET

To develop a Profile image of your program, transfer your mark from
each item of the Evaluative Checklist to this sheet. Connect the marked
squares by straight lines. Then turn the sheet to a horizontal position. This
will pictorially demonstrate the "peaks" and "valleys" of attainment for
your program.

WEAK ⟶ STRONG

Section I

Item									
A	1	2	3	4	5	6	7	8	9
B	1	2	3	4	5	6	7	8	9
C	1	2	3	4	5	6	7	8	9
D	1	2	3	4	5	6	9	7	8
E	1	2	3	4	5	6	7	8	9

Section II

Item									
A	1	2	3	4	5	6	7	8	9
B	1	2	3	4	5	6	7	8	9
C	1	2	3	4	5	6	7	8	9
D	1	2	3	4	5	6	9	7	8

Section III

Item									
A	1	2	3	4	5	6	7	8	9
B	1	2	3	4	5	6	7	8	9
C	1	2	3	4	5	6	7	8	9
D	1	2	3	4	5	6	9	7	8
E	1	2	3	4	5	6	7	8	9
F	1	2	3	4	5	6	7	8	9

Section IV

Item									
A	1	2	3	4	5	6	7	8	9
B	1	2	3	4	5	6	9	7	8

Section V

Item									
A	1	2	3	4	5	6	7	8	9
B	1	2	3	4	5	6	7	8	9
C	1	2	3	4	5	6	7	8	9

Section VI

Item									
A	1	2	3	4	5	6	7	8	9
B	1	2	3	4	5	6	7	8	9

Policies and Procedures for Selection of School Library Materials*

The following statement of policy making with regard to materials selection for school libraries is offered as a guide to those wishing to formulate a policy. It is believed that such a policy should be formally adopted by each school district as a basis for consistent excellence in choice of materials and as a document that can be presented to parents and other citizens for their further understanding of the purposes and standards of selection of school library materials.

PATTERNS OF POLICY MAKING

The governing body of a school is legally responsible for all matters relating to the operation of that school. It is recommended that assumption of responsibility and the delegation of authority be stated in a formal policy adopted by the legally responsible body.

SELECTION PERSONNEL

Materials for school libraries should be selected by professional personnel in consultation with administration, faculty, students and parents. Final decision on purchase should rest with professional personnel in accordance with the formally adopted policy.

TYPES OF MATERIALS COVERED

There should be criteria established for all types of materials included in a library collection. Such criteria should be available in written form.

* Approved by the Board of Directors of the American Association of School Librarians at the ALA Midwinter conference, February 3, 1961.

OBJECTIVES OF SELECTION

The primary objective of a school library is to implement, enrich and support the educational program of the school. Other objectives are concerned with: 1) the development of reading skill, literary taste, discrimination in choice of materials, and 2) instruction in the use of books and libraries.

The school library should contribute to development of the social, intellectual and spiritual values of the students.

CRITERIA FOR SELECTION

1. Needs of the individual school.
    a. Based on knowledge of the curriculum.
    b. Based on requests from administrators and teachers.
2. Needs of the individual student.
    a. Based on knowledge of children and youth.
    b. Based on requests of parents and students.
3. Provision of a wide range of materials on all levels of difficulty, with a diversity of appeal and the presentation of different points of view.
4. Provision of materials of high artistic quality.
5. Provision of materials with superior format.

SELECTION TOOLS

Reputable, unbiased, professionally prepared selection aids should be consulted as guides.

CHALLENGED MATERIALS

A procedure should be established for consideration of and action on criticism of materials by individuals or groups. The School Library Bill of Rights, endorsed by the Council of the American Library Association in July, 1955, is basic to this procedure. It follows:

SCHOOL LIBRARY BILL OF RIGHTS

School libraries are concerned with generating understanding of American freedoms and with the preservation of these freedoms through the development of informed and responsible citizens. To this end the American Association of School Librarians reaffirms the Library Bill of Rights of the American Library Association and asserts that the responsibility of the school library is:

> To provide materials that will enrich and support the curriculum, taking into consideration the varied interests, abilities, and maturity levels of the pupils served.
> To provide materials that will stimulate growth in factual knowledge, literary appreciation, aesthetic values, and ethical standards.
> To provide a background of information which will enable pupils to make intelligent judgments in their daily life.
> To provide materials on opposing sides of controversial issues so that young citizens may develop under guidance the practice of critical reading and thinking.
> To provide materials representative of the many religious,

ethnic, and cultural groups and their contributions to our American heritage.

To place principle above personal opinion and reason above prejudice in the selection of materials of the highest quality in order to assure a comprehensive collection appropriate for the users of the library.

EXAMPLES OF POLICY STATEMENTS

SCHOOL LIBRARY ASSOCIATION OF CALIFORNIA BULLETIN

The Value of a Statement of Policy and Procedure.

There are many reasons why a school district should have a written statement detailing a clearly defined procedure for the selection of library materials.

1. A written statement will make it easier for all school personnel—teachers, librarians, principals, supervisors, superintendents and members of the Governing Board—to be fully informed on the specific book selection practices of the district.
2. The responsibilities of participating individuals and the limits of their responsibilities will be explicitly stated.
3. If criteria are clearly detailed, and techniques for applying them are clearly set forth, those persons responsible for doing the actual selection will do a thorough and efficient job. Written criteria will serve as a basis for common agreement for those responsible for the selection of material.
4. The materials selected by such criteria and procedures will be better and more useful.
5. A written statement of policies and procedures is an aid in keeping the community informed on the selection of library materials. The confidence of the community in its schools will be increased by the knowledge of the thorough and reasoned philosophies and procedures underlying the selection of materials for its school libraries.

Suggested Contents for a Statement of Book Selection Policy.

On the local level, a statement of book selection policy should include:

1. A statement of the philosophy of book selection for school libraries such as is given in the *School Library Bill of Rights* of the American Association of School Librarians, or the *Book Selection Policy* (Tentative) of the School Library Association of California, Northern Section.
2. A statement that the Governing Board of the district is legally responsible for the selection of library materials.
3. A statement detailing the delegation of this responsibility to professionally trained personnel.
4. An outline of the procedures and criteria to be applied throughout the school or district in selecting library materials.
5. A routine procedure for handling library materials that may be questioned by individuals or groups within the community.

POLICY ON SELECTION OF MATERIALS FOR SCHOOL LIBRARIES*

We, as a group are in accord with the policy of the National Education Association's Commission to Defend Democracy through Education, which is to encourage young people to locate, use, and evaluate relevant materials of instruction as they identify and analyze significant contemporary problems and form judgments about them. However, it is not our duty to direct or compel any particular judgments. We do feel that it is a basic duty of the school library to make available materials of sound literary quality and authority presenting the history of American democracy and its underlying principles.

In formulating our policy we considered these subjects which have been topics of criticism: Religion, Ideologies, Sex, and Science.

1. Religion. Factual unbiased material which represents all major religions should be included in the library collection.
2. Ideologies. The library should, without making any effort to sway the reader's judgment, make available basic factual information on the level of its reading public, on any ideology or philosophy which exerts a strong force, either favorably or unfavorably in government, current events, politics, education, or any other phase of life.
3. Sex and Profanity. Materials presenting accents on sex should be subjected to a stern test of literary merit and reality by the librarian, who takes into consideration her reading public. While we would not in any case include the sensational or over-dramatic, the fact of sexual incidents or profanity appearing should not automatically disqualify a book. Rather the decision should be made on the basis of whether the book presents life in its true proportions, whether circumstances are realistically dealt with, and whether the book is of literary value. Factual material of an education nature on the level of the reader public should be included in the library collection.
4. Science. Medical and scientific knowledge should be made available without any biased selection of facts.

BASIC PRINCIPLES FOR THE SELECTION OF MATERIALS FOR THE EAST GREENBUSH CENTRAL SCHOOL DISTRICT SCHOOL LIBRARIES**

It is the policy of the East Greenbush Central School District to select materials for our libraries in accordance with the following:

1. Books and other reading matter shall be chosen for values of interest and enlightenment of all the students of the community. A

---

* Developed by a (Florida) County Organization of School Librarians.
** Adopted at a meeting of the Board of Education March 22, 1954, East Greenbush Central School District, Rensselar County, New York 12061.

book shall not be excluded because of the race, nationality, or the political or religious views of the writer.

2. There shall be the fullest practical provision of material presenting all points of view concerning the problems and issues of our times, international, national, and local; and books or other reading matter of sound factual authority shall not be prescribed or removed from library shelves because of partisan or doctrinal disapproval.

3. Censorship of books shall be challenged in order to maintain the school's responsibility to provide information and enlightenment.

Interpreting these principles in selection of reading material more specifically, the following will apply:

1. We believe it is the right and responsibility of teachers and librarians to select reading material which is carefully balanced to include various points of view on any controversial subject.

2. Since materials are selected to provide for the interest and needs of the school community and the school program, therefore, they will be selected cooperatively by teachers, principals, and librarians, sometimes with the assistance of students.

3. Selection of materials will be assisted by the reading, examination, and checking of standard evaluation aids; i.e., standard catalogs and book review digests.

4. Two basic factors, truth and art, will be considered in the selection of books and other library materials. This first is factual accuracy, authoritativeness, balance, integrity. The second is a quality of stimulating presentation, imagination, vision, creativeness, style appropriate to the idea, vitality, distinction.

5. Materials for the school library shall be examined to select those in which the presentation and the subject matter are suitable for the grade and the interest level at which they are to be used. They will be considered in relation to both the curriculum and to the personal interest of pupils and teachers.

Books and materials meeting the above standards and principles will not be banned but books or materials of an obscene nature or those advocating overthrow of the government of the United States by force or revolution shall not be recommended for purchase.

Criticisms of books that are in the library should be submitted in writing to the superintendent. The Board of Education will be informed. Allegations thus submitted will be considered by a committee among the faculty which will be appointed by the superintendent. This committee will be in the subject matter field of the book or material challenged and the challenged book or material will be judged by the committee as to its conformity to the aforementioned principles. The books or materials involved will be suspended pending a decision in writing by the above committee. Appeals from this decision may be made through the Superintendent to the Board of Education for final decision.

SELECTING MATERIALS FOR SCHOOL LIBRARIES*

Foreword

The passage of the Elementary and Secondary Education Act of 1965 re-emphasized the importance of careful selection of all types of materials for school libraries. Title II of the Act (PL 89-10) provides "grants for the acquisition of school library resources, textbooks, and other printed and published instructional materials for the use of children and teachers in public and private elementary and secondary schools." This title further provides that the state plan must "set forth the criteria to be used in selecting the library resources, textbooks, and other instructional materials to be provided under this title." As funds are made available under this Act, schools and school systems over the nation will be purchasing all types of print and non-print materials for their school libraries. Funds are being used now to purchase books and other materials eligible under the expanded provisions of Title III of the National Defense Education Act of 1964. In many schools these materials are being housed in and circulated from a central location—the school library or instructional materials center.

Personnel responsible for selecting items to be purchased under either of these acts need assistance in choosing quality materials. The explosion of knowledge and the tremendous increase in available books and other instructional resources make it impossible to examine and evaluate all materials before they are purchased. Therefore, a varied and extensive collection of authoritative selection aids is essential.

The American Association of School Librarians has prepared this publication to help individuals and groups in selecting appropriate library materials. Each individual or group must evaluate the selection sources which are listed in the publication in order to choose bibliographies which are pertinent to their local situation.

GUIDELINES FOR SELECTION OF SCHOOL LIBRARY MATERIALS

The expansion of school library programs to include a diversity of materials is a natural outgrowth of the acceptance of the concept of the library as an integral aspect of the instructional program of the school. It is the function of the library to provide materials which undergird the school curriculum, and it is no longer realistic to think of teaching and learning materials only in terms of the printed word. To support its educational program, a school needs material in many forms related to all curriculum areas.

Intelligent selection of these materials is a time consuming task which requires professional competence as well as the ability to profit by the professional competence of others. The first requisite is depth of knowledge of the curriculum and the second is knowledge of the needs, interests, and abilities of the school clientele. Related factors are the amount of money available, the materials already available in the school library, and materials available from other sources.

Selection of the type of material, printed, pictured, or recorded, should

* Prepared by *The American Association of School Librarians*. A Division of the American Library Association and a Department of the National Education Association. 1965.

be made on the basis of the medium available that most effectively conveys or interprets the content or the concept; in many instances, material in one format is useful in supplementing that in another. The same material may be needed in various media for use with individuals and groups with varying abilities and interests as well as to provide opportunities for variety in presentation. All materials selected for the school library, in whatever format, should meet high standards of excellence. Materials which deal with current topics should be up-to-date; those which reflect a biased point of view should make the prejudice recognizable.

The individual school library collection should include all facets of the curriculum with materials which reflect different points of view on controversial subjects and which provide opportunities for pupils and teachers to range far and wide in their search for information and inspiration. Since there is within a school little homogeneity of either ability or interest, the collection should contain both easy and difficult materials.

Selection is a cooperative process which should involve staff and pupils, though the final decisions are vested in the library personnel. Teachers are subject specialists with the added knowledge of the needs, interests, and abilities of their pupils. It is the responsibility of the library staff to consult with them, to provide them with as much bibliographic information as possible, and to secure their assistance in the evaluation of materials. Pupils can be encouraged to use bibliographic sources and to make recommendations for materials in which they are interested or which they need.

The safest method for selection is, of course, a first hand knowledge of the material itself; the next is the perceptive use of reliable lists. Factors to consider in evaluating lists include the reliability of the person or organization who prepared them and their recency. Many school districts now provide examination centers where books, films and filmstrips, tapes, and recordings may be previewed or examined. Where such service is available, teachers and librarians should be given the opportunity to become familiar with the materials and should avail themselves of this opportunity before recommending their purchase.

Many school districts, too, have developed statements of policy which govern their selection of materials. Such statements include the philosophy for selection, the agency and staff responsible for implementing the policy, the types of materials included, criteria and procedures for their selection, and procedures for handling problems which arise when a particular piece of material is questioned. When such statements are cooperatively developed, accepted and adhered to, they provide both guidance and protection for all who are involved in the selection of materials.

Three publications which are useful in the preparation of a policy statement are: *The School Library Bill of Rights* (endorsed by the American Association of School Librarians and The American Library Association, 1955); the joint statement of AASL-ACRL-DAVI on the relationship of all materials, adopted by the Executive Boards of the three organizations in 1958 (see p. 59 of *Standards for School Library Programs.* (ALA, 1960 $2.50); *Policies and Procedures for Selection of School Library Materials* (endorsed by American Association of School Librarians, 1961); and *The Students' Right To Read,* prepared by the National Council of Teachers of English in 1962 (Council, 25¢).

APPENDIX I

Model

SCHOOL LIBRARY PHILOSOPHY AND POLICY STATEMENT
AS ENDORSED BY THE EXLER SCHOOL BOARD*

The Exler School District believing that each American citizen is entitled
to a quality, optimum education has designed an educational program
which will encourage and enable each student to become intellectually and
socially competent, to value moral integrity and personal decency, and to
achieve self-understanding and self-realization.

The following objectives provide unity, direction, and guidance in both
the design and implementation of the educational program:

1. To provide ample opportunity for each student to build his
   "house of intellect" commensurate with his mental potential
2. To provide teaching experiences which will meet uniquely and
   adequately individual student needs, interests, goals, abilities,
   and creative potential
3. To provide learning experiences and teaching guidance which
   will enable and encourage each student to build a positive set of
   values
4. To provide teaching and learning experiences which will enable
   and encourage each student to understand, to appreciate, and to
   value his cultural, social, political, and economic heritage as an
   American, as a world citizen and as a human being

* Pennsylvania Department of Public Instruction. Division of School Libraries. *A Guide
for School Librarians.* Harrisburg, Pennsylvania: Department of Public Instruction, 1969.
pp. 16-20.

5. To provide teaching and learning experiences which have been structured as a progressive continuum of related fundamentals from kindergarten through grade twelve
6. To provide ample opportunity for each student to become conversant with the techniques of critical, analytical, reflective, logical, and creative thinking

The Exler school libraries function as an integral part of the total educational program. The goal of the school library program is to facilitate and expedite the realization and attainment of a quality, optimum education by each student. To reach this goal the following objectives give purpose and direction to the library program:

1. To provide an educationally functional and effective library program which will meet adequately the developmental needs of the curriculum and the personal needs, interests, goals, abilities, and creative potential of the students
2. To provide informed and concerned guidance in the use of library services and resources which will personalize teaching and individualize learning
3. To provide a planned, purposeful, and educationally significant program which will be integrated appropriately with the classroom teaching and learning program
4. To provide library resources which will stimulate and promote interest in self-directed knowledge building

LIBRARY INTEGRATION AND ENRICHMENT PROCEDURE

I. Programming for the purposeful and systematic use of library materials is the shared responsibility of teacher and librarian
   A. Teacher plans with librarian in a scheduled conference to
      1. Determine library contribution to unit development
      2. Determine library contribution to class and individual student achievement
   B. Teacher and librarian design cooperatively a media program to support the anticipated teaching program
      1. Exploring together the developmental needs of the unit
      2. Identifying specific topics, concepts, and skills to be introduced, reinforced, and extended
      3. Identifying specific teaching experiences and activities requiring supporting media
      4. Identifying specific learning experiences and activities requiring supporting media
      5. Identifying special student needs, interests, goals, and abilities requiring media accommodation
      6. Determining class, group, and individual student media usage patterns for knowledge building
      7. Designing a media usage sequence to match
         a. Specific topic, concept, and skill development patterns
         b. Specific teaching goals, experiences, and activities
         c. Specific learning needs, experiences, and activities

   C. Librarian searches for resources to support the teaching plan
1. Matching materials to specific topic, concept, and skill development needs
2. Matching materials to specific student needs, interests, goals, and abilities
3. Relating materials in a usage pattern of logical sequential order
4. Assembling, grouping, and relating materials

II. Implementing the media program is the shared responsibility of teacher and librarian
   A. Teacher orients his students to the specific contribution library resources are to make to the development of the teaching and/or learning plan
   B. Teacher pre-plans with librarian for class, group, or individual student use of the library
   C. Librarian serves as teacher
1. Orienting students to materials of special or unique value
2. Introducing students to new tools, techniques, or skills essential to building adequacy of understanding
3. Guiding students in their use, interpretation, extension, association, integration, and evaluation of information
   D. Librarian cooperates with classroom teacher
1. Evaluating effectiveness of student, group, and class use of media
2. Analyzing educational value of the media pattern and program
3. Determining program adjustment and modification

POLICIES AND PROCEDURES FOR SELECTING LIBRARY MEDIA:

While the legal responsibility for the purchase of all instructional materials is vested in the Exler School Board, the final responsibility for the selection of library materials has been delegated to the school librarians of the district.

The school librarians have been charged with the responsibility of identifying, ordering, and organizing materials which will implement, enrich, and support the educational program of the school and will meet the needs, interest, goals, concerns, and abilities of the individual students.

RATIONALE FOR THE EXLER MEDIA SELECTION POLICIES:

The administrative staff of the Exler schools endorses the tenets set forth in the School Library Bill of Rights:*

> "School libraries are concerned with generating understanding of American freedoms and with the preservation of these freedoms through the development of informed and responsible citizens. To this end the American Association of School Librarians reaffirms the 'Library Bill of Rights' of the American Library Association and asserts that the responsibility of the school library is:

---

* Based on procedures outlined in, *Policies and Procedures for Selection of School Library Materials,* American Association of School Librarians, 1961.

To provide materials that will enrich the curriculum, taking into consideration the varied interests, abilities, and maturity levels of the pupils served

To provide materials that will stimulate growth in factual knowledge, literary appreciation, aesthetic values, and ethical standards

To provide a background of information which will enable students to make intelligent judgments in their daily lives

To provide materials on opposing sides of controversial issues so that young citizens may develop under guidance the practice of critical reading and thinking

To provide materials representative of many religions, ethnic, and cultural groups and their contributions to our American heritage

To place principle above personal opinion and reason above prejudice in the selection of materials of the highest quality in order to assume a comprehensive collection appropriate for the users of the library."

PROCEDURE:

All library materials are to be ordered by the coordinator of library service or by librarians delegated this responsibility by the coordinator.

Administrators, supervisors, teachers, and students are to be encouraged to suggest materials to be added to the library collection and to share in evaluating materials being considered for purchase.

Whenever possible, both print and nonprint media are to be examined physically before purchase. If possible, materials should be bought "on approval" and, if judged unsuitable, returned to vendor for credit. Pilot testing of material in a classroom teaching situation is to be employed where class reaction and student use are to be determined.

Centralized ordering and processing of all school library materials are to be provided by the staff of the district instructional materials center.

The reviewing of books and the evaluating of nonbook materials are to be a team enterprise; librarians and teachers are to share their knowledge in selecting instructional media.

CRITERIA FOR SELECTING PRINTED AND NONPRINTED MEDIA:

1. Educational significance.
2. Need and value to the collection
3. Reputation and significance of author or producer
4. Clarity, adequacy, and scope of text or audiovisual presentation
5. Validity, accuracy, objectivity, up-to-dateness, and appropriateness of text or audiovisual presentation
6. Organization and presentation of contents
7. High degree of readability and/or comprehensibility
8. High degree of potential user appeal
9. High artistic quality and/or literary style
10. Quality format
11. Value commensurate with cost and/or need

QUESTIONED MEDIA:*

Review of questioned materials should be treated objectively, unemotionally, and as a routine matter. Criticisms of library books must be submitted in writing to the Superintendent, must be signed, and must include specific information as to author, title, publisher, and definite citation of objection.

A review committee will be appointed by the Superintendent to determine the validity of the objection. Appeals from the decision of the committee may be made through the Superintendent to the Board of Education for final decision.

DISTRICT SHARING OF LIBRARY RESOURCES

Each of the Exler school libraries is an integral component of the total district library program and is not an entity in and of itself.

All librarians are guided by the educational philosophy and standards of the district; all are guided by the district library philosophy, objectives, and procedural plan.

Budget funds are allocated on the basis of a district program of uniform excellence and the individual library's role in that program.

Each library collection is considered a segment of the total district library collection. All materials are shared; all materials are made available upon request to any school library in the district.

* Based on procedures outlined in, *Policies and Procedures for Selection of School Library Materials,* American Association of School Librarians, 1961.

Elementary Reading Interest Inventory*

Name_____ Grade_____Date_____

Please help us discover the kind of reading you enjoy so we can buy books which will have special appeal just for you.

STEP 1 Read the list carefully.

STEP 2 Read the list again and put a line through each type of story you would NOT enjoy reading.

Example: _____ Adventure

_____ Air Force   —This indicates you would **NOT**
_____ Airplanes   enjoy reading a book about the Air Force.

STEP 3: Read the list again and check the 5 types you would MOST enjoy reading.

Example: _____ Automobiles

__X__ Baseball   —This indicates that you have se-
_____ Basketball   lected baseball stories to be one of your **FIVE** most enjoyable
_____ Boating   types of reading.

* North Hills School District, Pittsburgh, Pennsylvania 15229.

TYPES OF FICTION OR STORY BOOKS

_____ Adventure	_____ Indians
_____ Air Force	_____ King Arthur
_____ Airplanes	_____ Knights
_____ Annapolis	_____ Middle Ages
_____ Automobiles	_____ Mountain life
_____ Baseball	_____ Mystery and detective
_____ Basketball	_____ Nurses
_____ Boating	_____ Orphans
_____ Camping	_____ Penguins
_____ Cats	_____ Pilgrims
_____ Caves	_____ Pirates
_____ Children in other lands	_____ Pony Express
_____ Circus	_____ Prehistoric man
_____ Colonial times	_____ Railroads
_____ Dinosaurs	_____ Ranch life
_____ Doctors	_____ Refugees
_____ Dogs	_____ School
_____ Donkeys	_____ Science
_____ Dragons	_____ Scouts
_____ Eskimos	_____ Sea
_____ Fairy tales	_____ Skiing
_____ Family life	_____ Skin diving
_____ Farm life	_____ Slaves
_____ Fishing	_____ Space
_____ Football	_____ Submarines
_____ Foreigners	_____ Swimming
_____ Frontier and pioneer life	_____ Tall tales
_____ Ghosts	_____ Teen-age
_____ Goblins	_____ Veterinarians
_____ Gypsies	_____ War
_____ Historical	_____ Whaling
_____ Holidays	_____ Wild animals
_____ Horses	_____ Witches
_____ Humorous	_____ Zoos
_____ Hunting	

STEP 4 Please list any other types you would enjoy reading but have not found listed above.

_____ _____
_____ _____
_____ _____
_____ _____
_____ _____

STEP 5 Please read the following list of nonfiction or factual books and put a line through any type you would NOT enjoy reading.

STEP 6 Please read the list again and check the 5 types you would MOST enjoy reading.

TYPES OF NON-FICTION OR FACTUAL BOOKS

_____ Annapolis	_____ Magic
_____ Aquariums	_____ Making a kite
_____ Archery	_____ Making a model airplane
_____ Astronauts	_____ Making a model automobile
_____ Astronomy	_____ Making a model boat
_____ Atomic energy	_____ Making a model ship
_____ Automobiles	_____ Making a motor
_____ Aviation	_____ Making a radio
_____ Ballet	_____ Making puppets
_____ Baseball	_____ Nature study
_____ Basketball	_____ Nurses
_____ Biography	_____ Painting
_____ Boating	_____ Parties
_____ Bowling	_____ Pets
_____ Camping	_____ Photography
_____ Chemistry	_____ Plays
_____ Children of other lands	_____ Poetry
_____ Collecting coins	_____ Radio
_____ Collecting dolls	_____ Rock collecting
_____ Collecting insects	_____ Science experiments
_____ Collecting seashells	_____ Scuba and skin diving
_____ Collecting stamps	_____ Scouting
_____ Computers	_____ Sewing
_____ Cooking	_____ Skiing
_____ Dinosaurs	_____ Space exploration
_____ Doctors	_____ Submarines
_____ Fishing	_____ Swimming
_____ Golf	_____ Teachers
_____ History	_____ Television
_____ Hockey	_____ Tennis
_____ Holidays	_____ Training a dog
_____ Horseback riding	_____ Veterinarians
_____ Jokes and riddles	_____ West Point
_____ Leathercraft	

STEP 7 Please list any other types you would enjoy reading but have not found listed above.

_____   _____
_____   _____
_____   _____
_____   _____
_____   _____

Streamlining for Service*

Changes in American education have increased the demand for more and better school library services. To provide library programs adequate to support instruction, school districts have devised special services to schools so that librarians, freed from routine and repetitive tasks associated with the organization and circulation of materials, can devote more of their time to work with pupils and teachers.

CENTRALIZED PROCESSING

Probably the most important school district service needed to eliminate duplication of effort in school libraries is the centralized ordering, cataloging, and physical preparation of materials for use. Centralized cataloging includes only the classifying of books and the supplying of full sets of catalog cards. Centralized processing includes both the cataloging and the physical preparation of books, i.e., marking call numbers on the books and putting cards and pockets in the books. The only step to be done at the local library is the filing of catalog cards. A complete centralized processing system includes ordering as well.

Several school districts have cataloged centrally for their schools for many years. Since 1944 the Georgia State Department of Education, through its State Catalog Card Service, has offered catalog cards to both school and public libraries in Georgia at nominal cost. In the 1963–64 fiscal year, 4 school districts and 1,413 individual schools participated. In a few states public libraries and area processing centers have offered similar services or more extensive ones, including ordering and physical preparation of books, to school libraries. More frequently, however, school districts have organ-

* Darling, Richard L. *School Activities and the Library*. Chicago, Illinois: American Library Association, 1965. pp. 1-2.

ized their own central cataloging or processing centers to serve all schools within their jurisdiction. In 1960–61, according to a U. S. Office of Education study, 467 school districts in the United States were providing centralized processing of school library materials for elementary schools, and 239 for secondary schools. No doubt the number of school districts with this service has increased since the study was made.

Practices in centralized processing differ from district to district. In some school districts centralized processing is supplied to elementary schools only. In others processing is done only for new schools; during the summer vacation; or for special materials, such as those purchased with National Defense Education Act funds. Some school districts provide only central ordering and cataloging, and leave full processing to the schools. Many now, however, are providing complete processing for all library books.

A few school districts also process nonprint materials, such as filmstrips, slides, and recordings. The Montgomery County Public Schools, Rockville, Maryland, for example, began by processing books only. As a second step the district started processing all films in the central office inventory and depositing complete sets of cards in each school library for interfiling in the card catalog. Now cards are being prepared for filmstrips, and soon recordings and other instructional materials will be fully processed. This development is probably typical of that in many school districts.

USE OF MACHINES FOR PROCESSING

Early in the development of centralized processing for school libraries, librarians administering the service turned to machines to increase output and economy of operation and to assure a standardized product. Most processing centers use pasting machines, call-number lettering machines, one of a variety of duplicating machines, and photographic equipment for producing duplicating masters. A few processing centers have added photocopying machines which will copy a full set of commercially printed or locally typed catalog cards for each additional copy of a book.

COMMERCIAL CATALOGING AND PROCESSING

Other school districts have turned to commercial sources for cataloging or processing. For many years school libraries have depended upon the Library of Congress and the H. W. Wilson Company for printed catalog cards for books. Some publishers now supply sets of catalog cards with their books. Some school districts are buying their books from suppliers who deliver them ready for use, completely processed. Several firms now process books before delivery, either according to a standardized procedure or tailored to fit customer specifications. One large eastern school district pays only 85¢ per book to receive its purchases preprocessed, and was able to contract at 65¢ per book for a large order for new schools. Ordinarily most schools would have to pay from 70¢ to $1.70 per book for this service, depending upon the type of material involved and the kind of processing demanded. The availability of printed cards and preprocessed books has great advantages for small school districts, for which the cost of equipment and the difficulties of employing staff for processing centers may be too great.

COOPERATION AMONG SCHOOL DISTRICTS

Whether each school district should set up its own processing center is doubtful, for an effectively administered processing center can easily serve more than one district. A state school library supervisor from a state where four large school districts operate central processing centers has indicated that she feels these four are probably sufficient to serve the state's smaller school districts, and is urging them to extend their service to the rest of the state's schools through cooperative arrangements.

In other states, particularly those with large numbers of small school districts, central processing centers to serve several districts might be organized as cooperative ventures and administered by one school district for all of them or by an intermediate unit of school administration. Support for these centers would have to be apportioned among the cooperating school districts, and legislative action could be sought to secure state assistance. It has also been found feasible for schools and public libraries in an area to cooperate in a processing endeavor.

DATA PROCESSING EQUIPMENT FOR ORDERING AND PROCESSING

As school districts adopt the use of data processing equipment, they will be able to process a far greater volume of school library materials more efficiently than they do now. Punched cards on which essential data have been coded make it possible to reduce the number of routine procedures to be done manually. Several school districts already use data processing equipment for acquisitions, and at least one school district has proposed to handle all processing of books by such machines, including the preparation of the book catalogs.

Montgomery County, Maryland, has begun a data processing program which will be used throughout the various steps involved in providing materials to schools. Though much of the plan remains to be implemented, it provides an outline of ways in which data processing can assist in streamlining procedures of evaluation, selection, ordering, and complete processing.

When the school district requests copies of instructional materials for evaluation or receives complimentary copies for its review program, punched cards are prepared for each title, including cards for control purposes, for reviews by members of the professional staff, for use in preparation of approved lists, and for ordering. After reviews have been written, additional data from them are punched into the cards, and masters are prepared by machine from which lists are duplicated. Orders submitted from schools are entered on punched cards so that the machines can produce combined purchase orders with materials correctly listed for each vendor, and can provide lists with the necessary information to expedite the processing and delivery of materials to each school.

PRINTED BOOK CATALOGS

A logical future step in planning might be the printed book catalog prepared by machine methods. Some public libraries have abandoned card catalogs in favor of book catalogs. Before school districts transfer their card catalogs to books, however, there should be a careful study made of their value for schools. Individual school libraries do not have the same relationship to the district central office that public library branches have to the main library with its large supporting collection. Nor has the exchange of materials, common within public library systems, become widespread in school districts. The book catalog facilitates this exchange. School districts also need to determine whether such exchange of materials is desirable for improving school library services. The answers to these questions are the important factors in deciding on book catalogs. Compared to these questions, technical problems are minor.

DATA PROCESSING FOR INFORMATION RETRIEVAL

Some schoolmen have proposed the use of data processing equipment for information retrieval systems for school libraries. The value of such retrieval for school libraries should be seriously questioned, since the consensus at present is that the mechanical storage and retrieval of information hold little promise for libraries with general collections.

Undoubtedly there are other ways in which school districts can streamline routines, such as by centralized production of some kinds of instructional materials. School librarians should explore innovations which promise greater efficiency. The sure test of the value of such innovations is that they free librarians for selection of materials and for service to students and teachers. The goal of streamlining must be improved instruction through better school library service.

Social Studies Skills:
A Guide to Analysis
and Grade Placement*

Helping young people develop and use skills effectively is one of the central purposes of social studies instruction. Indeed, without an adequate command of skills, it is doubtful that students can gain the insights concerning their society or develop the habits of intellectual and social behavior that constitute the ultimate goals of the social studies program. Skills are tools for learning, both in and out of school. The student who develops a command of social studies skills during his school years and carries these skills into the adult years has laid a firm basis for continued learning throughout his life.

The chart which appears in the following pages has been developed as an aid to social studies teachers who desire to improve their teaching of social studies skills.[1] It represents an illustrative analysis of major skills areas that should be developed in social studies programs. It is organized in two parts, as follows:

* Johns, Eunice and Fraser, Dorothy McClure. In *Skill Development in Social Studies*, edited by Helen McCracken Carpenter. Thirty-Third Yearbook. Washington, D.C.: National Council for the Social Studies, 1963.

[1] In preparing this chart, the authors have consulted a wide range of curriculum materials and professional literature, including: Baltimore (Md.) Public Schools. *Guide to Elementary Education*, 1955; Buffalo (N.Y.) Public Schools. *Curriculum Guide, Kindergarten–Grade Three*, 1959, and *Curriculum Guide, Grade Four–Six*, 1959; Minneapolis (Minn.) Public Schools. *Social Studies*, 1957; John U. Michaelis, editor. *Social Studies in Elementary Schools*. Thirty-Second Yearbook. Washington, D.C.: National Council for the Social Studies, a department of the National Education Association, 1962. Chapter VI; and the body of the *Yearbook* in which this Appendix appears. They wish to acknowledge a particular debt to the social studies committees of the Washington County (Md.) Public Schools and of the Wilmington (Del.) Public Schools, whose draft formulations of similar charts are reflected in this chart.

PART ONE. Skills which are a definite but shared responsibility of the social studies

    I. Locating information
    II. Organizing information
    III. Evaluating information
    IV. Acquiring information through reading
    V. Acquiring information through listening and observing
    VI. Communicating orally and in writing
    VII. Interpreting pictures, charts, graphs, tables
    VIII. Working with others.

PART TWO. Skills which are a major responsibility of the social studies

    I. Reading social studies materials
    II. Applying problem-solving and critical-thinking skills to social issues
    III. Interpreting maps and globes
    IV. Understanding time and chronology.

The chart also suggests a tentative grade placement for three levels of emphasis on each sub-skill that is identified: (1) introducing the specific skill, through planned readiness experiences; (2) developing the skill systematically; and (3) reteaching, maintaining, and extending the skill as necessary.

Thus, the chart outlines a planned, sequential program for skill development, one that cuts across subject lines and bridges the gap between the elementary and the secondary school. It may serve as a reminder to every teacher that effective teaching of skills should be part of a cumulative program running from the early school years through high school. It may help the teacher plan so as to reinforce whatever command of skills his pupils have already attained at the same time that he leads them to a higher level of performance.

The chart may also be used by groups of social studies teachers and their colleagues in other fields as a point of departure in formulating their own analysis and plan for the social studies skills program in their own school system.[2] When teachers thus clarify their own purposes for teaching skills, become sensitized to their pupils' needs for skill development, and identify ways of meeting those needs, major benefit to the instructional program will result that could never come from uncritical acceptance of an already formulated program.

Throughout this *Yearbook* the point has been made that pupils develop skills most effectively when there is systematic instruction and continuing application of the skills. The following principles of learning and teaching have been emphasized as a basis for the social studies skills program:

    1. The skill should be taught functionally, in the context of a topic of study, rather than as a separate exercise.

---

[2] Teachers and curriculum committees who wish to reproduce the chart, or portions of it, are hereby granted permission to do so by the National Council for the Social Studies, holder of the copyright. It is requested, however, that in all cases the introductory pages (pp. 310-312) be included, since this explanatory material provides the necessary frame of reference for the proper use of the chart.

2. The learner must understand the meaning and purpose of the skill, and have motivation for developing it.
3. The learner should be carefully supervised in his first attempts to apply the skill, so that he will form correct habits from the beginning.
4. The learner needs repeated opportunities to practice the skill, with immediate evaluation so that he knows where he has succeeded or failed in his performance.
5. The learner needs individual help, through diagnostic measures and follow-up exercises, since not all members of any group learn at exactly the same rate or retain equal amounts of what they have learned.
6. Skill instruction should be presented at increasing levels of difficulty, moving from the simple to the more complex; the resulting growth in skills should be cumulative as the learner moves through school, with each level of instruction building on and reinforcing what has been taught previously.
7. Students should be helped, at each stage, to generalize the skills, by applying them in many and varied situations; in this way, maximum transfer of learning can be achieved.
8. The program of instruction should be sufficiently flexible to allow skills to be taught as they are needed by the learner; many skills should be developed concurrently.

In applying these principles, teachers should keep two cautions in mind. First, although it is possible to make a general plan for continuity in skill development, it is impossible to set a particular place in the school program where it is always best to introduce a specific skill. Many factors enter into the final decision of the teacher, as he works with a specific class, and the general plan can serve only as a guide to what seems to be good practice. True continuity in skill development is that which is developed within the learner, not that which can be blocked out in a general plan. Furthermore, it can never be assumed that a child has gained command of a particular skill merely because he has been exposed to it. Review and reteaching of skills that have been stressed at an earlier grade level are often necessary, even with the most capable students.

Second, the suggested grade placements indicated in the chart which follows are based on a combination of current practice and the subjective judgments of many teachers, including the authors. Both of these reflect what young people seem to be able to achieve within existing patterns of instruction. It is possible that pupils could achieve earlier and more effective command of many aspects of social studies skills if new patterns and approaches for instruction were employed. More systematic and intensive readiness experiences, for example, might enable children to profit from systematic instruction in skills at an earlier age. If so, they would gain an earlier command of tools that could enhance their learning through the rest of their school years. On the other hand, it is possible that present practice calls for instruction in some skills before the learner has developed the necessary related concepts. If so, he may not only fail for the moment but be handicapped in later efforts to gain control of the particular skill. Almost no research evidence exists to guide the proper grade placement of skill instruction. Evidence of this kind is urgently needed as a basis for improving the teaching of social studies skills. It is the hope of the authors that their efforts in preparing this guide to the analysis and grade placement of skill instruction will stimulate such research in the years immediately ahead.

The chart follows:

SOCIAL STUDIES SKILLS: A GUIDE TO ANALYSIS AND GRADE PLACEMENT
(Code: EP, early primary; LP, late primary; EI, early intermediate;
LI, late intermediate; J, junior high school; S, senior high school)

PART ONE: Skills which are a definite but shared responsibility of the social studies

Skill	Introduce, through planned readiness experiences	Develop systematically	Reteach, maintain, and extend
I. Locating information			
A. Work with books			
1. Use title of books as guide to contents	EP	LP-LI	J-S
2. Use table of contents	LP	EI-J	S
3. Alphabetize	LP	EI-J	S
4. Use index	EI	LI-J	S
5. Use title page and copyright date	EI	LI-J	S
6. Use glossary, appendix, map lists, illustration lists	EI	LI-J	S
7. Distinguish between storybooks and factual books	LP-EI	LI-J	S
8. Choose a book appropriate for the purpose	LP-EI	LI-J	S
B. Find information in encyclopedias and other reference books			
1. Locate information in an encyclopedia by using key words, letters on volume, index, and cross references	EI	LI-J	S
2. Use reference works, such as *World Almanac*, atlases, *Who's Who*, *Statesman's Yearbook*	EI	LI-J	S
C. Make efficient use of the dictionary			
1. Alphabetize a list of words according to the first letter; according to the second and third letters	LP	EI-J	S
2. Use guide words	EI	LI-J	S
3. Learn correct pronunciation of a word	EI	LI-J	S
4. Understand syllabication	EI	LI-J	S

SOCIAL STUDIES SKILLS: A GUIDE TO ANALYSIS AND GRADE PLACEMENT—*Continued*
(Code: EP, early primary; LP, late primary; EI, early intermediate;
LI, late intermediate; J, junior high school; S, senior high school)

PART ONE: Skills which are a definite but shared responsibility of the social studies—*Continued*

Skill	Introduce, through planned readiness experiences	Develop systematically	Reteach, maintain, and extend
I. Locating information—*Con.*			
C. Make efficient use of the dictionary—*Con.*			
5. Choose the appropriate meaning of the word for the context in which it is used	EI	LI-J	S
D. Read newspapers, magazines, and pamphlets with discrimination			
1. Recognize these materials as sources of information about many topics, especially current affairs	LP	EI-LI	J-S
2. Select important news items	EI	LI	J-S
3. Select from these sources material that is pertinent to class activities	EI	LI-J	S
4. Learn the organization of a newspaper and how to use the index	LI	J	S
5. Learn about the sections of the newspaper	EI	LI	J-S
6. Recognize the differences in purpose and coverage of different magazines, papers, and pamphlets	LI	J-S	S
E. Know how to find material in a library, both school and public			
1. Locate appropriate books	EI	LI-J	S
2. Use a book card	EI	LI	
3. Use the card catalogue to learn that—			
a. A book is listed in three ways—by subject, by author, and by title	EI	LI-J	S
b. All cards are arranged alphabetically	EI	LI-J	S

c. Cards have call numbers in upper left-hand corner which indicate the location on the shelf	EI	LI–J	S
d. Some author cards give more information than the title or subject card	EI	LI–J	S
e. Information such as publisher, date of publication, number of pages and of illustrations, and usually some annotation are provided	EI	LI–J	S
	J	S	S
f. The Dewey Decimal System is a key to finding books	J	S	S
4. Use the *Readers' Guide to Periodical Literature* and other indexes	J	S	S
F. Gather facts from field trips and interviews			
1. Identify the purpose of the field trip or interview	EP	LP–J	S
2. Plan procedures, rules of behavior, questions to be asked, things to look for	EP	LP–J	S
3. Take increasingly greater initiative in the actual conduct of the field trip or interview	EP	LP–J	S
4. Evaluate the planning and execution of the field trip or interview	EP	LP–J	S
5. Find acceptable ways to open and close an interview	LP	EI–J	S
6. Express appreciation for courtesies extended during the field trip or interview	EP	LP–J	S
7. Record, summarize, and evaluate information gained	EP	LP–S	S
G. Be selective in using audiovisual materials	EP–LI	J	S
(See Acquiring information through listening and observing; and Interpreting pictures, charts, graphs, tables; Part One, Sections V, VII.)			
H. Use maps and globes in developing geographic skills	LP	EI–J	S
(See Interpreting maps and globes, Part Two, Section III.)			
II. Organizing information			
A. Make an outline of topics to be investigated and seek material about each major point, using more than one source	EI	LI–S	S

SOCIAL STUDIES SKILLS: A GUIDE TO ANALYSIS AND GRADE PLACEMENT—*Continued*
(Code: EP, early primary; LP, late primary; EI, early intermediate;
LI, late intermediate; J, junior high school; S, senior high school)

PART ONE: Skills which are a definite but shared responsibility of the social studies—*Continued*

Skill	Introduce, through planned readiness experiences	Develop systematically	Reteach, maintain, and extend
II. Organizing information—*Con.*			
B. Select the main idea and supporting facts	EI	LI-S	S
C. Compose a title for a story, picture, graph, map, or chart	EP	LP-LI	J-S
D. Select answers to questions from material heard, viewed, or read	EP	LP-J	S
E. Take notes, making a record of the source by author, title, page	LI	J-S	S
F. Classify pictures, facts, and events under main headings or in categories	LP	EI-J	S
G. Arrange events, facts, and ideas in sequence	EP	LP-J	S
H. Make simple outlines of material read, using correct outline form	LI	J-S	S
I. Write a summary of main points encountered in material	EI	LI-S	S
J. Make a simple table of contents	LP	EI-J	S
K. Make a bibliography	LI	J	S
III. Evaluating information			
A. Distinguish between fact and fiction	EP	LP-J	S
B. Distinguish between fact and opinion	LI	J-S	S
C. Compare information about a topic drawn from two or more sources to recognize agreement or contradiction	LP	EI-J	S

D. Consider which source of information is more acceptable, and why	LP	EI-S	S
E. Examine reasons for contradictions, or seeming contradictions, in evidence	J	J-S	S
F. Examine material for consistency, reasonableness, and freedom from bias	J	J-S	S
G. Recognize propaganda and its purposes in a given context	J	J-S	S
H. Draw inferences and make generalizations from evidence	EP	LP-S	J-S
I. Reach tentative conclusions	EP	LP-S	J-S
IV. Acquiring information through reading			
A. Skim to find a particular word, get a general impression, or locate specific information	LI	J-S	S
B. Read to find answers to questions	EP	LP-J	S
C. Make use of headings, topic sentences, and summary sentences to select main ideas and differentiate between main and subordinate ideas	EI	LI-J	S
D. Select the statements that are pertinent to the topic being studied	LP	EI-J	S
E. Make use of italics, marginal notes, and footnotes to discover emphasis by author	LI	J-S	S
F. Consciously evaluate what is read, using the approaches suggested in Section III above	LI	J-S	S
V. Acquiring information through listening and observing			
A. Listen and observe with a purpose	EP	LP-J	S
B. Listen attentively when others are speaking	EP	LP-J	S
C. Identify a sequence of ideas and select those that are most important	LP	EI-J	S
D. Relate, compare, and evaluate information gained through listening and observing with that gained from other sources of information	LP-EI	LI-J	S

SOCIAL STUDIES SKILLS: A GUIDE TO ANALYSIS AND GRADE PLACEMENT—*Continued*
(Code: EP, early primary; LP, late primary; EI, early intermediate; LI, late intermediate; J, junior high school; S, senior high school)

PART ONE: Skills which are a definite but shared responsibility of the social studies—*Continued*

Skill	Introduce, through planned readiness experiences	Develop systematically	Reteach, maintain, and extend
V. Acquiring information through listening and observing—*Con.*			
E. Adjust to a speaker's voice and delivery and to the physical conditions of the situation	LP	EI-J	S
F. Reserve judgment until the speaker's entire presentation has been heard	J	J-S	S
G. Take notes while continuing to listen and to observe	J	J-S	S
H. Analyze video and audio presentations, e.g., films, pictures, models, exhibits, and other graphic materials concerned with social studies topics	J	J-S	S
VI. Communicating orally and in writing			
A. Speak with accuracy and poise			
1. Develop an adequate vocabulary	EP	LP-J	S
2. Choose the appropriate word	EP	LP-J	S
3. Pronounce words correctly and enunciate clearly	EP	LP-J	S
4. Talk in sentences	EP	LP-J	S
5. Prepare and use notes in presenting an oral report, giving credit when material is quoted	EI	LI-S	S
6. Keep to the point in all situations involving oral expression	EP	LP-J	S
7. Develop self-confidence	EP	LP-J	S

8. Exchange ideas through discussion, either as leader or participant.	EP	LP-J	S
9. Respect limitations of time and the right of others to be heard.	EP	LP-J	S
B. Write with clarity and exactness			
1. Collect, evaluate, and organize information around a clearly defined topic (see Sections I-V above).	LI	J-S	S
2. Write independently, avoiding copying from references.	EI-LI	J-S	S
3. Give credit for quoted material.	LI	J-S	S
4. Use standard English.	LI	J-S	S
5. Include a bibliography to show source of information.	EI	LI-J	S
6. Include footnotes when necessary.	J	J-S	S
7. Apply the skills being developed in printing, writing, spelling, punctuating, capitalizing, and arranging written work.	LP	EI-J	S
8. Proofread and revise.	LI	J-S	S
VII. Interpreting pictures, charts, graphs, tables			
A. Interpret pictorial materials			
1. Recognize these materials as sources of information.	EP	LP-J	S
2. Distinguish between types of pictorial material, recognize the advantages of each, and recognize the need for objectivity in interpretation.	EI	LI-J	S
3. Note and describe the content of the material, both general and specific.	EP	LP-LI	J-S
4. Interpret by applying related information, and use the material as one basis for drawing conclusions.	EP	LP-J	S
B. Interpret cartoons			
1. Recognize these materials as expressing a point of view and interpret the view expressed.	LI	J-S	S
2. Note and interpret the common symbols used in cartoons.	LI	J-S	S
C. Study charts			
1. Understand the steps in development indicated.	LI	J-S	S

SOCIAL STUDIES SKILLS: A GUIDE TO ANALYSIS AND GRADE PLACEMENT—*Continued*
(Code: EP, early primary; LP, late primary; EI, early intermediate;
LI, late intermediate; J, junior high school; S, senior high school)

PART ONE: Skills which are a definite but shared responsibility of the social studies—*Continued*

Skill	Introduce, through planned readiness experiences	Develop systematically	Reteach, maintain, and extend
VII. Interpreting pictures, charts, graphs, tables—*Con.*			
C. Study charts—*Con.*			
2. Trace the steps in the process shown	LI	J–S	S
3. Compare sizes and quantities	LI	J–S	S
4. Analyze the organization or structure	LI	J–S	S
5. Identify elements of change	LI	J–S	S
D. Study graphs and tables			
1. Understand the significance of the title	EI	LI–J	S
2. Determine the basis on which the graph or table is built and the units of measure involved	EI	LI–J	S
3. Interpret the relationships shown	EI	LI–J	S
4. Draw inferences based on the data	EI	LI–J	S
E. Construct simple graphs, charts, tables, and other pictorial materials (including cartoons)	EI	LI–J	S
F. Relate information derived from pictures, charts, graphs, and tables with that gained from other sources	LI	J	S
VIII. Working with others			
A. Respect the rights and opinions of others	EP	LP–S	S
B. Understand the need for rules and the necessity for observing them	EP	LP–S	S

Skill	Introduce, through planned readiness experiences	Develop systematically	Reteach, maintain, and extend
C. Take part in making the rules needed by the group	EP	LP–S	S
D. Accept the role of leader or follower, as the situation requires	EP	LP–S	S
E. Profit from criticism and suggestions	EP	LP–S	S
F. Distinguish between work that can be done most efficiently by individuals and that which calls for group effort	EP	LP–S	S
G. Use the rules of parliamentary procedure when needed	LI	J	S

PART TWO: Skills which are a major responsibility of the social studies

Skill	Introduce, through planned readiness experiences	Develop systematically	Reteach, maintain, and extend
I. Reading social studies materials			
A. Understand an increasing number of social studies terms	EP	LP–S	S
B. Learn abbreviations commonly used in social studies materials	EI	LI–J	S
II. Applying problem-solving and critical-thinking skills to social issues			
A. Recognize that a problem exists	EP	LP–J	S
B. Define the problem for study	EP	LP–J	S
C. Review known information about the problem	EP	LP–J	S
D. Plan how to study the problem	EP	LP–J	S
E. Locate, gather, and organize information. (For detailed analysis, see Part One, Section I.)	EP	LP–J	S
F. Interpret and evaluate information. (For detailed analysis, see Part One, Section III.)	EP	LP–J	S
G. Summarize and draw tentative conclusions	EP	LP–J	S

SOCIAL STUDIES SKILLS: A GUIDE TO ANALYSIS AND GRADE PLACEMENT—*Continued*
(Code: EP, early primary; LP, late primary; EI, early intermediate; LI, late intermediate; J, junior high school; S, senior high school)

PART TWO: Skills which are a major responsibility of the social studies—*Continued*

Skill	Introduce, through planned readiness experiences	Develop systematically	Reteach, maintain, and extend
II. Applying problem-solving, etc.—*Con.*			
H. Recognize the need to change conclusions when new information warrants	EP	LP-J	S
I. Recognize areas for further study	EP	LP-J	S
J. Use problem-solving techniques in meeting personal and societal problems	EP-LP	EI-J	S
III. Interpreting maps and globes			
A. Orient the map and note directions			
1. Use cardinal directions in classroom and neighborhood	LP	EI-J	S
2. Use intermediate directions, as southeast, northwest	EI	LI-J	S
3. Use cardinal directions and intermediate directions in working with maps	EI	LI-J	S
4. Use relative terms of location and direction, as near, far, above, below, up, down	EP	LP-J	S
5. Understand that north is toward the North Pole and south toward the South Pole on any map projection	LP-EI	LI-J	S
6. Understand the use of the compass for direction	EI	LI-J	S
7. Use the north arrow on the map	EI	LI-J	S
8. Orient desk outline, textbook, and atlas maps correctly to the north	EI	LI-J	S

9. Use parallels and meridians in determining direction	EI	LI-J	S
10. Use different map projections to learn how the pattern of meridians and that of parallels differ	EI	LI-J	S
11. Construct simple maps which are properly oriented as to direction	EI	LI-J	S
B. Locate places on maps and globes			
1. Recognize the home city and state on a map of the United States and on a globe	EI	LI-J	S
2. Recognize land and water masses on a globe and on a variety of maps—physical-political, chalkboard, weather, etc.	LP	EI-J	S
3. Identify on a globe and on a map of the world, the equator, tropics, circles, continents, oceans, large islands	EI	LI-J	S
4. Use a highway map for locating places by number-and-key system; plan a trip using distance, direction, and locations	EI	LI-J	S
5. Relate low latitudes to the equator and high latitudes to the polar areas	EI	LI-J	S
6. Interpret abbreviations commonly found on maps	EI	LI-J	S
7. Use map vocabulary and key accurately	EI	LI-J	S
8. Use longitude and latitude in locating places on wall maps	LI	J	S
9. Use an atlas to locate places	LI	J	S
10. Identify the time zones of the United States and relate them to longitude	EI	LI-J	S
11. Understand the reason for the International Date Line, and compute time problems of international travel	J	S	S
12. Consult two or more maps to gather information about the same area	EI	LI-J	S
13. Recognize location of major cities of the world with respect to their physical setting	EI	LI-J	S
14. Trace routes of travel by different means of transportation	EI	LI-J	S
15. Develop a visual image of major countries, land forms, and other map patterns studied	EI	LI-J	S
16. Read maps of various types which show elevation	EI	LI-J	S

SOCIAL STUDIES SKILLS: A GUIDE TO ANALYSIS AND GRADE PLACEMENT—*Continued*

(Code: EP, early primary; LP, late primary; EI, early intermediate; LI, late intermediate; J, junior high school; S, senior high school)

PART TWO: Skills which are a major responsibility of the social studies—*Continued*

Skill	Introduce, through planned readiness experiences	Develop systematically	Reteach, maintain, and extend
III. Interpreting maps and globes—*Con.*			
B. Locate places, etc.—*Con.*			
17. Understand the significance of relative location as it has affected national policies	LI	J–S	S
18. Learn to make simple sketch maps to show location	LP	EI–J	S
C. Use scale and compute distances			
1. Use small objects to represent large ones, as a photograph compared to actual size	EP	LP–J	S
2. Make simple large-scale maps of a familiar area, such as classroom, neighborhood	EP	LP–J	S
3. Compare actual length of a block or a mile with that shown on a large-scale map	EI	LI–J	S
4. Determine distance on a map by using a scale of miles	EI	LI–J	S
5. Compare maps of different size of the same area	EI	LI–J	S
6. Compare maps of different areas to note that a smaller scale must be used to map larger areas	EI	LI–J	S
7. Compute distance between two points on maps of different scale	EI	LI–J	S
8. Estimate distances on a globe, using latitude; estimate air distances by using a tape or a string to measure great circle routes	LI	J	S
9. Understand and use map scale expressed as representative fraction, statement of scale, or bar scale	LI	J	S
10. Develop the habit of checking the scale on all maps used	EI	LI–J	S

D. Interpret map symbols and visualize what they represent

1. Understand that real objects can be represented by pictures or symbols on a map	EP	LP-J	S
2. Learn to use legends on different kinds of maps	EI	LI-J	S
3. Identify the symbols used for water features to learn the source, mouth, direction of flow, depths, and ocean currents	EI	LI-J	S
4. Study color contour and visual relief maps and visualize the nature of the areas shown	LI	J	S
5. Interpret the elevation of the land from the flow of rivers	LI	J	S
6. Interpret dots, lines, colors, and other symbols used in addition to pictorial symbols	EI	LI-J	S
7. Use all parts of a world atlas	J	S	S

E. Compare maps and draw inferences

1. Read into a map the relationships suggested by the data shown, as the factors which determine the location of cities	EI	LI-J	S
2. Compare two maps of the same area, combine the data shown on them, and draw conclusions based on the data	EI	LI-J	S
3. Recognize that there are many kinds of maps for many uses, and learn to choose the best map for the purpose at hand	EI	LI-J	S
4. Understand the differences in different map projections and recognize the distortions involved in any representation of the earth other than the globe	LI	J	S
5. Use maps and the globe to explain the geographic setting of historical and current events	LI	J	S
6. Read a variety of special-purpose maps and draw inferences on the basis of data obtained from them and from other sources	J	J	S
7. Infer man's activities or way of living from physical detail and from latitude	EI	LI-J	S

IV. Understanding time and chronology

A. Develop an understanding of the time system and the calendar

1. Learn to tell time by the clock	EP	LP	LI
2. Use names of the days of the week in order	EP	LP	EI

SOCIAL STUDIES SKILLS: A GUIDE TO ANALYSIS AND GRADE PLACEMENT—*Continued*
(Code: EP, early primary; LP, late primary; EI, early intermediate; LI, late intermediate; J, junior high school; S, senior high school)

PART TWO: Skills which are a major responsibility of the social studies—*Continued*

Skill	Introduce, through planned readiness experiences	Develop systematically	Reteach, maintain, and extend
IV. Understanding time and chronology—*Con.*			
A. Develop an understanding of the time system and the calendar—*Con.*			
3. Use names of the months in sequence	EP	LP	EI
4. Use calendar to find dates of special events and to determine length of time between important dates	EP	LP-LI	J
5. Associate seasons with particular months in both northern and southern hemispheres	EP	LP-LI	J-S
6. Understand the relation between rotation of the earth and day and night	LP	EI-J	S
7. Understand the system of time zones as related to the rotation of the earth	LP	EI-J	S
8. Understand the relation between the earth's revolution around the sun and a calendar year	LP	EI-J	S
9. Accumulate some specific date-events as points of orientation in time	EI	LI-S	S
10. Comprehend the Christian system of chronology—B.C. and A.D	EI	LI-J	S
11. Use the vocabulary of definite and indefinite time expressions			
a. Use such definite time concepts as second, minute, yesterday, decade, century	EI	LI-J	S
b. Use such indefinite time concepts as past, future, long ago, before, after, meanwhile	EP	LP-J	S
12. Acquire a sense of prehistoric and geological time	J	J-S	S
13. Learn to translate dates into centuries	EI	LI-J	S

B. Develop an understanding of events as part of a chronological series of events and an understanding of the differences in duration of various periods of time

1. Recognize sequence and chronology in personal experiences, as the school day, weekly schedule, etc.	LP	EI-LI	
2. Learn to arrange personal experiences in order	EP	LP-LI	
3. Comprehend sequence and order as expressed in first, second, third, etc.	EP	LP-LI	
4. Learn to think of the separation of an event from the present in arithmetical terms	EI	LI-J	S
5. Learn to figure the length of time between two given dates	EI	LI-J	S
6. Understand differences in duration of various historical periods	J	J-S	S
7. Understand and make simple time lines	EI	LI-J	S
8. Use a few cluster date-events to establish time relationships among historic events	EI	LI-S	S
9. Learn to relate the past to the present in the study of change and continuity in human affairs	EI	LI-S	S
10. Learn to formulate generalizations and conclusions about time in studying the development of human affairs	J	J-S	S

APPENDIX M

Facilities Planning*

Any administrator faced with the responsibility of designing a new school library facility or for renovating existing facilities, should involve the librarian in all phases of this planning. Too often the librarian—most intimately concerned with the functional plant—is consulted after decisions are made and rectification of mistakes financially unfeasible.

Before one fact is placed on a worksheet or one line on a preliminary layout sketch, the librarian should review the basic principles of functional school library design. The United States Office of Education** and the Educational Facilities Laboratories***, a nonprofit corporation established and funded by the Ford Foundation, provide excellent sources of such guidance.

With background from these or similar sources, plus knowledge of numbers of students and faculty to be served and of the kind of library program anticipated, the librarian will be prepared to preplan the school library physical plant intelligently. The function-facilities-space worksheet included here can serve as pattern for such preplanning.

A blueprint, North Hills Middle High School Library Complex, is included to assist the librarian in visualizing the relation of function to design and to space allocation.

Just as consultation with the librarian should precede facilities layout, so consultation with other members of the library staff should precede detailing plant facilities and furnishings. Therefore, included here also for librarian guidance is the In-Service Secondary Library Staff Meeting Agenda which directed the North Hills secondary library staff in determining details of plant facilities and furnishings.

* Scholl, Mrs. Joyce B. School Library Development Advisor, Western Area Branch, Division of School Libraries, Pennsylvania Department of Public Instruction, Harrisburg, Pennsylvania.
** Taylor, James L. et al. *Library Facilities for Elementary and Secondary Schools.* United States Department of Health, Education and Welfare, OE-15050 Special Publication No. 10: Washington, D.C., 1965.
*** Ellsworth, Ralph E. and Hobart D. Wagener. *The School Library.* Educational Facilities Laboratories: New York, 1963.

A FUNCTION-FACILITIES-SPACE WORKSHEET FOR PREPLANNING THE SCHOOL LIBRARY PHYSICAL PLANT*

I. RECEPTION OR CIRCULATION AREA

FUNCTION:	FACILITY-CONSIDERATIONS:	FOR _____ STUDENTS SPACE REQUIRED:
A. Controlling library complex	1. Central location 2. Safety glass view panels 3. Uninterrupted view 4. Access to corridor 5. Access to suite components 6. Library complex intercom control 7. Library complex master light switch	
B. Admitting and dismissing library users	1. Unimpeded traffic flow 2. Ample entrance/exit	
C. Charging out and receiving back instructional materials	1. Book depository 2. Depressible book truck 3. Check out surface (two level for elementary) 4. Charging machine 5. Electrical outlet 6. Book truck passage 7. Storage shelves/bins	
D. Accommodating reserve instructional materials	1. Back counter shelving 2. Reserve stacks	
E. Maintaining circulation mechanics	1. Card files 2. Lockable drawers 3. Book trucks	
F. Scheduling, training, supervising clerical help	1. Clerical stations 2. Duty posting board	
G. Giving directions and announcements	1. Display spaces 2. Bulletin board	
H. Providing temporary storage for library users' personal effects	1. Storage lockers	
I. Providing for copying of print materials	1. Copying equipment 2. Coin changer 3. Supplies dispenser	

Reception or Circulation Area Space Required _____

* Compiled by Mrs. Joyce B. Scholl, School Library Development Advisor, Western Area Branch, Division of School Libraries, Pennsylvania Department of Public Instruction, Harrisburg, Pennsylvania. 1969.

II. GENERAL USE AREA

FUNCTION:	FACILITY-CONSIDERATIONS:	FOR _____ STUDENTS SPACE REQUIRED:

A. Providing for individual
    reading
    writing
    examining
    analyzing
    comparing
    contrasting
    thinking
    enjoying
    questing
	1. Location convenience
	2. Ease of control
	3. Unimpeded traffic flow
	4. Adjustable shelving
	  a. Perimeter and double
	    faced
	  b. Full and counter
	    height
	  c. Sized for
	    (1) Standard books
	    (2) Quarto books
	    (3) Picture books (for
	       elementary)
	  d. Provided with
	    (1) Backs
	    (2) Section, shelf
	       labels
	    (3) Book supports
	    (4) Step stools
	5. Work surfaces
	  a. Tables
	  b. Carrels
	  c. Picture book tables
	    with wells (for ele-
	    mentary)
	  d. Index/reference
	    tables (for secon-
	    dary)
	6. Seating
	  a. Chairs
	  b. Picture book table
	    stools (for elementary)
	  c. Storytelling cushions/
	    hassocks (for ele-
	    mentary)
	  d. Rocking chairs (for
	    elementary)
	  e. Shelf-side benches/
	    stools
	7. Files
	  a. Card catalog
	  b. Pamphlet
	  c. Graphics
	8. Dictionary stands
	9. Atlas stands
	10. Globes
	11. Portable, expandable
	    display screens	

B. Providing for directions, announcements, display

1. Intercom connection
2. Clock
3. Chalkboard/tackboard
4. Bulletin board
5. Display surface/rack

General Use Area
Space Required____

III. SPECIAL USE AREAS

FUNCTION:	FACILITY-CONSIDERATIONS:	FOR _____ STUDENTS SPACE REQUIRED:
A. Providing for librarian office	1. Library suite and corridor access 2. Safety glass control panels 3. Desk, posture chair 4. Files 5. Shelving/counter 6. Electrical outlets 7. Telephone 8. Conferee chair 9. Coat storage	
B. Providing for conference, seminar, small group instruction	1. Library suite access 2. Safety glass control panels 3. Electrical outlets 4. T-V viewing screen 5. Projection screen 6. Overhead projector and projection cart 7. Chalkboard/tackboard 8. Map/chart rack 9. Shelving 10. Table 11. Seating	
C. Providing for large group instruction	1. Library suite and corridor access 2. Electrical outlets 3. T-V viewing screen 4. Projection screen 5. Overhead projector and projection cart 6. Chalkboard/tackboard 7. Shelving 8. Writing/work surfaces 9. Seating 10. Professional station 11. Podium/lectern	

D. Providing for listening and viewing

1. General use area juxta-position
2. Maximum privacy, light controlled carrels
   a. Free standing
   b. Wall hung
3. Electrical outlets
4. Individual projection surfaces
5. Seating
6. Dial access equipment
7. Equipment carts
8. Phonographs with ear-phones
9. Listening posts with ear-phones
10. Tape recorders with ear-phones
11. Projectors
    a. Film
    b. Filmstrip
    c. Rear screen
    d. Single concept
    e. Sound filmstrip
    f. Slide
12. Shelving/storage
13. Media aide station

FUNCTION:	FACILITY-CONSIDERATIONS:	FOR _____ STUDENTS SPACE REQUIRED:

E. Providing for AV media previewing	1. Viewers
	   a. Filmstrip
	   b. Slide
	   c. Transparency	

F. Providing for practicing, recording, seminar activities	1. General use area juxta-position 2. Acoustical privacy 3. Safety glass control panels 4. Carrel/work surface 5. Seating 6. Storage/shelving 7. Electrical outlets 8. Typewriter(s) 9. Tape recorder(s) 10. Waste disposal 11. "In use" light	

G. Providing for periodical use	1. General use area juxta-position
	2. Shelving
	   a. Periodical display
	   b. Periodical stacks
	3. Microreader stations	

     4. Electrical outlets
     5. Microreader
     6. Microreader-printer
     7. Newspaper display rack
     8. Files/file boxes
     9. Seating
     10. Media aide station

H. Providing professional
    library facilities

     1. Library suite and corri-
        dor access
     2. Electrical outlets
     3. Shelving/stacks
     4. Files/storage cabinets
     5. Work surfaces
     6. Seating

Special Use Area
Space Required____

IV. WORK/STORAGE AREA

FUNCTION:	FACILITY-CONSIDERATIONS:	FOR _____ STUDENTS SPACE REQUIRED:
A. Providing for media the facilities to select order receive examine process organize schedule evaluate circulate inventory repair store	1. Corridor access 2. Dollies 3. Book trucks 4. Waste disposal 5. Sink, running water 6. Counter, two level 7. Electrical outlets 8. Adjustable shelving 9. Bins 10. Drawers 11. Storage cabinets 12. Files a. Movable card b. Letter and legal vertical c. Jumbo d. Map e. Portable card catalog f. Recordex visual 13. Work stations 14. Chairs/stools 15. Library suite access 16. Safety glass view panels 17. Telephone 18. Hat, coat racks 19. Typewriter desk 20. Posture chair 21. Typewriter 22. Adding machine 23. Labeling machine 24. Pencil sharpener 25. Stapler	

B. Providing for supplies the facilities to select order receive house distribute inventory	1. Storage cabinets 2. Dispensers a. Adhesive b. Label c. Cord d. Plastic jacket e. Tape f. Paper 3. Tote boxes
C. Providing for media accessibility	1. Adjustable perimeter shelving 2. Stacks 3. Bins a. Equipment b. Realia c. Kit d. Object 4. Counters 5. Rolling equipment floor space 6. Cabinets a. Disc b. Film c. Filmstrip d. Flat graphic e. Microform f. Programmed instruction g. Slide h. Stencil, master i. Tape j. Transparency 7. Book truck passage space 8. Files

Work/Storage Area
Space Required____

V. PRODUCTION AREA

		FOR _____ STUDENTS
FUNCTION:	**FACILITY-CONSIDERATIONS:**	**SPACE REQUIRED:**
A. Facilitating *all* production activities in each of the following areas	1. Library suite and delivery entrance access 2. Job rated electrical wiring 3. Light control 4. Electrical outlets 5. Sinks, running water 6. Heat and stain resistant, sound deadening flooring	

    7. Exhaust, ventilating fans/direct fume vents
    8. Humidity control
    9. Dollies, hand trucks
   10. Waste disposal
   11. Work surfaces/counters
   12. Cabinets/shelving/bins/drawers
   13. Files
      a. Standard
      b. Jumbo
      c. Map
      d. Special
   14. Packaging equipment
      a. Wrapping paper dispenser
      b. Tape dispenser and moistener
      c. Cord dispenser
   15. Media specialist stations

B. Providing for graphics production

    1. Typewriter desk, chair
    2. Typewriters
      a. Standard
      b. Special keyboard
      c. Primary
    3. Mimeograph
    4. Mimeograph stencil files
    5. Mimeograph light board
    6. Spirit duplicator
    7. Three-hole punch
    8. Paper cutter
    9. Electric stapler
   10. Collator
   11. Spiral binding equipment
   12. Dry mount press and tacking iron
   13. Transparency production systems
   14. Transparency viewer
   15. Overhead projector/screen
   16. Sink, running water
   17. Drying racks
   18. Laminator
   19. Airbrush
   20. Ventilating shield and hood
   21. Drawing board
   22. Mechanical lettering devices
   23. Sign making equipment
   24. Multilith

C. Providing for photographic production	1. Dark room
	2. Dark room equipment
	  a. Electric warning signal
	  b. Acid resistant, multi basin sinks, running water
	  c. Timer
	  d. Paper cutter
	  e. Drying rack
	  f. Photo modifier and stand
	  g. Photo copier and stand
	  h. Slide reproducer
	3. Cameras with accessories
	  a. 35mm
	  b. 16mm
	  c. 8mm
	  d. 35mm still
	  e. Rapid process (Polaroid)
	4. Flood lighting equipment
	5. Light box
	6. Film rewind
	7. Film splicers
	8. Tape splicer
	9. Portable chalkboard
	10. Composing stick and print

D. Providing for three-dimensional construction (ETV stage sets, dioramas, mock-ups)	1. Sink, running water
	2. Work bench
	3. Carpentry tools
	  a. Hand
	  b. Power
	4. Paint spray equipment
	5. Heating equipment

E. Providing for electronic production and retrieval	1. Coaxial cable outlets
	2. Acoustical privacy
	  a. Sound proof floor
	  b. Sound proof walls
	  c. Sound proof ceiling
	3. TV studios
	  a. "On camera"
	    (1) Camera and accessories
	    (2) Monitor
	    (3) Video taping equipment
	    (4) Warning light
	    (5) Storage

       (6) Trolley for
           drapes
     b. Rehearsal
  4. TV office
  5. TV properties storage
  6. Dial access
     a. Control console
     b. Storage center
  7. Computerized learning
     laboratory
  8. Language laboratory
     area

Production Area
Space Required____

Total Suite Space
Required _____

IN-SERVICE SECONDARY LIBRARY STAFF MEETING
North Hills School District
Chairman, Helen Rea

AGENDA: Staff examination of the blueprint (see plan) to decide the following for the North Hills Middle High School Library Complex:

1. About student convenience lockers in the range inside the main library entrance:
   What size should each locker be?
   How many lockers should there be in this section?
   Should all lockers have doors or should some be merely convenience boxes for the placing of extra student books while the student is working in the library?
   How many lockers should have locks in anticipation of the student needing to protect his tape recorder or portable typewriter until he returns to work in the library?
   What other recommendations should be made pertaining to these lockers?

2. About the charging desk:
   What sections would you suggest being placed in the charging desk?
   Would you recommend two wells for charging machines?
   Where would you recommend placing the charging machine or machines?

3. About electricity controls:
   Would you recommend having switches

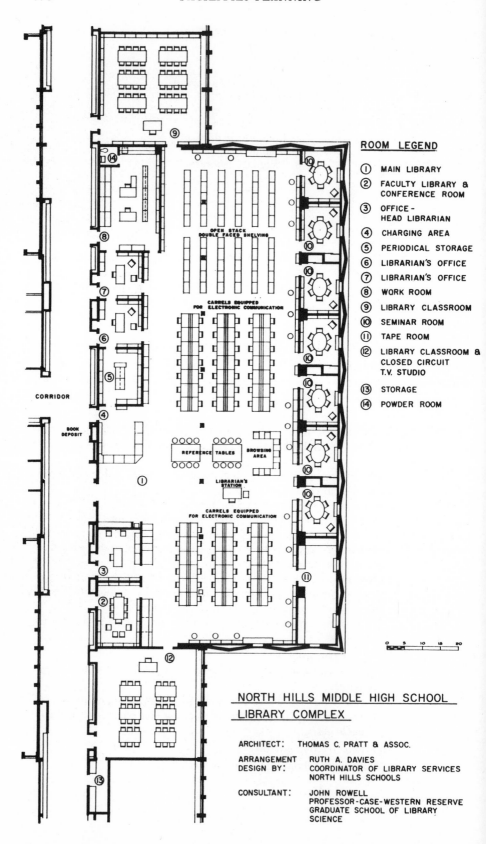

ROOM LEGEND

① MAIN LIBRARY
② FACULTY LIBRARY & CONFERENCE ROOM
③ OFFICE - HEAD LIBRARIAN
④ CHARGING AREA
⑤ PERIODICAL STORAGE
⑥ LIBRARIAN'S OFFICE
⑦ LIBRARIAN'S OFFICE
⑧ WORK ROOM
⑨ LIBRARY CLASSROOM
⑩ SEMINAR ROOM
⑪ TAPE ROOM
⑫ LIBRARY CLASSROOM & CLOSED CIRCUIT T.V. STUDIO
⑬ STORAGE
⑭ POWDER ROOM

NORTH HILLS MIDDLE HIGH SCHOOL
LIBRARY COMPLEX

ARCHITECT: THOMAS C. PRATT & ASSOC.

ARRANGEMENT DESIGN BY: RUTH A. DAVIES
COORDINATOR OF LIBRARY SERVICES
NORTH HILLS SCHOOLS

CONSULTANT: JOHN ROWELL
PROFESSOR-CASE-WESTERN RESERVE
GRADUATE SCHOOL OF LIBRARY
SCIENCE

in each area of the main room?

in each conference room?

in each seminar room?

Would you recommend having a master light switch for control of the lights in the total library complex?

Would you recommend a master control at the charging desk to shut off the school intercom when tapes are being made?

4. About storage:

How much and what width shelving would you recommend for each librarian's office?

Should magazine shelving be placed in the main shelving area or in a special magazine floor rack?

Where and how should newspapers be housed?

What kind of record storage should be provided: cabinet or shelving, open or closed?

Would it be feasible to house microfilm in the periodical-reserve storage room and have students request it at the desk?

Would you recommend storage of anything else in the periodical room?

What type of locker for coats, etc., do you recommend for the workroom and the librarian's office?

5. About furniture:

What type and what items of furniture would you recommend for the faculty library?

What style and how many chairs do you recommend for

the main reading room?

the conference room?

the seminar rooms?

the workroom?

Do you favor placing a Howe table with electronic listening well in each of the seminar rooms?

Do you recommend one or more reference type tables?

Would you recommend hassock type stools at reference tables?

Would you favor putting the 120-drawer card catalog against the periodical room wall?

Would you recommend a separate card catalog for the faculty library?

6. About equipment:

What type typewriter should be specified for

Librarian's office?

Workroom?

Seminar room?

Other area needs?

Would you recommend placing microfilm readers on carrels?

For record players, what are your recommendations on

Number needed for use in library?

Make and model?

Make and model of listening post?

Make and model of earphones?

For tape recorders, what are your recommendations on
Number needed for use in library?
Make and model?
7. About other furnishing for library complex:
What do you recommend?

Learning to Learn
in School Libraries*

Not surprisingly, discussions of changes being effected in school library
programs by curricular and instructional developments, educational technology and facilities, automation, federal and state legislation, networks of
library resources and services, computerized information services, and innovations too numerous to mention lead frequently to a consideration of
teaching the use of the library and its resources. This venerable subject of
library instruction is currently getting new nomenclature (*methods of inquiry*, for example), attracting critical examination and reappraisal, and
generating some controversy.

PHILOSOPHY AND PRACTICE

Learning, with its many elements and variables of what is to be learned and
how it is to be learned, what is to be taught and how it is to be taught, constitutes a complex discipline—the core of the educative process. Teaching
study and research skills represents but a small segment, and teaching the
use of the library and its resources falls within that segment.

Determining the objectives, content, and methodology of library instruction in contemporary elementary and secondary education is not the simple
matter that it may appear to be, and our traditional approaches, shaped by
long service and practice, may be affording librarians a specious form of
security. The current emphasis in the schools on self-directed learning, inquiry, and independent study all too often contribute to an automatic
solidifying of these established methods, with little or no critical evaluation
of their current appropriateness.

With the widespread interest in and exploration of techniques for teaching learning, the art and methods of instruction, and the psychology of
learning, it can reasonably be assumed that some agreements concerning
the program of teaching study skills and methods of inquiry might eventually be reached in much the same way that decisions have been made in the
last decade in planning programs in numerous substantive fields of the curriculum. (Analysis of these curricular programs for implications and suggestions for study, learning, and research skills holds great value.) It is true that
designs for library instruction have been constructed on local and system
levels, involving librarians, teachers, and curriculum specialists, but it seems

* Henne, Frances. *School Libraries*. American Association of School Librarians. vol. 15.
no. 4, May 1966. pp. 15-23.

timely that a systematic study on a national basis be implemented, utilizing techniques of discussion (symposia), study, and experimentation that the various commissions or other deliberative groups in the substantive fields have employed.

For the specifics of content (types of knowledge and skills) to be acquired by individual students and the decisions regarding the appropriate time, place, and methods for acquiring them can best and only be determined by the pooled judgments of experts in the academic subject fields, in curriculum construction, in instructional methods, in the psychology of learning, and in school librarianship. (This suggestion is a variation, and a significant variation, of one of the proposals made at the Conference within a Conference.) The expectations of college specialists would also be relevant. This recommendation in no sense rules out the importance of the school librarian's participation in the planning and implementing of programs thus evolved; but instruction relating to study skills and methods of inquiry, including the use of the library and its resources, is always a means to an end, and this end and the ways to reach it must involve the philosophy and experiences of curriculum specialists and specialists in the theory of learning.

Until we have the benefits of deliberations of the kinds suggested above, the nature of teaching library instruction will be shaped primarily on a local level. (It should be emphasized that the proposals noted here do not rule out the desirability of or the need for making adjustments necessary for the individual school. The integration with the school's curriculum would always be local in a very real sense.) Some current theories and developments that are occupying the attention of many school librarians in the area of library instruction are presented in the remainder of this paper. Many represent topics that have been with us a long, long time, but now seem to be pressing forward for action and decision on a wide scale.

THE NATURE OF LIBRARY SERVICE

Recommendations about the nature of library instruction will affect, and also be affected by, philosophy concerning the scope of library services. Current thought about the distinctions to be made between independent use of the library by students and desirable library services provides an example. *In the viewpoint of many school librarians the mere process of locating and finding materials in the library holds little intellectual benefit for students, and time thus spent is generally wasted time.* The many processes involved in what students do with materials—evaluation, synthesis, reflection, thinking, appreciation, or whatever—are the important factors, not the searching, locating, and assembling of materials.

At points like these, it is essential for new thinking and new decisions in order to determine how much students should know about the use of the library and its resources, how consistently and persistently they must apply their skills and knowledge independently and without assistance from librarians, when this independent pursuit of materials results in a waste of time, and what variations should be recommended for different groups of students. Deploring the spoon-feeding of students, as librarians so frequently do, may actually mean deploring a more intelligent use of a student's time and efforts; and self-directed study or learning is not necessarily synonymous with self-directed finding of materials.

Thus expanded location, information, and bibliographic services are being recommended, and in some cases in actual operation, on school building and system levels for both teachers and students. The centralized bibliographic and abstracting services developed by Leonard Freiser in Toronto are well known. The potential of system and regional centers, with their bibliographic apparatus, retrieval machinery, and specialized service is briefly described in the national standards for school libraries. All of these developments, on-going and projected, can make materials and the content of materials more accessible and facilitate and expand information and other library services. The philosophy of expanded library services for teachers and students pertains to the library program in the school, and is not restricted to centralized system operations.

HOW MUCH, FOR WHOM, WHEN, AND WHERE?

In the program of library instruction, the recognition of individual abilities (individualization) is stressed. Various designs in curriculum construction (ungraded schools, track curricula, advanced placement and accelerated programs, provisions for exceptional children, among others) are geared to the individual and varying abilities existing among students, and so must the library program of instruction. These adaptations will vary from school to school and within schools. For the most able students, regardless of whether they are economically able to go to college, the school's program of research skills is required in full. For others, the amount of instruction may range from practically nothing to other levels, depending upon the abilities and characteristics of the students. For some students, and in certain schools this may be many students, the only library skill that they should have to acquire is an awareness, imprinted indelibly and happily upon them, that the library is a friendly place where the librarians are eager to help. To these students, the delights of periodical indexes and other library tools must ever remain closed. When the program of library instruction is truly integrated with classroom instruction, the needs of the retarded, the slow, the underachieving, the average, and the academically talented are taken care of in a realistic and natural way.

When decisions about what students need to know are reached by the school, their implementation requires careful planning by the school's administrators, teachers, and librarians that is comparable to, but obviously not identical with, the planning required for the substantive areas of the curriculum. The principal assumes responsibility for this area as seriously as he does for other parts of the instructional program. The head school librarian can serve, and frequently does, as the chairman of the school's committee (or equivalent) that plans and implements the school's program of teaching study skills and methods of inquiry. This committee includes teachers representing the various subject areas and grade levels in the school. All faculty members, of course, are ultimately involved in the program.

Local circumstances may necessitate or commend variations on the principles enumerated above, but basic objectives and desired outcomes remain essentially the same. For example, a system curriculum coordinator may work with the school committee. In some school systems the school library supervisor or coordinator develops the study and research skills program with the cooperation of the system subject and area specialists or with librarians and teachers representing each of the schools. Whether plans are developed at building, system, or state levels, the program must be geared to meet the needs of the objectives and instructional methods of the individual schools, and the administration, librarians, and faculty of the school must become actively involved in these procedures.

ANALYSIS OF ASSIGNMENTS

Whether in conjunction with developing a research skills program or in some other context, analysis and evaluation of assignments are high priority pursuits in many schools. Since the program of library instruction is integrated with the curriculum and objectives and content of the component parts of the curriculum determine the kinds of library resources to be used and any skills needed for their use, an analysis of all assignments made in the school proves useful. Theoretically, analyses of curricular content should reveal the kinds of study and research skills to be taught, but this cannot be assumed to apply to every school. In any event, knowledge of the assignments provides information needed to indicate an appropriate integration of the program with curriculum content.

This analysis also enables the librarians to evaluate the adequacy of the library's resources to meet student needs. For the program of teaching study skills and the methods of inquiry involves not just teaching the types of knowledge and skills entailed, but also opportunities to put them into operation through the use of a wide variety of school library resources. Independent research and inquiry are important in themselves, whether the student locates the necessary materials or has them located for him, and the library's resources must therefore be comprehensive and adequate for his purpose. Analysis of assignments can be and frequently is delegated to the head school librarian when the major objective relates to determining the adequacy of the school library resources. This form of evaluation is kept up-to-date by the teacher's reporting assignments to the school librarian on a continuing basis, and by having the librarians serve on the school's curriculum committees. A long history in the school of such reporting and representation will obviate the need for innovating a systematic analysis of assignments in terms of available library resources.

Scrutiny of assignments is important, as experience has frequently shown, for reasons other than those already noted, including locating busywork, pointless duplication, antiquated exercises, and sheer foolishness—and then making the improvements in order.

TEACHING STUDY SKILLS

No matter how the school may allocate the responsibilities for teaching the various study skills, whether to teachers alone, or librarians alone, or a combination of both—the librarians' responsibilities and opportunities for observing and helping students in the use of materials (and, in the process, evaluating their competencies) are clearly indicated. This principle applies to all schools. In those schools where independent study and self-directed learning are carefully planned for the students, these activities of the librarians represent key factors in a successful program. The librarian is the one who has the opportunity to observe, among other matters, the student's ability to use materials, to take notes, to outline, and to evaluate and synthesize materials. The school librarian's role in the program of study skills and methods of inquiry is that of a teacher and guidance specialist. The librarian's follow-up services in seeing how effectively students are using the library materials they have selected for their immediate needs are strategic and valuable ones.

All of which means that school librarians must have a knowledge of recent developments and approved techniques concerning the skills and psychology of learning and related topics. More is implied here than the content covered in the educational or teaching requirements commonly required for the certification of school librarians. From part of the school librarian's double-pronged certification requirements, comes some understanding, enriched later through experience, of teaching methods and developments; but the content prescribed in the principle stated above goes beyond this rudimentary preparation. (Being taught how to construct lesson plans is not the point intended!)

THE LEARNING CENTER

The library forms a natural environment for the kind of guidance that has just been described, and the 'designation of the school library as a study or learning laboratory does not need to have the chill connotation that some attach to it. A library *is* a learning center, and learning embraces reading a book for fun or aesthetic enjoyment as much as it does examining materials to abstract information or ideas for a term paper. It is not unnatural that in many schools the library is called the Learning Center. The Learning Center evolves directly and purely from the recent emphasis in the educational programs of the schools on the processes of learning: learning skills and competencies to be acquired by students; the materials and apparatus to be used by them (including traditional library resources as well as newer media); and the careful planning of time for study in the students' schedules —now done in some schools by computers. Inquiry, independent or individual study, and self-directed learning occupy a strong position in the philosophy of modern education, and in this development the school library's resources and its program of teaching study and research skills form a key and integral part at all levels of elementary and secondary education.

Along with the new focus on the library as a learning center, we can note changes in the attitude toward the library as the place for study. The image of the old-fashioned library study hall rightly evokes chilling horror in the hearts of school librarians, and the comments that follow do not apply to this concept. Today, students should and must have the opportunity to study, to learn, in a library and not in the bleak and barren environment of a study hall. Now, with the developments in school library facilities—library areas, resource centers, and all the multi-dimensional forms they take—the goals have changed. The idea portrayed in the oft reiterated cliché that curricular and instructional changes have made modern high school libraries comparable to those in many liberal arts colleges of yesteryear and to junior college libraries of today is true, and it must be put into operation in all respects, not just in raising the maturity level of the resources collections. Making it possible for all students to study and work in a library environment requires certain conditions, since no one is asking for a return to the old-fashioned library study hall with its frequently attendant policing and disciplinary problems. The minimal conditions include: sufficient quarters and facilities for the library, sufficient staff, sufficient resources, and, if students have scheduled study periods, intelligently and carefully planned programs for study. Let it be stressed that current national standards for school libraries relating to facilities and to staff do not sufficiently provide for an automatic conversion of library areas into study halls or vice versa.

THE I.M.C. AND THE SKILLS OF LEARNING

With more and more school libraries becoming instructional materials centers with fully equipped facilities and with functional programs of service, the librarian's role has expanded. Students, in the pursuit of their studies, use a cross-media or multi-media or single medium approach, and receive appropriate guidance from the school librarians in the selection of these materials and in their effective use. This principle means more than showing a student how to use a filmstrip viewer, or machinery for teaching tapes, or an 8mm sound film projector, or the micro-reader, or the apparatus for listening to recordings, or the dial equipment for banks of resources now making their appearance, or the apparatus for making transparencies, or machines and devices for programmed instruction. The program of teaching the use of library resources includes guidance in teaching students viewing and listening skills. Opportunities to help students to acquire film literacy are rapidly increasing for school librarians.

Learning how to view and how to listen and acquiring the skills of perception that evaluation and appreciation of the media require represent abilities that young persons have to acquire through time, effort, and guided experiences, in much the same manner they master the mechanical skills and developmental aspects of reading. Such instruction includes guidance in helping students to turn naturally to media other than print as the best and possibly the only appropriate or artistic forms of communication, to realize when audiovisual media complement printed materials, and to know when they have no relevance or are inferior for the purposes at hand. School librarians also have exciting opportunities to present to students the realm of the cinema as an art form.

ACADEMIC CREDIT

Unfortunately, the importance attached to the skills of learning and methods of research sometimes results in the revival of outmoded techniques of the implementation of undesirable practices. No academic credit at any grade level should be given for instruction in the use of the library and its resources. Logically, this principle is a superfluous one, since the well-planned program, fully integrated with the curriculum, would not make such an eventuality possible. Library skills are means to other educational ends, and not ends in themselves. Library skills do not represent a separate substantive discipline and hence should not be designated as course content carrying academic credit. Nonetheless, there seems to be a growing and alarming tendency to formalize this instruction. Even when no academic credit is given, no justification exists for having either courses in this area or a detached string of lessons. Ironically enough, the use of programmed aids and of audiovisual materials in conjunction with library instruction often contributes to the perpetuation of arbitrary, nonintegrated instruction.

ACCESSIBILITY

The materials of learning are made easily accessible to students, and the schools provide the necessary materials, time, facilities, and staff, that give students optimum benefits in the pursuit of their studies and for nonacademic purposes as well.

This principle covers many vital parts of the school library's program. For library facilities, the following developments can be noted: the expansion of library quarters (main library areas, resource centers, learning areas, and other space provisions) and new organizational patterns for library areas on a subject or grade level basis. Equipment has been expanded to include wet and dry carrels, language laboratories, teaching machines, micro-readers, audiovisual equipment of all types, machinery for the production and reproduction of materials, and other items. Experiments with electronic machines for dialing materials, or comparable devices, are under way.

In order to meet the needs of students, the resources of school libraries are constantly being improved and expanded. Particular emphasis is being given to developing reference resources (including those in the elementary schools, since the requests of teachers and children constantly require consultation and use by the librarians of resources that are far from being elementary), the periodical collections, the collections of audiovisual materials, and the professional materials for teachers. In secondary schools a major drive has been made to provide the resources needed for accelerated, advanced placement, honors, and enriched courses. In order to satisfy quantitative demands for particular materials school libraries are providing materials in sufficient duplication. The acquisition and use of paperbacks in school libraries have rightly assumed sizable proportions.

Making materials easily accessible can also be seen in the current circulation policies of school libraries that are elastic and flexible, making it possible for students to withdraw all kinds of materials easily, and some kinds of equipment. Further evidence can be noted in the extension of the hours and days that many school libraries are open for student use. Even recent movements toward printed book catalogs and new classification arrangements have a direct bearing on making materials accessible.

The need to meet, at the very least, existing national standards for size of library staff becomes critically imperative, since so much individual work with students in the school library and group work with them in the library areas and elsewhere form a basic part of the research and study skills program—and this but one part of the school library's services.

Quite probably, the notoriously substandard conditions relating to size of school library staff that have persistently plagued school libraries—and not the lack of carefully delineated philosophy of library instruction—have led to an over-emphasis on teaching and requiring students to work independently in libraries, rather than providing them with library services that would do much of this location and collection of materials.

STUDENT USE OF OTHER LIBRARIES

Amidst what must be millions of words written and spoken about students crowding into public libraries, the essential points are sometimes lost in the welter of verbiage. As far as elementary and secondary school students are concerned, the most immediate fact to recognize and concentrate upon is that school libraries must be developed and they must meet the standards for resources and programs. The important goal to reach and to be concentrated upon is that of bringing school libraries up to these standards as quickly as possible. Providing substitutes for these measures, no matter how noble the intents, simply means supporting the perpetuation of inferior conditions in the schools. When the schools fully meet their responsibilities in providing the resources of teaching and learning, in having library programs and services that meet recognized standards, and in making the school library resources and services truly accessible, lamented pressures on the public library might even fade away; and colleges would no longer have to give elementary and secondary school level courses in library instruction.

If endeavors to improve school library conditions fail or improvements come too slowly, and if the public libraries continue to assume responsibilities for providing services and resources to meet curricular needs of students, then what implications can be drawn? One would be that the principles outlined for teaching students about study skills and methods of inquiry must be recognized and followed by the public library in its own program of service. This is relatively simple in those numerous instances where students attend schools that have programs of library instruction but still flock to the public library because of inadequacies in the collections of the school libraries, the inaccessibility of the school libraries, or for other reasons. Otherwise it is not simple, and even quite unmanageable, because library instruction must be related to curricular content and assignments, must stress the multi-media approach in the process of learning, and must provide group and individual guidance of many kinds—clearly functions of the schools and the educational process. *(It is not as simple a matter as just knowing in advance what the assignments are.)*

In the current scene, a paradox emerges. On the one hand, we have the numerous references to the problems created by student use in libraries other than those in schools (most often public, but sometimes college, university, and special libraries), and on the other we have a proliferation of community, regional, and state plans setting forth various proposals for reference and research resource centers to serve all groups (including students) and also proposals for other types of cooperative library services. As we hear more and more about the latter (not infrequently, with the pleasant jingle of federal and state funds in the background), we hear less and less about the evils emanating from students swarming into libraries outside their schools.

There is no question that the future holds changes, even marked changes, in the forms of library services, the audiences served, the organizational and administrative patterns, and the kinds of cooperative planning. The philosophy behind some of these possible trends was introduced decades ago. A plea is made that proposals for cooperative resources and services be based on sound evidence and sound theories. The viewpoint is submitted that we have not yet assembled all the essential facts and that we will never have a true picture of conditions until school libraries reach recommended standards for resources, facilities, and services. Only then will we be in a position to collect the data needed for planning. We do not even know enough now about the nature of the materials that students use for their academic purposes in the school library or elsewhere, or about the number and characteristics of students using or not using library resources. As part of their responsibilities in planning the programs of study skills and methods of inquiry, school librarians might well find out about the specific materials used by students, the purposes for which they use them, where they get them, and the reasons for using resources other than the school library.

We tend to assume that students need materials for their curricular purposes that are too rare or too scholarly or too expensive or too infrequently used to justify their inclusion in school library collections, and this assumption is probably fallacious. (We also tend to assume that all public library collections are superior to all school library collections, and this is definitely fallacious.) We tend to ignore existing and proposed school system and multi-school system plans for materials centers, for centralized processing, and for other cooperative library services among schools. Too often the creators of state and regional library plans have little real understanding of what a good school library program is or the reasons why modern schools must have the resources of teaching and learning. Under any circumstance, state, regional, and local planning for libraries should actively involve school administrators and other educators, and too often this has not been the case.

Plans and practices that ‚perpetuate substandard conditions in school libraries or that recommend organizational patterns which violate the educational objectives and services that are uniquely characteristic of school libraries, do a disservice to students and teachers. There are innumerable reasons why this is true, but the one to conclude with here is that learning to learn in libraries forms a natural part of the education of youth, best achieved where a richness of materials is easily accessible and under the guidance of teachers and librarians expert in their knowledge of the students, the curriculum, the ways of teaching, and the ways of learning.

Poetry Unit

Subject: Language Arts
Grade: Six
Library-based Unit: Exploring Poetry

GOALS

To provide an opportunity before going to junior high school for each child to become conversant with poetry which is uniquely appropriate to the elementary level.

To provide ample opportunity for each child to find satisfaction, stimulus, enjoyment, and challenge through poetry.

OBJECTIVES

To encourage the pupils to discover the power and beauty of poetic imagery.

To encourage the pupils to interpret poetry in a variety of ways: verbally, pictorially, musically, dramatically, etc.

To encourage the pupils to experiment with poetic expression.

To encourage each child to become acquainted with a wide variety of poetry and anthologies of poetry.

To encourage the pupils to become acquainted with those poets uniquely appropriate for elementary children.

To encourage the pupils to become acquainted with illustrators uniquely appropriate for elementary children.

To encourage the pupils to appreciate song as poetry.

To encourage the pupils to read poetry as a form of recreation.

To encourage the pupils to compile an anthology of favorite poems.

INTEREST SAFEGUARDS

Stress enjoyment, minimize mechanics, terminology, memorization, analysis, biographical data.

Encourage each child to explore widely and to select that which has special significance and appeal for him.

Encourage each child to express his understanding in a manner compatible with his abilities and interests.

Encourage each child to experiment with rhyming *when he is alone and away from other pupils.*

Encourage each child to experiment interpreting poetry verbally, pictorially, musically, and dramatically, and to share his interpretation with the class *if he wishes.*

Encourage each child to experiment making a tape of his favorite poem or poems.

Note: No child should be required to write poetry.
No child should be required to interpret poetry for the class or for the teacher.

TERMINOLOGY

anonymous	imagery
anthologist	light verse
anthology	limerick
biographical note	mood
compile	nonsense verse
compiler	pen name
description	pictorial interpretation
dust jacket	poetry
editor	prose
emotion	rhyme
figures of speech	rhythm
illustrated edition	stanza
illustrator	verse

STUDY SKILLS

Introduce the term "anthology":

explain the difference between an anthology and a collection of the works of one poet;
explain the difference between anthologist and author.

Determine the significance of the title page noting:

"Compiled by"	"Illustrated by"
"Edited by"	"Selected by"

Examine and discuss the following kinds of indexes:

author index	first line index
title index	subject index

Discover and discuss the poetic uses of indention and capitalization.
Discover and discuss the biographical note included in many anthologies.
Discover and discuss the significance of biographical information on the dust jacket.

Discover and discuss the uniquely individualistic style of contemporary illustrators:

Marguerite De Angeli	Peter Spier
Ed Emberley	Tasha Tudor
Gyo Fujikawa	Tomi Ungerer
Paul Galdone	Brian Wildsmith
E. H. Shepard	

Discover and discuss the proper way to compile a table of contents.
Discover and discuss the proper way to make a title sheet.
Discover and discuss the proper way to capitalize the title of a poem.
Discover and discuss the proper way to organize an anthology.
Discover and discuss the various ways to index an anthology.

CLASSROOM-BASED LEARNING EXPERIENCES

Introduce pupils to the unit.
List poets and poems suggested by the pupils.
Have pupils define poetry from their own understanding of the term.
Have pupils discuss the frequent use of poetry:
    in advertising like jingles on TV or radio;
    in recreation like singing games;
    in expressing ideas, emotions, patriotism, etc.

LIBRARY-BASED LABORATORY EXPERIENCES

Acquaint the class with the section of the library where the poetry collection is housed.
Prove that some informational books are written in poetic form and, therefore, might not be given a poetry call number:
    biography like *The Book of Americans* by Rosemary and Vincent Benet;
    etiquette like *Your Manners Are Showing: A Handbook of Teenage Know-How* by Betty Betz;
    geography like *High Hills: A Book of Eskimo Poems* with photographs by Guy Mary-Rousseliere;
    science like *A Dozen Dinosaurs* by Richard Armour.
Introduce the various approaches to discovering poetry through the card catalog:
    POETRY—as main subject heading;
    POETRY—as subdivision heading.
Introduce the anthology as a source of poetry written by a number of poets.
Introduce this basic list of poets uniquely appropriate to the elementary level.

Dorothy Aldis	Rachael Field
Richard Armour	Aileen Fisher
Margaret Wise Brown	Rose Fyleman
Lewis Carroll	Edward Lear
Elizabeth Coatsworth	Katherine Love
William Cole	A. A. Milne
Walter De La Mare	Eve Merriam
Eugene Field	Phyllis McGinley

| Mary O'Neill | James Whitcomb Riley |
| Laura E. Richards | Robert Louis Stevenson |

Introduce and discuss basic vocabulary listed above under *Terminology*.
Introduce, compare, and analyze different kinds of illustrations like:

cut paper or cloth figures	stick figures
line drawings	wash drawings
photographs	wood cuts

Introduce the following nonbook poetry sources:

| disc recordings | transparencies |
| tape recordings | |

Discuss the various ways of interpreting poetry by:

compiling an anthology	making dioramas
constructing a mobile	making tape recordings
designing a book jacket	making transparencies
designing a greeting card	painting a mural
dramatizing a poem	writing a rhyming commercial
drawing illustrations	

Bibliography

The AAAS Science Book List for Children. Washington, D.C.: American Association for the Advancement of Science, 1963. (Footnote 147)

The AAAS Science Book List for Young Adults. Washington, D.C.: American Association for the Advancement of Science, 1964. (Footnotes 146, 148)

Adler, Irving. "The Cambridge Report: Blueprint or Fantasy." *The Arithmetic Teacher,* 13 (1966):185-6. (Footnote 158)

American Association of School Librarians. *Standards for School Library Programs.* Chicago: American Library Association, 1960. (Footnotes 26, 27, 30, 31, 32, 35, 73, 175, 186, 211, 220)

American Association of School Librarians and the Department of Audiovisual Instruction. *Standards for School Media Programs.* Chicago: American Library Association and Washington, D.C.: National Education Association, 1960. (Footnotes 73, 78, Figure XII)

American Association of School Librarians and The National Commission for Teacher Education and Professional Standards. *The Teachers' Library: How to Organize It and What to Include.* rev. ed. Washington, D.C.: National Education Association, 1968. (Footnote 83)

American Library Association, Committee on Post-War Planning. *School Libraries for Today and Tomorrow.* Chicago: American Library Association, 1945. (Footnote 70)

American School Counselor Association. *Statement of Policy for Secondary School Counselors.* Washington, D.C.: American Personnel and Guidance Association, 1964. (Footnote 171)

Anderson, Paul S. *Language Skills in Elementary Education.* New York: Macmillan, 1964. (Footnote 104, Examples VI, VII)

Anderson, Verna D. *Readings in the Language Arts.* New York: Macmillan, 1964. (Footnote 109)

Association for Supervision and Curriculum Development. *Leadership for Improving Instruction.* Washington, D.C.: National Education Association, 1960. (Footnotes 204, 205, 206, 207)

Aylesworth, Thomas G. *Planning for Effective Science Teaching.* Columbus, Ohio: American Education Publications/A Xerox Co. 1964. (Footnote 143)

Bacon, Francis. *The Essays of Francis Bacon.* Edited by Clark S. Northup. Boston: Houghton, Mifflin, 1936.

Benjamin, Harold. *The Saber-Tooth Curriculum.* New York: McGraw-Hill, 1939. (Footnote 8)

Berman, Louise M. and Usery, Mary Lou. *Personalized Supervision: Sources and Insights.* Washington, D.C.: Association for Supervision and Curriculum Development, 1966. (Footnote 208, Appendix C)

Bloom, Benjamin S., ed. *Taxonomy of Educational Objectives: The Classification of Educational Goals.* Handbook I, Cognitive Domain. New York: David McKay, 1956. (Footnote 20, Appendix C)

Blough, Glenn O. and Schwartz, Julius. *Elementary School Science and How to Teach It.* New York: Holt, 1964. (Footnote 145)

Boula, James A. "Guidelines for Instructional Materials." *Illinois Journal of Education.* October 1963. (Figure X)

Bowker Annual. New York: R.R. Bowker, 1968.

Brain, George B. *Increasing Your Administrative Skills in Dealing with the Instructional Program.* Englewood Cliffs, N.J.: Prentice-Hall, 1966. (Footnote 213)

Bruner, Jerome S. *The Process of Education.* Cambridge, Mass.: Harvard University Press, 1960. (Footnotes 15, 16, 17, 18, 19, 55, 56, Appendix C)

Burnham, Reba M. and King, Martha L. *Supervision in Action.* Washington, D.C.: Association for Supervision and Curriculum Development, 1961. (Footnotes 203, 209)

Burton, William H. *The Guidance of Learning Activities: A Summary of the Principles of Teaching Based on the Growth of the Learner.* 3rd ed. New York: Appleton-Century-Crofts, Educational Division, Meredith Corp. 1962. (Footnotes 36, 38, 42, 53, 54, 88, 187, 188, 189, 190, Appendix C)

Burton, William H. and Brueckner, Leo J. *Supervision Is a Social Process.* 3rd ed. New York: Appleton-Century-Crofts, Educational Division, Meredith Corp. 1955. (Footnote 202)

Burton, William H., et al. *Education for Effective Thinking.* New York: Appleton-Century-Crofts, Educational Division, Meredith Corp. 1960. (Footnotes 62, 87, 91, 92, 93, 102, 103, 142, Table XVIII, Checklist XII)

California Association of School Librarians. *Instructional Materials: Selection Policies and Procedures.* Daly City, Calif.: California Association of School Librarians, 1965 (Footnote 79)

Carpenter, Helen M., ed. *Skill Development in Social Studies.* Thirty-Third Yearbook. Washington, D.C.: National Council for the Social Studies, 1963. (Footnotes 110, 118, 119, 120, 179, 182, 183, 185, 191, Appendix L)

Cartwright, William H. and Watson, Richard L., Jr., eds. *Interpreting and Teaching American History.* Thirty-First Yearbook. National Council for the Social Studies, Washington, D.C.: 1961. (Footnote 115)

Chicago University, Graduate Library School. *Youth, Communication and Libraries: Papers Presented Before the Library Institute at the University of Chicago, August 11-16, 1947.* Chicago: American Library Association, 1949. (Footnote 71)

Commission on Imperatives in Education. *Imperatives in Education.* Washington, D.C.: American Association of School Administrators, 1966. (Footnotes 127, 172, 173, 174, 176)

Committee of Ten. *Madison Conference Report.* 1892. As quoted in *Teaching of History in Elementary and Secondary Schools* by Henry Johnson. New York: Macmillan, 1915. (Footnote 64)

Committee on High School-College Articulation. *High School-College Articulation of English.* Champaign, Ill.: National Council of Teachers of English, 1963. (Footnotes 111, 112, 113)

Committee on Science in the Promotion of Human Welfare. American Association for the Advancement of Science. "Science and Human Welfare." *Science,* vol. 132, July 8, 1960, p. 69.

Conner, Forrest E. and Ellena, William J. *Curriculum Handbook for School Administrators.* Washington, D.C.: American Association of School Administrators, 1967. (Footnotes 44, 92, 93, 130, 135, 144, 166)

Cook, Luella B. "Criteria for Selecting and Evaluating Reading Materials." *Materials For Reading: Proceedings of the Annual Conference on Reading.* Vol. XIX. Chicago: University of Chicago Press, 1937. (Footnote 100)

Curriculum Development Council for Southern New Jersey. *Teaching Study Skills: A Handbook for Teachers and Administrators of Grades K-12.* Glassboro, N.J.: Glassboro State College, 1965. (Checklist IX, Tables XI, XX)

Curriculum Materials. 1968 Annual. Washington, D.C.: Association for Supervision and Curriculum Development. Annual.

Dale, Edgar. "Educating for Flexibility." *ALA Bulletin* 57 (1963): 134.

Davies, Ruth A. and Metz, Vernon W. *A Guide to the Use of Primary Sources in Teaching and Interpreting American History.* Pittsburgh: North Hills School District, 1967. (Checklist X)

De Grazia, Alfred and Sohn, David A., eds. *Revolution in Teaching: New Theory, Technology, and Curricula.* New York: Bantam Books, 1964. (Footnote 212)

Department of Audiovisual Instruction. "The Changing Role of the Audiovisual Process in Education: A Definition and a Glossary of Related Terms." *AV Communication Review,* vol. 2, no. 1. January-February, 1963. (Appendix C)

Department of Audiovisual Instruction. *Quantitative Standards for Audiovisual Personnel, Equipment and Materials.* Washington, D.C.: National Education Association, 1966. (Footnote 75)

Detroit Board of Education. *A Program of Social Studies Instruction, Grades 1-12.* Detroit: Detroit Board of Education, 1961. (Footnote 116)

Dewey, John. *Experience and Education.* New York: Macmillan, 1938. (Footnote 40)

Editors of *Education U.S.A. The Shape of Education for 1964: A Handbook on Current Educational Affairs.* Washington, D.C.: National School Public Relations Association, N.E.A., 1964. (Footnotes 29, 129, 132, 134)

Educational Policies Commission. *The Central Purpose of American Education.* Washington, D.C.: National Council for the Social Studies, 1963. (Footnote 180)

Ellsworth, Ralph E. and Wagener, Hobart D. *The School Library.* New York: Educational Facilities Laboratories, 1963. (Appendix M)

The Encyclopedia: A Resource for Creative Teaching and Independent Learning. Chicago: Field Enterprises, 1968. (Figures I, II)

Enrichment Mathematics for the Grades. Twenty-Seventh and Twenty-Eighth Yearbooks. Washington, D.C.: National Council of Teachers of Mathematics, 1963. (Footnotes 162, 163, 164, 167, 168)

Erickson, Carlton W. H. *Administering Audio-Visual Services.* New York: Macmillan, 1959. (Checklist IV)

Fargo, Lucille F. "Training High School Students in the Use of the Library." *Addresses and Proceedings, 1913.* Salt Lake City, 1913. (Footnote 65)

Fleming, Robert S., ed. *Curriculum for Today's Boys and Girls.* Columbus, Ohio: Charles E. Merrill, 1963. (Appendix C)

Fraser, Dorothy McClure and West, Edith. *Social Studies in Secondary Schools: Curriculum and Methods.* New York: Ronald Press, 1961. (Appendix D)

Frazier, Alexander, ed. *Learning More About Learning.* Washington, D.C.: Association for Supervision and Curriculum Development, 1959.

Gardner, John W. *Excellence: Can We Be Equal and Excellent Too?* New York: Harper & Row, 1961. (Footnotes 21, 23)

Garry, Ralph. *The Psychology of Learning.* Washington, D.C.: Center for Applied Research in Education, 1963. (Footnote 39)

General Education in a Free Society: A Report of the Harvard Committee. Cambridge: Harvard University Press, 1945. (Footnotes 4, 13, 106, 107, Appendix A)

Goals for School Mathematics, The Report of the Cambridge Conference on School Mathematics. Boston: Educational Services, 1963. (Footnote 157)

Good, Carter V., ed. *Dictionary of Education.* 2d ed. New York: McGraw-Hill, 1959. (Footnotes 193, 201, Appendix C)

Grossnickle, Foster E. et al. *Discovering Meanings in Elementary School Mathematics.* 5th ed. New York: Holt, 1968. (Footnotes 156, 160, 165, 178)

A Guide for Teaching Social Studies, Kindergarten Through Grade Seven. Minneapolis, Minn.: Minneapolis Public Schools, 1957. (Appendix E)

Hall, Mary E. "The Development of the Modern School Library." *Library Journal,* September 1915, p. 672. As quoted in *Selected Articles on School Library Experience* by Mary Wilson. New York: H.W. Wilson, 1925. (Footnotes 66, 67, 68)

Hanna, Paul R., ed. *Education: An Instrument of National Goals.* New York: McGraw-Hill, 1962. (Footnotes 34, 219)

Harris, Lewis E. and Moore, Clyde B. *Keys to Quality.* Quest for Quality Series, booklet no. 14. Washington, D.C.: American Association of School Administrators, 1960. (Footnote 194)

Henne, Frances. "School Libraries." *Library Surveys.* Edited by Maurice F. Tauber and Irene R. Stephens. New York: Columbia University Press, 1967. (Footnote 198)

"High School Paperback Survey." *Product Information for Schools.* 2d quarter, 1966, pp. 36-39. (Footnote 80)

Hook, J.N. *The Teaching of High School English.* 3rd ed. New York: Ronald Press, 1965. (Footnotes 86, 90, 114, 218, Figure VI)

Hopkins, L. Thomas. *Interaction: The Democratic Process.* Boston: D. C. Heath, 1941. (Table XV)

Huck, Charlotte S. and Kuhn, Doris Young. *Children's Literature in the Elementary School.* 2d ed. New York: Holt, 1968. (Footnote 101, Example II)

Hurd, Paul De Hart. *Science Teaching for a Changing World.* Chicago: Scott, Foresman, 1963. (Footnotes 128, 131, 140, 141)

I Want to Be. Series. Chicago: Children's Press, 1956–1962.

International Paper Company. *How to Get the School Library Your Child Needs.* New York: International Paper Company, 1965. (Checklist XIV)

Jarolimek, John. *Social Studies in Elementary Education.* 2d ed. New York: Macmillan, 1963. (Footnotes 43, 46, 47, 51, 121, Figure VII, Appendix C)

Jefferson, Thomas. *The Writings of Thomas Jefferson.* Edited by A. E. Bergh. Washington, D.C.: Thomas Jefferson Memorial Association, 1907. (Footnotes 1, 2)

Johnson, B. Lamar and Lindstrom, E., eds. *The Librarian and the Teacher in General Education: A Report of Library-Instructional Activities at Stephens College.* Chicago: American Library Association, 1948.

Johnson, Henry. *Teaching of History in Elementary and Secondary Schools.* New York: Macmillan, 1915. (Footnotes 12, 64, 69)

Kenworthy, Leonard S. *Guide to Social Studies Teaching in Secondary Schools.* Belmont, Calif.: Wadsworth, 1962. (Footnote 122, Table XXI)

Knight, Douglas M. "Foreword." *Library Services for the Nation's Needs: Toward Fulfillment of a National Policy.* Report of the National Advisory Commission on Libraries, 1968. As quoted in *Libraries at Large,* ed. by E. Shepley Nourse. New York: R. R. Bowker Co., 1969.

Lee, J. Murray and Dorris M. *The Child and His Curriculum*. New York: Apple-
    ton-Century-Crofts, Educational Division, Meredith Corp. 1960. (Figure III)
MacCampbell, James C. and Peck, Elinor, eds. *Focus on Reading*. Cambridge,
    Mass.: New England School Development Council, 1964. (Footnotes 95, 96, 97)
MacDonald, James B., ed. *Theories of Instruction*. Washington, D.C.: Association
    for Supervision and Curriculum Development, 1965. (Footnote 214)
Macintosh, Helen K. et al. *Administration of Elementary School Programs for
    Disadvantaged Children*. Disadvantaged Children Series No. 4. Washington,
    D.C.: United States Department of Health, Education and Welfare, 1966.
    (Footnotes 98, 99)
McLuhan, Marshall. *Understanding Media: The Extensions of Man*. New York:
    New American Library, 1964. (Footnote 76)
Madison, James. *The Complete Madison: His Basic Writings*. Edited by Saul K.
    Podover. New York: Harper & Row, 1953. (Footnote 3)
Mahar, Mary Helen, ed. *The School Library as a Materials Center: Educational
    Needs of Librarians and Teachers in Its Administration and Use*. Washington,
    D.C.: U.S. Department of Health, Education and Welfare, 1963. (Footnotes
    60, 61, 84, 85, 86, 215)
Mann, Horace. *Life and Works of Horace Mann*. vol. 3. Boston: Lee and Shep-
    ard, 1891. (Footnotes 11, 63)
Michaelis, John U. *Social Studies for Children in a Democracy: Recent Trends and
    Developments*. 3rd ed. New Jersey: Prentice-Hall, Inc., 1963. (Footnotes 48,
    50, 52, 117, 124, 125, 184, Table XIX)
Michigan Curriculum Program assisted by the Michigan Library Association. *Mr.
    Administrator: What Is Your Library Service Profile?* Lansing, Mich.: Michi-
    gan State Library, 1960. (Figure XII)
Miel, Alice. "Learning More About Learning: A Key to Curriculum Improve-
    ment." *Learning More About Learning*, edited by Alexander Frazier. Wash-
    ington, D.C.: Association for Supervision and Curriculum Development, 1959.
Miles, Matthew B., ed. *Innovation in Education*. New York: Teachers College
    Press, Columbia University, 1964. (Footnote 9)
Minneapolis Public Schools. *A Guide for Teaching Social Studies, Kindergarten
    Through Grade Seven*. Minneapolis: Minneapolis Public Schools, 1957. (Ap-
    pendix E)
Murray, Marguerite. "Knapp Project Evaluated." *Library Journal*, 15 September
    1967, p. 3127.
National Archives Accessions. No. 57. June 1963, p. 33. (Footnote 123)
National Education Association. The Joint Project on the Individual and the
    School. *A Climate for Individuality*. Washington, D.C.: National Education
    Association, 1965. (Footnotes 57, 58, 217)
National Science Teachers Association. *Planning for Excellence in High School
    Science*. Washington, D.C.: National Science Teachers Association, 1961. (Foot-
    notes 133, 136)
National Science Teachers Association. *New Developments in Elementary School
    Science*. Washington, D.C.: National Science Teachers Association, 1963.
    (Footnote 150)
National Study of Secondary School Evaluation. *Evaluative Criteria*. 4th ed. Wash-
    ington, D.C.: National Study of Secondary School Evaluation, 1969. (Footnote
    195)
National Study of Secondary School Evaluation. *Evaluative Criteria for Junior
    High Schools*. Washington, D.C.: National Study of Secondary School Evalua-
    tion, 1963. (Footnote 89)
National Study of Secondary School Evaluation. *Evaluative Criteria for Junior
    High Schools*. 2d ed. Washington, D.C.: National Study of Secondary School
    Evaluation, 1970. (Footnote 195)
New York Library Association, School Libraries Section. *Evaluating the School*

Library: Suggestions for Studying the School Library in Action. New York: New York Library Association, 1962. (Footnotes 77, 199)

Patterson, Franklin, ed. *Citizenship and a Free Society: Education for the Future.* Thirtieth Yearbook. Washington, D.C.: National Council for the Social Studies, 1960. (Footnote 126)

Pennsylvania Bureau of General and Academic Education. *Mathematics Education in Pennsylvania.* Harrisburg, Pa.: Department of Public Instruction, 1967. (Footnotes 154, 155, 161)

Pennsylvania Division of School Libraries. *A Guide for School Librarians.* Harrisburg, Pa.: Department of Public Instruction, 1969. (Footnotes 25, 210, Checklist V, Appendices B, I)

Pennsylvania Governor's Committee on Education, Pennsylvania, 1960, Task Force on Curriculum. "The School Library–Keystone of Quality Education." In *A Guide for School Librarians.* Pennsylvania Division of School Libraries. Harrisburg, Pa.: Department of Public Instruction, 1969. (Footnote 25)

Pooley, Robert C. "The Professional Status of the Teacher of English." *English Journal,* vol. XLVIII, September 1959, p. 311. (Footnote 105)

Price, G. Baley. "Progress in Mathematics and Its Implications for the Schools." *The Revolution in School Mathematics: A Challenge for Administrators and Teachers.* Washington, D.C.: National Council of Teachers of Mathematics, 1961. (Footnotes 151, 152, 153, 159)

Product Information for Schools. 2nd quarter, 1966. (Footnote 80, Table V)

Project on Instruction. National Education Association. *Schools for the 60's.* New York: McGraw-Hill, 1963. (Footnotes 10, 74, 177, 181, 182, 183)

Public Papers of the Presidents of the United States, Containing the Public Messages, Speeches of the President. John F. Kennedy, January 1 to November 22, 1963. Washington, D.C.: United States Government Printing Office, 1964.

The Pursuit of Excellence: Education and the Future of America. "America at Mid-Century Series," Special Studies Project Report V, Rockefeller Brothers Fund. Garden City, N.Y.: Doubleday & Co., 1958. (Footnotes 5, 14, 33, 170, Appendix A)

Putnam, John F. and Chismore, W. Dale. *Standard Terminology for Instruction in State and Local School Systems: An Analysis of Instructional Content, Resources, and Processes.* State Educational Records and Reports Series, Handbook 6, 3rd draft. Washington, D.C.: U.S. Department of Health, Education and Welfare, 1967. (Footnotes 45, 49, Appendix C)

Ranking, Paul T. "The Importance of Listening Ability." *English Journal.* Chicago, Ill.: University of Chicago Press. vol. 17, October, 1929, p. 629. (Footnote 108)

The Report of the President's Commission on National Goals, from *Goals for Americans.* The American Assembly, Columbia University, New York. Englewood Cliffs, N.J.: Prentice-Hall, 1960.

Resources for the Teaching of English. Distributed by The National Council of Teachers of English, Champaign, Ill. Annual.

"Role of Paperbacks in Schools Today." *School Management Magazine,* vol. 2, September 1967, pp. 1-6. (Footnote 81)

Rufsvold, Margaret I. *Audio-Visual School Library Service: A Handbook for Librarians.* Chicago: American Library Association, 1949. (Footnote 72)

Santayana, George. *The Life of Reason or The Phases of Human Progress.* vol. 1. 2d ed. New York: Scribner, 1922.

School Activities and the Library. Chicago: American Library Association, 1965. (Appendix K)

The School Library Program and Instructional Resources. Bulletin 640. Austin, Tex.: Texas Education Agency. 1964. (Footnote 196)

The School Library Program and Instructional Resources 1965–66: Standards and Guidelines for Texas Schools. Bulletin 659. Austin, Tex.: Texas Education Agency, 1965. (Footnote 197)

Scott, Marian, ed. *Periodicals for School Libraries: A Guide to Magazines, Newspapers, and Periodical Indexes.* Chicago: American Library Association, 1969. (Footnote 82)

Shores, Louis. *Instructional Materials: An Introduction for Teachers.* New York: Ronald Press, 1960. (Appendix C)

Smith, Edward W. et al. *The Educator's Encyclopedia.* Englewood Cliffs, N.J.: Prentice-Hall, 1963, (Footnote 37)

Smith, Eugene R. et al. *Appraising and Recording Student Progress.* New York: Harper & Row, 1942. (Footnote 28)

Strang, Ruth et al. *Gateways to Readable Books: An Annotated Graded List of Books in Many Fields for Adolescents Who Find Reading Difficult.* New York: H.W. Wilson, 1966. (Table VIII)

Taylor, James L. et al. *Library Facilities for Elementary and Secondary Schools.* Washington, D.C.: U.S. Department of Health, Education and Welfare, 1965. (Appendix M)

Torrance, E. Paul. *Education and the Creative Potential.* Minneapolis: University of Minnesota Press, 1963.

Toynbee, Arnold J. *A Study of History.* Abridged by D. C. Somervell. New York: Oxford University Press, 1946. (Footnote 41)

U.S. National Advisory Commission on Libraries. "Report." *ALA Bulletin.* vol. 63, January, 1969, pp. 67-94. (Footnote 216)

U.S. News and World Report. May 20, 1968, p. 50. (Footnote 169)

Victor, Edward. *Science for the Elementary School.* New York: Macmillan, 1965. (Footnotes 137, 138, 139, 149)

Webster's Third New International Dictionary of the English Language. New York: Merriam-Webster, 1961. (Appendix C)

Wesley, Edgar B. and Wronski, Stanley P. *Teaching Social Studies in High Schools.* 5th ed. Boston: D. C. Heath, 1964. (Figure VIII, Appendix C)

Wisconsin Department of Public Instruction. *Elements of an Effective Audiovisual Program: A Handbook for Wisconsin Educators.* Madison, Wis.: State Department of Public Instruction, 1966.

Index

A

Acculturation, 46
Activities, *see* Learning, activities
Adler, Irving, 176-77
Administering Audio-Visual Services, 70-71
Administration of Elementary School Programs for Disadvantaged Children, 106
Affective area of learning, 15, 187-88, 191
American Association for the Advancement of Science (AAAS), 160, 167
American Association of School Administrators (AASA), 210
American Association of School Librarians (AASL), 17, 18, 20, 21, 26-27, 62-63, 64, 78, 92, 106-07, 192, 203, 221, 225, 235, 248, Appendices F, H, N
American Library Association (ALA), 61, 62
American School Counselor Association (ASCA), 188-89
Anderson, Paul S., 120-22
Anderson, Verna D., 127-28
Anthropology, 137, 138
Appraising and Recording Student Progress, 20
Arithmetic Teacher, 176-77
Assignments, 206-08, Appendix N
Association for Supervision and Curriculum Development (ASCD), 228-34
Audiovisual media, *see* Instructional materials
Audio-Visual School Library Service, 62
Aylesworth, Thomas G., 166

B

"Believing and Behaving," 59
Benjamin, Harold, 7
Berman, Louise M., 234
Bills, Robert E., 59

Biographee Profile Rating Scale, 116-17, 120
Biography Reading Summary Form, 122
Biography Unit, 113-15
Bloom, Benjamin, 13
Blough, Glenn O., 166
Blueprint for excellence, 11-12
Blueprint for Literacy, 185
Book reports, 119-20, 155
Book selection, *see* Instructional materials—Selection
Boula, James A., 215
Bowker Annual, 79
Brain, George B., 227
Brueckner, Leo J., 228
Bruner, Jerome S., 11-12, 55
Budget, 91-92, 93-95
Burnham, Reba M., 229, 235
Burton, William H., 27, 32, 41, 53, 59, 86, 99, 119, 165, 168-69, 203-04, 206, 228

C

California Association of School Librarians, 65, Appendix H
Cambridge Conference on School Mathematics, 176-77
"The Cambridge Report," 176-77
Carpenter, Helen M., 127-28, 143, 199, 200-01, 202, 208, Appendix L
Cartwright, William H., 137
Central Purpose of American Education, 199
Centralized processing, Appendix K
Challenge to the Social Studies, 156
Changing Concepts of Instruction and the School Library as a Materials Center, 58, 81-82
Characteristic Differences in Emphasis Between the Subject and Experience Curriculum, 157
Chase, William, 20

Checklists, 150, 210; see listing in Contents
Chicago University, Graduate Library School, 62
Child and His Curriculum, 35
Children's Literature in the Elementary School, 84-85, 118-19
Chismore, W. Dale, 44, 46-48
Circulation, see Instructional materials—Circulation
Citizenship and a Free Society, 156
Civil War Pretest, 153-54
Civil War Resource Unit, Appendix D
Classroom Experiences in Listening, 124
Classroom libraries, 80-81
Cohen, Wilbur J., 137
Commission on Imperatives in Education, see Imperatives in Education
Community resource file, 78-79
Conant, James, 4
Conner, Forrest E., 43, 99, 160, 161, 166, 180
Cook, Luella B., 108
Council on Library Resources, 62
Courses of study, 11, 49, 53, 72-74, 134
Criteria, 210
    Determining appropriateness of supporting media, 74
    Determining evaluative excellence, 210-11
    Evaluating literature, 117-19
    Evaluating units, 53-54
    Learning activities and experiences, 54
    Science curriculum, 163-64
    Selecting and evaluating reading materials, 104, 105, 176
    Selecting books for adolescent retarded readers, 107
    Selecting equipment, 70
    Supervisory appraisal, 231
Criteria Relating to Educational Media Programs in School Systems, 64, Appendix G
Critical thinking skills, see also Study skills
    Characteristics, 165-66
    Checklist, 146
    Guidelines for teaching, 204
    Patterns, 205
    Science, 161-62, 164-65, 168
    Social Studies, 143, 145-48
Cross media kits, see Instructional materials—Kits
Curriculum
    Change, 43
    Definition, 43-45
    Experience, 157
    Fused, 134-35, 147, 157
    Guides, 45-54
    Materials, 79
    Organization, 147
    Planning, 56
    Study and revision, 41-43, 55
    Subject vs. experience, 157
Curriculum Development Council, 124, 125, 205

Curriculum Handbook for School Administrators, 43, 99, 160, 166, 180
Curriculum laboratories, see Subject laboratories
Cyclo-teacher, 182

D

Dale, Edgar, 25, 159
Darling, Richard L., Appendix K
DAVI, see Department of Audiovisual Instruction
Davies, Ruth A., 146
Definitions, 43, 47-48, Appendix C
Department of Audiovisual Instruction (DAVI), 62, 63, 64, 92, 225, Appendix G
Designing Courses of Study, 90
Detroit Board of Education, 139
Dewey, John, 39, Appendix C
Dictionary of Education, 210, 228, Appendix C
Discovering Meanings in Elementary School Mathematics, 176, 178, 180
Discovery method, 12-13
Diversification, 57, 179-80

E

East Greenbush Central School District, Appendix H
Economics, 138, 147
"Educating for Flexibility," 25, 159
Education, see also Educational program
    Aim, 17-18, 199-200
    Archaic, 7, 9
    Challenge, 187-88
    Change, 41
    Class approach, 10
    Democratic concern, 3-16, 243
    Equality of opportunity, 5
    Excellence, 5, 11-13
    Goals, 3-16
    Individualized, 14, 15, 57, 178, 187
    Objectives, 20, 23
    Purpose, 59, 199
    Textbook veneration, 9
Education: An Instrument of National Goals, 25, 248
Education for Effective Thinking, 59, 86, 99, 119, 165, 168, 203
Education and the Creative Potential, 227
Education, U. S. A., 20, 159, 160
Educational Policies Commission, 199
Educational program
    Characteristics, 45
    Climate, 15
    Excellence, 5, 11-13
    Individualization, 57
    Innovation, 7, 15, 23
    Outcomes, 46
    Spiral, 12
    Traditional, 7, 15
    Transition, 15
"Educational Program in Transition," 15

Educational Research Information Center (ERIC), 79

Educators Encyclopedia, 29-31

Elan, 247-48

Elementary and Secondary Education Act (ESEA), 63, Appendix H

Elementary School Science and How to Teach It, 166

Ellena, William J., 43, 99, 160, 161, 166, 180

Encyclopedia: A Resource for Creative Teaching, 12

English, 97; *see also* Listening, Literature, Reading, Speaking
  Aims, 99
  Biography unit, 112
  Book reports, 119-20
  Communication, 97-98
  Courses of study, 134
  Curriculum organization, 147
  Goal, 99
  Guiding principles, 98
  Integration with other subjects, 12, 134, 147, 148, Appendix O
  Interest safeguards, 119-20
  Laboratory, 83, 133
  Poetry unit, Appendix O
  Program, 97
  Research paper, 132
  Teacher, 97
  Trends, 99

Enrichment Mathematics for the Grades, 179, 181

Equipment selection, 70

Erickson, Carlton W. H., 70

ERIC, *see* Educational Research Information Center

ESEA, *see* Elementary and Secondary Education Act

Evaluating the School Library, 64, 218

Evaluation, 209-26
  Action plans, 225
  Criteria, 210-11, Appendix G
  Definition of terms, 210
  Evaluative Checklist, Appendix G
  Evaluative Criteria, 211, 212
  Evaluative Criteria for Junior High Schools, 98, 211, 212
  Find Your School Library Service Profile, 217
  Find Your School Media Center Service Profile, 221
  Library Self Evaluation Scale, 215
  Master plan, 225
  Necessity, 213
  Procedure, 218, 225
  Professional excellence of the librarian, 224
  School Library Checklist, 216
  School Library Service Profile, 217

Evaluative Checklist, Appendix G

Evaluative Criteria, 211, 212

Evaluative Criteria for Junior High Schools, 98, 211, 212

Excellence: Can We Be Equal and Excellent Too?, 13, 14, 187

Experience and Education, 39

F

Facilities, *see* School library—Facilities

Fargo, Lucille, 60

Ferguson, W. Eugene, 177

Field Educational Publications, 183

Find Your School Library Service Profile, 217

Find Your School Media Center Service Profile, 221

Focus on Reading, 100-01

Forms of Curriculum Organization, 147

Frazier, Alexander, 41

Fulton, W. R., Appendix G

Fused Library-Based unit: Transportation, 148

G

Gardner, John, 13, 14, 187

Garry, Ralph, 36-38

Gateways to Readable Books, 107

General Education in a Free Society, 4-6, 10, 120, Appendix A

Geography, 138, 147

Goals, Contest, Method, Media Shape Unit and Course Design, 55

Goals for Americans, 4-5, 6, 15, 58, 100, 209, 224, Appendix A

Goals for School Mathematics, 176

Good, Carter V., 210, 228, Appendix C

Grambs, Jean D., 156

Grossnickle, Foster E., 176, 178, 180

Growth Characteristics of Pupils, Appendix E

Guidance, 187-98
  Career, 47
  Integration with teaching program, 192-93
  Laboratory, 196
  Personal, 189-92
  Purpose, 188
  Types, 189
  Vocational, 192-95

Guidance of Learning Activities, 27, 32, 41, 53, 86, 206

Guide for School Librarians, 71, Appendices B, I

Guide to Social Studies Teaching in Secondary Schools, 145, 224

Guidelines for Instructional Materials, 215

H

Hall, Mary E., 60

Hanna, Paul, 25, 248

Harris, Lewis E., 211

Harvard Report, see *General Education in a Free Society*

Henne, Frances, 213, Appendix N

High School—College Articulation of English, 132

High School Paperback Survey, 75
Hook, J. N., 83, 97, 99, 135, 247
Hopkins, L. Thomas, 75
Houston Independent School District, 69
"How to Do It" series, 156
How We Think, Appendix C
Huck, Charlotte S., 84, 118
"Humanist Goals," 248
Hurd, Paul D., 159, 160, 163, 164

I

"I Want to Be" series, 192
Imperatives in Education, 156, 189, 191, 192, 193
"Implementing the New Mathematics Program," 177
"Importance of Listening Ability," 123
Increasing Your Administrative Skills in Dealing with the Instructional Program, 227
Independent study, 81-82
Individual differences, 14-15, 36, 56
Individualizing the Teaching Design, 56
Innovation, 7, 15, 23-24
Innovation in Education, 7
Instructional materials
  Adequacy, 20-21
  Appropriateness, 74
  Budget, 91, 93, 221
  Circulation, 184, Appendix N
  Classroom collections, 80-81
  Collection evaluation, 221, Appendix G
  English program support, 99, 113
  Guidance program support, 195
  Kinds, 89
  Kits, 169
  Mathematics program support, 177, 181, 182, 184
  Microforms, 77
  Multi media approach, 15, 21, 23, 63, 95, Appendix F
  Non print, 10, 15, 21, 23, 60, 63, 69
  Paperbacks, 74-77
  Periodicals, 77-78
  Planned use, Appendix I
  Primary sources, 93, 145, 153
  Programming, 85, 95, 182
  Reading program support, 101-02, 108-13
  Science program support, 166-70, 184
  Selection, 65, Appendices H, I
    Audio-Visual Materials Evaluation Guide, 69
    Book Selection Guide, 66
    Criteria, 74, 104
    Policies and Procedures for Selection of School Library Materials, Appendix H
    Principles, 144, Appendix H
    Reading materials, 108
    Self Evaluation in Media Selection, 71
    Student participation, 65-66, Appendix H

    Teacher participation, 65-66, Appendix H
    Textbook Evaluation Form, 67
  Social studies program support, 90, 93, 143, 155-56
  Study Skills Support, 200-03, 208
  Systems approach, 89
Instructional materials center, *see* School library—Instructional materials center concept
Instructional Materials: Selection Policies and Procedures, 65, Appendix H
Instructional materials specialist, *see* School librarians
Instructional outcomes, 46-47
Interaction: The Democratic Process, 157
Interest inventory, Appendix J
International Paper Company, 216
Interpreting and Teaching American History, 137-39
Itemized Media Budget Request, 93

J

Jarolimek, John, 42, 44, 49, 138, 145
Jefferson, Thomas, 4
Johnson, B. Lamar, 199
Johnson, Henry, 9, 60, 61

K

Kennedy, John F., 3, 145
Kenworthy, Leonard, 145, 224
Keys to Quality, 211
King, Martha L., 229, 235
Kits, *see* Instructional materials—Kits
Knapp Foundation, 17, 62-63
Knight, Douglas M., 246
Knowledge proliferation, 8
Kuhn, Doris Y., 84, 117-18

L

Laboratories, *see* Subject laboratories
Language arts, *see* English, Listening, Literature, Reading, Speaking
Language Skills in Elementary Education, 120, 121, 122
Leadership for Improving Instruction, 229, 230, 231
Learning
  Activities, 54
  Guides, 90
  Principles, 36
Learning laboratory, *see* School library—Learning laboratory
Learning More about Learning, 41, 59
Learning to learn, *see* Study skills
Learning to Learn in School Libraries, Appendix N
Lee, Murray and Dorris, 34
Lerner, Max, 248
Librarian, *see* School librarian
Librarian and the Teacher in General Education, 199
Library—based units, *see* Units

Library-research paper, 132
Library Self Evaluation Scale, 215
Library Services for the Nation's Needs, 246
Library Surveys, 213
Life and Works of Horace Mann, 9
Life of Reason, 137
Listening, 123
  Classroom experiences, 124
  Evaluation checklist, 125
  Skills, Appendix M
Listening and Speaking, 127-29
Listening Skill Evaluation Checklist, 125
Literature
  Biography unit, 113-15
  "Biography Summary," 122
  Book Reports, 119-20, 121, 122, 155
  Criticism, 119
  Evaluating, 117-19
  Integration with social studies, 154-55
  Interest safeguards, 119
  Recordings, 126-27
  Trends to discourage, 120
Lohrer, Alice, 241

M

MacCampbell, James C., 100, 101
Macintosh, Helen K., 106
McLuhan, Marshall, 63
Madison Conference, 9, 60
Madison, James, 4
Magazines, *see* Periodicals
Mann, Horace, 9, 59
Mathematics
  Cambridge Conference, 176
  Computer influence, 175
  Differentiated instruction, 178, 181
  Enrichment, 178-82
  Gifted students, 181-83
  Goals, 175
  Integration with other subjects, 12
  Learning aids, 178
  Learning to Use Roman Numerals, 182
  Modern program, 174-75
  Principles, 176
  Programmed instruction, 182
  Units, 178-80
Mathematics Education in Pennsylvania, 175, 178
Media, *see* Instructional materials
"Medium is the message," 63
Memorization, 13, 15
Mersand, Joseph, 97, 135
Metz, Vernon, 146
Michaelis, John, 45, 49, 51, 140, 155, 201, 204
Michigan Curriculum Program, 217, 221
Michigan Library Association, 217, 221
Microforms, 77
Miel, Alice, 41
Miles, Matthew, 7
Minneapolis Public Schools, Appendix E
Multi media kits, *see* Instructional materials
  —Kits
Murray, Marguerite, 17

N

National Advisory Commission on Libraries, 246
National Archives Accessions, 145
National Commission for Teacher Education, 78
National Council for the Social Studies (NCSS), 127, 137, 143, 155, 156, 199, 200-01, 202, Appendix L
National Council of Teachers of English (NCTE), 132
National Council of Teachers of Mathematics (NCTM), 174, 178, 181
National Defense Education Act (NDEA), 63, Appendix H
National School Boards Association (NSBA), 210
National Science Teachers Association (NSTA), 160, 161, 170
National Study of Secondary School Evaluation, 98, 211, 212-13, 214
Newark Public Schools, 61
New Developments in Elementary School Science, 170
New England School Development Council, 100, 101
New Jersey Curriculum Development Council, *see* Curriculum Development Council
New York Library Association, 64, 218
Non print media, *see* Instructional materials —Non print
North Hills School District, 66, 90, 146

O

Occupational guidance, *see* Guidance—Vocational
One Day in an Elementary Instructional Materials Center, 84
Open-ended learning, 85
Outline of a Resource Unit, 93

P

Paperback books, 74-77
  High School Paperback Survey, 75
  Role of Paperbacks in Schools, 76
Peck, Eleanor, 100, 101
Pennsylvania Division of School Libraries, 17, 71, 221, Appendices B, I, M
Pennsylvania Governor's Committee on Education, 17
Periodicals, 77-78
Periodicals for School Libraries, 77
Personalized Supervision, 234
Pittman learning guides, 90, 182
Pittman, Shirley A., 90, 182
Planned Instructional Outcomes for Pupils, 46
Planning for Effective Science Teaching, 166
Planning for Excellence in High School Science, 160-61

*Policies and Procedures for Selection of
    School Library Materials,*
    Appendix H
"Pony Express" programmed guide, 90
Pooley, Robert C., 120
President's Commission on National Goals,
    see Goals for Americans
President's Committee on Libraries, 137
Pretest: "Civil War," 153-54
Price, G. Baley, 174
Primary source materials, 93, 145
Principal's responsibility to library program,
    237-38
Problems approach, 145, 161, 164, 168
Process of Education, 11, 55
Product Information for Schools, 75
Profession, 26
Professional library, 78-80
Program of Social Studies Instruction, 139
Programmed learning guides, 89-91, 182-83
Project Head Start, 190
Project on Instruction, *see Schools for the
    Sixties*
Programming, *see* Instructional materials—
    Programming
Psychology of Learning, 36
Pullen, Thomas G., Jr., 227
Pursuit of Excellence, 5-6, 11, 25, 188, Ap-
    pendix A
Putnam, John F., 44, 46-48, Appendix C

                    Q

Quarters, *see* School library—quarters
Quantitative Standards for Audiovisual Per-
    sonnel, Equipment and Materials,
    63

                    R

Rankin, Paul T., 123
Reading program, 99-135
    Adolescent retarded readers, 107
    Biography Reading Summary, 122
    Biography unit outline, 121
    Characteristics, 100-01
    Disadvantaged learner, 106
    Enrichment, 104, 108
    Interest inventory, 123, Appendix J
    Literature, 108
    Media support, 105, 106, 107, 108-13
    Read for Fun, 121
    Recordings, 126-27
    Report forms, 116, 121, 122
    Tenets, 100
Recordings, 126-27
Research paper, *see* Library-research paper
Resources, *see* Instructional materials
Resources for the Teaching of English, 133
Revolution in School Mathematics, 174, 177
Rockefeller Report, see *Pursuit of Excel-
    lence*
Role of Paperbacks in School Today, 76
Rufsvold, Margaret I., 62
Russell, David H., and Elizabeth, 127

                    S

Saber-Tooth Curriculum, 7, 19
San Diego County Schools Textbook Evalua-
    tion Form, 67
Santayana, George, 137
Schedule, *see* School library—Schedule
Scholl, Joyce B., 221, Appendix M
School Activities and the Library,
    Appendix K
School librarian, 25-40, 41-58, 59-96
    Agent for curricular change, 41
    Attitude, 32, 40
    Certification, 26-27
    Cooperates with teachers, 20, 32-34, 83,
        134-35, 154-56, Appendix I
    Curriculum consultant, 19, 23, 41, 72-73
    English program, 123, 133
    Expedites learning, 23-24, 36, 38
    Guides students, 22
    Guidance program, 195
    Humanizes teaching, 197
    Image, 244-46
    Job description, Appendix B
    Knowledge of the educational program,
        25, 72
    Literature program implementation, 108,
        123
    Materials specialist, 19, 26, 32-33, 59-96,
        238, Appendix F
    Mathematics program implementation,
        177, 180, 184
    Media selection, 71, 74, Appendices H, I
    Mediating agent for educational excel-
        lence, 25-40
    Personalizes teaching, 34
    Plans with teachers, 72-73, 83, 95, 153, Ap-
        pendix I
    Professional excellence, 224
    Professional preparation, 26-27
    Profile, 39
    Quality, 25-26
    Responsibility, 19
    Science program implementation, 159-86
    Self-evaluation, 71
    Self-image, 32, 40
    Social studies program implementation,
        137-58
    Speech program implementation, 129-32
    Study skills program implementation, 208
    Team teacher, 15, 19, 20, 23, 32
    Thought-energizer, 23
    Traditional function, 15
    Training, 26
    Unit development and implementation,
        32-33
School Libraries, Appendix N
"School Libraries," 213
"School Libraries as Instructional Materials
    Centers," 241, Appendix F
School library, 17-24
    Actualizes educational goals, 17
    Agent for educational effectiveness, 17
    Aim, 18

Budget, 91-92, 93
Design, 18-19, 243-44
District program, 63-65, 244
English program support, 97
Evaluation, 209, Appendix G
Facilities, 92, Appendix M
Find Your School Media Center Service Profile, 221
Goals, 25, 248
History, 60
Instructional materials center concept, 61, Appendices F, H, N
Keystone of a quality educational program, 17, 25, 58
Learning laboratory, 19, 22, 23, 32, 34, 59, 95, 133, 185, 243, Appendix N
Literature program support, 108
Mathematics program support, 177, 180, 184
Objectives, 17, 21-22
Philosophy, Appendix I
Planning-steering committee, 64
Policy statements, Appendices H, I
Principal's role, 238
Program, 64, 82, 225
Purposes, 18
Quarters, 92, Appendix M
Reading program support, 99-102
Requisites, 243
Research paper, 132
Schedule, 83-85
Science program support, 159, 184
Social studies program support, 137-58
Staff, 82, 217
Standards, 17, 26, 62
Supervisor, 227-242
Traditional, 19, 23, 60
School Library as a Materials Center, 58, 81, 82, 241
School Library Bill of Rights, 21-22, Appendices H, I
School Library Program and Instructional Resources, 213
Schools for the Sixties, 8, 63, 194, 200
Schurz, Carl, 243
Science
  Abilities, 161
  Appreciations, 163
  Attitudes, 162
  Book Lists, 167
  Content, 159
  Critical thinking, 165
  Curriculum
    Criteria, 163
    Organization, 147
  Definition, 6, 159, 161
  Goals, 160
  Integration with other subjects, 12
  Kits, 169
  Knowledge explosion, 159-60
  Laboratory, 185
  Library-based units, 170-74
  Library support, 165-67, 177

Literacy, 159
  Open-ended learning, 161
  Problem solving skills, 161, 164, 168
  Skill development, 161, 164
"Science and Human Welfare," 159
Science Booklist for Children, 167
Science Booklist for Young Adults, 167
Science for the Elementary School, 161
Science Teaching for a Changing World, 159, 160, 163, 164
Scott, Marian, 77
Self-directed learning, 81-82
"Self-Evaluation in Media Selection," 71-72
Shape of Education for 1964, 20, 159, 160
Skill Development in the Social Studies, 127, 143, 199, 200, 201, 202, 208, Appendix L
Skills, *see* Study skills
Smith, Edward W., 29
Smith, Eugene, 20
Social studies, 137-58
  Appreciations, 137, 142
  Attitudes, 142
  Civil War pretest, 153-54
  Civil War Resource Unit, Appendix D
  Concepts, 138, 141
  Content, 138
  Critical thinking, 143
  Curriculum, 137, 138, 147
  Definition, 138
  Design, 137
  Emphasis, 157
  Goals, 137
  "How to Do It" series, 155-56
  Integration with other subjects, 12, 154
  Laboratory, 155
  Learning guides, 90
  Library support, 137
  Literature integration, 154
  Media selection, 144
  Objectives, 139-40
  Pittman guides, 90
  Primary sources, 93, 145
  Problems approach, 145
  Purposes, 141
  Resources, 90, 93, 143, 155
  Skill development, 139, 141, 146
  Speech program integration, 127-28
  Transportation unit, 148
  Understandings, 137, 139, 140
  World Cultures topic checklist, 151
Social Studies for Children in a Democracy, 45, 49, 51, 140, 155, 201, 204
Social Studies in Elementary Education, 42, 49, 138
Social Studies in Elementary Schools, 204
Sociology, 137, 138
Speaking, 97, 127
Speech unit, 129
Spiral of Education, 12
Sputnik, 5
Standard Terminology for Instruction, 44, 46, Appendix C

Standards for School Library Programs, 17, 18, 20, 21, 24, 62, 91-92, 192, 203, 221, 235, 248
Standards for School Media Programs, 63, 64, 77, 91-92, 221
Stephens College library program, 199
Stephens, Irene R., 213
Strang, Ruth, 107
Streamlining for Service, Appendix K
Study of History, 41
Study skills, 199-208; *see also* Critical thinking skills
  Assignments and skill development, 206, Appendix N
  Classroom resources support, 81
  Comprehension, 199
  Content development, 201
  Continuum, Appendix L
  Integration with educational program, 199, 201, Appendix N
  Learning to learn, 13, 243, Appendix N
  Library support, Appendix N
  Philosophy, Appendix N
  Primary source approach, 145
  Problems approach, 145, 164, 168, 204
  Program design, 202
  Science program integration, 161, 164, 168
  Social studies program integration, 141, 144-46
Subject laboratories, 81
  English, 83, 133
  Guidance, 196
  Mathematics, 185
  Science, 185
  Social studies, 155
Supervision, 227-42
  Criteria for Supervisory Appraisal, 231
  Definition, 229
  Educational function, 229
  Evaluation, 234
  Group action, 232
  Historical role, 227
  Impact on teacher, 234
  Library supervisor, 235, 237-38
  Principal's role, 235-36
  Responsibilities, 228
  Role perception, 231
  Saber-tooth variety, 227
  School library supervisors, 235
  Tasks, 229
  Tenets, 235
Supervision in Action, 229, 235
Supervision Is a Social Process, 228
Supervisor, *see* Supervision
Systems approach, 89-90

T

Tauber, Maurice F., 213
Taxonomy of Educational Objectives, 13

Teacher
  Assignments, 206
  Characteristics, 28-29, 224
  Plans with librarian, 73, 82, 95, 153, Appendix I
  Quality, 13, 28-29
  Requisites, 27
  Selects media, 65
Teachers' Library, 78, 79
Teaching of High School English, 83, 97, 99, 135
Teaching of History in Elementary and Secondary Schools, 9, 60-61
Teaching Social Studies in High School, 147
Teaching Study Skills, 124, 125, 205
Team teaching, 14, 15, 23, 24, 32, 33, 58, 123
Terminology, 88, Appendix C
Texas Educational Agency, 212-13
Textbook Evaluation Guide, 67
Torrance, E. Paul, 227
Toynbee, Arnold J., 41
Transportation unit, 148
Trump, J. Lloyd, 58, 81, 82

U

U. S. News and World Report, 188
Understanding Media: The Extensions of Man, 63
Units
  Biography, 112
  Civil War, Appendix D
  Design, 51-55
  Development, 151
  Evaluation, 53
  Exploring Our Universe, 170
  Learning activities, 54
  Money, Interest, Banking, and Investments, 180
  Outline of a Resource Unit, 49
  Poetry, Appendix O
  Speech, 129
  Transportation, 148
  World Cultures, 151
United States Chamber of Commerce, 156
Usery, Mary Lou, 234

V

Victor, Edward, 161-62, 168

W

Weaver, Warren, 6
Wesley, Edgar B., 147
World Cultures topic checklist, 151
Writing, 132
Wrouski, Stanley P., 147

Y

Youth Communications and Libraries, 62

Z

Zito, Genevieve P., Appendix D